Hui-Ling Chen

CHARTER SCHOOLS IN ACTION

Charter Schools in Action

RENEWING PUBLIC EDUCATION

With a new preface by the authors
Chester E. Finn, Jr.,
Bruno V. Manno, and
Gregg Vanourek

PRINCETON UNIVERSITY PRESS

PRINCETON AND OXFORD

Copyright © 2000 by Princeton University Press
Published by Princeton University Press, 41 William Street,
Princeton, New Jersey 08540
In the United Kingdom: Princeton University Press,
3 Market Place, Woodstock, Oxfordshire OX20 1SY

Fourth printing, and first paperback printing, with a new preface, 2001
Paperback ISBN 0-691-09008-4

The Library of Congress has cataloged the cloth edition of this book as follows

Finn, Chester E., Jr. 1944–
Charter schools in action : renewing public education /
Chester E. Finn, Jr., Bruno V. Manno, Gregg Vanourek.
p.   cm.
Includes bibliographical references and index.
ISBN 0-691-00480-3 (cloth : alk. paper)
1. Charter schools — United States. I. Manno, Bruno V.
II. Vanourek, Gregg.   III. Title.
LB2806.36.F527   2000
371-01 — dc21   99-32344

British Library Cataloging-in-Publication Data is available

This book has been composed in Sabon

Printed on acid-free paper. ∞

www.pup.princeton.edu

Printed in the United States of America

4   6   8   10   9   7   5

CONTENTS

List of Tables
vii

List of Interviews and Profiles
ix

Preface to the Paperback Edition
xi

Introduction
3

PART I: CHARTER SCHOOLS IN ACTION

Chapter 1: What's a "Charter School"?
13

Chapter 2: Field Trips
23

Chapter 3: Where Did They Come From?
53

Chapter 4: How Are They Working?
74

Chapter 5: Trials by Fire
100

Chapter 6: The Accountability Puzzle
127

PART II: RENEWING PUBLIC EDUCATION

Chapter 7: The Case against Charter Schools:
A Ten-Count Indictment
151

Chapter 8: Political Battlegrounds
169

Chapter 9: Beyond the Schoolhouse Door:
Changing Systems
192

Chapter 10: Beyond the Schoolhouse Door:
Building Communities
220

Chapter 11: The Great Issues
237

Chapter 12: Will Charter Schools Save
Public Education?
248

Epilogue
265

Appendix: Survey Results and Methodology
269

Index
281

TABLES

Table 2–1. State Charter School Activity (September 1999)   24
Table 4–1. At-Risk Youth in Charter Schools and Regular Schools   81
Table 4–2. Students' Rating of Their Performance (by Race/Ethnicity)   83
Table 4–3. Students' Charter School Likes and Dislikes   84
Table 4–4. Reasons Parents Chose Charter School (by Income)   86
Table 5–1. Mississippi's Charter Law: Weakest in the Nation (as of February 1999)   103
Table 5–2. Financial Profile: Academy of the Pacific Rim (Start-Up Costs and First-Year Operating Costs, 1997– 98)   106
Table 5–3. Financial Profile: Texas Academy of Excellence (Start-Up Costs and First-Year Operating Costs, 1996–97)   107
Table 5–4. Illustrative Shortfalls in Charter School Operating Funds   108
Table 5–5. Barriers Facing Charter Schools (Federal Sample, 1996–98)   111
Table 5–6. Charter School Start-Up Issues   114
Table 5–7. Charter School Allies — Public, Private, and Nonprofit   120
Table 5–8. Per-Pupil Facilities Funding for Charters (as of January 1999)   121
Table 6–1. Accountability in the Financial and Education Sectors   142
Table 7–1. Estimated Percentages of Enrollment in Charter Schools (1997–98) and All Public Schools in the Twenty-four Charter States (1996–97) by Racial/Ethnic Category   161
Table A-1. Students' Comparison with Previous School   269
Table A-2. Parent Demographics   270
Table A-3. Parent Satisfaction with Charter School   271
Table A-4. Parents' Rating of Charter School vs. School Child Would Otherwise Attend   272
Table A-5. Charter School vs. School Child Would Otherwise Attend, Rated by Parents of Special Needs Students   273
Table A-6. Parents' Rating of Child's Overall Performance   274
Table A-7. Students' Educational Challenges (Identified by Parents)   275
Table A-8. Teacher Demographics   276
Table A-9. Teacher Satisfaction with Charter School   277
Table A-10. Teachers' Views on Charter School Success   278

LIST OF INTERVIEWS
AND PROFILES

CHAPTER 2. FIELD TRIPS

Profile: Clarise Armisted (11ᵗʰ Grade Student, Sequoia School, Mesa, AZ) 35
Profile: Julie Veeneman (Parent, Excel Charter Academy, Grand Rapids, MI) 41
Interview: Jennie Dearborn (Student, Excel Charter Academy,
Grand Rapids, MI) 42
Interview: Doug Lemov (Principal, Academy of the Pacific Rim, Boston, MA) 50

CHAPTER 3. WHERE DID THEY COME FROM?

Profile: Jim Goenner (Director, Charter Schools Office, Central Michigan
University, MI) 67

CHAPTER 4. HOW ARE THEY WORKING?

Profile: Mickey Bruns (Student, Lowell Middlesex Academy, MA) 79
Profile: Janice Cross (Student, Charter School of San Diego, CA) 82
Profile: Karen J. Holden (Parent, Renaissance School, Douglas County, CO) 87
Interview: Keith Grauman (Teacher, Guajome Park Academy, Vista, CA) 89

CHAPTER 5. TRIALS BY FIRE

Interview: Harry Fair (Board Member, Renaissance Charter School,
Douglas County, CO) 111
Interview: Linda Brown (Pioneer Institute, Boston, MA) 118
Profile: Mark Kushner (Leadership High, San Francisco, CA) 123

CHAPTER 6. THE ACCOUNTABILITY PUZZLE

Interview: Lisa Graham Keegan (State Superintendent of Public Instruction,
Arizona) on "Accountability Arizona-Style" 129
Interview: Scott W. Hamilton (Former Associate Commissioner for Charter
Schools, Massachusetts) on "Accountability Massachusetts-Style" 130
Profile: ACHIEVE — A School-Based "Performance Information System" 134

Chapter 8. Political Battlegrounds

Interview: Mary Hartley (State Senator, Arizona)   186
Interview: Lisa Graham Keegan (State Superintendent of Public
   Instruction, Arizona)   188

Chapter 9. Beyond the Schoolhouse Door: Changing Systems

Interview: Dr. Richard O'Connell (Superintendent, Douglas County School
   District, CO)   198
Profile: Vernon Robinson (Director, North Carolina Education Reform
   Foundation)   206
Interview: Dr. James Zaharis (Superintendent, Mesa Public Schools, AZ)   210

Chapter 10. Beyond the Schoolhouse Door: Building Communities

Interview: Rev. Ellis L. Smith (Founder, Colin Powell Academy, Detroit, MI)   221
Profile: Nina Lewin (Parent, Chelmsford Public Charter School, MA)   229
Profile: Sarah Kass (President, City On A Hill Charter School, Boston, MA)   233

Chapter 12. Will Charter Schools Save Public Education?

Interview: Lyndon Hernandez (Mythical Former Executive
   Director, MCREA)   256

We have known for a while that charter schools operate on a fast-changing field, but it is breathtaking to us to step back and reflect on how much has changed in the charter movement in the months since the initial publication of this book. What a difference a single year can make in this fascinating world of educational innovation.

During the 2000 presidential election, both candidates were falling over themselves trying to demonstrate which was more "pro-charter" and who could do more to advance this movement. Then–Governor Bush proposed a Charter School Homestead Act that would provide $3 billion in loan guarantees to assist two thousand charter schools. Then–Vice President Gore vowed to triple the number of charter schools by 2010. Children from Houston's celebrated KIPP Academy charter school starred at the Republican convention, basked in the spotlight on *Sixty Minutes*, and landed on the front page of the *New York Times*.

Congress nearly doubled the appropriation for the federal charter start-up program (now $195 million); about four hundred new charter schools opened their doors (boosting the total above two thousand); and the nation's charter enrollment rose a whopping 20 percent, now surpassing half a million youngsters.

As is to be expected, research on charter schools continues apace, and much of it points to positive results. According to a new study by the Goldwater Institute in Arizona, charter schools in that state seem to be outperforming their public school counterparts: "In sum, charter schools do consistently better in reading. They do no worse in math. . . . Charters do better the longer kids attend them, but students who return to a traditional public school still benefit from having attended a charter school. . . . There is no evidence of charters creaming the best students, or of the worst performing charter students being the ones who leave."[1] A meta-review by the Center for Education Reform found that fifty out of fifty-three research-based studies of charter schools concluded that charter schools have been "innovative, accountable, and successful and have created both opportunities for the children who attend them and a 'ripple' effect on

---

[1] Lew Solmon et al., *Does Charter School Attendance Improve Test Scores?*, (Phoenix, Ariz.: Goldwater Institute, 2001).

traditional public schools within their jurisdiction."[2] In March 2001, *USA Today* reported that three new studies document large gains in charter schools: "After a decade of mixed results, new studies show strong academic gains in test scores for children in charter schools, with some of the biggest improvements among the lowest-performing students."[3]

Despite these encouraging findings, the caps (or limits or moratoriums) on the number of charter schools in some jurisdictions have become a serious problem in such diverse places as Massachusetts, Ohio, Michigan, North Carolina, Utah, Kansas, Idaho, Arkansas, Connecticut, Texas, Chicago, and rural Alaska. The demand for charters continues to exceed the available — or permissible — supply.

Perhaps this flurry of activity should not be surprising, considering the dynamism that has characterized the charter movement from the outset. Here we pause to catch up with recent developments, review three contentious topics in the charter school story, and preview several issues that bear on the future of public education in America.

TAKING STOCK

As we write in spring 2001, nearly twenty-one hundred operating charter schools enroll upwards of 518,000 children. If all those students were joined in a single school system, it would be the country's third largest, trailing only New York and Los Angeles. Judged by numbers alone, the charter movement is a force to be reckoned with. What's more, it is clearer than ever that charters are compatible with other important school reforms underway in the United States: with "standards-based" reform and its approach to accountability (which is the focus of a lively debate catalyzed by President Bush's proposals to transform federal education policy); with the intensifying focus on school results rather than inputs; with the effort to offer families more choices among more diverse schools; with the trend toward contracting and outsourcing education services and school makeovers; with the diversity and feisty independence of the growing home schooling movement; with the impulse to provide more small schools for children for reasons of both education and safety; and with accelerating change on the technology front.

Charter schools, in fact, turn out to be astonishingly adaptable and well suited to other reform initiatives, even as they point the way toward a reconceptualization of education policies with yet larger implications. Consider, for example, Bush's proposal to allow "charter states" to interact with Washington according to the now-familiar norms of operational flexibility and results-based accountability.

[2] Center for Education Reform, *What the Research Reveals about Charter Schools,* 2 November 2000, http://www.edreform.com/pubs/charters.htm.
[3] Tamara Henry, "Score Goes Up for Charters," *USA Today,* 28 March 2001.

None of this means that charter schools are yet the object of a political or educational consensus. Indeed, for all its growth, dynamism, and plasticity, what to make of the charter movement still depends on whom one asks. Views differ sharply. If you query the Ford Foundation and Harvard's John F. Kennedy School of Government, they think well enough of this reform idea to have awarded one of their coveted "Innovations in American Government" awards — some call these the Oscars of public service — to Minnesota's pioneering charter law. If you ask the National School Boards Association, on the other hand, they will thrust at you a recent study of "fact and fiction about charter schools" that stresses how little has been accomplished by this "expensive experiment" and that recommends ways that state and local officials should clamp down on charters.[4]

Whether one salutes it or seeks to throttle it, the charter movement has indisputably widened its reach. Five years ago, nearly 80 percent of all charter schools could be found in Arizona, California, and Michigan. Today, their portion is just 40 percent. In nearly every state with a "strong" charter law, the number of schools continues to grow, save where "caps" preclude this.

Yet the United States may have reached a plateau of sorts, at least with regard to the number of states with charter programs. Remaining jurisdictions seem reluctant to join the movement, whether due to political crosscurrents or lack of demand. Consider the state of Washington. After a half-dozen years of grassroots efforts (led by Jim and Fawn Spady) to pass a charter law over the opposition of powerful interest groups (see chapter 8), the Evergreen State came within a whisker of passing a charter referendum initiative in 2000, earning 48 percent of the statewide vote. Yet the measure lost. We'd call it "Spady and Goliath," except that Goliath still commands the field. Beyond Washington, there have also been charter school rumblings of late in Maryland, but as we go to press it remains among the thirteen states without a charter law.

NAVIGATING THE RAPIDS

From the beginning, charter schools have had to navigate treacherous rapids. Some capsize along the way. Some charter schools are ill-conceived, poorly planned, or badly led. A few have misbehaved. Some misjudged the student market in their communities. Others simply failed to surmount the challenges of starting and persevering with such a complex enterprise.

According to the Center for Education Reform, which tracks charter schools nationally, "As of December 2000, the number of failed charter

---

[4] Thomas L. Good and Jennifer S. Braden, *Charting a New Course: Fact and Fiction about Charter Schools* (Washington, D.C.: National School Boards Association, 2000).

schools stands at 86, and makes up 4 percent of the overall number of charter schools ever opened in the U.S."[5] Further analysis reveals that 38 percent of those that closed did so because of mismanagement, 37 percent for financial reasons (such as debt, inadequate enrollment, or unexpected costs), 15 percent for facility woes (such as losing their lease or failure to obtain necessary permits), 8 percent for academic reasons (such as accreditation issues and poor student academic performance), and 1 percent (a single school) due to a dispute between the hired management firm and the school's administration. In addition to outright closures, twenty-six charter schools were consolidated into their local school districts for various reasons, and at least another fifty have failed to open, whether because they changed their minds, got cold feet, or saw their facility plans crumble.

As if to illustrate the fragility of some charter schools, in spring 2001 the *New York Times* reported how a promising school in the Bronx foundered after the abrupt resignation of a popular teacher: "[The] departure shows how the careful plans on which charter schools are constructed can be disrupted by the same forces that often cause instability at traditional public schools in poor neighborhoods. . . . Operating outside a larger bureaucracy can make charter schools more dependent on individual personalities and thus more vulnerable to such surprises, though it may also give them more flexibility to rebound."[6]

We have known for a while that the rapids hold dangers for charter schools (see chapter 5), but several of the rocks in this channel now loom larger than before: allegations of tribalism, charges of profiteering, and the problem of "partial success."

Tribalism

While just about everyone acknowledges that charter schools are — and are supposed to be — public schools (albeit of a new sort), there is mounting concern that some charter laws enable private interests to rupture the common weal and inject social division into communities. One reviewer of this book acknowledged that "The robust charter school movement offers one of the most intriguing civic revivals of the past decade," but cautioned that "the charter financing mechanism is being used to strengthen not only local communities but also private tribes."[7]

How to reconcile this tension between fostering community and promoting tribalism? We acknowledge the concern, and we embrace the

---

[5] Center for Education Reform, "Closures: The Opportunity for Accountability," December 2000, http://www.edreform.com/pubs/cs_closures.htm.

[6] Jody Wilgoren, "Bronx Prep Reels as a Teacher Quits," *New York Times*, 14 March 2001.

[7] Bruce Fuller, review of *Charter Schools in Action*, forthcoming in *Education Matters*, Summer 2001.

American conviction that public schooling should serve to bridge society's differences rather than widen them. Most charter schools of our acquaintance build robust spans as they invite disadvantaged youngsters who rely on a strong education to cross over onto the shores of success rather than remain stranded on islands of despair. Examples abound, but notable among them are the Academy of the Pacific Rim and City on a Hill Charter School, both of which are not only examples of successful integration and community-building but also educational excellence.

Yet some charter critics insist that choice inevitably leads to discrimination and invidious selection. One points to charter schools' ability to "select their students" by creating "curriculums that have racial or ideological biases (of the left or the right)."[8] However, levels of integration in charter schools are more a function of residential housing patterns than any sub-rosa plot among charter operators to discriminate against groups of children. The essential point is that charter schools are undeniably serving minority communities and, in many cases, serving them better than regular public schools.

Some skeptics cite the recent experience of New Zealand, recounted by authors Edward Fiske and Helen Ladd, as a "cautionary tale" for charter schools.[9] They aver that the Antipodean school system has become more stratified and segregated as a result of educational choice.

Yet the New Zealand parallel is not all that pertinent. For example, choice schools in New Zealand were able to select their students, which U.S. charters may not do. They also consisted of "conversions" of existing schools, not like the new "start-up" schools that comprise the overwhelming majority of the U.S. charter rolls. In addition, New Zealand's schools of choice had limited autonomy, remained subject to nationwide union contracts, gained scant control over financial and personnel decisions, and were constrained even in curriculum and governance. We would not call that a free marketplace of choice schools nor draw from it many lessons for American charters.

Profiteering

Along with concerns about balkanization, hostility toward for-profit companies using the charter mechanism to make a buck at taxpayers' ex-

---

[8] Howard Gardner, "Paroxysms of Choice," *The New York Review of Books*, 19 October 2000, 44–48. See also Bruce Fuller, ed., *Inside Charter Schools: The Paradox of Radical Decentralization* (Cambridge: Harvard University Press, 2001).

[9] See Gardner, "Paroxysms of Choice." See also Edward B. Fiske and Helen F. Ladd, "The Invisible Hand as Schoolmaster," *The American Prospect*, 22 May 2000, 19. See also review of Ladd and Fiske by Mark Harrison, forthcoming in *Education Matters*, Summer 2001.

pense often confronts charter schools.[10] (It also greeted this book.) While most such disputes have specific, local roots, they typically reflect deep-seated beliefs and assumptions. In our view, they reflect a romantic conception of a "public" education system that refuses to recognize the extent to which that system is already driven by financial interests and competitive dynamics (for example, textbook companies, technology providers, food-service companies, and transportation providers, not to mention teachers' unions and school boards).

A favorite lightning rod for critics of the profit motive in education is Edison Schools (formerly the Edison Project), now the country's largest charter management company. This firm has been under fire from coast to coast. In New York City, Edison was voted down when it offered to manage some of the city's worst-performing public schools under contract. In Florida (where Edison pioneered the practice of giving company stock options to school employees), the firm was criticized for forming a partnership with the United Teachers of Dade to launch ten charter schools in Miami-Dade County. Three thousand miles away, as we write, the San Francisco school board is on the verge of booting out the Edison Charter Academy, evidently untroubled by the fact that pupils in that school have made impressive academic gains in reading and math under Edison's management. When asked about his opposition to the school, considering how much better its students were doing, one San Francisco board member flatly stated, "I am philosophically against a corporation running a school. . . ." A parent shot back, "What part of success don't you understand?"[11]

And so goes the debate, with critics insisting that the profit motive does not belong in public education. Never mind that barely 10 percent of all charter schools are managed under contract by for-profit companies. Never mind that most such agreements take the form of performance-based contracts negotiated at arms-length between private firms and the nonprofit organizations that actually hold the charter and remain accountable for its success. Never mind that most of these school management companies have yet to turn a profit—and that they will make a profit only if they deliver the goods. And never mind that the goods haven't been delivered by the public school system in these areas for thirty years.

Here we reiterate our point (from chapter 10) that charter schools represent a "third way," a middle ground between the poles of outright privatization and barren government bureaucracy. When all is said and done, it is likely that a system of public-private partnerships, driven by the con-

[10] See Fuller, review of *Charter Schools in Action*. See also Richard Rothstein, "Double Standards," *The American Prospect*, 31 July 2000.

[11] Debra J. Saunders, "Edison Is Ground Zero in Education Battle," *San Francisco Chronicle*, 28 January 2001. Michael Bazeley, "S.F. School Committee Suggests Edison Academy Warrants Probe," *San Jose Mercury News*, 23 February 2001. Ann Grimes, "San Francisco's School Board Seeks to Revoke Edison's Charter," *The Wall Street Journal*, 20 February 2001.

sumers of education (parents and students), will lead the way out of tired old debates.

Partial Success

Perhaps due to the high-voltage controversies associated with charter schools due to such allegations of tribalism and profiteering, not to mention cloudy pictures of student performance, charter accountability arrangements often get framed in binary terms: either a school succeeds and is renewed or it fails and gets shut down. But as we move further along the learning curve, it is clear that many charter schools today are in the gray area of partial success.

What is to be done with a school that makes solid progress toward its stated objectives but doesn't actually attain all of them within the allotted time—a school, for example, that rashly promised that all its graduates would be ready for college? Suppose just half of them are? If the school is serving kids who otherwise wouldn't be headed for college at all, half is an awesome gain. Yet it is a considerable distance from the goal the school wrote into its charter. Should such a school be praised or closed—or given more time?

This wrenching question is illustrated by the Cesar Chavez Public Charter School in our nation's capital. The school has been lauded for the great strides it has made and its commitment to high standards, but it has also been criticized for lagging test scores and overpromising in its charter contract. Its dynamic principal, Irasema Salcido, held back two-thirds of her ninth graders in spring 1999 and half the ninth graders and a quarter of the tenth graders in spring 2000, yet her students still may not reach the ambitious goals of the school's charter. One problem: when they entered Cesar Chavez in 1998, some ninth graders were reading at third-grade level and could not recite their multiplication tables. The D.C. Public Charter School Board will soon have to decide whether to close the school down, put it on probation, give it a provisional renewal and mandate an improvement plan, or let the school continue along its current path.[12] This is a story that we should expect to see repeated in every community and state with a charter program, and it's one that cannot be sufficiently addressed by the simplistic mantra that "either the school succeeds or it must close."

THE FRONTIER OF SCHOOL REFORM

While these three controversies are lively and important, we sense that the true measure of the charter movement's value to this country will be in its ability to point the way toward a better—more effective, efficient, and dynamic—model of public education. In particular, three frontier issues

[12] Siobhan Gorman, "Great Expectations," *National Journal,* 9 September 2000.

are being pushed forward by charter schools: transparency, technology, and "portability."

The Promise of Transparency

While several elements of this book proved controversial, one concept that has been applauded by readers and commentators across the political spectrum is our proposal for "accountability via transparency," also known as "GAAPE" (Generally Accepted Accountability Principles for Education).

To be sure, "accountability" is all the rage in statehouses and along the Potomac. But what we propose is more than a slogan. We sought to outline a paradigm for education accountability with applications far beyond the charter movement. We believe that chapter 6, "The Accountability Puzzle," can serve as a guide for policymakers and educators seeking to push the envelope in holding all schools to account for their results without regulating them into oblivion.

Some people view this approach as a fig leaf covering a stealth regimen of regulation. One reviewer asserted that we "propose rigorous accountability for charters but fail to recognize this for the public regulatory scheme it is."[13] In our view, it is critical to distinguish between public regulatory schemes as currently constituted, focused chiefly on inputs such as attendance, "seat time," class size, per-pupil expenditures, and the like, and transparent accountability schemes that invite the world to observe a school's record of academic achievement and fiscal soundness. Transparency relies on market forces — not regulatory compliance — but insists that the various markets be fully informed. This is a way of solving the country's problem of insufficient educational accountability without enmeshing schools in innumerable rules, contracts, clauses, and ordinances.

With transparency, policymakers can take the approach of "trust but verify" with their charter schools — and perhaps with other schools. Indeed, state and federal education programs could benefit from a healthy dose of transparency in their operations. Transparency could also go a long way to resolve the problem of partial success. If the information is public and the market is regulating, which includes "signaling" the schools about what needs to change, maybe there would be diminished need for the "all or nothing" approach to accountability.

E-Charters

We noted above that charters are adaptable to the electronic world. Clearly, big changes lie ahead as technology gradually severs the ancient

[13] Rothstein, "Double Standards," 52.

link between educating kids and insisting that they sit in physical schools. The day is coming when parents will be able to obtain almost any kind of education they want for their children, twenty-four hours a day and seven days a week, any place they happen to be, including the home, day care center, workplace, cottage by the sea, YMCA, or local community college. This is already happening in higher education, usually called "distance learning." It is coming fast to K–12 education and is fraught with implications for absolutely every aspect of this field.

As in so many arenas, charter schools seem to be at the head of the parade. There are already about a dozen "virtual" charter schools operating in the United States that are bending our notions of attendance, "seat time," school day, school year, count days, school funding, grade level, individualized instruction, child-centered learning, school community, record-keeping, privacy, assessment, and the measurement of learning. At Choice 2000 Online Charter School (www.choice2000.org) in Perris, California, classes are conducted synchronously over the Internet using an electronic whiteboard and real-time audio. At the Electronic Classroom of Tomorrow (www.ecotohio.org) in Ohio, over twenty-five hundred students signed up for the school in its first period of operation in the 2000–01 school year.[14] (There are also more than fifty home-based charter schools that are similarly pointing the way toward new conceptions of schooling, in which parental involvement is no longer a platitude but rather an integral part of a school's instructional program.) As the Internet reaches beyond the schools themselves, communities are no longer inhibited by home-grown resources, local talent, or the physical capacity of aging buildings. World-class content can be delivered on demand. What does tomorrow hold? We cannot be sure, but charter schools are proving to be fertile soil for experimentation.

Portability

By challenging so many traditional assumptions, charter schools highlight any number of discrepancies between America's educational aspirations and its customary practices. We've seen this with the dynamics of choice, with transparency, with accountability, and with technology. But nowhere is it truer than in the Byzantine world of school funding. Charter schools — and other forms of school choice — call attention to a basic defect in America's education finance system, which was designed for a world with no choice.

School funding in most places is heavily geographic, based on a district where certain people live, which has certain property located within its

---

[14] Two of the authors are affiliated with K12 (www.K12.com), an online school that is slated to open in September 2001.

boundaries and certain tax revenues based on that property. That arrangement was okay when all kids attended district-operated schools located in the district where they lived. But the charter movement is based on the premise that you can go to school practically anywhere and that the money should be attached to the child, not the district. Will the finance system catch up? Michigan and California have already turned school finance into a state-level responsibility. But other states like New York and Ohio continue litigating and politicking over financial equity.

One solution lies in the concept of "portability," which entails strapping the money to the child's back and letting these dollars accompany that child to the school of the family's choice. It's simple enough in concept, but it has massive implications for the entire financing scheme of U.S. public education. This principle is already in place in Arizona, which also happens to be the epicenter of charter school activity in the United States. It is, effectively, the charter principle carried to its logical fiscal conclusion. If it were applied more generally to public education in other states, there would be tectonic shifts. Thus, we are left wondering what an education system might look like if it were based on the charter model.

THE FUTURE OF CHARTER SCHOOLS

It is by raising such profound questions about transparency, technology, and school finance that charters are helping Americans glimpse a very different educational future. Instead of viewing charters as pressure release valves for pent-up steam in the boiler, we hear talk about "chartering" every single public school in a community, about "charter districts" (a few of which now exist in California, Georgia, and Florida), and about charter states. We even hear about charter universities and charter "ed schools."

Is it possible that the charter concept is becoming a preview of tomorrow's central educational design? In this book's concluding chapter, we sketch such a future by depicting an entire metropolitan area whose education system is imbued with the precepts, dynamics, and energy of charter schools.

The charter movement is a strikingly fluid and dynamic venture that keeps surprising us, solving one problem and opening another, redefining key terms, and creating new opportunities. While all this poses a mighty challenge to the analyst and author, it is also a sign of something alive and organic, and well worth watching closely. How intriguing that American education, for so long such an inert mass, could sprout (and tolerate) this kind of a dynamic offshoot — both a near-term opportunity to offer more choices for families and boost children's academic performance, and a long-term re-sequencing of the DNA of public education itself. The question is whether such a quirky and contentious movement ends up isolated by a system intent on preserving its old ways or turns out to be compelling and resilient enough to tug its host in new directions. It may be another decade before we know for sure.

Washington, D.C.
April 2001

CHARTER SCHOOLS IN ACTION

INTRODUCTION

The point is that it's time to question or justify every assumption we have had about schooling for the last 150 years. . . . This is . . . likely to produce some very new models.

Albert Shanker, 1988

THIS BOOK emerges from three and a half years of immersion in the world of charter schools under the auspices of the Educational Excellence Network. The first two of those years we devoted to a research project called "Charter Schools in Action," generously supported by the Pew Charitable Trusts and housed at the Hudson Institute. We conducted that study with Louann Bierlein, now the education policy advisor to Louisiana Governor Mike Foster. (We're pleased that Louann also appears in chapter 11.)

Our purpose was to examine practical and policy issues surrounding the creation and operation of charter schools, to begin to appraise what was, in 1995, still a new and poorly understood education reform strategy. During those two years, we visited about one hundred charter schools, interviewed hundreds of people involved with the charter movement, surveyed thousands of parents, students, and teachers, and familiarized ourselves with the policy dilemmas, political environments, and implementation problems of more than a dozen states. A sizable and well-conceived federal charter school study is now underway, but as of now, to the best of our knowledge, we have gathered and analyzed more information about this reform strategy than anyone else. While the charter scene is too dynamic for any account to remain definitive for long, we respectfully suggest that these pages come as close as is presently possible.

Numerous reports and articles emerged from our fieldwork and analysis.[1]

---

[1] "What Are We Learning About Charter Schools?" *Jobs & Capital* (Spring 1996): 11–17; "Finding the Right Fit: America's Charter Schools Get Started," *Brookings Review* (Summer 1996): 18–21; "Better Schools," *The San Diego Tribune*, 22 September 1996, G1, G6; "Charter Schools: What Have We Learned?" *Aberdeen Daily World*, 25 October 1996, A4; "Not Getting It Quite Right on Charter Schools," *Pacific Research Institute Briefing Paper* (October 1996): 1–9; "The Empire Strikes Back," *The New Democrat* (November/December 1996): 8–11; "Accountable Education," *The Washington Post*, 15 December 1996, C1, C2; "The False Friends of Charter Schools," *Education Week*, 30 April 1997, 60; "Charter

But something else happened along the way. We found ourselves tantalized by the charter phenomenon and its potential to transform American public education. We also found ourselves amazed by the variety of problems that people were using charter laws to solve, alarmed by early signs of trouble in some schools, and absorbed by the complex politics surrounding them.

So we continued our investigations. The data soon bulged out of our files, and friends and relatives tired of our propensity to jabber incessantly about charter schools. By the time we published the Charter Schools in Action "final report" in summer 1997, it was clear that this story deserved a full-fledged book.[2] With the encouragement of Peter J. Dougherty, our exemplary editor at the Princeton University Press, we undertook the present work, which, predictably, kept changing as each avenue of analysis led to another. Our fieldwork continued, too, as we updated our information, revisited schools, interviewed charter experts and foes, and enlisted dozens of others to enrich (and correct) our thinking.

Schools Show Great Promise," *Triangle Business Journal*, 2 May 1997, 38; "Learning in Charter Schools," *Journal of Commerce*, 5 May 1997, A11; "Giving North Carolina Charter Schools a Chance to Reinvent Education," *Charlotte Observer*, 30 April 1997, A11; "Chartering a New Course," *Washington Post Outlook*, 31 August 1997, C1–2; "Creating America's New Public Schools," *The World & I*, (September 1997): 317–29; "The New School," *National Review*, 15 September 1997, 48–52; "Norma Cantu Strikes Again," *The Weekly Standard*, 27 October 1997, 14–16; "Do the Right Thing for Marcus Garvey and All Charter Schools," *The Washington Post*, 31 October 1997, A25; *Charter School Accountability: Findings and Prospects* (Bloomington, Ind.: Phi Delta Kappa Educational Foundation, 1997); "Charter Schools: Accomplishments and Dilemmas," *Teachers College Record 99*, no. 3 (Spring 1998): 537–57; "How Charter Schools Are Different," *Phi Delta Kappan 79*, no. 7 (March 1998): 489–98; "Charter Schools as Seen by Students, Teachers, and Parents," in *Learning from School Choice*, eds. Paul E. Peterson and Bryan C. Hassel (Washington, D.C.: Brookings Institution Press, 1998), 187–211; "A School Reform Whose Time Has Come," *City Journal 8*, no. 3 (Summer 1998): 73–80; "The Real Story on Charter-School Success," *The Seattle Times*, 3 April 1998; "The Twelve Labors of Charter Schools," *The New Democrat,* July/August 1998: 10–12; "Support Your Local Charter School," *Policy Review* September/October 1998: 18–25; "Charter Schools Survive Garvey," *Washington Business Journal*, 3–9 July 1998, 58; "Charters: After Marcus Garvey," *The Washington Post*, 7 July 1998, A13; "Who's Afraid of Charter Schools?" *The Washington Post*, 9 September 1998, A 19; "Mayoral Hopefuls Should Back Charter Schools," *Washington Business Journal*, 11–17 September 1998, 107; "Your Money and Your Life," *Philanthropy* September/October 1998: 18–22; "Charter Schools Help Change Public Education," *The Anniston Star*, 11 October 1998, F3.

    [2] Three reports were published under the auspices of that project: Chester E. Finn, Jr., Bruno V. Manno, and Louann A. Bierlein, *Charter Schools in Action: A First Look* (Indianapolis: Hudson Institute, January 1996); Chester E. Finn, Jr., Bruno V. Manno, and Louann A. Bierlein, *Charter Schools in Action: What Have We Learned?* (Indianapolis: Hudson Institute, 1996); and Chester E. Finn, Jr., Bruno V. Manno, Louann A. Bierlein, and Gregg Vanourek, *Charter Schools in Action: Final Report* (Indianapolis: Hudson Institute, July 1997). Two of these reports are on-line at http://www.edexcellence.net/topics/charters.html.

THE PAGES AHEAD

The twelve chapters that follow are organized in two parts. The first part, "Charter Schools in Action," begins with a description (in chapter 1) of the charter phenomenon. In chapter 2, we tour five operating schools that illustrate this movement—warts and all—better than a thousand generalizations or statistics. Even this humble sampling includes small schools and large, urban and suburban, for-profit and nonprofit, progressive and traditional, "real" and "virtual." Here, as throughout this volume, the reader will make the acquaintance, via interviews and profiles, of people active in the charter movement: parents and operators, students and teachers, board members and state officials.

Next (in chapter 3), we examine the theory of charter schools, the idea's origins, the education environment in which it has taken root, and some powerful parallels in other spheres of contemporary life. We then (in chapter 4) ask how well charter schools are actually working and report some of the evidence concerning their strengths and weaknesses. (More data appear in the appendix.)

Chapter 5 explains why it is so difficult to launch successful charter schools, but then shows some of the ways that plucky charter founders overcome adversity and find solutions to their start-up problems. The book's first half concludes with chapter 6, which sets forth a unique concept of school accountability that would, we believe, make for a healthier charter movement—not to mention a blueprint for change among conventional schools.

Part II is called "Renewing Public Education." Here we step back to view what is happening beyond the perimeter of individual charter schools. Whatever good many of them are doing, it is vital to establish the context within which they are doing it and to look toward the future.

The charter movement remains plenty controversial, and we seek not to duck the accusations that are hurled at it but, rather, to grapple directly with them. In chapter 7, we weigh the principal arguments against charter schools. And in chapter 8, we plunge into the political arena within which they exist.

Chapter 9 opens with another tour, this time to two school districts that have been strongly influenced by the charter movement. Then it examines other ways in which this movement is leveraging change in state and local education systems and reshaping the national policy debate. Chapter 10 travels beyond the customary boundaries of education policy and examines the interplay between charter schools and their communities. Neither conventionally governmental nor essentially private, charters tap into Americans' propensity for civic engagement and channel that impulse into education reform. In so doing, they affect civil society itself.

Where is the charter movement headed? In chapter 11, with the help of three notable experts from different states and with different political perspectives, we examine the great issues facing the charter reform strategy. Will it remain a sideshow, a welcome refuge for a few hundred thousand youngsters but peripheral to the larger world of K–12 education? Or will charter schools move into the center ring, becoming a major option for millions of American children and reinventing public education along the way?

In the book's final chapter, we imagine what that "major option" might actually look like in practice by sketching a picture of public education reinvented along charter precepts. We take an imaginary tour of a major city around the year 2010 and illustrate the ways in which education is different under this new regime. This chapter is followed by an Epilogue in which we tease out key features of the reinvented system. Finally, we conclude the book with an Appendix that provides more data on the students, parents, and teachers of charters schools and describes the concept and methodology of our multiyear study.

Like all authors, we hope that everyone who picks up this volume will read it from cover to cover. But here are some suggestions for those short on time:

Parents wanting to know more about charter schools should concentrate on Part I, particularly chapters 1, 2, 4, and 5, and perhaps peek at the discussion of the intersection between these schools and their communities in chapter 10.

Teachers, principals, and other educators will be especially interested in the first five chapters, together with chapters 9 and 12. And brave folks considering starting a charter school ought to look with special care at chapters 1, 2, 5, 6, and the Epilogue.

Policymakers weighing a charter program for their state or community would be wise to review the evidence on school success that is supplied in chapter 4, the analysis of weak and strong charter laws in chapter 5, and the discussion of accountability in chapter 6. They may also benefit from a look at the political climate (chapter 8), key issues as seen by veteran policymakers (chapter 11), and our rendering of a charter-based future (chapter 12).

ACKNOWLEDGMENTS

Our debts are more numerous and varied than can be repaid in a few paragraphs. To those interviewed or profiled in the book, we are immeasurably thankful for their willingness to appear in print and by name, including several thoughtful individuals who are less than enraptured with charter schools.[3] We will but name them here, as they are identified where

---

[3] Interviews appearing in this book were conducted by sending charter students, teachers,

they appear in the pages that follow: Linda Brown, Harry Fair, Jim Goenner, Keith Grauman, Scott Hamilton, Mary Hartley, Karen Holden, Sarah Kass, Lisa Graham Keegan, Mark Kushner, Doug Lemov, Nina Lewin, Joe Lucente, Richard O'Connell, Marilyn Keller Rittmeyer, Vernon Robinson, Ellis Smith, Fawn and Jim Spady, Deborah Springpeace, Irene Sumida, Julie Veeneman, James Zaharis, and students at Lowell Middlesex Academy, the Charter School of San Diego, Sequoia School, and Excel Charter Academy. (In the interests of privacy, we have changed the names of individual students, and thus are unable to thank them by name.) Several other wonderful people went through the arduous process of being interviewed, but then, due to space considerations, had their profiles or interviews left on the cutting-room floor. They deserve both our gratitude and apologies.

The five schools that we "visit" in chapter 2, and the two districts that we "tour" in chapter 9, are real places full of real people who went far beyond the call of duty to inform us, correct our errors, keep us up to date, and influence our thinking. Special thanks to Joe Lucente and Irene Sumida of California's Fenton Avenue Charter School, Stacey Boyd and Doug Lemov of Massachusetts's Academy of the Pacific Rim, Randy Gaschler and Keith Alpaugh of California's Horizon Instructional Systems, Bill Knoester and Barb Bliss of Michigan's Excel Charter Academy, and Don Flake of Arizona's Sequoia School. In Douglas County, Colorado, we are greatly indebted to superintendent Rick O'Connell and his team, particularly Pat Grippe and Laura Harmon. In Kingsburg, California, we are sincerely grateful to Ron Allvin, Mark Ford, and Jim Haslip.

We cannot begin to name the hundreds of other people around America — adults and kids alike — who graciously let us visit their schools, interview them at length, observe their classes, peer over their shoulders, sit in on their meetings, harass them by mail, fax, e-mail, and phone, and otherwise get in their way. Without them, however, our only information about charter schools would be what we could read, which is no way to learn about so varied and complex an education reform strategy. We are as appreciative as can be.[4]

Throughout our fieldwork, we were immensely aided by state-level charter leaders and experts who shepherded us around, helped us determine with whom to talk, explained the idiosyncrasies of their state's charter program, and gave us periodic updates. We single out Arizona's John Kakritz, Kathi Haas, Mary Gifford, and Lisa Keegan; California's Eric Premack, Sue Burr, Sue Bragato, Pam Riley, and Kay Davis; Colorado's Jim Griffin and Bill Windler; Wisconsin's Senn Brown; Massachusetts's Scott

---

parents, directors, policymakers, analysts, and critics a list of questions and then obtaining either oral or written responses. Profiles were created by sending them a list of questions and then weaving the responses of each individual into a vignette about that person.

[4] The Hudson Institute reports cited in footnote 2 contain many names of people we interviewed.

Hamilton, Jose Alfonso, Linda Brown, and Jim Peyser; Minnesota's Peggy Hunter; Michigan's Jim Goenner and Bob Whittmen; Texas's Brooks Flemister; New Jersey's Sarah Tantillo; the District of Columbia's Nelson Smith, David Mack, and Eunice Henderson; Kansas's Phyllis Kelly; North Carolina's Jim Watts, Richard Clontz, Roxanne Premont, and Thelma Glynn; and Florida's Frank Brogan, Tracey Bailey, and Brewser Brown.

Special thanks are due to Louann Bierlein, Gary Hart, and Tom Patterson for, in effect, co-authoring chapter 11 with us. Louann bears an extra burden of responsibility and thus deserves an extra measure of gratitude, as she was our star partner during much of the research phase and did much to shape our thinking and make sense of our data. Gary Hart and Tom Patterson, one a Democrat, the other a Republican, can be termed the legislative fathers of charter schools in the two states (California and Arizona) with the most extensive charter programs today.

The Pew Charitable Trusts underwrote much of this endeavor. The former director of Pew's education program, Bob Schwartz, had the vision and courage to break ranks with more charter-wary foundations and support a major investigation of a controversial topic by strong-minded people. We are sincerely grateful to him and his successors and colleagues. Similarly, the Hudson Institute, on whose research staff we served during much of this period, was a grand home for such a study. Former Hudson president Leslie Lenkowsky and current president Herb London were supportive of the work, genuinely interested in our findings, and helpful in a hundred ways. Debbie Hoopes kept track of the money. Sam Karnick lent a hand with publications. Expert secretarial and administrative assistance came from Sheryl McMillian and Irmela Vontillius. John Barry, Adam Goldin, Jan Oliver, and Rebecca Arrick pitched right in, as did a multitude of wonderful interns, including Rebecca Gau, Jake Phillips, Brad White, Mark Scheffler, and Diana Schloegel. Bruno Manno also wishes to thank the Lynde and Harry Bradley Foundation and the Annie E. Casey Foundation for their support of his participation. Chester Finn is grateful to the John M. Olin and Thomas B. Fordham Foundations, which sustain his work.

As the data arrived, analysis was needed. After surveying nearly 5,000 students, 3,000 parents, and 500 teachers, we turned to the Information Technology Services division of the Brookings Institution for help in processing and analyzing that data. Special thanks to Tibor Purger, Winnie Alvarado, and Jane Fishkin for their excellent, professional work.

With draft in hand, we sought advice about how to improve it. Nine wonderful friends gave us timely and perceptive help with this manuscript: Stacey Boyd, charter (and business) founder without peer; Scott Hamilton, formerly the Bay State's charter maestro and a longtime colleague; Eric Hanushek, one of the nation's truly distinguished education economists; Paul Hill, the single most inventive education policy thinker we know;

Caroline Minter Hoxby, a fast-rising economics star with special insight into education choice issues; Marci Kanstoroom, a young political scientist and colleague, now at the Manhattan Institute and Thomas B. Fordham Foundation; Mike Petrilli, a passionate and astute young education reformer (and Manhattan/Fordham colleague); Diane Ravitch, America's premier education historian, our longtime partner, and co-founder (back in 1981) of the Educational Excellence Network; and Bill Schambra of the Lynde and Harry Bradley Foundation, who is an acute analyst and tireless restorer of civil society in the United States.

Like all authors, we needed help now and again, and there was always someone to turn to. Special thanks to Jeanne Allen and Dave DeSchryver of the Center for Education Reform, Bryan Hassel, Jim Peyser, Robert Vanourek (Gregg's father), and a host of students at the Yale School of Management. We are also grateful for the help and hard work of the team at Princeton University Press, including Jodi Beder, our able copy editor.

Chester Finn offers an extra bouquet to his wife, Renu Virmani, who has learned rather more than she ever intended about charter schools and who cheerfully tolerated this additional intrusion into family life.

Bruno Manno is grateful to his wife, Linda Hammond, and granddaughter, Ashli Kaye, for their forbearance through many long months of research and writing, and to his parents who saw to it that all four of "the kids" were given the best educational opportunities they could receive. Ashli Kaye has also helped him appreciate how important it is for this nation to have public schools that meet the diverse and special needs of all its youngsters.

Gregg Vanourek would like to thank his family — Bob, June, and Scott — for encouraging him to pursue his dreams.

Washington, D.C.
Baltimore, Maryland
New Haven, Connecticut
September 1999

Part I

CHARTER SCHOOLS
IN ACTION

1

WHAT'S A "CHARTER SCHOOL"?

> The charter school concept has the potential to utterly trans-
> form public education. Thanks to charter schools, the public
> is getting used to the idea that a school does not need to be
> operated directly by government in order to be public.
>
> *Scott W. Hamilton, former Associate Commissioner,*
> *Massachusetts Department of Education*

CHARTER SCHOOLS are the liveliest reform in American education.
"When I was elected President," Bill Clinton observed in July 1998,
"There was only one such school in the country. . . . We're well on our
way to meeting my goal of creating 3,000 such schools by the beginning of
the next century."[1] Connecticut Democratic Senator Joseph Lieberman
writes: "Competition from charter schools is the best way to motivate the
ossified bureaucracies governing too many public schools. This grass-roots
revolution seeks to reconnect public education with our most basic values:
ingenuity, responsibility, and accountability."[2] An Arizona official terms
charter schools "the most important thing happening in public education."

Before these unconventional public schools vaulted into the spotlight in
the mid-1990s, education reform in the United States was nearing paral-
ysis—stalemated by politics, confused by the cacophony of a thousand
schemes working at cross-purposes, and hobbled by most people's inability
to imagine anything very different from the schools they had attended decades earlier.

More than a generation of schoolchildren have passed through U.S.
schools since the National Commission on Excellence in Education warned
in 1983 that America's well-being was menaced by the mediocrity of our

---

[1] Remarks of President Bill Clinton in the Rose Garden, Washington, D.C., Office of the
White House Press Secretary, 24 July 1998.

[2] Joseph Lieberman, "Schools Where Kids Succeed," *Readers' Digest,* January 1999. Lieberman was the sponsor of the first federal Charter School Grant Program and co-sponsored
the 1998 Charter School Expansion Act.

K–12 education system.[3] Yet little has changed for the better. Despite bushels of effort, barrels of good intentions, and billions of dollars, most reform efforts have yielded meager dividends. Test scores are generally flat, and U.S. twelfth graders lag far behind their international counterparts in math and science, although our school expenditures are among the planet's highest. Combining large budgets and weak performance, American schools can fairly be termed the least productive in the industrial world.[4]

Countless parents, especially the poor, minorities, and inhabitants of our central cities, are worried about their children's education—and urgently seeking alternatives.[5] Too many students are shortchanged by the current system, emerging without decent preparation for citizenship, college, and the workforce. Hordes of good teachers are frustrated and overwhelmed. Some abandon the field after just a few years.

Enter charter schools in 1991, a seedling reform that grew into a robust tree, then a whole grove. The trees are still young, and the grove attracts plenty of lightning strikes, but it is steadily expanding and mostly thriving.

Even if the charter forest doesn't come to dominate our education ecosystem, the idea behind it has powerful implications for the entire enterprise of public schooling. In this book, we tease out those implications by explaining where charter schools came from, what they are like, how they function, and how they are doing so far. We also describe their potential to renew and redefine public education in the United States—and show how difficult it will be to turn that potential into reality.

What, Exactly, Is a Charter School?

Few outside the charter movement are clear about what a charter school is. A workable starting definition is that a charter school is an "independent public school of choice, freed from rules but accountable for results."

A charter school is a new species, a hybrid, with important similarities

---

[3] National Commission on Excellence in Education, *A Nation at Risk: The Imperative for Educational Reform* (Washington, D.C.: U.S. Government Printing Office, 1983).

[4] Herbert J. Walberg, *Spending More While Learning Less: U.S. School Productivity in International Perspective* (Washington, D.C.: Thomas B. Fordham Foundation, 1998). See also Harold W. Stevenson, *A TIMSS Primer* (Washington, D.C.: Thomas B. Fordham Foundation, 1998) and Diane Ravitch, *National Standards in American Education: A Citizen's Guide* (Washington, D.C.: The Brookings Institution, 1995), 59–97.

[5] On the 1998 Gallup survey of public attitudes toward education, for example, 46 percent of public school parents indicated that they would send their child to a different school if the government paid the tuition. Thirty-nine percent indicated a preference for a private or parochial school. Lowell C. Rose and Alec M. Gallup, "The 30th Annual Phi Delta Kappan/Gallup Poll of the Public's Attitudes Toward the Public Schools," *Phi Delta Kappan*, September 1998, 45–6.

to traditional public schools, some of the prized attributes of private schools — and crucial differences from both.

As a public school, a charter school is open to all who wish to attend it (i.e., without regard to race, religion, or academic ability); paid for with tax dollars (no tuition charges); and accountable for its results — indeed, for its very existence — to an authoritative public body (such as a state or local school board) as well as to those who enroll (and teach) in it.

Charter schools are also different from standard-issue public schools. Most can be distinguished by five key features:

- They can be created by almost anyone.
- They are exempt from most state and local regulations, essentially autonomous in their operations.
- They are attended by youngsters whose families choose them.
- They are staffed by educators who are also there by choice.
- They are liable to be closed for not producing satisfactory results.

Charter schools also resemble private schools in two important particulars. First, they are independent. Although answerable to outside authorities for their results (far more than most private schools), they are free to produce those results as they think best. They are self-governing institutions. They, like private schools, have wide-ranging control over their own curriculum, instruction, staffing, budget, internal organization, calendar, schedule, and much more. Second, like private schools, charter schools are schools of choice. Nobody is assigned against his will to attend (or teach in) a charter school. Parents select them for their children, much as they would a private school, albeit with greater risk because the new charter school typically has no track record.[6]

The "charter" itself is a formal, legal document, best viewed as a *contract* between those who launch and run a school and the public body that authorizes and monitors such schools. In charter-speak, the former are "operators" and the latter are "sponsors."

A charter operator may be a group of parents, a team of teachers, an existing community organization such as a hospital, Boys and Girls Club, university or day-care center, even (in several states) a private firm. School systems themselves can and occasionally do start charter schools. Sometimes an existing school seeks to secede from its local public system or, in a few jurisdictions, to convert from a tuition-charging private school to a tax-supported charter school. In those instances, the parents, staff, or

---

[6] In the case of "conversion" schools, it is usually taken for granted that the pre-charter student body will remain, and individuals must take steps to opt out and go elsewhere. But we have not found a single charter school where the exit door is barred. And "start-up" charters are nearly always full-fledged "schools of choice" that must begin from scratch in attracting students.

board of an existing school apply for a charter. The application spells out why the charter school is needed, how it will function, what results (academic and otherwise) are expected, and how these will be demonstrated. The operator may contract with someone — including private companies or "education management organizations" — to manage the school, but the operator remains legally responsible to the sponsor.

The sponsor is ordinarily a state or local school board. In some states, public universities also have authority to issue charters, as do county school boards and city councils. If the sponsor deems an application solid, it will negotiate a more detailed charter (or contract) for a specified period of time, typically five years but sometimes as short as one or as long as fifteen.

During that period, the charter school has wide latitude to function as it sees fit — at least if its state enacted a strong charter law (see chapter 5) and did not hobble charter schools with many of the constraints under which conventional public schools toil. Key features of the charter idea include waivers from state and local regulations, fiscal and curricular autonomy, the ability to make independent personnel decisions, and responsibility for delivering the results pledged in the charter.

If a school succeeds, it can reasonably expect to get its charter renewed when the time comes. If it fails, it may be shut down. And if it violates any unwaived laws, regulations, or community norms during the term of its charter, it may be shut down sooner. (Thirty-two charter schools had, for various reasons, ceased operation by the beginning of the 1998–99 school year.)[7]

We think of charters as "reinventing public education." Traditionally, Americans have defined a public school as any school run by the government, managed by a superintendent and school board, staffed by public employees, and operated within a public-sector bureaucracy. "Public school" in this familiar sense is not very different from "public library," "public park," or "public housing project."

Now consider a different definition: a public school is any school that is open to the public, paid for by the public, and accountable to public authorities for its results. So long as it satisfies those three criteria, it is a public school. It need not be *run* by government. Indeed, it does not matter — for purposes of its "publicness" — who runs it, how it is staffed, or what its students do between 9 and 10 A.M. on Tuesdays.

Charter schools are part of a bigger idea: reinvented public education in which elected and appointed officials play a strategic rather than a func-

---

[7] RPP International, *The State of Charter Schools: Third-Year Report* (Washington, D.C.: U.S. Department of Education, 1999), 10. See also Dave DeSchryver, "Charter Schools: A Progress Report, Part II: The Closures," Center for Education Reform, Washington, D.C., February 1999, http://www.edreform.com. In chapter 6, we take a closer look at charter closings.

tional role.[8] Charter schools mean public support of schooling without governmental provision of schools.

REVOLUTION OR EVOLUTION?

Enthusiasts and opponents often depict charter schools as a revolutionary change, a policy earthquake, an unprecedented and heretofore unimaginable innovation.[9] Boosters seize on such colorful rhetoric because it dramatizes the historic significance of their crusade. Enemies deploy the same terminology for the opposite purpose: to slow this movement's spread by portraying it as radical, risky, and unproven. Both groups tend to stand too close to the objects they are describing.

Viewed from a few inches away, charter schools *do* represent sharp changes in the customary practices of today's public school systems, especially the large ones. But with more perspective, we readily observe that charter schools embody three familiar and time-tested features of American education.

First, they are rooted in their communities. They are the essence of local control of education, not unlike the village schools of the early 19th century and the one-room schoolhouses found across the land through much of the 20th century. They resemble America's original public schools in their local autonomy, their rootedness in communities, their accountability to parents, and their need to generate revenues by attracting and retaining families. Creatures of civil society as much as agencies of government, charter schools would have raised no eyebrows on Alexis de Tocqueville.

Second, charter schools have cousins in the K–12 family. Their DNA looks much the same under the education microscope as that of lab schools, magnet schools, site-managed schools, and special focus schools (e.g., art, drama, science), not to mention private and home schools. Much the same, but not identical. The Bronx High School of Science is selective, while charter schools are not. Hillel Academy and the Sancta Maria Middle School teach religion, while charter schools cannot. The Urban Magnet School of the Arts was probably designed by a downtown bureaucracy and most likely has prescribed ethnic ratios in its student body, whereas most charter schools do not. Yet similarities still outweigh differences.

Third, these new schools reveal a classic American response to a problem or opportunity: institutional innovation and adaptation. In that respect, they resemble community colleges, which came into being (and

---

[8] Another contemporary example is the practice of school districts contracting with private "education management organizations" to operate individual public schools. For a thoughtful and complete treatment of this concept, see Paul T. Hill, Lawrence C. Pierce, and James W. Guthrie, *Reinventing Public Education* (Chicago: The University of Chicago Press, 1997).

[9] We have occasionally been guilty of this ourselves.

spread rapidly and fruitfully) to meet education needs that conventional universities could not accommodate.

As an organizational form, then, charter schools are not revolutionary. They are part of what we are and always have been as a nation.

WHERE DID CHARTER SCHOOLS COME FROM?

Most experts agree that the phrase was first used by the late Albert Shanker, long-time president of the American Federation of Teachers, in a 1988 speech to the National Press Club and a subsequent article. This is ironic, in view of the teachers unions' continuing hostility to the charter movement (see chapter 8). But it was not unusual for the brilliant and venturesome Shanker to suggest education reforms well in advance of their time.

Basing his vision on a school he had visited in Cologne, Germany, Shanker urged America to develop "a fundamentally different model of schooling that emerges when we rethink age-old assumptions — the kind of rethinking that is necessary to develop schools to reach the up to 80 percent of our youngsters who are failing in one way or another in the current system." He contemplated an arrangement that would "enable any school or any group of teachers . . . within a school to develop a proposal for how they could better educate youngsters and then give them a 'charter' to implement that proposal." "All this," he wrote,

> would be voluntary. No teacher would have to participate and parents would choose whether or not to send their children to a charter school. . . . For its part, the school district would have to agree that so long as teachers continued to want to teach in the charter school and parents continued to send their children there and there was no precipitous decline in student achievement indicators, it would maintain the school for at least 5–10 years. Perhaps at the end of that period, the school could be evaluated to see the extent to which it met its goals, and the charter could be extended or revoked.[10]

Shanker was echoed in a 1989 article called "Education by Charter" by Ray Budde.[11] Then a Minnesota legislator named Ember Reichgott Junge launched this idea in her state. By 1991, Minnesota had enacted the nation's first charter law.[12] Several dozen states have followed suit, and by September 1999 about 1,700 charter schools were up and running.

That scrap of history doesn't do justice to the many tributaries that fed into the charter idea. In chapter 3, we explore this topic in detail. For now,

---

[10] Albert Shanker, "Restructuring Our Schools," *Peabody Journal of Education* 65, no. 3 (Spring 1988): 97–98.

[11] *Charter Schools: A New Breed of Public Schools,* North Central Regional Educational Laboratory (NCREL), Report 2, 1993.

[12] Louann A. Bierlein, "The Charter School Movement," in *New Schools for a New Century: The Redesign of Urban Education,* eds. Diane Ravitch and Joseph P. Viteritti (New Haven: Yale University Press, 1997), 39–40.

suffice to say that we would not likely have any charter schools if Americans were content with their elementary-secondary education system or confident that more conventional reform efforts would work. Surveys show that education has become the country's number-one worry. It may also be our next great civil-rights frontier. Former New York Democratic Congressman Rev. Floyd Flake suggested as much when he said of today's education reform debate, "Masses of uneducated children represent a serious threat to the security of the country. . . . *Brown v. Board of Education* was about opportunity. So is school choice. . . ."[13]

Though widespread complacency about schools remains, particularly among the suburban middle class, one would have to be comatose not to detect the mounting ardor for alternatives, most intensely among minority groups and city dwellers. That is why some once rock-solid political supporters of traditional public schooling are becoming advocates for bold innovations. For example, U.S. Senator Robert Byrd recently remarked to his Senate colleagues:

> I have been voting for Federal aid to education for decades — not just years, for decades — since 1965, to be exact. . . . But, we still seem to be losing the battle against mediocrity. I do not want to vote against spending for education. But, Mr. President, when do we admit that we are doing poorly, and try something new?[14]

That is also why many parents are "voting with their feet" — and pocketbooks — and taking charge of their children's education. Private school enrollments are rising. Home schooling is burgeoning, by some estimates now accounting for 1.5 million U.S. youngsters. And we find widening use of other strategies for enriching children's learning, such as after-school tutoring (frequently provided by private firms), educational software for home computers, summer programs for gifted youngsters, and much more.

"Education reform" has itself become a growth industry in recent years, as we have devised a thousand innovations and spent billions to implement them. We have tinkered with class size, fiddled with graduation requirements, sought to end "social promotion," pushed technology into the schools, crafted new academic standards, revamped teacher training, bought different textbooks, and on and on. Most alterations were launched with good will and the honest expectation that they would turn the situation around.

Some say these reforms haven't had time to gain traction. Others claim that they haven't been adequately funded. No doubt there is some truth in those explanations. Our sense, however, is that the chief explanation for their failure is their incrementalism.

---

[13] Wendy Costa, "Public Acceptance of Vouchers Is Growing Rapidly," *The Fresno Bee*, 11 November 1998, B5.

[14] U.S. Senator Robert Byrd, speech on the Senate floor, 23 April 1998.

The conventional reforms of the past two decades do not fundamentally alter our approach to public education. They do not replace the basic institutional arrangements, shift power, or rewrite the ground rules. That is acceptable if one believes the old structures remain sound. But that is not how we read the evidence. We judge that the traditional delivery system is obsolete. To be sure, there are some fine schools within the "regular" system and a number of exceptional ones on its periphery. But the system itself is failing because its basic mechanisms and structures *cannot* change in the ways needed to meet today's education needs and societal demands.[15] Its many "stakeholders" and interest groups fight every significant alteration. Yet if that delivery system doesn't change profoundly, the very concept of public education may be doomed in America. And many youngsters will be doomed with it.[16]

YESTERDAY'S DILEMMA, TODAY'S SOLUTION

Stop reading here if you believe that the traditional operating system of U.S. public education simply needs an upgrade. The chapters that follow will only aggravate you. If you don't believe in any form of public education, you, too, will likely be upset by our take on this complicated topic; by our conviction that there is a promising alternative to the conventional school system as it has evolved over the past century; and by our belief that the community still has an obligation to see that today's unlettered children become tomorrow's educated adults. At day's end, this book defends the principle and function of public education while arguing for a top-to-bottom makeover of its ground rules and institutional practices.

The alternative we depict is a way out of a wrenching dilemma. Until recently—really until charter schools came along—the only clear competitor to the government-run, bureaucratic system of public education was wholesale privatization: leave people who want schooling for their children to purchase it with their own money, or redeploy government dollars in the form of "vouchers" to subsidize families making private purchases from private vendors.[17]

---

[15] For a magisterial explanation of "the system's" inability to change itself, see John E. Chubb and Terry E. Moe, *Politics, Markets, and America's Schools* (Washington, D.C.: The Brookings Institution, 1990).

[16] See E.D. Hirsch, Jr., *The Schools We Need and Why We Don't Have Them* (New York: Doubleday, 1996); Charles J. Sykes, *Dumbing Down Our Kids: Why America's Children Feel Good About Themselves but Can't Read, Write, or Add* (New York: St. Martin's Press, 1995); Chester E. Finn, Jr., *We Must Take Charge: Our Schools and Our Future* (New York: The Free Press, 1991).

[17] The libertarian case for complete privatization is made eloquently, logically, and with much historical backing by Andrew J. Coulson in *Market Education: The Unknown History* (New Brunswick, New Jersey: Transaction Publishers, 1999); for additional versions, Eli J. Lake, "Christians Plot Course to Vacate Public Schools," *Education Daily*, 19 August 1998,

Privatization appeals to libertarians and free-marketeers, but it also has shortcomings. Here are a half-dozen that we find most compelling:

- Americans believe in "public education." They don't necessarily believe in big government–style education, and they surely don't crave costly, ineffectual education. But when they conclude that a reform scheme (or candidate for office) would undermine the *principle* of public education, they nearly always turn away.
- Many political interests are arrayed against the privatization of K–12 education. The weight of much history (and vast systemic inertia) is on their side.
- Constitutional inhibitions remain, not so much at the national level as in the states, where every single constitution charges the state itself with delivering a basic education to its citizenry.
- Despite their aura, private schools don't do all that great a job. Yes, for the most part their students are safer, happier, higher-scoring, and more likely to go to college than their public-school counterparts. But that margin isn't very wide, particularly with respect to academic achievement. Moreover, the supply of private schools is limited, and they are often reluctant to grow, add a second campus, or otherwise respond to demand even when their waiting lists begin to bulge.
- Absent generally agreed-upon academic standards and measures, it is risky to trust the marketplace alone to improve the quality of education. It can surely inject dynamism and enterprise, while lubricating the engines of reform. But so long as people lack vital consumer information, especially comparative data on school performance, the marketplace will not work perfectly.
- Though economists will quarrel until Doomsday about whether education is a "private good" or a "public good," we judge that it is both. The individual receiving it surely benefits, but so does the larger society gain in myriad ways — civic and cultural as well as economic — from having an educated citizenry. Hence society, acting through its instrumentalities of public policy, retains an interest in K–12 education and an obligation to see not only that it is provided but also that its lessons penetrate the minds of the young.

For these reasons, wholesale privatization does not seem likely. The public interest will not evaporate from K–12 education, nor will the state foreswear its obligation to see that children get educated. Thus arose the Hobson's choice that has long paralyzed serious education reform: the

1; Douglas D. Dewey, "An Echo, Not a Choice," *Policy Review*, November/December 1996, 28–32; and Ronald L. Trowbridge, "Devil's Deal. . .," *National Review*, 15 September 1997, 56–62.

choice between a moribund government-run system and the chimera of privatization. *The purpose of this book is to introduce the reader to a third option: the reinvention of public education via charter schools.*

Our purpose in what follows is not to advocate charter schools per se. Neither are we promoting any specific school design, curriculum, or pedagogy. Rather, we believe that the charter idea is worthy of being examined and tested and that its central assumptions — schooling based on choice, autonomy, and accountability — can undergird a new model for public education.

Today, America is blessed with many high-profile strategies for reforming education, such as vouchers, contracting, standards, and accountability, in addition to charter schools. Most are exciting and controversial; each invites us to reexamine obsolete education assumptions and practices. This is as it should be.

As yet, there is no "one best reform" strategy — and perhaps none will emerge. This is a big, diverse land, and our children's education is too important to give any single idea a monopoly. But charter schools seem to us the most vibrant force in education today, not only because of their broad appeal and their roots in the principle of *public* education, but also because they are themselves so diverse. These are public schools that invite a thousand innovations and move us toward a powerful new framework of educational accountability. Perhaps most heartening, charter schools are providing a worthy alternative to conventional district schools for those who need it most — families whose children are stuck in failing schools.

In this book we seek to unlock the secrets of the charter schools. We begin by visiting five of them.

2

FIELD TRIPS

In this chapter, we briefly survey the charter landscape and then visit five real schools in four states. Nationally, we can spot about 1,700 charter schools in September 1999, located in 32 states and the District of Columbia. Approximately 350,000 children attend them—and all these numbers are rising fast. By mid-1999, 36 states and the District of Columbia had enabling legislation for charter schools. Two and a half times as many such schools were operating in September 1998 than just two years earlier. While the country will not reach President Clinton's ambitious target of 3,000 schools by century's end, it is likely to do so within the first few years of the next decade.

Today, charter schools are distributed widely but unevenly (see Table 2-1). Arizona is the Grand Canyon of charter states, with 348 in 1999, but we also find 234 in California, 175 in Michigan, and 168 in Texas. Florida, Colorado, North Carolina, Wisconsin, Minnesota, Massachusetts, New Jersey, and Pennsylvania also have a healthy crop of charter schools. New states are climbing aboard the charter-mobile, too. New York passed charter legislation late in 1998, Oklahoma and Oregon did so early in 1999, and that year's legislative session saw several other states come close. Today, charter schools are found in all kinds of communities: cities, suburbs, and rural areas; industrial towns, deserts, and Indian reservations; ethnic neighborhoods, commuter towns, even in cyberspace.

A complete tour of the charter landscape does not stop at the U.S. border. Charter schools or charter-like developments can be found in the United Kingdom, Canada, New Zealand, Australia, Chile, and Pakistan. (See chapter 4.) And there are signs of interest in Japan and Argentina.

However, while the idea now crosses national boundaries, this book is concerned with charter schools in the United States. Who starts them? Who attends them? Why do people seek them? How do they work? How are they different from other schools? How are they doing?

Generalizations are difficult, for these schools are breathtakingly diverse. There is no "typical" example. Accordingly, the best way to begin to answer all these questions is to tour several actual (and in one case "virtual")

TABLE 2–1. State Charter School Activity (September 1999)

State	Year Charter Law Passed	Stronger Law	Weaker Law	Number of Schools Opened
Alaska	1995		√	18
Arkansas	1995		√	0
Arizona	1994	√		348
California	1992	√		234
Colorado	1993	√		68
Connecticut	1996	√		17
Delaware	1995	√		5
District of Columbia	1996	√		28
Florida	1996	√		112
Georgia	1993	√		32
Hawaii	1994		√	2
Idaho	1998	√		8
Illinois	1994	√		19
Kansas	1995		√	15
Louisiana	1995	√		17
Massachusetts	1993	√		39
Michigan	1993	√		175
Minnesota	1991	√		57
Mississippi	1997		√	1
Missouri	1998	√		14
Nevada	1997		√	5
New Hampshire	1995	√		0
New Jersey	1996	√		52
New Mexico	1993		√	3
New York	1998	√		3
North Carolina	1996	√		83
Ohio	1997	√		48
Oklahoma	1999			2
Oregon	1999			1
Pennsylvania	1997	√		45
Rhode Island	1995		√	2
South Carolina	1996	√		10
Texas	1995	√		168
Utah	1998		√	8
Virginia	1998		√	0
Wisconsin	1993	√		45
Wyoming	1995		√	0
Nationwide Totals	—	24	11	1,684

[a]Source: Center for Education Reform, Washington, D.C., February 1999, http://edreform.com. The "stronger" versus "weaker" law distinction is explained in chapter 5. The Oklahoma and Oregon charter laws were unranked as we went to press.

schools. In the next few pages, we introduce five of these, beginning — as so many things in America now do — in Southern California.

Fenton Avenue Charter School
LAKE VIEW TERRACE, CALIFORNIA

1998–99 Enrollment: 1,331
Percentage of students who are:
  White 2.7%
  Black 16.8%
  Hispanic 77.7%
  Asian 0.9%
  Other 1.9%
Grades served: PreK through 5

First year as charter school: 1994
Estimated total expenditure per pupil: $6,112
Type of charter: conversion
Charter sponsor: Los Angeles Unified School District
Current charter expires in 2003
Founded by: teachers

"Climbing new heights together." This motto, chosen by the struggling Fenton Avenue School when it decided to "go charter," hints at what has occurred there since 1994. Located in an inner-city neighborhood in the northeast San Fernando Valley, Fenton Avenue was a troubled Los Angeles public elementary school when Joe Lucente was assigned as its principal. It had the usual urban ills: meager pupil and teacher attendance, weak achievement, scant parent involvement, gang activity, scruffy facilities, unstable leadership, and so on.

Lucente knew that a major challenge faced him. "I heard stories of how bad it was at the school," he recalled. "It went through four principals in five years. But I never realized it was as bad as it was until that day I met with the superintendent and he told me for just over an hour in graphic terms about the school."

The new principal struggled mightily to turn his school around. Things did improve, but the system cramped Lucente and his team in too many ways. Key staff members left in frustration. He, too, "began to think about leaving. We had reached the point where we couldn't go any further unless we got the state and the district with all their rules and regulations and bureaucracy off our back. The charter approach offered us a way to do that."

LAUNCHING AN AUTONOMOUS SCHOOL

Lucente and his colleagues began to talk about becoming a charter school shortly after California passed enabling legislation in 1992. As they moved through the process of writing a charter, they engaged parents and other members of the school community.

They agreed that their charter request would seek complete freedom for the school, including: governance, fiscal planning and budget, instruction and staff development, parent involvement, employment of support staff, even food services and transportation. (Only a handful of California charter schools enjoy this much autonomy from their districts.)

Ninety-five percent of Fenton Avenue's professional staff voted by secret ballot to seek charter status. In effect, they signed a declaration of independence. The school filed its application with the Los Angeles board of education in April 1993. It was revised twice, as the district added more conditions. With these modifications, the charter was approved in late July 1993.

Rather than rush into reopening as a charter school, however, Fenton staff took time, as Lucente says, "to do it right the first time and hit the ground running." Fenton Avenue began functioning as a PreK–6 charter school in January 1994. (It is now PreK–5.) In retrospect, he sees this half-year planning process as important to developing the staff consensus that molded the school into a cohesive community.

WHAT IS DIFFERENT

Fenton Avenue now controls 97 percent of its operating budget, $8.2 million in 1998–99. It contracts with the county board of education for payroll and other fiscal services as well as liability insurance, and contracts out for health and welfare benefits, offering employees several choices not available through the district.[1]

The school operates year-round. By cycling three platoons of students and staff through the calendar year, it can serve over 1,300 youngsters, making this one of the largest U.S. charter schools. Those youngsters are 78 percent Hispanic and 17 percent African-American. Over three-fifths have limited English proficiency. Eighty-five percent qualify for federal Title I services, and all students are fed a free breakfast and lunch. After-school enrichment classes, "academic clinics," and study halls are offered for those who want or need assistance. Since converting to charter status, the school has gone from serving 52 to 140 disabled students.

Forging a strong bond with parents is central to the school's success. At the start of each year, they receive information (in English and Spanish) on school policies and standards. The home-school contract is discussed at a parent orientation meeting. It includes homework policy, the student responsibility code (including mandatory uniforms), a textbook contract, and an Internet-use contract. Parents and students sign a statement saying that they agree to comply with these provisions.

Saturday workshops for parents, led by Fenton teachers, focus on techniques for working with students at home. They cover such topics as homework and discipline. The school also has a Family Center that offers classes in citizenship, English, computers, parenting, and adult literacy. It operates a food pantry and offers help with legal and health matters. As a

---

[1] Fenton and the district have not yet been able to resolve several complex finance and legal issues, including the school's "fair share" of employee retirement benefits.

Fenton staffer explains the school's approach to parents, "We're clear with them about what we expect. . . . And no matter how limited they are in their own knowledge, they want the best school right here for their kids and they know that's exactly what we're trying to create."

School leadership is shared by Lucente, now the executive director, and Irene Sumida, director of instruction. His role is akin to that of a chief financial officer, including school operations and external relations. She is primarily responsible for the education program. They can fill in for each other on any issue at a moment's notice. Lucente says of this approach, "Not everyone could run a school like we do here at Fenton. . . . People aren't prepared to run schools with all the autonomy and teamwork we have."

Fenton Avenue has 65 teachers, all state-certified. Approximately 30 percent hold advanced degrees or multiple credentials. There are several teacher-leader positions: mentor teachers, grade-level chairs, and school standards consultants, with extra compensation provided. Teachers have their own budgets for educational materials, and grade-level teams are provided $2,000 to spend on projects or professional development.

The school negotiated a "sidebar" agreement with the United Teachers of Los Angeles and another union that enrolls teacher assistants, instructional aides, and classified employees. The unions agreed "to subrogate current L.A. Unified School District contractual rights to those procedures established by the Fenton Avenue Charter school governing body." On June 30, 1998, all former L.A. Unified School District employees working at Fenton were forced to resign from the school district — they had been on leave — due to a district-union agreement that teachers must choose between the district and the charter school. Yet morale remains high. An evaluation report commissioned by the district comments: "By almost all accounts, the school has created a collaborative and collegial climate for its staff [that] is supported by codes of professional conduct which . . . are guided by the needs of students."[2]

A fence surrounds Fenton's large campus. Though it appears uninviting, Lucente says, "The parents know how to get in and that they can come anytime. The fence sends a message to those who might be troublemakers to keep out." Fenton's original building included 14 permanent classrooms designed to house 420 students. The school now has 46 classrooms, most of them portable units.

The governance structure might also strike a newcomer as uninviting. It has worked well, however, and has been modified over the years. The school now has four working councils of teachers, parents, staff, and community members. Their mandates span budget, facilities, and safety; curriculum and assessment; personnel; and school-community relations.

[2] WestEd, *LAUSD Charter School Evaluation: Case Study — Fenton Avenue Charter School,* Los Angeles Unified School District, LEARN Office, 30 June 1998, 1.

Overseeing them is the Council of Councils, with twenty voting members — sixteen staff, three parents, and one business or community member.

Sumida explains: "The council structure makes it possible for members of the school community to provide direction for the school. This is what we always envisioned. One of the things we've found is that council members have reached the point where they trust each other to make sound decisions. At first, there was a great deal of fear about what might transpire at the meetings. But no more. We no longer have to belabor every issue or point." Lucente adds: "It's been fascinating to see what happens when you give staff more freedom than they're accustomed to having. The big surprise to me has been you never know who will push the envelope and move into uncharted paths. And when it comes to staff who don't meet our standards, their peers communicate to those who aren't making it that this school is not for them. Their peers do a better job moving them out than we could do." A teacher added that "It's been a lot of hard work. But we've been able to do it."

CLIMBING NEW HEIGHTS

The school's autonomy has led to accomplishments that would have been impossible under the thumbs of district and union. These include:

- boosting pupil test scores more than 20 percent in its first two years;
- raising the school's academic rank so that in four years it went "from the bottom to the top" (compared to other district schools with similar characteristics);[3]
- reducing class size from 30 to 20 in grades K–3 and to 25 in grades 4–5;
- cutting its students' transiency rate from 57 to 32 percent in 1996–97;
- paying $85,000 in bonuses in 1995–96 to all employees;
- repaving the playground area using private contractors at one-fourth the cost quoted by the district;
- providing accident insurance for students and disability insurance for employees;
- adding after-school and Saturday programs;
- managing the school's own food service;
- reducing administrative personnel by 25 percent, redeploying those dollars to hire a music teacher and a technology assistant;
- restoring a 10 percent district-wide staff pay cut;
- implementing a school-wide phonics instruction program in English and Spanish;

[3] Ibid., 2.

- creating an on-site broadcasting studio (the first in any California elementary school);
- decreasing teacher absenteeism by 80 percent; and
- adding five mentor teacher positions.

Perhaps Fenton's most visible achievement has been in the area of technology, which began with a "Writing to Read" lab underwritten by the Riordan Foundation. This primary language-arts program uses computers to reinforce the connection between speech and print, and it catalyzed expanded use of technology in instruction at Fenton. In 1996, the school had no multimedia computers or network. In less than two years, all classrooms were networked and each had at least four multimedia computers, a television with VCR and CD-I player, satellite connection, and cable access. An on-site studio allows students and staff to broadcast presentations on a closed-circuit TV channel—Fenton Charter Broadcasting. This effort was financed from Fenton's operating budget and an innovative financing partnership with two corporations. Six upper-grade classrooms model Fenton's ultimate technology goal: a computer on every student's desk. This will soon become a reality with the help of a $2.3 million federal loan.

In 1997, Fenton Avenue was named a California Distinguished Elementary School. In the words of an outside evaluator hired to assist the school in preparing for its charter renewal, "Fenton has come a long way from its reputation as a 'hellhole.' "[4] State Superintendent Delaine Eastin called it "one of the nation's finest schools."[5] The district's evaluation of Fenton summarizes its accomplishments: "Students have shown gains in both standardized student achievement test scores and in other outcome measures since becoming a charter school, . . .with those . . . who stay with the school for longer periods of time show[ing] more growth. . . ."[6] In 1998, the school had its charter renewed for five years.

Sequoia School
MESA, ARIZONA

1998–99 Enrollment: 1,184	First year as charter school: 1996–97
Percentage of students who are:	Estimated total expenditure per
White 87%	pupil (1997–98): $4,998
Black 2%	Type of charter: start-up
Hispanic 8%	Charter sponsor: Higley
Asian 1%	Elementary School District
Native American 2%	Current charter expires in 2013
Grades served: K–12	Founded by: parents

[4] Diane R. Becket, *Fenton Avenue Charter School: Evaluation Report* (Los Angeles: University of Southern California Center on Educational Governance, 1997), 7.

[5] Alicia Doyle, "Superintendent Lauds Fenton," *Los Angeles Daily News*, 8 November 1996, 24.

[6] WestEd, *LAUSD Charter School Evaluation*, 39.

To visit the Sequoia charter school in Mesa, Arizona, you drive out of Phoenix on the busy Superstition Freeway, into the booming eastern half of what state tourism boosters call the "Valley of the Sun." Then you weave through a working-class neighborhood to a plot of pancake-flat land alongside the freeway. On it sits a three-year-old school with a complex and controversial history, plenty of start-up problems, and a mixed record of success. It deserves a visit, though, because of its curricular diversity, its bubbling entrepreneurialism and boundless vision, and its illustration that not every charter saga is a smooth and painless tale.

School head Don Flake and board chairman David Wade both have large families themselves, and some of their children were not thriving in the local public schools. They sought alternatives in a place with few private school options. They are also both veteran education activists. Flake chaired Arizona's state charter school board in its early days and remains a major player in the statewide charter movement. (He recently spearheaded the effort by the charter school association to create its own accreditation system.) But he wanted to do "retail," too. An engineer by profession, he is passionate about education, and poured himself into the creation of Sequoia, one of the country's largest start-up charter schools, which opened its doors in 1996.

By the fall of its third year, most of the school was housed in parallel rows of those dull but functional structures known in the education world as "portables." As Sequoia's enrollment exceeded their capacity, the school temporarily obtained spillover space in a nearby church. That arrangement left much to be desired, however, so in mid-1998 the school arranged a several million dollar construction loan to erect three permanent buildings on its original site, doubling its physical capacity and improving its facilities. By early 1999, everyone was back together on the campus alongside the freeway.

THE WORLD CAPITAL OF CHARTER SCHOOLS

The east valley of Phoenix is one of the areas of fastest growth in America, both in population and in charter activity. Sitting in a charter school not far from Sequoia, we were told that "within a ten-mile radius, there are sixty-six charter schools," a far greater concentration than can be found anywhere else. It's the sort of place where the desert is being bulldozed into new housing developments, where you can see cows in one lot, half-built homes on the next lot, and a tidy suburban neighborhood just across the street.

Mesa itself is an older suburb with nowhere left to grow. It is also home to the largest public school system in Arizona, headed by a formidable superintendent named James Zaharis. (See interview in chapter 9.) Zaharis is an executive who likes to be in charge—and does a good job with the schools he runs—so the loose, autonomous nature of charter schools is not his glass of lemonade. But their proliferation in his backyard, and their magnetic effect on many Mesa families, obliged him to respond. Proud as he is of the Mesa Public Schools, the eruption of charter schools caused him to alter the system's familiar ways.

Zaharis is one of the handful of U.S. school superintendents savvy enough to recognize that traditional school systems must change to survive in this brave new world of education choices. He estimates that Mesa has lost 3,000 students to charters, though he believes the number will stabilize at 5 percent of total enrollment.[7] Still, the Mesa Public Schools have taken steps to woo their "customers," a novel concept for most public school administrators. This includes advertising schools on billboards, in movie theaters, and over the radio—ads that contain digs at charter schools for not requiring "certified" teachers—and, more importantly, starting new academic programs to appeal to families that might otherwise opt for charters. A new Montessori program has recently begun, as have full-day kindergarten options, an enrichment program for home-schoolers, an arts program, and several clones of Mesa's long-popular (and severely oversubscribed) "basics" school. Comments a local reporter, "The district began listening more closely to parents' wishes."[8]

CHOICES WITHIN A SCHOOL OF CHOICE

Sequoia is one of the rare charter schools in America with internal education choices. A family doesn't just decide to enroll its child at Sequoia. It must also determine which program to place her in—and some families have youngsters in more than one.

The school began with two options—a back-to-basics curriculum and a progressive "Project" program—at the elementary level. Then it added a third, creating some confusion. By the 1998–99 school year, Sequoia's able new principal, Jack Graham, had refashioned these into five reasonably coherent options: the large "Basic" program and four smaller "learning families," each with several teachers and about eighty youngsters spanning a range of ages, and each with its own curricular focus. One such learning family is science-centered, another literature-based, and so forth. They resemble miniature magnet schools within the larger charter school.

The secondary program has choices, too, including an academically oriented continuation of the "Basic" program, and an effort to extend the hands-on "Project" approach. About half of Sequoia's high school stu-

---

[7] Other close watchers of the local education scene estimate that as many as 8,000 charter pupils in the East Valley would otherwise be attending the Mesa Public Schools—equivalent to more than eleven percent of the system's enrollment.

[8] Kelly Pearce, "Charters' Growth Shows No Signs of Slowing," *The Arizona Republic*, 7 March 1999.

dents are simultaneously getting college credit in advanced courses. Meanwhile, Messrs. Flake and Wade have obtained a second charter for Sequoia Choice Schools, which serves hearing-impaired youngsters and others with nontraditional needs. This new school is still small, but it is heavy on technology and individualized instruction and will soon offer distance-learning classes in conjunction with other schools.

Sequoia also opened a branch K–12 campus in 1998 in the faraway town of Linden, and Sequoia College will soon enroll its first students. "We're working to create a college program," explains planner Clark Smithson. "People want a small-college environment for the same reasons they come to a charter school."

Though Sequoia lacks the intimacy found in many charters, with nearly 1,200 pupils it can afford to offer options. The school was intended from the outset to demonstrate the efficacy and appeal of a different kind of institutional arrangement rather than a single curriculum or pedagogy. Meeting students' varied needs is its core value, and that has led the school to develop alternatives, sometimes launching them before they are quite ready. As Don Flake says, "We have the attitude that kids come first and programs second. If we become too program-centered, we lose the ability to be child-centered."

Birth Pains

These are ambitious people with seemingly boundless energy, educational entrepreneurs and (perhaps in the Mormon tradition) missionaries whose already bright eyes take on even more of a gleam as they describe Sequoia's mission and bold future designs, with still more campuses, sister schools, far-flung "distance learning" programs, their own college, and more.

But they also encountered problems aplenty in launching the school, some of them traceable to their zeal to start big and fast. Three proved especially vexing.

First, a schism developed during the school's first year, and the team that initially led the "Basic" program split off to found its own pair of nearby charter schools, taking hundreds of Sequoia students with them. (Those new schools subsequently ran into troubles of their own.)

Second, other enrollment fluctuations kept Sequoia off balance. The dual impulse to start with a K–12 program and to serve youngsters who had not thrived elsewhere led the school to recruit and admit dozens of teenagers who would not or could not comply with Sequoia's academic standards and puritanical norms of behavior (and dress). Moreover, this happened three times! The first year, it could be explained by naivete. But it happened again in the fall of 1997, due to the school's need to make up the pupil shortfall caused by the aforementioned schism. And then it happened again around Christmas 1997 when another charter school abruptly closed, stranding hundreds of adolescents, many of whom sought admission to Sequoia. The school welcomed them even though it was barely able to ensure a first-rate education for those it already had. (By 1998–99, the enrollment appeared to have stabilized.)

Third, the school had problems with its charter, which was originally obtained from the Ganado Unified School District on the distant Navajo reservation. This meant that Sequoia was an early participant in one of the most controversial aspects of the Arizona charter program: the practice of local districts issuing charters to schools in other parts of the state. The districts that did most of this were small, predominantly Native American school systems that had educational and economic troubles of their own. Their motivation was primarily economic; one of them — Window Rock — briefly became notorious for "selling" charters for fat fees to distant school operators over whom it then exercised little oversight. (By fall 1998, Window Rock had foresworn chartering altogether.) But district sponsorship is also financially beneficial for charter schools, due to a statutory wrinkle that allows them to obtain larger transportation reimbursements than by dealing directly with the state.

Ganado was more conscientious than Window Rock, but when new leadership took over the district in late 1997, it chose to vacate the charter field. District officials advised Sequoia (and a half dozen other schools) that they would have to find new sponsors.

There was more to the story. Several Ganado charters, including Sequoia, had stirred controversies of their own, having especially to do with sloppy handling of money, over-hasty procurements, and, in Sequoia's case, the question of whether the contiguous Mormon "seminary" that many students attend during free periods was or wasn't part of the charter school itself.[9] Sequoia's initial ownership and governance structure also created opportunities for financial entanglements that a punctilious auditor (and fired-up newspaper reporters) could — and did — take exception to.[10]

Orphaned by Ganado, in early 1998 Sequoia went shopping for a new sponsor. It found one in the tiny elementary school district of Higley, with just 230 students of its own, which decided to reinvent itself as a district of charter schools. By September 1998 it had agreed to sponsor 28 of them

[9] It is common in heavily Mormon communities such as Mesa for the Latter Day Saints church to operate a religious education program adjacent to a public high school and for youngsters to leave school at various times to attend "seminary." But it is impermissible for a public school — charter or otherwise — itself to deliver religious education. Sequoia — with a student body perhaps half Mormon — stepped too close to that line for the comfort of Ganado officials.

[10] In June 1998, together with the charter school business management firm called Arizona Benefits Solutions, Sequoia acquired a full-time chief financial officer to keep track of its $5 million budget. Don Flake reports that this has lifted a huge burden from his shoulders and made for a much better managed school.

all over Arizona, including many of the refugees from Ganado and Window Rock. Suddenly, Higley emerged with more than 3,500 students on its books. The fees paid to it by the charter schools — a sliding scale from $10,000 to $100,000 per annum, based on enrollment — more than cover the district's costs. In fact, Higley is making a tidy pile of money from this arrangement, which has enabled it to hire a new principal, upgrade its technology, and add a business office. "This is a new business," says Superintendent Larry Likes. "It is a business. Let's not kid ourselves."[11]

Sequoia, meanwhile, had the new sponsor that it needed. And America had yet another example of the changes being wrought by the charter phenomenon in the customary structures and operations of public education.

The Quest for Stability

Despite its stormy start, Sequoia remains a dynamic place. In fact, it is a bit too dynamic for some of its constituents, who wish that Messrs. Flake and Wade would pause in their ambitious plans and tidy up the school's day-to-day functioning.

Initial academic results were not as strong as everyone hoped. Sequoia pupils lost ground on the state's Stanford 9 tests between the school's first and second years, a worrying development, to be sure, though it may have had more to do with pupil turnover than with teaching and learning. Don Flake explains that each year Sequoia has found itself enrolling more difficult students from less supportive families, noting that intensifying competition for pupils among East Valley charters makes it harder to attract and retain good students. With Sequoia's new focus on academic results, however, and additional staff development for teachers, he expects solid improvement in test scores.

Withal, those scuffed portables house a lively and exciting education program. The visitor who walks into a "Basic" classroom at the elementary level encounters quiet rows of children working at carefully prepared lessons. The curriculum is old-fashioned, yet delivered with precision, enthusiasm, and manifest affection.

In the more child-centered parts of the school, by contrast, one finds considerable hubbub, as (in mid-1998) some 200 children of many ages shared one large space (and some small side rooms) with eight teachers and various aides and volunteers. Excitement was in the air. And a method seemed to underlie the apparent looseness.

The method is harder to find in the high school program, although efforts are underway to strengthen and stabilize it. Though some fine college-level classes are offered — the kids get college credit, too, if they pay

---

[11] Pearce, op. cit. By January 1999, however, Higley was encountering financial troubles of its own and the legislature was considering limiting districts' ability to charter distant schools.

the tuition — the high school program was stumbling when we visited. It had suffered facility woes and staff changes, and still had a jerry-built curriculum. "I've had three math teachers in just one year," griped one high school student. "The turnover is too high."

PROFILE

Clarise Armisted (11th Grade Student, Sequoia School)*

Clarise's first year at Sequoia was 1997–98, when she was a tenth grader. The daughter of a realtor and a homemaker, she had been home-schooled through fourth grade and again in ninth, but attended public schools from fifth through eighth. (Many Sequoia students have complicated patterns like this.) Her parents chose the charter school because there were fewer students and "the quality of the education was better."

Clarise finds the schoolwork more difficult at Sequoia than in her previous schools, but suspects that is because she is in "all advanced classes," including several that yield college credit. The teachers are good, but not necessarily better than she had experienced elsewhere. Her biggest beef is the science program, due to the shortage of labs: "It's very difficult to learn biology and chemistry this way." Although she finds the school a bit disorganized, she's philosophical about it: "It will take time to work out some of the problems, but every school has problems they need to work out . . . especially one that is only three years old."

Her greatest personal accomplishment at Sequoia: "I was able to get up enough courage to run for Student Body President. I did not win, but for me, getting up and talking in front of the school was very hard."

Discipline remains a problem at the high school level, too. During the first half of the 1997–98 year, Sequoia let more than a hundred pupils go. As one student put it, "A ton of people got expelled."

Nobody seems embarrassed by this turnover, however. As Flake says, "Our orientation is to counsel out those who don't uphold the standards of the school. We make our standards very clear before new students enroll. Those who struggle with these standards either step up or step out." Though charter critics contend that this makes it "too easy" to run a successful school, Flake views expulsions as a clear signal to all students (and parents) that the school is serious about its norms and will protect those who honor them from the temptations, dangers, and dysfunctions of ordi-

---

* Names of students have been changed.

nary high schools. Some of the students are grateful for this. "I feel safe here," reported one who had not felt that way in her previous schools.

Some of the facility and program constraints of charter schools started to vex high school students in search of interscholastic sports and other big-time extracurricular activities. "I miss some of the public school opportunities, such as being in a musical and playing basketball," remarked a Sequoia student. "We don't have any equipment for science or math," noted another.

But the school's leadership is nothing if not responsive and adaptable. By fall 1998, the high school program was back on the main campus. New buildings were under construction. More science teachers were hired. Labs were functional. And Sequoia had joined the Arizona Interscholastic Association in order to give its students access both to statewide high school athletic leagues and to programs in forensics, music, drama, and the like. "We're never going to be a football powerhouse," Flake remarks, "but we'll do pretty well in basketball."

As for Sequoia's academic standards, they are getting attention, too. In Flake's view, the school's next big challenge is to "raise the bar" academically, especially in the high school. "A significant percentage of kids are still here to be baby-sat," he comments. "We still have many kids who are exerting zero academic effort."

With higher standards, he has no doubt, Sequoia will attract plenty of able students. The college-level courses already do some of that. Still, Flake notes, "Our students are a U-shaped curve, but still weighted to the low end. We intend to emphasize our strong academic curriculum, and challenge the districts — and the other charters — for their best students."

Sequoia's ambitious plans took another hit in summer 1998, when the school was featured in a series of muckraking articles in a suburban newspaper. These contained some errors and gave short shrift to the many successes of Arizona's burgeoning charter program, but they also exposed a number of problems. The state's permissive charter law, which the legislature came close to tightening in 1999, allows practices that other states do not permit and that, when exposed to light, look dubious even if legal. The reporter alleged, for example, that Flake and Wade and a former partner had profited inappropriately from Sequoia and had employed family members at the school's expense.[12]

They quickly responded, both by converting Sequoia to a nonprofit organization with ownership of its own assets, and by installing a CFO to keep closer track of the school's finances. And Sequoia's enrollment was unaffected. "If anything," Flake comments, "the critical publicity brought us more inquiries from families."

[12] Kirk Mitchell, "$500 Down, $90,000 Profit," *The Mesa [Ariz.] Tribune*, 23 August 1998, A-8.

Despite its star-crossed past, hundreds of East Valley families now find Sequoia a satisfactory option for their children. In hindsight, it seems clear that the school's founders would have been more prudent to "grow their own" high school program rather than starting one *de novo*. They would have been more prudent to get one or two academic programs running smoothly before adding more. They would have been prudent not to recruit — and then expel — dozens of teenagers who were poorly suited to this particular school. They certainly could have avoided some grief if they had been more meticulous from day one in their handling of the school's finances. But such prudence was trumped by their missionary zeal, their enterprise, and, perhaps, by their hope to make a bit of money. Today, they seem unlikely to pocket much financial gain, but their ardor for education gains appears undimmed. There are kids needing to be educated, programs needing to be started, and new education reform frontiers begging to be explored. And despite the turnover in students and staff, a great many students and parents are delighted with their Sequoia experience. "We could have moved to Utah," said Keith and Debbie Redford, who lead the school's parent advisory committee. "We stayed in Phoenix largely because of this school."

Excel Charter Academy and the National Heritage Academies
GRAND RAPIDS, MICHIGAN

1998–99 Enrollment: 625
Percentage of students who are:
  White 80%
  Black 13%
  Hispanic 6%
  Asian 1%
Grades served: K–8
First year as charter school:
  1995–96

Estimated total expenditure per
  pupil: $5,450
Type of charter: start-up
Charter sponsor: Grand Valley
  State University
Current charter expires in 2000
Founded by: National Heritage
  Academies

John Charles (J.C.) Huizenga wants to change the way America educates children. That's probably true of a lot of people, but Huizenga is putting his money where his mouth is. And he has some money.

Huizenga is a multimillionaire businessman, the son of a high school dropout who created the core of what would become the world's largest waste disposal company. But he's been restless lately. Reflecting on his financial success, his toddler son, and his middle age, he has become eager to give something back. He explains, "I'm at a point where I'm looking at the balance of my life and looking at what I can do to make a difference."[13]

Huizenga sees a great opportunity to do just that — and perhaps make

---

[13] Quoted in Roland Wilkerson, "J. C. Huizenga Runs Four Schools," *The Grand Rapids Press*, 6 April 1997, E1.

still more money—via charter schools. He has poured millions of dollars into thirteen Michigan schools, all managed by National Heritage Academies (NHA), a for-profit management firm that he founded in 1995.[14]

His vision is simple: build a twenty-first century school system that can provide a better education for children by drawing on marketplace incentives to make schools more responsive, accountable, and efficient. Huizenga explains: "Competition does two things: It increases quality and lowers cost. It's worked in every other sector of society. Why not education?"[15] But it's not just about competition. Huizenga's charter schools focus on academics, parent participation, and character education.[16]

Huizenga's first charter school, the Excel Charter Academy, made quite a splash in the community, not least because its students made significant academic gains. Three more charter schools—all run by NHA—followed in rapid succession and, by 1998–99, there were thirteen.

Principal Bill Knoester is in charge at Excel. He is viewed affectionately by parents and children at the school, which is located on the fringe of an urban area of about half a million people (many of them immigrants) that was once the nation's furniture manufacturing center.

Knoester is himself an immigrant. Netherlands-born, he reached the United States in 1950 at the age of six. He grew up in Grand Rapids and attended Calvin College, down the street from today's Excel.

Knoester is no stranger to public education. He worked in the local school system for thirty years as teacher, counselor, coach, principal, and central office administrator. He gushes about the potential for his charter school to improve the lives of its pupils. And he says with conviction and without hubris that Excel is by far the best school in his experience. In all the conventional schools where he had worked, he lacked the autonomy to develop the curriculum, set the basic policies, or pick the staff. Everything was done from the top down, and seniority was the name of the game. At Excel, it is just the opposite. Knoester was able to select a top-notch staff. Once on board, these teachers helped him develop the school's policies and curriculum.

Excel is one of seventeen charter schools in Grand Rapids. Yet the public school system is not in crisis. Many of its pupils receive a good education. And there is a thriving parochial school system in town. A whopping 37 percent of Grand Rapids children attend private schools (compared to a national average of 11 percent). Many parents seek not only demanding

---

[14] The firm was originally called the Educational Development Corporation.

[15] In Wilkerson, "J. C. Huizenga Runs Four Schools."

[16] Some observers are uncomfortable with Huizenga's involvement with charter schools, given his openly religious beliefs. See Daniel Golden, "Old-Time Religion Gets a Boost at a Chain of Charter Schools," Wall Street Journal, 15 September 1999, A1. NHA schools have a "character education" program (as do many conventional public schools), but it is not religious in nature.

academics but also a moral focus. Thus, many are bailing out — both from the public schools and the private schools — to participate in Grand Rapids's charter experiment.

They seem to be getting what they want at Excel. The student/teacher ratio is 24 to 1. About three-quarters of its students came from public schools, about a fifth from parochial schools, and a small percentage were home-schooled. Excel now draws children from two dozen districts, including one child who lives 25 miles away.

Academic success is a substantial part of the reason for this popularity. In the school's first year, students gained an average of nearly two grade equivalents. In its second year, they progressed an average of about 1.3 years in reading, language, and math, as measured by a national achievement test (the MAT-7). In its third year, they gained an average of 1.4 grade equivalents. Besides this praiseworthy growth in academic attainment, Excel's overall MAT-7 scores came in about one year above the national average, with gains chalked up by both minority and white youngsters.

But Excel and NHA look for more than just academic achievement. NHA's president, Pete Ruppert, a businessman with a Harvard MBA, remarks, "Ultimately, our customers will determine whether or not we are successful." In 1997, the company set out to assess satisfaction by polling the parents of 2,146 students in eight charter schools. More than 95 percent of respondents said they would recommend their child's charter school to friends, 95 percent said their children's teachers exhibit effective teaching skills, and 95 percent indicated that their children are getting a better education at their charter school than they would otherwise get.[17]

Knoester has identified several reasons for his school's success: a dedicated and able teaching staff, a challenging curriculum (including Open Court language arts and University of Chicago math), lots of time on task (three hours of math and reading every day), committed and involved parents, and the character education program.

Especially striking is Excel's level of parent involvement. About 85 percent of parents volunteer in some capacity, and 99 percent made it in for the last round of parent-teacher conferences. The school has a varied array of committees that parents can serve on, including Assessment, Library, Technology, Moral Focus, Fundraising, Health/Sex Education, Volunteer Coordination, Building/Playground, Carnival, and Hot Lunch.

EDUCATION AND ENTREPRENEURSHIP

How do these traditional aspects of schooling and parent volunteerism coexist with a for-profit company managing the school? NHA's charter

[17] Earlene McMichael, "Charter School Firm Plans for Growth," *Kalamazoo Gazette*, 11 January 1998.

schools receive a set amount of state money per student and can keep as profit anything they don't spend to operate the school. While the mere notion of profit from schooling riles some, NHA officials point out that if they don't succeed in educating the kids and satisfying their parents, they will surely go out of business.

The company is considering "going public" to raise additional capital so as to place itself on the growing list of education management firms that have a national reach. By 2006, NHA hopes to have as many as 200 charter schools operating nationwide.

The combination of education and entrepreneurship is part of what makes Excel Charter Academy run smoothly. But this wasn't always so. The path was sometimes bumpy, and the school didn't obtain its building until a month before the first bell rang. Knoester was not hired until mid-July, and he had precious little time to put a staff together before the pupils arrived. At first, basic materials — even desks — were missing. And there was tension between school staff and the business office: nobody was sure who was in charge.

But an early watershed event eased the tension. The business office was keen on a phonics curriculum called SRA (Science Research Associates, a "direct instruction" model), but the newly hired instructional staff favored Open Court.[18] Nobody wanted to give in. Eventually, though, the corporate staff acknowledged that their job was to make sure the bills got paid and the classrooms were supplied, and that the principal and teachers needed to select a curriculum. And so it went. Now, there is a company-wide curriculum committee led by the principals.

Armed with a solid education vision and an entrepreneurial spirit, Huizenga and Ruppert would like to turn National Heritage Academies into a recognizable "brand name." As Ruppert puts it, "We want to build a national network of schools based on a similar model but customized to the local community. That way, if a family moves from Michigan to Arizona, they'll know what to expect from a National Heritage Academies school in a new community."

The company maintains a strong belief in specialty schools that focus on academics and character. That clear mission makes it easier for parents to decide whether this learning environment is right for their child. And having such a coherent focus gives staff members a shared vision and common ground for team-building.

But NHA goes beyond espousing leadership philosophies and business principles. It puts them into practice at the building level. Consider Excel's performance-based pay system. Each year, teachers undergo a three-part appraisal: an evaluation by the principal, an assessment of their measurable results (including student test scores and parent surveys), and an eval-

---

[18] Both SRA and Open Court are published by McGraw-Hill.

uation of the school's overall performance. These factors are weighed in determining teacher effectiveness, calculating end-of-year bonuses, and identifying shortcomings.

Besides incentives for performance and a focus on achievement, NHA also attends to efficiency. Due to the peculiarities of Michigan's charter law, Excel receives 30–40 percent less money than neighboring public schools. Furthermore, in 1997–98 a whopping one-third of the school's budget went toward the lease of its buildings. The school was squeezed financially.

One creative solution was to find alternate ways to construct a new school building to house all of Excel's students. Most schools are built of bricks or cinder blocks. Instead, NHA chose the pole-barn structure, which uses thick drywall. This means the company can afford to construct new buildings for its students—the average Grand Rapids public school building is 54 years old—that are safe and bright at about a third of the usual cost. NHA spent about $4 million for a building (which opened in the fall of 1998) that houses 650 students, whereas school districts would typically pay well over $10 million for a facility that size.

PROFILE

Julie Veeneman (Parent, Excel Charter Academy)

Julie Veeneman's eighth-grade daughter has been at the Excel Charter Academy for several years. Prior to that, she attended local Christian schools—and Veeneman faced tuition bills of about $4,000 per year. She has a post-graduate education and used to be a teacher and social worker. She now works part-time for the Kent County Probate Court. (She is also recovering from cancer.)

Veeneman chose Excel not because she was unhappy with her daughter's private school, but because she wanted to become involved with changing public education. She was also seeking a school that fostered parental involvement.

So far, she says, her daughter's education at Excel is comparable to the one she was receiving at her former private school. She is happy, challenged, and staying at or above grade level in all her classes. What Ms. Veeneman especially likes about the school is that "As parents we feel useful, respected, consulted, like decision makers." Asked her biggest worry about her child's education, she replied, "Where will she go to high school?"

When it comes to the bigger picture, Veeneman believes Excel is having an impact on its neighboring schools. She said it has "made the traditional public schools listen to parents," and that the district opened a new middle school to compete with the charter schools.

CHAPTER 2

INTERVIEW

Jennie Dearborn (Student, Excel Charter Academy)*

Jennie was a seventh-grader at Excel in 1998–99, her third year at the charter school. She previously attended a regular public school. She has a big family (six brothers and three sisters). Her parents are "a stay-home mom and my dad is an x-ray technician." Her interests are eclectic; she loves "to play soccer, watch surgery, ride horses, and run."

What are three ways in which this school is different from your previous school? This school teaches morals. We learn more here and are taught stuff better.

Are your teachers here better than those at your last school, or worse? My teachers here are better because they understand us, and listen to us, and have control of the class.

What do you like least at school? We don't have a whole lot of after-school sports.

Are you learning more at this school than at your old school? How do you know? Yes, we're learning more here and I know that because we take more tests.

What else would you like to say about this school? I think Excel is the best in teaching kids to read because they make it fun. It's a really cool school and there should be more charter schools that teach morals and have great, understanding teachers and principals.

Horizon Instructional Systems
LINCOLN, CALIFORNIA

1998–99 Enrollment[19]: 2,661
Percentage of students who are:
  White 64%
  Black 4%
  Hispanic 7%
  Asian 0.5%
  Native American 1%
  Other[20] 23.5%
Grades served: K–12

First year as charter school: 1993–94
Estimated total expenditure per pupil: $3,821
Type of charter: start-up
Charter sponsor: Western Placer Unified School District
Current charter expires in 2003
Founded by: teachers and parents

Randy Gaschler never expected to find himself in education. He had been a college football coach, a cabinet maker, then the proprietor of an auto parts store. But he wanted to work with kids. So he made a career shift,

* Names of students have been changed.
[19] As we write, the school's enrollment has jumped to 3,200.
[20] "Other" includes answers that were not reported.

receiving his first full-time classroom assignment in 1990: teaching world history (and coaching football) at Lincoln High School.

Before long, Gaschler became "increasingly frustrated with a system that has a one-size-fits-all philosophy to what education should be. I was convinced that this wouldn't work over the long haul. More and more kids and families have needs that don't fit into the ways most schools are organized. . . . For me, public education is a public service that should meet the needs of kids and not the other way around."

This led him to become an instructor in California's independent study program, which allows families to contract with teachers for a personal study plan that uses a district's curriculum but does not require actual classroom attendance. He worked in the Western Placer Unified School District, not far from Sacramento.

After California passed its charter law in 1992, Gaschler saw an opportunity to "create a situation where parents had different individualized educational opportunities for their kids, one that had high academic standards, that uses the best of modern technology to deliver most instruction, but that isn't bound to a traditional classroom structure."

Gaschler approached the Western Placer superintendent with his idea and was told to proceed with a plan. The main reason for the district's support was straightforward: it would gain revenues by bringing back onto its rolls youngsters who were being home-schooled or had dropped out. Moreover, because the charter school would use technology to deliver instruction, the district could enroll students from beyond its boundaries, further increasing revenues.

Gaschler wrote the school's charter with assistance from parents, and the district board okayed it. The school would be mostly autonomous but would purchase some services (e.g., budget and payroll) from the district.

Horizon Instructional Systems (HIS) opened in August 1993 as a K–12 charter with fifteen students. Word spread quickly, and within a few months, enrollment was nearly 200 students. The name sent a message: This "school" would be different, a system rather than a building, using technology to span several counties. It would have multiple sites where students could meet for instruction delivered by satellite. Keith Alpaugh, an administrator, says, "We're different. We don't want to be a school in the usual sense, least of all a place. We're whatever instructional design helps parents and kids meet the educational needs that kids have."

HIS uses the charter as an umbrella under which a number of programs are offered. All emphasize a "back to basics" curriculum with a detailed plan for each student that sets forth the knowledge and skills to be mastered. Progress is assessed through a monthly collection of student work and annual portfolios. Instructional strategies include home-based learning; the state's independent study program; the Electronically Assisted Student Teaching (EAST) Program, which blends home-based computers with distance learning and satellite technology; and small-group instruction (called contract classes) for five to fifteen students who need special tutoring or want enrichment courses.

Not only is the school tuition-free, but participating families may actually tap a $1,150 scholarship for each student from the HIS operating budget. This money can be used for any valid educational expenses, such as purchasing contract classes, leasing a home computer, taking field trips, or ordering supplementary materials. This combination of multiple education options and the consumer power that comes from a hefty scholarship has brought together parents with widely divergent views under the banner of choice in education.

In 1998, HIS enrolled 2,661 students spread over six counties, with a waiting list of more than 550. The school is governed by a committee of four parents, three education specialists (two from HIS and one from the district), a local business representative, and the superintendent's designee. Teachers are called "education specialists." All are credentialed and each has a laptop furnished by HIS. They also have individual contracts with the HIS board. On average, each specialist is assigned twenty students. They meet with youngsters and their families from once a week to once a month, depending upon the students' programs.

Nearly all communications and record-keeping are carried out electronically. HIS administrators designed their own management information system to track attendance, purchasing, use of scholarships, and other record-keeping activities. Whatever they can do electronically, they do. Staff development, however, usually involves face-to-face contact.

Finding a facility was not problematic, since HIS does not need a conventional school building. Students learn on-line, or in individual arrangements with an instructor or parent, or via some combination of approaches. Most meetings with students occur at the regional sites or in their homes.

HIS has a modest office in downtown Lincoln. A nearby resource center houses books and other materials used by students. Adjacent to the office is a technology center with 40 computers for students and staff. Free Internet service is provided for students and staff. They also developed a web site that offers parents current information on classes and field trips, school newsletters, forms, and documents.

A HIGH-PROFILE LEGAL BATTLE

HIS's start-up problems, such as making sure that it had adequate staff, textbooks, software, and hardware, were mostly connected to its rapid growth. But the school also endured a two-year conflict with the state education department, a saga that included temporary revocation of its charter and a march on the statehouse by 300 HIS supporters led by a state assemblyman.

This problem arose from a 1993 "budget trailer" bill meant to close a loophole in California's independent study program: Some districts were enticing families by offering free enrollment gifts. The result was that these "things of value" — such as cash rebates, videocassettes, and computers — accrued to some students but not to all. The districts' motivation was clear: more state money accompanied each student. Such independent study programs could be "cash cows" for districts, since a single teacher could supervise as many as fifty students. Moreover, there were no facility costs. The legislature's response was to say that districts couldn't claim state funding for independent study by a pupil if "things of value" were not also provided to students in regular classes. Furthermore, the geographic area from which a district could draw independent study students was limited.

In June 1994, someone — to this day, nobody knows who — complained to the state department of education that HIS was in violation of the new restrictions. HIS was enrolling students from several counties and providing them with "things of value" (e.g., computers) without substantially similar goods and services being provided to other district students. This led to a decision by the state that the district must reimburse the state for all the funding it had received for HIS students. A huge controversy ensued.

The Western Placer district was threatened with a cut-off of state education funds — in effect, bankruptcy — if it didn't comply with state demands that HIS stop its "illegal" activities. The county office of education determined that HIS and Western Placer were in noncompliance during 1993 and 1994, thereby denying them about $900,000 in funding.

Western Placer then took steps to revoke the HIS charter. Meanwhile, in November 1994 the state ruled that another school similar to HIS — providing lessons via computer to students at home — could be classified as distance learning, thereby avoiding the problems inherent in the "things of value" debate. Yet the department would not consider HIS in those terms.

Both the State Attorney General and former state senator Gary Hart, lead author of California's charter law (see chapter 11), disagreed with the agency's narrow interpretation. In April 1996, an agreement was finally signed by the state department of education and the Western Placer trustees saying, in essence, that the district and HIS did not violate the law. HIS may provide students with computers and other materials not available to other district pupils. As of this writing, however, the issue of what happens to the $900,000 that the state withheld earlier has not yet been settled.

This protracted battle took an enormous toll. Gaschler laments, "We lost two years of time and energy on fighting the bureaucracy when we could have spent it growing our program and helping the kids. We were forced to limit our programs to home-based instruction and independent study and had to put our notion of contract classes on hold. And we couldn't give computers to kids while we battled the state. The parents and the kids adjusted. But what a shame."

ON THE HORIZON

HIS has been approved by the Western Association of Colleges and Schools as a candidate for accreditation. Gaschler and his staff are developing an achievement index to measure student learning across the core content areas. The school's charter renewal request reported that HIS "students have scored as well as, or better than, students in its sponsoring district and have performed above the 'average' for the state of California." HIS is also seeking to open its classes to students from neighboring districts and to create links with state colleges. It will offer the state "challenge exams" so that HIS students can receive university credit by exam. The staff wants to become an Advanced Placement testing site, thinking that this will prompt more students to consider AP exams.

HIS had its charter renewed in February 1998 by Western Placer. Gaschler commented, "I never dreamed that I'd be able to create a place like HIS. And all of a sudden we found out that we had been doing it for five years."

Academy of the Pacific Rim
BOSTON, MASSACHUSETTS

1998–99 Enrollment: 150
Percentage of students who are:
  White 19%
  Black 61%
  Hispanic 9%
  Asian 9%
Grades served: 6–8
First year as charter school: 1997–98

Estimated total expenditure per
  pupil: $7,500
Type of charter: start-up
Charter sponsor: Massachusetts
  Board of Education
Current charter expires in 2002
Founded by: community activists

The Academy of the Pacific Rim debuted in 1997–98 with 100 sixth and seventh graders, mostly poor and minority. They will "grow" into the Academy's own high school; by the fall of 2000, "PacRim" plans to serve 350 students through grade 12.

This charter school vows to meet the toughest challenge in American education: providing inner-city youngsters with a world-class education. It begins with the premise that *all* kids can learn to high standards, and it accepts no excuses for failure. It also backs up its promise with a money-back guarantee, something not previously glimpsed in U.S. public education: If students don't pass their 10th grade state assessments, the Academy will allow their parents to pick another school and will transfer to that school the $7,500 that the state pays for each charter pupil.[21]

By anyone's count, promising a world-class education for inner-city children and backing it up with a money-back guarantee is a bold gambit. But at PacRim this promise is buttressed by resources and strategies that appear likely to make it work: a clear academic mission, lots more time on task, firm discipline within a nurturing environment, impressive technology, fine teachers, and committed parents.

These assets would not likely have been assembled without the energetic leadership of founding director Stacey Boyd, who had recently earned twin Harvard masters' degrees (in business administration and public policy) after having taught in Japan.[22] Boyd brought to the Academy a sound business plan and quickly assembled a team of like-minded and equally driven people.

Like most start-up charters, however, PacRim has traveled a road with plenty of bumps and curves. The biggest challenge was finding a facility. The school actually received its charter in March 1995 and had hoped to open in the fall of 1996, but could not find an available building in time. After a year's delay, PacRim finally found usable, low-rent space on the second floor of a Hyde Park Catholic school with shrinking enrollments.

Governance was a challenge, too, as for many charter schools. As board member George Cha explains, "Somehow, after we received the charter and as we moved through the process of getting organized, some of the core people who were part of this effort from the start really weren't paid much attention to anymore. The new folks moved on to other issues and wanted to get on with things while some of the original folks wanted a slower, steady-as-you-go pace." Once the school opened its doors, however, it didn't take long for things to gel.

A WORLD-CLASS EDUCATION FOR ALL

PacRim's mission statement promises "to empower urban students of all racial and ethnic backgrounds to achieve their full intellectual and social potential by combining the best of the East—high standards, discipline, and character education—with the best of the West—a commitment to individualism, creativity, and diversity." It may seem odd that a school called the Academy of the *Pacific* Rim is located a few miles from the Atlantic, but several founders were prominent in Boston's Asian-American community and dreamed of a school that resembled the best in their ancestral lands and that looked and felt global.

The Academy also affirms the Asian conviction that "All young people,

[21] Public dollars won't actually be used for this purpose. Donations from foundations and the school's founders have been used to establish the guarantee fund.

[22] She is also a friend and former colleague of the authors.

not just the privileged or the exceptionally talented, can achieve to the highest standard. Effort, not ability, determines success." One-third of its students qualify for the federal subsidized lunch program, and over three-quarters are minority. All pupils were tested prior to matriculation so that PacRim would have accurate baseline data. Their initial scores resembled those of students in the Boston Public Schools.

Well before it opened, the school developed its own high academic standards. These draw upon some of the best models in the world, including the International Baccalaureate program, Japanese and Taiwanese standards, and some of the better U.S. state standards. But they don't stop there. The staff also interviewed twenty corporate leaders about the competencies they seek in new employees and turned their answers into practical "work-skill" standards.

All PacRim students take English, math, science, civics/geography/history, and Mandarin every day. (Yes, Mandarin. The teacher had previously taught comparative literature in China for a decade, then at Harvard.) Since the courses are tough, the teaching staff has to make sure that students keep up. Every teacher meets weekly with the principal to discuss each student's academic progress and see that none falls through the cracks. This functions as an early warning system. At critical intervals (the end of grades 8 and 12), PacRim also plans to administer external academic audits that students must pass before they move on or graduate.

Pupils take five hour-long core academic courses each day. The day begins at 8:00 A.M. and ends at 4:10 P.M., two hours more than the Boston norm. The year is 210 days long (compared to the typical 180). The upshot is that PacRim students attend school the equivalent of over a hundred more days a year than the Boston average, and those who stay at the Academy from grades 6 through 12 will receive the equivalent of four and a half additional Boston Public School years of education.

To get entering students up to speed—and accustom them to the school's exacting standards for academics and behavior—Boyd launched a summer program designed for youngsters who scored poorly on the baseline exam. The idea was to help level the playing field. The result was a stunning success: in just six weeks, the Academy's summer students improved their reading, writing, and math skills, in some areas as much as a full academic year (based on Stanford 9 test results).

But the extra help didn't end on Labor Day. For students who are still struggling, the Academy offers after-school tutoring sessions in reading, writing, and math, and trained volunteers from the acclaimed City Year program tutor youngsters five days a week.[23]

---

[23] City Year gives a "living stipend" to young adults aged 17 to 23 who perform ten months of full-time community service in the Boston area.

An Environment That Fosters Success

PacRim's discipline policy is strict, but it treats parents as full partners in fostering character and good conduct. Children must leave class if they are disruptive. They go to the director's office, where they are asked to evaluate their behavior (in writing) and discuss alternate behaviors with a teacher. If the disruption was serious, they are sent home and can only return when accompanied by a parent who signs a readmission contract. Although this procedure is used frequently, it has not resulted in the permanent loss of a single pupil.

To be sure, parents resisted at first. So did some teachers. But the administration stuck to its guns, confident that the "tough love" approach would pay dividends in the long run. And it has. Now parents, teachers, and children all speak proudly of the policy.

PacRim's tough discipline is balanced by a nurturing learning environment, including some unconventional approaches. Once a week, all students gather in their homerooms for 25 minutes of Tai Chi, a traditional Chinese exercise used to calm body and mind.

Even more important is the daily *gambatte* award. *Gambatte* is a Japanese word that has been adopted as the school's motto. It means "persevere" or "don't give up," and is intended to teach youngsters that opportunity is not a corollary of race, station in life, or luck, but rather a product of effort, discipline, and perseverance. One high point in the school's first year occurred when a sixth grader with a history of discipline problems earned the *gambatte* award for turning in a dollar that he had found on the restroom floor.

Committed (and Busy) Teachers

It is unlikely that a world-class education can be provided without a world-class faculty. That is why Boyd threw her net far and wide. In the end, the Academy's staff of 12 was selected from a pool of 600 applicants from 10 countries.

None of the full-time teachers has less than three years experience, though only a few are certified in Massachusetts. There are 25 students in each classroom, and teachers teach three or four classes per day, not six or seven as in many schools. That means they get two hours daily to prepare lessons.

Teaching at the Academy includes helping with many aspects of the school. For example, Doug Lemov, who succeeded Boyd as school director during the 1998–99 school year (see profile below), worked thirteen-hour days as a teacher. Prior to the school's opening, he was responsible for purchasing much of its technology. (All teachers have voice mail, Internet access, and e-mail, plus use of photocopying equipment.) He also took the lead in developing the discipline policy, which he directed as Dean of Students while teaching English and history/civics/geography.

Doug Lemov (Principal, Academy of the Pacific Rim)[24]

A former journalist, Doug has bachelor's and master's degrees in English. Prior to joining the PacRim staff, he worked for three years as a teacher and soccer coach at the Princeton Day School, an independent school in New Jersey. He also worked in admissions and directed a peer-counseling program for ninth graders. After that, he taught Introductory Composition at Indiana University, where he also did a lot of tutoring.

Why did you decide to teach at this school? Control. I wanted to be able to build a school where the faculty made the decisions, where adjustments and changes and innovations were not only encouraged but expected. It's always struck me that teachers want autonomy and independence as much or more than they want better compensation. It's the paradox of the airplane: they tell us that flying is safer than riding in a car, but there in your seat, you look out at the problem — the ground far below you — and know you have absolutely no control over its solution. You feel a lot more anxious and tense than you do driving your own car, when you call the shots. Well, professionally, I'd rather drive. I think letting schools drive themselves — and be held very responsible for the results of their decisions — makes for a much better trip. People come through our school and they can't believe how hard we work. But of course we do it that way — we're deeply invested in the product because it is ours.

Was it a difficult decision for you? What worried you the most? The decision was a bit risky. The school could have been a disaster, a total flop. I guess I did it anyway because there was so much to gain.

How is teaching here different from teaching elsewhere? Hours are longer, and faculty members are more cohesive and supportive. Professionalism is very high. There is no dead wood here.

How many hours per week do you work at this school? I work much longer hours than I used to. I rarely work less than a 12-hour day — that's 12 hours at school, then there's grading at home.

---

[24] This interview was conducted while Lemov was a teacher (and Dean of Students) at the Academy — before he became principal.

How is the school working? I think amazingly well but I'd rather talk about what still needs to be done. One thing we need to do is make parents feel more welcome and involved in the school. We've tried to give parents constant information about their students' progress (weekly progress reports, etc.), but that's not a substitute for face-to-face contact. I think we get a lot out of our technology, but it's not a substitute for shaking hands and meeting people.

The Academy nurtures its classroom talent. Every other week, teachers observe each other's classes, providing a regular feedback loop and maximizing teamwork. All teachers are paid a competitive base salary (commensurate with Boston public school rates), but how they perform (largely measured by how well their students progress) determines their bonus. (The maximum is 15 percent of base salary.)

Evaluations work the other way, too. One of Boyd's toughest challenges during the school's first year was firing a teacher—a twenty-year classroom veteran—who could not maintain order. The school tried to help her succeed, including giving her detailed feedback and advice. But eventually it became clear that she had to go. While that produced a strain on the entire staff, in the end it signaled that this school is serious about achievement and accountability for staff as well as students.

Still, teachers cannot do it alone. They rely heavily on parents as partners. At the end of the first summer, the school hosted a seven-hour orientation for parents (98 percent of whom showed up), during which they discussed PacRim's academic program and discipline policy and were invited to become intimately involved with the school. Parents are also required to sign a contract in which they pledge to supervise their children's school work, provide a desk for homework, participate in school activities, get their children to school on time, and speak with their children's academic advisor at least thrice annually.

All these novel approaches appear to be working. PacRim sixth graders gained an average of 1.7 years in math and 0.7 years in English on the Stanford 9 exam in 1997–98, while seventh graders gained an average of 1.7 years in math and 1.8 years in English. Sixth and seventh graders who received after-school tutoring gained an average of 3.4 years in English, based on the Wide Range Achievement Test.

PacRim still faces obstacles. With high school students on the horizon, PacRim is outgrowing its present facility. There are signs of staff burnout, and more governance woes have surfaced. So far, however, these challenges have not diluted the education that youngsters are receiving.

With its unique blend of Western and Eastern thought, pioneering learning guarantee, high standards, and rigorous discipline, PacRim is destined to make waves in the seas of school reform. Those seeking a glimpse of the charter movement's potential are well advised to begin their quest at the Academy of the Pacific Rim.

THESE five examples, chosen from hundreds, barely scratch the surface of the charter movement. What secrets and scars do the nation's other charter schools contain? What potential do they have to renew — or undermine — American education? In the next chapter, we describe the transformation of education thinking that underlies charter schools, examine their origins, and look at some intriguing counterparts in other fields.

3

WHERE DID THEY COME FROM?

Any organization . . . needs to rethink itself once it is more than forty or fifty years old. It has outgrown its policies and its rules of behavior. If it continues in its old ways, it becomes ungovernable, unmanageable, uncontrollable.

Peter Drucker, "Really Reinventing Government"

NEITHER Sarah Kass nor Ann Connelly Tolkoff looks like a subversive bent on undermining public education. Kass came to the Boston area from teaching in the Chicago public schools. Tolkoff was a suburban school committee member and teacher. They met in the Chelsea, Massachusetts public high school where they both taught. Chelsea was so educationally moribund that its school system was taken over by the state and placed under the control of Boston University in the hope that B.U.'s hard-nosed president, John R. Silber, could salvage it.

After a two-year struggle in Chelsea, both Kass and Tolkoff were desperate for a change. They wanted to teach in a place where learning would be the top priority. Kass recalls that "The public school system . . . couldn't deliver. The system wouldn't give. We felt like we were banging our heads against the wall. We thought that what we needed was a 'zero-based approach' to public education—none of the old rules or regulations apply and judge us on how much our kids know and can do. Ann and I wanted to create a different kind of school where we were free to teach young people to be literate citizens in a democratic society."

When Kass and Tolkoff heard about the Commonwealth's new charter law, they knew it was the opportunity they had been seeking. Tolkoff saw the law "as a chance to start from scratch. We no longer had to do things the old-fashioned way." They decided to submit a proposal to start an urban high school with a strong core curriculum and emphasis on civic education, using the city of Boston as a primary educational resource. Kass says that she and Tolkoff "weren't opting out of public education, but opting in—in a different kind of way."

The school they opened in 1995 overturns many conventions about how a public school functions. Teachers run it, not a conventional principal. An independent board of parents, teachers, and community representatives governs it, not a collection of politicians and bureaucrats. It holds to the conviction that all children can achieve world-class standards. And it invites outsiders to evaluate students' work directly to ensure that they are learning enough. Today, City On A Hill is arguably the best-known charter school in America. It all started with Kass and Tolkoff huddled at the kitchen table, dreaming of something better.

How did things get to the point that two dedicated teachers felt they must start from scratch to create a school worth teaching in? In this chapter, we examine the system to which charter schools are an alternative, look at profound changes in education that gave rise to the charter idea, and glimpse parallel developments in other sectors.

"One Best System"

Today's system of public schooling is a mid-nineteenth century invention. In the 1840s and 1850s, states began to establish schools as a direct activity of government. Until Horace Mann and his associates crossed that bridge, there had been no real distinction between public and private schools in America. All were community institutions, run under lay or religious control, funded by a mix of town and private funds, and managed in whatever manner each community thought best. As historians David Tyack and Elisabeth Hansot explain the pre-1850 view of education, "Many forms of schooling deserved the favor of government [and] citizens tended to have an attitude toward education that Americans today have toward religion: attend the school of your choice."[1]

This began to change when reformers such as Mann inaugurated the "common school" which was, in Tyack's accounting, "to be public in political control and economic support, to include children of all classes, sects, and ethnic groups, and existed to produce literate, numerate, and moral citizens."[2] The precursor of today's "public" school, it typically took the form of a one-room schoolhouse in rural communities and a multi-classroom institution in cities. It wasn't long before public education adopted a new mandate: forging a common identity from America's growing and diversifying population.

In some places, the older institutions remained. Many of today's best-

---

[1] David B. Tyack and Elisabeth Hansot, *Managers of Virtue* (New York: Basic Books, 1982), 28–29. See also David B. Tyack, Michael W. Kirst, and Elisabeth Hansot, "Educational Reform: Retrospect and Prospect," *Teachers College Record* 81, no. 3 (Spring 1980): 253–69; Diane Ravitch, *The Schools We Deserve: Reflections on the Educational Crises of Our Times* (New York: Basic Books, 1985), 185–88.

[2] Tyack, Kirst, and Hansot, "Educational Reform," 256.

known private schools—Andover and Exeter, for example—began as community schools that served youngsters from their towns and, gradually, from elsewhere. Other schools—Boston Latin, for example—were melded into the new "public" system. Vestiges of the original arrangement linger today in northern New England where some communities, rather than running public high schools of their own, pay tuition for youngsters to attend private academies.[3]

The transfer of responsibility and control from community to government took a giant leap in the late nineteenth and early twentieth centuries, as progressive reformers applied to education the scientific management notions and factory models of the industrial age. This move to centralize, standardize, and make schooling more efficient and orderly was deemed necessary both to counter municipal corruption and to assimilate millions of immigrants into American culture. Tyack terms the result "the one best system," and summarizes it this way:

> [A]n interlocking directorate of urban elites—largely business and professional men, university presidents and professors, and some "progressive" superintendents—joined forces to centralize the control of schools. They campaigned to select small boards composed of "successful" people, to employ the corporate board of directors as the model for school committees, and to delegate "experts" (the superintendent and his staff) the power to make most decisions concerning the schools. . . . [T]his movement glorified expertise, efficiency, and the disinterested public service of the elites.[4]

In hindsight, we can see that the reformers were naïve in thinking they could insulate schools from politics. By shifting power from local communities and elected officials to "professionals"—and the potent state and national organizations they would create—they swapped one form of politics for another. Decision-making power was transferred from aldermen to associations of teachers, principals, and the like.

As the "one best system" spread, the states became deeply involved with education, legislating such features as compulsory school attendance to a specified age and universal availability of public schools. Although families could comply with attendance laws without patronizing government-run schools, those schools were free, courtesy of the taxpayer, while the other kinds cost parents money. Today, nearly nine out of ten children attend

---

[3] See, for example, Amity Shlaes, "School Choice Isn't a New Idea," *The Wall Street Journal*, 1 October 1998, for an account of St. Johnsbury Academy in Vermont.

[4] David Tyack, *The One Best System* (Cambridge: Harvard University Press, 1974), 7. For the status of blacks during much of the period discussed by Tyack, see James D. Anderson, *The Education of Blacks in the South, 1860–1935* (Chapel Hill, N.C.: The University of North Carolina Press, 1988). For a study of a more recent time, see Vanessa Siddle Walker, *Their Highest Potential: An African American School Community in the Segregated South* (Chapel Hill, N.C.: The University of North Carolina Press, 1996).

the tax-financed, government-run schools: 46 million youngsters enrolled in 85,000 public schools.

The state also began to specify qualifications for teachers and administrators, turning school instruction and administration into "expert" fields requiring specialized university degrees. It also set graduation requirements for students seeking high school diplomas. But (except for Hawaii) the state entrusted the actual management of its public schools to "local education agencies," mostly organized at the municipal level. Today, on average, 93 percent of public school funding comes from state and local tax funds. (The rest comes from Washington, chiefly as assistance for low-income and disabled youngsters.)

As the state strengthened its grip on the delivery of education, in the interest of efficiency it also abolished (or "consolidated") huge numbers of local school agencies. Whereas the United States had more than 127,000 separate school systems as recently as 1931, today it has about 15,000, each with its own board and superintendent. The total public school payroll numbers around five million persons, and the schools spend about $255 billion. Viewed as a single enterprise, U.S. public education is one of the largest bureaucracies in the world.

In its midst, private schooling survived. America's 26,000 private schools are living proof that diverse, self-governing educational institutions can exist — and serve millions of youngsters every year — without government control or bureaucratic management. The issue, of course, is that without public subsidy they are, for the most part, accessible only to reasonably well-off families, a different situation than we see in countries that routinely finance attendance in privately operated schools. Still, the perseverance of a private sector within U.S. education shows that the "one best system" never took over completely. It simply took over about 90 percent.

The Factory Model in a Post-Industrial Era

For much of this century, that system served America well enough. It helped fuel economic growth and generally furthered cultural unity and democratic government. Access to education was expanded and more services were extended to nearly everyone. For example, just 6 percent of American adults finished high school in 1900. By the mid-1960s, half the adult population over the age of 25 had high school diplomas. Today, nearly 95 percent of young adults have completed high school or the equivalent. A K–12 education is available to all who want it.

This was an extraordinary accomplishment. Yet that is like remarking on the success of an immense horse-and-buggy factory in providing everyone with a one-hoss shay. The system is universal but antiquated. One form of obsolescence can be glimpsed in a poignant 1995 article by

Jacques Steinberg titled "Time Stands Still in Some School Boiler Rooms," printed in the *New York Times*. It profiled Brunel Toussaint, the coal stoker at Junior High School 99 on East 100th Street in Manhattan. There he shovels anthracite into the school's twin boilers, installed in 1924. Coal furnaces are still the primary source of heat in more than a quarter of New York City's thousand-plus public school buildings. Steinberg noted that "It could have been a scene out of early industrial England."

It isn't just the heating arrangements that are outdated. So is the education production-and-delivery system. The system runs in classic bureaucratic fashion, satisfying some but also frustrating many parents who seek something different for their children, and thwarting teachers like Kass and Tolkoff who yearn for autonomy and prize their professionalism. Its notable accomplishments on the quantitative side — the provision of almost boundless educational services to all — have been offset by thirty years of accumulating evidence that the *quality* of its products is shoddier than the country can afford.

While there are exceptions to this bleak description, these are often the products of idiosyncratic, even heroic efforts by maverick principals and exceptional superintendents. Even the late Albert Shanker, a lifelong teachers' union leader, said, "It's time to admit that public education operates like a planned economy, a bureaucratic system in which everybody's role is spelled out in advance, and there are few incentives for innovation and productivity. It's no surprise that our school system doesn't improve. It more resembles the communist economy than our own market economy."[5]

Consider the plight of Reginald Moss, veteran principal of one of the best schools in the troubled District of Columbia system. Because he could not get funding for some needed extras at Alice Deal Junior High School, which he has led for two decades, he devised an innovative money-raising plan: letting Domino's Pizza sell food on campus at lunchtime in return for a 30 percent share of the proceeds, which would go directly to the school. The resulting $44,000 helped pay for extra staff, Christmas gifts, and so forth. But when the D.C. Inspector General got wind, he investigated Moss and, in March 1999, urged his firing. Why? Because the principal's entrepreneurial ways did not conform to the regulations and procedures concerning public school funding in the nation's capital.

Is this the model we want to take with us into the twenty-first century, where, Peter Drucker tells us, "Education will become the center of the knowledge society, and the school its key institution"?[6] A quartet of outdated assumptions forms the foundation on which today's public education edifice rests:

---

[5] Albert Shanker cited in *The Wall Street Journal* (editorial), 2 October 1989.
[6] Peter Drucker, "The Age of Social Transformation," *Atlantic Monthly*, November 1994.

Old Assumption # 1
Public schools are instrumentalities of government, managed in a
bureaucratic fashion.

States organize public schools into geographically defined systems or districts, ruled by a (usually elected) board of education. That board is empowered by the state to own and operate public schools. It sets their policies and establishes their rules, subject to innumerable additional regulations from state and federal governments. The board also employs state-licensed professionals to staff its schools, using civil-service-style personnel procedures. The local board customarily hires a superintendent to oversee a central office staff that acts as the board's administrative arm.

Money flows into the district's coffers from local, state, and federal tax receipts. Much of it has strings attached. Money for textbooks can be spent only to purchase books on a state-approved list. The elementary school principal must be picked from among individuals certified by the state licensing board. If a school receives money from Washington for bilingual education, it must follow the prescriptions of the federal bilingual program about who is eligible for services, what methods teachers must use, and so on.

Labor relations are industrial-style. In most districts, collective-bargaining agreements control teacher assignments, working hours, class size, evaluation procedures, and so forth. Uniform salary schedules treat everyone alike, no matter whether they are good, bad, or mediocre at their jobs. Salary increases are given for time spent in the system. Lifelong employment (i.e., tenure) often comes after two or three years.

Schools run this way—managed by government, staffed by public employees, and overseen by lay boards—were meant to escape from circa-1890 patronage and municipal corruption. But the structure has grown an insulated political culture of its own.

Old Assumption # 2
Public school systems are near-monopolies that typically deliver education
through standard-issue schools. Only the well-to-do have ready access to
alternatives for their children.

In the words of analyst Ted Kolderie, "Public education is organized as a pattern of territorial exclusive franchises."[7] Only school boards can run public schools in their territory, typically assigning youngsters to them according to geography, grade level, and building capacity. This monopoly doesn't allow families the option of fleeing a bad public school. Prosperous

[7] Ted Kolderie, *The States Will Have to Withdraw the Exclusive* (St. Paul, Minn.: Center for Policy Studies, 1990), 1.

families can break free by residing elsewhere or paying tuition at private schools. Other families are stuck with what they are given.

District boards also control the education process within schools. That control is usually used to sustain an outmoded design. According to David Osborne and Ted Gaebler,

> Public education's customers — children, families, and employers — have changed dramatically over the past 50 years. Yet most schools look just like they did 50 years ago. We still require most children to attend the school closest to their home, as we did in the days of the horse and buggy. We still organize school calendars as if children were needed on the farm all summer. We still schedule the day as if Mom will be home at 3 P.M. We still put each student through the same 12-year program, grade by grade. We still measure students' progress in course credits, using a system designed in 1910. And we still put teachers in front of rows of children, primarily to talk.[8]

Exceptions require bureaucratic end-runs, often blocked by provisions of the union master contract and other special interests. Add the conviction that uniformity is a virtue — in the name of social equity, cultural unity, and so forth — and it is no surprise that most schools are basically alike. So are most efforts to reform them. Changing the practices of a bureaucratic monopoly means laboriously changing the whole enterprise at once. The belief behind what is today termed "systemic reform" is that education can be rationalized and upgraded by a command-and-control system so long as all schools receive the same marching orders.[9]

Old Assumption # 3
Education quality is properly gauged by inputs, resources, and compliance with rules. Results-based accountability is largely absent.

Today's public school enterprise lacks clear standards and expectations for most students and employees. Where states specify outcomes, the list is often vague about knowledge and skills and more attentive to attitudes and behavior (resulting in a backlash against standard-setting itself).[10] Per-

[8] David Osborne and Ted Gaebler, *Reinventing Government: How the Entrepreneurial Spirit Is Transforming the Public Sector* (Reading, Mass.: Addison-Wesley, 1992), 314–15.

[9] Paul T. Hill, Lawrence C. Pierce, and James W. Guthrie, *Reinventing Public Education* (Chicago: University of Chicago Press, 1997), 105–6 (see 105–14 for a thorough critique of the "systemic education reform" model); see also Paul T. Hill and Mary Beth Celio, *Fixing Urban Schools* (Washington, D.C.: Brookings Institution Press, 1998), 20–21.

[10] This is manifest most visibly in the reaction to "outcome-based education." See the following for an elaboration of this point: Bruno V. Manno, "The New School Wars: Battles Over Outcome-Based Education," *Phi Delta Kappan*, May 1995, 720–26; Bruno V. Manno, "Outcome-based Education: Has It Become More Affliction Than Cure?" in *Certain Truths: Essays About our Families, Children and Culture,* ed. Mitchell B. Pearlstein (Minneapolis: Center of the American Experiment, 1995), 177–220.

formance standards for personnel are almost nonexistent, though innumerable rules specify who may do what.

Neither do external audits furnish clear, comparable, and timely information about education results. At the levels that matter most, there is simply no auditor. We have decent national and international data on student achievement, and there is ample information about school resources and programs. Yet anyone seeking solid data on education performance at the student, classroom, school, or district level won't find much.

Nor do consequences predictably follow from performance. Nobody loses their job when test scores drop. Indeed, the school where they plummet is apt to be sent additional money on the theory that this will solve its problems. Great educators rarely get bonuses—and in many schools they are hassled by their peers for stepping out of line. Outside a handful of elite schools and selective colleges, students, too, find few rewards for studying hard and excelling academically—and few sanctions for coasting. To the extent that any accountability procedures are in place, these typically concentrate on measuring services provided and regulatory compliance.

Old Assumption # 4
Power properly rests with the producers, not the consumers.

One might assume that public education is accountable to the public for its performance. Yet most operational power rests with the producers of education, not with consumers, taxpayers, or citizens. Most decisions are made by an education "establishment" that includes the two big teachers' unions; groups representing principals, superintendents, and other school employees; state departments of education; textbook publishers and software vendors; colleges of education; the custodians and coal stokers; the bus drivers and cafeteria workers; school psychologists; even the boards of education themselves. They are frequently joined by (slightly sheepish) business groups and even by a docile PTA. Political scientist Terry Moe observes: "American public bureaucracy is not designed to be effective. The bureaucracy arises out of politics, and its design reflects the interests, strategies, and compromises of those who exercise political power."[11]

Power in the hands of producers means power withheld from consumers. Yes, schools profess to want more parent involvement and often solicit help with fundraisers and field trips. They may even require attendance at parent-teacher conferences. But parents seldom have real influence over which school their child attends or what happens in it. Those who want their child to attend a different school must fight a system that

---

[11] Terry M. Moe, "The Politics of Bureaucratic Structure," in *Can the Government Govern?* eds. John E. Chubb and Paul E. Peterson (Washington, D.C.: The Brookings Institution, 1989), 267, 269.

assumes that parents don't know what is best for their children. In America today, families routinely choose where to live, shop, and work. They decide what to feed their child, what clothes to put on his back, what doctor will heal his infirmities, and which church will care for his soul. But unless they are rich, lucky, or uncommonly aggressive, they may not decide what school that child will attend.

EVOLUTION OF THE CHARTER ALTERNATIVE

The charter school idea points toward a new conception of public education that discards the factory model, rejects the "one best system," cracks the monopoly, views stakeholders in a fresh light, and replaces the old axioms about how public education is delivered. The new conception rests on its own quartet of assumptions:

- *A public school is any school that is open to the public, paid for by the public, and accountable to the public. It need not be run by government.*
- *Public schools should be different in myriad ways, and all families should be able to choose among them.*
- *What matters most is not the resources a school commands or the rules it obeys, but the results it produces.*
- *Each school is a self-governing community in which parents and teachers have valued roles.*

We will say more about these new assumptions later in this chapter. First, though, we try to explain what brought on this different view of public education. We look both within the field of education and beyond it. Within education, five momentous developments of the past several decades paved the way for the charter idea:

- A shift in focus from school inputs to outputs
- Setting higher standards
- The excellence movement
- New school designs
- Choice and competition

GREATER INPUTS ≠ STRONGER OUTPUTS

In 1965, President Lyndon Johnson signed into law the Elementary and Secondary Education Act, the apogee of the Great Society's strategy for improving American public education. Its premise was that schools were underfunded and more money for them would produce better results, especially for disadvantaged children. This reflected the era's conventional wisdom that the discrepant performance of youngsters arose from inequities in the allocation of resources to their schools; that spending more would cause children to learn more; and that education quality is properly judged in terms of inputs — intentions and efforts, programs and services, resources and activities.

A year later, sociologist James S. Coleman stunned the education world with his massive study, *Equality of Educational Opportunity*, which found no reliable relationship between the resources that go into a school and the learning that comes out.[12] Looking back on his work, Coleman later wrote, "The major virtue of the study [was] shifting policy attention from . . . inputs (per pupil expenditure, class size, teacher salaries, and so on) to a focus on outputs."[13] If one could not count on additional resources to yield better results, then — it stood to reason — anyone concerned about poor results would have to devise some other way of strengthening them. But this, of course, would be harder. Coleman saw the task of "overcoming . . . inequalities in the opportunity for educational achievement . . . [as] far more ambitious than has ever been attempted by any society."[14]

Coleman's insight raised a profound question. If some schools produce better results than others, what accounts for the difference? If not explicable by inputs, could the wide gap in educational attainment be traced to school and classroom practices, and to students' family backgrounds and economic circumstance?

The eminent Harvard education researcher, John B. Carroll, said yes. He observed that schools commonly hold constant such key instructional elements as teaching time while accepting wide differences in achievement results. Carroll suggested that more equal outcomes might be possible if instructional practices were tailored to the varied needs of students.[15]

Other scholars sought to understand which school practices worked best, particularly with poor and minority children. This line of inquiry was dubbed "effective schools" research.[16] Effective schools, it turned out, have

[12] James S. Coleman, *Equality of Educational Opportunity: Summary Report* (Washington, D.C.: Department of Health, Education, and Welfare, 1966).

[13] James S. Coleman, "The Evaluation of 'Equality of Educational Opportunity,'" in *On Equality of Educational Opportunity*, eds. Frederick Mosteller and Daniel Patrick Moynihan (New York: Vintage Books, 1972), 149–50.

[14] James S. Coleman, "Toward Open Schools," *The Public Interest* 9 (Fall 1967): 24–25.

[15] John B. Carroll, "A Model of School Learning," *Teachers College Record* 64, (1963): 723–33. See also the following: William G. Spady, "Outcome-Based Education," in *School Improvement Programs: A Handbook for Educational Leaders*, eds. James H. Block, Susan T. Everson, and Thomas R. Guskey (New York: Scholastic, 1995), 387–88 and Thomas R. Guskey, "Mastery Learning," 91–108; Benjamin S. Bloom, *Every Kid Can Learn: Learning for Mastery* (Washington, D.C.: College/University Press, 1973); and Camilla Persson Benbow and Julian C. Stanley, "Inequity in Equity: How 'Equity' Can Lead to Inequity for High-Potential Students," *Psychology, Public Policy, and Law* 2, no. 2 (1996): 249–92.

[16] See the following examples: Michael Rutter et al., *Fifteen Thousand Hours: Secondary Schools and Their Effects on Children* (Cambridge: Harvard University Press, 1979); Ronald R. Edmonds, *An Overview of School Improvement Programs* (Ann Arbor, Mich.: Michigan

certain predictable (and commonsensical) features, whether public or private. They have a clear, focused mission; a core curriculum with high expectations for all students (and teachers); an organizational climate that supports the school's mission and expectations; and strong leadership. Thanks to that leadership, most have also wrested a measure of autonomy from the system and have carved out a zone within which they can shape their own destinies.

Higher Standards for All

A loud, clear voice through this entire period, especially on behalf of black youngsters, was that of the iconoclastic psychologist Kenneth B. Clark, whose study of the malign effects of school segregation was cited in the Supreme Court's landmark 1954 decision, *Brown v. Board of Education.* Clark wrote extensively to refute the view that minority youngsters are intellectually inferior and require watered-down education standards. He had little stomach for the "racism of double standards [caused by] . . . the sloppy sentimentalistic good intentions of educators."[17]

Clark also had no patience with the way that urban school systems educated minority children, and argued for the need to rethink these systems. He called for "realistic, aggressive, and viable competitors" to the present public school system that would strengthen "that which deserves to survive," arguing "that public education need not be identified with the present system of organization of public schools."[18] He also believed that effectiveness and efficiency were two paramount criteria that public schools should adhere to, because in the future they would "be judged in terms of performance, not opportunity alone."[19] While not the only spokesman for this view, his was a respected and articulate voice in favor of challenging standards for all children. His writings showed how excellence and equality are complementary goals and how any effort to teach to higher standards must link expectations to assessments and consequences.

State University, 1983); Marshall S. Smith and Stewart C. Purkey, "Effective Schools — A Review," *Elementary School Journal* 83 (March 1983): 427–52; Andrew Greeley, *Catholic High Schools and Minority Students* (New Brunswick, N.J.: Transaction Books, 1982); James S. Coleman, Thomas Hoffer, and Sally Kilgore, *Public and Private Schools* (New York: Basic Books, 1987); Anthony S. Bryk, Valerie E. Lee, and Peter B. Holland, *Catholic Schools and the Common Good* (Cambridge: Harvard University Press, 1993); Paul T. Hill, Gail E. Foster, and Tamar Gendler, *High Schools with Character* (Santa Monica, Calif.: Rand, 1990).

[17] Kenneth B. Clark, "Efficiency as a Prod to Social Action," *Monthly Labor Review,* August 1969, 55–56.

[18] Quoted in Howard Fuller, "Milwaukee Choice Program," *Network News and Views,* December 1996, 66.

[19] Kenneth B. Clark, *An Intensive Program for the Attainment of Educational Achievement in Deprived Areas of New York City* (New York: MARC Education Group, 1967), 6.

THE "EXCELLENCE MOVEMENT"

In 1983, President Ronald Reagan's National Commission on Excellence in Education produced its landmark report, *A Nation at Risk.* It captured the country's attention by calling in blunt language for fundamental reforms to boost pupil achievement. The Commission asserted that America's young people were not learning nearly enough and that the conventional wisdom of the mid-1960s had failed to improve the education system's performance. Its report placed unprecedented pressure on policymakers to boost school standards and performance. Elected officials and business leaders set out to force changes on a change-averse public education establishment. This quest came to be called the "excellence movement."[20]

The nation's governors played a big part. Beginning in 1986, they issued a series of influential reports called *Time for Results.*[21] In 1989, President George Bush invited all fifty governors to an "Education Summit," where they set six ambitious national education goals. In the words of summit participants, "We want to swap red tape for results."[22] That would become the exact theory of charter schools.

The swap included freeing schools to make more decisions for themselves, a reform undertaken in a number of communities — dramatically so in Chicago — and frequently dubbed "site-based management" (SBM).[23] The idea was that authority over key decisions must shift from the central office to individual schools. Each would have an SBM committee comprised of school and community "stakeholders" (particularly teachers and parents), empowered by new decision-making roles. The concept is close kin to the charter school idea. (SBM alone rarely worked out in practice because effective control over such crucial domains as budget and personnel usually remained with the central office bureaucracy and the master union contract.)[24]

---

[20] Denis P. Doyle and Terry W. Hartle, *Excellence in Education: The States Take Charge* (Washington, D.C.: American Enterprise Institute, 1985). See also Thomas Toch, *In the Name of Excellence: The Struggle to Reform the Nation's Schools, Why It's Failing, and What Should Be Done* (New York: Oxford University Press, 1991).

[21] National Governors' Association, *Time for Results: The Governors' 1991 Report on Education* (Washington, D.C.: National Governors' Association, 1986). For an overview of the 1980s, see Denis P. Doyle, Bruce S. Cooper, and Roberta Trachtman, *Taking Charge: State Action and School Reform in the 1980s* (Indianapolis, Ind.: Hudson Institute, 1991).

[22] The Statement by the President and the Governors, "A Jeffersonian Compact," *New York Times*, 1 October 1989.

[23] On Chicago, see Anthony S. Bryk, "Policy Lessons from Chicago's Experience with Decentralization," in Diane Ravitch, ed., *Brookings Papers on Education Policy 1999* (Washington, D.C.: Brookings Institution Press, 1999), 67–99.

[24] Hill et al., *Reinventing Public Education*, 99–105; see also Hill and Celio, *Fixing Urban Schools*, 7–8, 21–23.

New School Designs

Not only was yesterday's "one best system" yielding unsatisfactory results; the "one standard model" was also proving dysfunctional. America is too big and varied a country to expect a single model to fit everyone, especially when that model is a half-century old. So, following our national penchant to tinker and invent new models, people set about creating new kinds of schools.

This was the notion behind the New American Schools Development Corporation, created in 1991 by private businesses in response to an invitation by President Bush to develop "break the mold" schools based on wholly different ideas about what a first-class education might be.[25] Other ventures set out to do much the same thing, including Theodore Sizer's "essential" schools, Henry Levin's "accelerated" schools, and Christopher Whittle's "Edison" schools. The message they sent was that even if we "fixed" every U.S. school according to the old design, we would still be in trouble. We also needed to create new types of schools, schools never before imagined.

Competition and Choice

In the mid-1950s, the Nobel prize-winning economist Milton Friedman stunned the education community when he proposed a competitive model of schooling based on the premise that government should not provide education directly. Families would instead receive from the state a certificate or voucher for a specific amount of money that could be redeemed for education at any state-approved school. These voucher schools would meet certain standards set by government. But Friedman did not depend on the state for quality control. He believed that failing institutions would be forced out of business by market pressures that would also motivate mediocre schools to higher performance levels. In this education marketplace, consumers would be sovereign. Competition would create a more efficient system of public schooling in which financial and human resources would focus on maximizing pupil performance.[26]

Friedman was echoed by prominent voucher advocates on the Left, including the sociologist Christopher Jencks. Jencks believed that giving poor families tuition grants so they could opt out of failing public schools would spread power and help equalize opportunity.[27]

[25] Susan Bodilly, *Lessons from New American Schools Development Corporation's Demonstration Phase* (Santa Monica, Calif.: Rand, 1996).

[26] Milton Friedman, *Capitalism and Freedom* (Chicago: University of Chicago Press, 1962), 85–107.

[27] Christopher Jencks, "Is the Public School Obsolete?" *The Public Interest*, 2 (Winter 1966): 18–27. See also Theodore Sizer and Philip Whitten, "A Proposal for a Poor Children's Bill of Rights," *Psychology Today*, August 1968.

In 1990, John Chubb and Terry Moe published a stinging and influential analysis of public education's faltering delivery system, urging instead a lively marketplace of private choices.[28] They focused on the bureaucratic and political institutions that shape public education and shield it from accountability. These arguments have recently been extended and given added historical grounding by Andrew J. Coulson, who makes a persuasive case for the superiority of "market education" to government schooling.[29] They have gained moral force and political momentum from such eloquent spokesmen for minority youngsters as Dr. Howard Fuller and Rev. Floyd Flake. Today, there are publicly funded voucher experiments underway in Milwaukee and Cleveland, the first statewide program coming on line in Florida, and about 50 privately supported programs.

PARALLEL UNIVERSES

Besides these portentous changes within the education realm, developments elsewhere in American society helped clear a path for charter schools. In the corporate sector, traditional bureaucratic structures and top-down management systems were being rendered obsolete by the heaving transition to the information age and the flexibility demanded by the global economy's fierce competitiveness. Whole industries were transformed, including automobiles, telecommunications, and steel. Corporate restructuring and, in some cases, massive downsizing have been brought on by international competition, technological advances, productivity breakthroughs, and tremendous pressure for profits. Comfortable lifetime jobs vanished in this new world of temporary employees, outsourcing, and "just-in-time" production schedules.

Many enterprises have transformed themselves, dispensing with top-down control, slashing middle management, and scrapping thick manuals of procedures. Taking a cue from organization experts, corporations have changed themselves from clumsy dinosaurs to fleet-footed tigers. Rigid, hierarchical management pyramids have been supplanted by flexible management systems that benchmark results, offer incentives for success, and develop strategies for continuous improvement.[30]

Most of today's successful companies run according to a "tight-loose" strategy: they are tightly controlled with respect to their goals and stan-

[28] John E. Chubb and Terry M. Moe, *Politics, Markets, and America's Schools* (Washington, D.C.: The Brookings Institution, 1990). For a review of the Chubb and Moe book by former U.S. Commissioner of Education Harold Howe II, see "Thoughts on Choice," *Teachers College Record* 93, no. 1 (Fall 1991): 167–73. The review is noteworthy because Howe calls for the "design [of] some new [education choice] trials [to] see how they work."

[29] Andrew J. Coulson, *Market Education: The Unknown History* (New Brunswick, N.J.: Transaction Publishers, 1999).

[30] Examples include General Electric, Xerox, IBM, Motorola, and the big-three automakers.

dards—the results they must achieve, and the information by which performance is tracked—but they are loose as to the *means* by which those results get produced. Individual units within the firm have wide latitude to operate as they see fit, so long as they deliver the desired bottom line. Responsibility and accountability are now vested in each operating unit. James Q. Wilson summarizes these changes:

> [I]n general the strategies emphasize empowering lower-level employees and their immediate supervisors to make more decisions, flattening the firm's hierarchy so that messages and orders travel shorter distances, designing compensation schemes that reward good performance, and developing an organizational culture based on such concepts as total quality management.[31]

PROFILE

Jim Goenner (Charter Schools Office, Central Michigan University)

Jim Goenner is Mr. Charter Schools for Michigan, the state with the country's third largest charter program. After serving as president of the Michigan Association of Public School Academies (Michigan's term for charter schools), he now directs the charter schools office at Central Michigan University. He has seen more than his fair share of charter activity, including a debate over the constitutionality of charter schools that ended with the Michigan Supreme Court ruling in their favor.

Goenner has been a teacher, a baseball coach, and a salesman. His mother was a public school teacher, and his father a school superintendent and university professor. Why did he get involved with charter schools? Goenner reflects:

My involvement with charter schools developed from personal experience in business and teaching and a strong family history in education. While in business, I became sold on the power of America's free enterprise system. That lesson stayed with me when I began teaching and coaching and saw that education could benefit from free enterprise. Recalling how competition drove innovation and excellence in business, I saw charter schools as a promising way to transfer entrepreneurship to education.

Goenner sees obvious parallels between the principles that drive the charter movement and the forces that have been reshaping the U.S. economy:

Charter schools offer the opportunity to improve American education by infusing the system with competition and market forces. The nature of a market-

---

[31] James Q. Wilson, "Can the Bureaucracy Be Deregulated? Lessons from Government Agencies," in *Deregulating the Public Service: Can Government Be Improved?* ed. John J. DiIulio, Jr. (Washington, D.C.: The Brookings Institution, 1994), 37.

based, entrepreneurial environment means that charter schools must be effective and efficient in order to exist. Michigan residents all know the story of how the domestic automobile industry was transformed by persistent foreign competition that taught customers to expect excellence. The same situation can occur in our public schools. Indeed, it must.

REINVENTING GOVERNMENT

Corporate restructuring, "tight-loose" management, and employee empowerment may be keys to private-sector success, but what about the public sector? Government often follows the opposite formula: it is rigid about how things get done but laid back as to whether the desired results are produced. It is more concerned with procedures than outcomes. Its institutions last forever.

On closer inspection, however, the management revolution has infiltrated government, too. Osborne and Gaebler called this movement "reinventing government." It involves transforming public agencies into "steering organizations . . . [that] set policy, deliver funds to operational bodies (public and private), and evaluate performance—but they seldom play an operational role themselves."[32] Osborne and Gaebler posit that many public services can be delivered efficiently without being provided directly by government agencies. Instead, government outsources the services to private providers, which in turn are held accountable for their results, not for compliance with procedures.

The reinventing government movement was embraced by the Clinton administration after it was pioneered by various state and local governments. For example, Indianapolis has experienced much success with privatizing welfare and other municipal services. Mayor Stephen Goldsmith employs the "Yellow Pages test": if the city is performing a function that is listed in the Yellow Pages, he will consider outsourcing that function. Phoenix put its Public Works Department in head-to-head competition with private companies for services such as trash collection and road repair. The Michigan Department of Commerce hired a customer-service chief, trained employees in consumer relations, and embraced Total Quality Management.[33] (Reinventing government need not mean privatization. It can also mean a different approach to government.) Wisconsin's welfare program, a work-based system of public aid that contracts with public and

[32] Osborne and Gaebler, *Reinventing Government*, 40. See also John E. Brandl, *Money and Good Intentions Are Not Enough: OR Why a Liberal Democrat Thinks States Need Both Competition and Community* (Washington, D.C.: Brookings Institution Press, 1998); Mark Schneider, Paul Teske, and Michael Mintrom, *Public Entrepreneurs: Agents for Change in American Government* (Princeton: Princeton University Press, 1995); Howard Davies, *Fighting Leviathan: Building Social Markets That Work* (London: The Social Market Foundation, 1992).

[33] Osborne and Gaebler, *Reinventing Government*, 17.

private organizations to help low-income families become self-sufficient, is widely touted as a success.

A central tenet of the reinventing government movement is that public agencies, like private corporations, must be mission-driven. According to Osborne and Gaebler, mission-driven organizations are more efficient, effective, innovative, and flexible, and have higher morale than rule-driven organizations.

TECTONIC CHANGES

Besides transformations in education, business, and government, other societal changes helped create a hospitable climate for charter schools. First, beginning in the 1960s, there was broad liberalization of American culture, what political scientist Hugh Heclo grandly terms an "awakening . . . to a plurality of authenticities."[34] Its elements have included, for better or worse, the decline of traditional authority, the exaltation of personal freedom, the rise of tolerance as a supreme value, and the spread of pluralism, multiculturalism, and diversity.

With all these forces chipping away at the industrial age's tendency toward centralization and standardization, it grows ever more peculiar that K–12 schooling remains essentially authoritarian and uniform. If we no longer accept "one best system" in other parts of our lives, why in education? Families have a thousand colleges to choose among. Why should they not have plenty of options in the schools their children attend?

A political sea change has also come over the United States in recent years. Candidates win elections by vowing to cut taxes, curb "big government," restore freedom, and offer people more choices. The conviction is spreading that government is only one among many ways of delivering public goods and services.[35]

Accompanying this political shift has been rekindled interest in the vitality of "civil society." The civic order is recognized as a third path — neither governmental nor strictly private — to meet human needs and solve community problems. Mediating institutions — e.g., churches, Neighborhood Watch groups, and organizations such as the Red Cross and the Girl Scouts — can help us solve intractable social problems while strengthening community bonds. The world of K–12 education is no exception. What better place than the school to reaffirm the ties between parent and child, to anchor communities, to teach children about citizenship, and to bring people together in common cause?

These many tributaries have fed a river of change in public education,

---

[34] Hugh Heclo, "The Sixties' False Dawn: Awakenings, Movements and Postmodern Policymaking," *Journal of Policy History* 8, no. 1 (1996): 46.

[35] See Lamar Alexander and Chester E. Finn, Jr., *The New Promise of American Life* (Indianapolis, Ind.: Hudson Institute, 1995).

which in chapter 1 we termed "reinventing public education." Charter schools are today's most prominent expression of that process. They change the emphasis from inputs to results by focusing on student achievement. They flip the structure from rule-bound hierarchy to decentralized flexibility by allowing individual schools to shape their own destinies.

Reinventing America's Schools

We now examine the four new assumptions on which charter schools rest, axioms that closely parallel the changes we have observed elsewhere in American society.

New Assumption # 1
A "public" school is any school that is open to the public, paid for by the public, and accountable to the public. It need not be run by government.

The charter idea begins with the conviction that sound public school choices can be provided to families without being owned and managed directly by government. A charter school can be created and run by parents, teachers, or civic organizations. The charter lays out how the school will organize and govern itself and what results it will produce.

We have long accepted this approach at the post-secondary level. Public higher education in most states is no chain of identical institutions run by a bureaucracy. Rather, it is a loose confederation of diverse, self-governing colleges and universities that are accountable to public authorities (as well as to the marketplace) in various ways. It is a flexible system that allows for such dissimilar campuses as the University of Michigan, Wayne State, and Bay de Noc Community College to coexist comfortably in the same state.

The charter idea keeps K–12 education public, too. But like public colleges and universities, these schools are free to be different.

New Assumption # 2
Public schools should be different in myriad ways, and all families should be able to choose among them.

The charter idea recognizes that people differ along countless dimensions, from the loftiest (values, beliefs, and goals) to the most mundane (daily schedules and work lives).

Whatever else the charter movement has accomplished since 1991, it has unwrapped the imaginations of thousands of individuals and organizations that have made these schools seedbeds of policy and educational innovation. The charter idea assumes that schools should differ from each other so that the diverse needs of a pluralistic society can be met. It allows for "back to basics" schools, "progressive" schools, virtual schools, Montessori schools, Waldorf schools, Comer schools, Core Knowledge schools, Advantage schools, Hope Academies, schools for at-risk kids, alternative schools, and all manner of public-private hybrids.

Rather than prescribing a single model of how a school ought to look, a charter law lays out certain ground rules — an "opportunity space"[36] — within which a school must be designed. Within those parameters, schools are free to differ in curricula, instruction, and assessment; internal organization; leadership and governance; staffing; parent and community involvement; scheduling; technology; financing; and much more. Some charters also incorporate comprehensive efforts to take many of the intersecting elements that make up a school, from staffing to organization, from schedule to budget, from curriculum to testing, and rework the whole design. With a charter school, you can start from scratch and build an entire new house or you can renovate only the kitchen.

Simple diversity is not the point, however. Efficacy counts for even more. Not all children acquire skills and knowledge in the same ways or at the same rates. Not all thrive in the same settings. Not all have the same interests and needs. The reason to encourage schools to be different is so that all youngsters, not just those who blossom under the "one best system," will have the kinds of education that enable them to learn.

New Assumption # 3
What matters most is not the resources a school commands or the rules it obeys, but the results it produces.

The genius of the charter concept is that it is demanding with respect to results but relaxed about how those results are produced; tight as to ends, loose as to means. Yet success in attaining results can be found only if there are clear standards, good assessments, and consequences for everyone.

Charter accountability is dual: to the customers (families) and to the public authority that sponsors the school. The charter approach does not mean blind faith in the invisible hand. While market forces are necessary, they may not be sufficient to assure quality. Neither is the charter strategy an example of "privatization." The public retains an interest in the successful delivery of education services paid for by public funds.[37]

Charter sponsors are responsible for setting academic, fiscal, and other performance standards for their schools and then holding operators accountable for meeting those standards. They should also be able to warn, intervene in, and, if necessary, withdraw public funds from any school that egregiously fails to meet those standards. While public officials thus retain

[36] RPP International, *A Study of Charter Schools: Second Year Report* (Washington, D.C.: U.S. Department of Education, 1998), 39.
[37] Brandl, *Money and Good Intentions Are Not Enough*, 84–85.

the power to close schools, they do not directly manage the schools or tell them how to allocate their resources, whom to employ, or how to teach. The charter idea views public authorities as purchasers — and monitors — of services, not providers of those services. They steer but don't row.

Charter operators, meanwhile, benefit from the "looseness as to means." This includes the vital domain of personnel. In most states, charter schools are not obliged to limit their pool of potential instructors and principals to graduates of teacher (or administrator) training programs. Individuals with sound character who know their subjects and want to teach children can work in many charter schools. This opens the classroom door to scientists and engineers who are expert in biology, chemistry, physics, or math, who are interested in teaching, and who are willing to work with a master teacher to acquire the necessary pedagogical tools. It also allows individuals trained in the leadership, management, and financing of other kinds of organizations to apply their knowledge and skills to public education. These nontraditional teachers and managers are creating a new education profession where individuals are paid (and retained) on the basis of their performance and are encouraged to innovate.

Assumption # 4
Each school is a self-governing community in which parents and teachers have valued roles.

The charter idea concentrates on individual schools, not school systems. Each school is a "production unit." It makes its own decisions so long as its results are solid. This emphasis places a premium on having a coherent vision and shared values.

Parents are ordinarily involved with charter governance, but so are teachers and other educators. In fact, the word "professional" takes on new meaning in this context. Since schools are autonomous, educators are free from the oversight and constraints that come with central bureaucracies. To them are ceded a wide array of decisions and responsibilities. So long as students attain the promised results and the customers remain satisfied, the school's staff can operate as it thinks best.

The scale is usually more intimate than in conventional schools, too. Though the charter world is beginning to develop some multi-site operations and chains of schools, most charter schools are self-contained and small.

The act of selecting one's school — whether that choice is made by a student, a parent, or a teacher — has great power, too, in terms of one's "buy-in" and commitment. Schools of choice are more apt to elicit parental engagement than schools of geographic assignment, since parents select schools not only for their academic programs but also because of their mission and values.

THE CHANGING EDUCATION ECOSYSTEM

"When paradigms change," Thomas Kuhn once remarked, "the world itself changes with them." The charter concept is no exception. When Sarah Kass and Ann Connelly Tolkoff decided to throw out the rulebook and start City On A Hill Charter School from scratch, they probably did not realize that the ideas that moved them were also beginning to transform American public education as a whole.

Some see the charter idea as a dangerous predator in the education ecosystem, one that will gradually consume and thereby destroy public education. But that isn't the only way to view this dynamic change.

Stephen Jay Gould's discussion of the "cropping principle" in evolution offers a different perspective. The conventional wisdom about the appearance of a new plant- or meat-eating animal — a "cropper" — into a territory is that it shrinks the number of species in the area. But science has found that precisely the opposite occurs. The cropper actually tends to enrich, not decimate, the ecosystem. In Gould's words, "A well-cropped ecosystem is maximally diverse, with many species and few individuals of any single species. Stated another way, the introduction of a new level in the ecological pyramid tends to broaden the level below it."[38] We believe this is the effect that the charter idea will have — indeed is beginning to have — on public education: enriching and broadening the entire ecosystem.

The charter paradigm is indisputably starting to change the education world. But how much of that change is for good? How well is it working? Are these successful enterprises? Are they boosting student achievement? How innovative are they? We saw partial answers at the five schools we visited in chapter 2, but most of the charter iceberg remains under the water. In the next chapter, we put on our diving gear and plunge in to survey more of its mass.

[38] Stephen Jay Gould, *Ever Since Darwin: Reflections in Natural History* (New York: W. W. Norton & Company, 1977), 123–24.

4

HOW ARE THEY WORKING?

Hᴏᴡ ᴡᴇʟʟ are America's charter schools doing? The answers are necessarily tentative. That the most ancient among them are barely seven years old — and the vast majority are in their first few years of operation — means that definitive data are scarce, particularly concerning pupil achievement.[1] Though organizational flaws can sometimes be glimpsed within weeks or months of a school's launch, no clear judgment can be made about any school's effectiveness after only a year or two with students. As Arizona State Superintendent Lisa Graham Keegan cautions, "I don't think one claims victory until [one sees] three to five years of sustained improvement."[2]

Efforts to appraise charter schools' efficacy are also handicapped by the information vacuum that weakens our entire public education system. Conventional public schools are derelict when it comes to documenting their performance. State and local systems are awash in data about inputs (e.g., teacher credentials, expenditures, and graduation rates), but the gaps are wide when comparing schools or districts on their effectiveness. American education still has no agreed-upon system of performance accounting, and the partial evaluation systems that exist render schools anything but transparent. Charter schools, like other schools, function with this information deficit. Thus the evidence presented here is suggestive, not dispositive.

In this chapter, we first examine such achievement data as can be obtained, followed by a demographic profile of charter students. Next, we examine satisfaction levels among students, teachers, and parents, and look at the innovativeness and efficiency of these schools. Finally, we report on the demand for charter schools both in the United States and abroad.

---

[1] According to the U.S. Department of Education, 70 percent of charter schools were brand new organizations. RPP International, *The State of Charter Schools: Third-Year Report* (Washington, D.C.: U.S. Department of Education, 1999), 14.

[2] Statement of Lisa Graham Keegan to U.S. Senate Committee on Labor and Human Resources, 31 March 1998, published by the Education Leaders Council, Washington, D.C., 4.

ACADEMIC ACHIEVEMENT

Everyone craves hard data on the academic performance of charter schools. As California Education Secretary Gary Hart (see chapter 11) says, "[T]he time is rapidly coming when people are going to be saying, 'Well, we've given you all of this freedom, what are you able to show for it?' . . . [T]he tradeoff has always been outcomes versus deregulation. And if we can't demonstrate the outcomes, we're not entitled to the deregulation."

Of the sparse outcomes data we have today, most are positive. In 1998, the Center for School Change at the University of Minnesota studied academic achievement in over thirty schools in eight states and came to these conclusions:

- "Charters are showing that they can improve student achievement. This report cites 21 charter schools which improved achievement."
- "Nine schools did not send enough comparable data from one year to the next to determine whether academic gains were made. Two schools provided no data."
- "Seven charters in the group have had their contracts renewed because of improved student achievement and six schools received an award for outstanding performance."[3]

That two-thirds of these schools had documented achievement gains was certainly encouraging. As this book goes to press, however, these are the only multi-state achievement data that we have. Fortunately, several states have already started to appraise the educational effectiveness of their charter schools, and more have plans to do so. In light of wide variability in testing programs, state-level data will likely be most illuminating.

Most charter statutes require the schools to participate in the state's assessment program. Arizona charters, for example, must take part in both the new Arizona Instrument to Measure Standards and the familiar Stanford 9 test. Colorado charters are included in the Colorado Student Assessment Program. Georgia charters must administer the Iowa Test of Basic Skills. Texas charter schools are obliged to participate in the Texas Assessment of Academic Skills (TAAS). And so forth.

What does the early state-level evidence show? In Colorado, a 1998 study found that charter performance (in the 32 schools that had been operational for at least two years) "is stronger than state averages, stronger than sponsoring district averages, and stronger than the averages of other schools in the sponsoring districts who [sic] serve a population of

[3] Stella Cheung, Mary Ellen Murphy, and Joe Nathan, *Making a Difference? Charter Schools, Evaluation, and Student Performance*, Center for School Change, University of Minnesota, March 1998.

students roughly comparable to the population served by charter schools."[4] Moreover, the "great majority" of Colorado charter schools "are meeting — or exceeding — the performance goals defined in their individual charters and school improvement plans."

In Minnesota, a 1999 study found that 40 percent of charter pupils met the state's graduation requirements for math (compared with 71 percent of students statewide) and that 43 percent of charter pupils met the state standards for reading (compared to 68 percent statewide). Attendance and graduation rates were also lower for charter schools. But Minnesota officials note that half the charter students were economically disadvantaged (compared with 24 percent statewide), that at least half were new to their charter school, and that most were from the Minneapolis-St. Paul area, and thus not representative of the entire state.[5]

The results are mixed in Arizona, too. According to the Goldwater Institute, 35 charter sites made Stanford 9 gains (between 1996–97 and 1997–98) in reading, math, and language, while 20 declined in all three subjects. Analyzing two years of test data, the Morrison Institute's Lori Mulholland concluded that "Overall, . . . charter schools are not performing very differently than other regular public schools."[6] Two years of achievement data are not much, though and, as in Minnesota, officials note that demographic differences must also be weighed. It is notable, too, that of Arizona's seventeen highest-performing schools in 1997–98, eight were charters.

In Texas, nine charter schools showed across-the-board gains (from 1997 to 1998) in the percentages of students passing the Texas Assessment of Academic Skills (TAAS) in all grades tested. Two showed mixed results, and two showed losses.[7]

California data are spotty, also. According to a 1997 evaluation, "[T]he available data do not allow us to draw definitive conclusions about charter schools' performance, in part because it is too early in the reform process and in part because the available data are insufficient."[8] A recent Los An-

---

[4] Colorado Department of Education, *1998 Colorado Charter Schools Evaluation Study: The Characteristics, Status, and Student Achievement Data of Colorado Charter Schools*, Denver, January 1999, i.

[5] "Minnesota Study Finds Charter Schools Don't Measure Up," *Education Daily*, 7 January 1999. State officials suggested that comparisons of test results in charter schools against their own goals, against schools with similar demographic characteristics, and changes in test results over time would be more relevant. See "Comparisons of Minnesota State-Wide Test Results for 1998," Minnesota Department of Education, 1999.

[6] Lori A. Mulholland, *Arizona Charter School Progress Evaluation*, Morrison Institute for Public Policy, Arizona State University, March 1999, 42.

[7] Preliminary (unpublished) data from the Texas Education Agency.

[8] Judith Powell, Jose Blackorby, Julie Marsh, Kara Finnegan, Lee Anderson, "Evaluation of Charter School Effectiveness Part I," SRI International, December 1997, 6. The report is available on-line at: http://www.lao.ca.gov/sri_charter_schools_1297-part1.html.

geles study by the WestEd Regional Education laboratory found that "[S]tudents in these five charter schools maintain or slightly improve their performance over time with respect to students in a comparison group of non-charter District schools, with a few exceptions."[9]

Early signs are encouraging in Massachusetts. In December 1998, the state released data comparing the performance of twenty-one charters and their host districts on tests taken the previous spring. Although these "baseline" scores do not show value added, analysts reported that "charter schools, overall, performed well." In English, "Most charter schools scored higher than or as well as their host districts at the 4th and 8th grade levels." In math, "Most charter schools performed the same or higher at the 4th grade, and the same or lower in the 10th grade. The strongest performance was at the 8th grade, where almost half of the charter schools had significantly higher scores." As for science, "Most charter schools scored the same or higher than their host district at 4th and 8th grades (with particularly strong performance at the 8th grade)."[10]

Individual Schools

Because it is so difficult to generalize about charter performance, individual school stories can be helpful. At the nation's first charter school, City Academy in St. Paul, according to the University of Minnesota study, "Students (on average) have made at least three years' academic gain in both reading and math" during the 1996–97 school year.[11]

At Boston's City On A Hill Charter School, eleventh graders gained an average of 2.7 years in both reading and language during the 1996–97 school year. In ninth grade, 52 percent of the charter students scored at or above grade level in reading, compared to 29 percent in the Boston Public Schools (B.P.S.), and over three times as many youngsters scored at or above grade level in math.[12]

But the news is not always bright. At Renaissance School in Douglas County, Colorado, after three years of experience, lackluster scores on district tests (especially in math) alarmed the parents and governing board, triggering an abrupt change in the school's leadership at the end of the 1997–98 school year. (The organizationally troubled charter school had yet another administrative turnover the following year.) We explore other such examples in the next chapter.

[9] WestEd, *The Findings and Implications of Increased Flexibility and Accountability: An Evaluation of Charter Schools in Los Angeles Unified School District*, 30 June 1998, 47.

[10] Massachusetts Department of Education, "MCAS Scores — Charter Schools," 9 December 1998.

[11] Cheung, Murphy, and Nathan, 1998.

[12] "City On A Hill Charter School Annual Report 1996–97," Boston, Massachusetts, 1997.

These school stories are only vignettes. Evaluating charter effectiveness school-by-school is what parents need to do, but it does not lead to broad conclusions about the charter phenomenon as a whole. One also needs more information about students. Were they high- or low-achieving pupils elsewhere? Is the school adding value or reflecting their prior achievement levels? These are important questions — with mostly incomplete answers today.

Time Horizons and Playing Fields

It takes time for children to make achievement gains and, especially, to overcome earlier deficits. Though Americans are eager to evaluate education innovations before the paint is dry, most experts agree that it is unreasonable to expect a new school — district, private, charter, whatever — to demonstrate significant gains for several years, preferably four or five. Accordingly, most analysts do not expect big jumps in test scores and other indicators during the first couple of years. After three or four years have passed, however, it is legitimate to seek hard evidence.

Michigan's test scores illustrate the issue. According to that state's fall 1996 assessment (MEAP), "Michigan's charter schools scored far lower than the state's schools as a whole."[13] Journalists and charter critics hastened to break the news that charter schools — a pet reform strategy of Governor John Engler — are worse than regular schools. Most did not mention that 34 of Michigan's charter schools had only been open for a few months when the test was taken, 39 had been operating for just a year, and only four had been open for even as much as two full years. The 1996 data actually revealed as much or more about where charter pupils came from — and the deficits they brought — as about how their new schools were doing.

The following year's MEAP results underscore the point. Improvements were documented in the fourth, fifth, seventh, and eighth grades in charter schools. Charter pupils gained an average of 24 points in fourth grade math (compared to 13 points statewide), 8 points in fourth grade reading (compared to 10 points), 6 points in fifth grade science (compared to 3), 8 points in seventh grade math and reading (compared to 10 points and 9 points, respectively), and 5 points in eighth grade science (compared to 4 points statewide). Declines in fifth and eighth grade writing scores were not as severe for charter students as for public school students.

Explains Jim Goenner (see profile in chapter 3), director of Central Michigan University's Charter Schools Office, "We said last year that the 1996–97 MEAP scores — the first for most schools — weren't a true reflec-

---

[13] Lynn Schnaiberg, "Michigan Tests Show Charter Schools Lagging Behind," *Education Week*, 24 September 1997, 5.

tion of the charters, many of which were open only a couple of months when the tests were given. The increases in these [1997–98] scores better illustrate the progress that charter schools make possible for Michigan children."

HAVENS FOR STRUGGLING CHILDREN

When comparing schools, it is also important to match pupil demographics. Big differences in student characteristics—poverty, parent education, and family stability, for example—are apt to echo in test scores and other performance data.

Critics predicted that charter schools would gain special advantage from an "uneven playing field" by enrolling children from well-off and motivated families. Dire warnings were voiced that these new schools would skim off the most fortunate students from regular public schools.

This has not happened. In fact, many charters attract youngsters with more problems and deficits than the conventional schools to which they are compared. These new schools are havens for children who were struggling in (or had dropped out of) their previous schools and for families alienated by the system. Some charters feel besieged by troubled youngsters whom the "regular" schools are glad to offload. As a Massachusetts charter founder commented, "This school is for kids no one else wants. And even if they had them, they wouldn't know what to do with them."

A hefty fraction of charter pupils would not otherwise be enrolled in any form of public education. According to Hudson Institute data, 19 percent of students enrolled in charter schools in 1996–97 had not been under the public education umbrella the prior year: 11 percent attended private schools, 3 percent were home-schooled, and 5 percent had dropped out. (Another 17 percent had not attended any U.S. school because they were too young, were recent immigrants, etc.)

PROFILE

Mickey Bruns (Student, Lowell Middlesex Academy, Massachusetts)*

Mickey graduated from Lowell Middlesex Academy Public Charter School in June 1998. Like his classmates, he had dropped out of regular high school but then decided to earn a diploma. He has two brothers and a sister, and his mom works in a convenience store. He says he enjoys "playing and watching sports, but my main interest is spending time with my son, who is two years old."

He attended the Academy for two years and chose this school "because of its small size and its reputation for helping kids like me. I feel

---

* Names of students have been changed.

very safe here. The school is much smaller than the local high school, and everyone here is here to learn, so we all get along. Many of the people at the regular high school were just there to hang out and start trouble." He learned "much more at this school than at my other school. My grades are very high, and I want to learn more."

What Mickey liked most about the Academy was "the teachers. They are more like friends. They are more involved here with individual students, and you can talk to them about anything. They actually care about what happens to you."

His "greatest success has been being named valedictorian of this year's graduating class." What he liked least about the school "is that it doesn't get enough recognition." If he could change one thing, it would be "that all the teachers would get a raise."

How one views this flow of youngsters into public education via the charter route naturally depends on one's vantage point. A state budget director may see the influx as an unanticipated outlay of tax dollars. But those who believe that public education is one of America's most important institutions should be elated.

How about at-risk children? It appears that between 37 and 41 percent of charter students come from low-income families, almost the same percentage as among regular public school pupils. About half of charter pupils belong to minority groups (compared to 41.3 percent in conventional schools). Ten to thirteen percent have limited English proficiency (compared to 10.7 percent in regular schools), and between 8 and 13 percent are special education students (compared to 11 percent in regular schools). See Table 4–1.

In the aggregate, charter schools are serving at least their "share" of disadvantaged youth. That should not be surprising. According to the U.S. Department of Education, one in five charter founders cited their desire to serve a special population of students as the most important reason for creating the school.[14] And that is exactly what many charters are doing. The federal study reported in 1998 that

> ... almost all the children in a significant number of charter schools are minorities, economically disadvantaged, or students with disabilities. We estimate that approximately one-fifth of charter schools may serve such a particular student population. At least 32 charter schools serve more than two-thirds African-American students, 13 serve more than two-thirds Native American children, 22 have more than two-thirds Hispanic students, and eight serve more than 50 percent students with disabilities.[15]

---

[14] RPP International, *The State of Charter Schools: Third-Year Report*, 42.
[15] RPP International, *A Study of Charter Schools: Second-Year Report* (Washington, D.C.: U.S. Department of Education, 1998), 74.

TABLE 4–1. At-Risk Youth in Charter Schools and Regular Schools[a]

	All Public School Students 1994–5/1996–97	Charter Students (Federal Sample) 1997–98	Charter Students (Hudson Sample) 1996–97
Eligible for federal lunch program	37.6%	36.7%	40.5%
Minorities	41.3%	48.2%	49.6%
Limited English	10.7%	10.1%	13.1%
Special Education	11.2%	8.3%	12.6%

[a]Federal subsidized lunch program eligibility and Limited English Proficiency data in the first column (All Public School Students) are from 1994–95. Minority and special education data in that column are from 1996–97. The first two columns supply data from RPP International, *The State of Charter Schools: Third-Year Report* (Washington, D.C.: U.S. Department of Education, 1999), 30–39. Hudson sample data (in third column) come from Gregg Vanourek, Bruno V. Manno, Chester E. Finn, Jr., and Louann A. Bierlein, "The Educational Impact of Charter Schools," *Charter Schools in Action Final Report, Part V,* Washington, D.C., July 1997, 2. The Hudson special education figure is the sum of the number of students (as reported by their schools) who have a formal IEP at their charter schools, the number who do not now have an IEP but probably would have at conventional public schools, and the number of other students with serious learning impediments.

Some states encourage—or even compel—charter schools to serve at-risk children. About a dozen have statutes that directly address such children's needs. Missouri's new charter law, for example, requires that each sponsor must grant at least one-third of its charters to schools targeting dropouts or at-risk kids. In Texas, there is a much looser cap on the number of "at-risk charters" than on other kinds.

According to the federal study, "Our data contain no evidence to support the concern that charter schools disproportionately serve white and economically advantaged students."[16]

But how well are charters serving their children? While hard data on achievement are sparse, there seems little doubt in the minds of charter students that they are doing better academically.

According to a Michigan student, "The people in this charter school really care about what I learn. At my other school, it was easy to hang back and do nothing; no one really pushed you to try harder." Another charter student said, "I used to be able to slack off quite a bit in my former school. Not here. They don't let you. They're always challenging you to reach new heights."

The academic success that students report crosses racial and ethnic lines. For example, with the change to charter schools the number of students

[16] RPP International, *The State of Charter Schools: Third-Year Report,* 2.

reporting that they are doing "excellent" or "good" work rose 20 percent for white students, 23 percent for African-American students, 22 percent for Hispanic students, 16 percent for Asian students, and 11 percent for Native American students. (See Table 4–2.)

The same trend is evident when the data are broken down by income level. In fact, self-reported performance gains are most significant among low-income children.

PROFILE

Janice Cross (Student, Charter School of San Diego)*

Janice Cross graduated from the Charter School of San Diego in June 1998, having completed her coursework for grades 7 through 12 in four years. The school enrolls about a thousand students, operates year-round, and spans the equivalent of grades 6–12.

Janice has two half-brothers and two half-sisters. Her dad is an estimator for a contracting company, and her mom is a day care provider. She had previously attended a regular public school but "wasn't getting the help I needed from teachers. My family and I decided that I should attend the charter school so I could receive the help I needed on a one-on-one basis from my teacher. Here, my teacher is the best. When I need help, she sits down with me and helps me understand. In regular school I was told to ask a student, but a student doesn't know any more than I do. That's why he's a student. My teacher makes a whole lot of difference in my life. . . . I've seen myself and others improve their grades and their attitudes toward school. I have gained much confidence in myself and have learned to get along with different ethnic groups and different personalities. Even my mother has seen the difference in me."

Satisfying the Clients

Charter schools have enjoyed bipartisan approval. But it is one thing for an idea to command support when it is new and another to sustain that ardor as it ages. Charter foes are watching like hawks, ready to swoop down on the smallest scrap of trouble. These schools will only retain their broad political base if their customers remain satisfied.

In contrast with the sparse achievement data, much is known about what students, parents, and teachers think of their charter schools. Such evidence must naturally be taken with a pinch of salt, as it is vulnerable to what economists call "revealed preferences" and the biases of self-selection. (Satisfaction with a charter school is influenced by the fact that few people would have chosen the school if they didn't expect to like it.)

---

* Names of students have been changed.

TABLE 4–2. Students' Rating of Their Performance (by Race/Ethnicity)[a]

		Excellent	Good	Average	Poor	Failing
All Students	Previous School	16.0%	26.7%	26.3%	13.3%	10.3%
	Current Charter School	20.9%	41.2%	24.4%	5.3%	1.8%
	Change	+4.9%	+14.5%	−1.9%	−8.0%	−8.5%
White	Previous School	19.0%	27.6%	24.8%	12.7%	10.0%
	Current Charter School	23.4%	43.2%	22.2%	4.6%	1.4%
	Change	+4.4%	+15.6%	−2.6%	−8.1%	−8.6%
African American	Previous School	12.5%	22.7%	28.0%	14.9%	10.2%
	Current Charter School	20.2%	38.4%	24.0%	5.7%	2.5%
	Change	+7.7%	+15.7%	−4.0%	−9.2%	−7.7%
Hispanic	Previous School	12.2%	25.3%	27.1%	14.1%	12.8%
	Current Charter School	18.6%	40.7%	26.2%	7.0%	1.8%
	Change	+6.4%	+15.4%	−0.9%	−7.1%	−11.0%
Asian	Previous School	13.3%	28.7%	26.7%	12.7%	15.3%
	Current Charter School	18.0%	40.0%	29.3%	6.0%	2.0%
	Change	+4.7%	+11.3%	+2.6%	−6.7%	−13.3%
Native American	Previous School	14.6%	29.5%	36.6%	10.9%	5.3%
	Current Charter School	15.4%	39.9%	35.1%	5.3%	1.0%
	Change	+0.8%	+10.4%	−1.5%	−5.6%	−4.3%

[a] "Sample A" student survey respondents from 39 charter schools across 10 states; N = 4,954 (February 1997); percentages may not add to 100 due to invalid and non-responses.

TABLE 4–3. Students' Charter School Likes and Dislikes[a]

"Likes"		"Dislikes"	
Good teachers	58.6%	Poor sports program	29.4%
Teach it until I learn it	51.3%	Not enough other activities	29.4%
Don't let me fall behind	38.5%	Food	28.6%
Computer & technology	35.7%	Too much homework	28.5%
Nice people running the school	34.9%	Boring	23.4%
Teacher's attention	33.9%	Not enough computers/	
Class size	33.9%	technology	21.8%
Curriculum	33.3%	Too strict	19.7%
Safety	27.5%	Difficult commute	14.5%
School size	25.4%	Poor facilities	12.1%
Other out-of-school activities	19.8%	I could be learning more	11.7%
A lot is expected of me	19.7%	Bad teachers	9.1%
Opportunities for parent		School too big or too small	7.5%
participation	15.9%	Not enough homework	6.9%
Sports program	15.8%	Classes too big or too small	6.7%
Food	12.0%	Too tough academically	6.7%
		Not safe enough	6.3%
		Not strict enough	6.0%

[a]"Sample A" student survey respondents from 39 charter schools across 10 states; N = 4,954 (February 1997).

But that is not just a form of bias; it is also evidence that what charter schools offer appeals to many people. Hence their rapid growth trajectory and waiting lists. Satisfaction surveys can thus be useful both in appraising the success of these schools in pleasing their clients and in identifying the charter attributes with greatest allure (and those most in need of improvement).[17]

Hudson Institute's 1997 survey of nearly 5,000 charter pupils revealed impressive satisfaction levels.[18] We asked students what they like (and dislike) about their charter school. Table 4–3 shows the most frequently cited "likes": "good teachers" (59 percent), "they teach it until I learn it" (51 percent), and "they don't let me fall behind" (39 percent). The next cluster

[17] It has been noted for years that parents nearly always give higher marks to their own child's school than to schools in general. This is both a form of "revealed preference" (many middle-class Americans in some sense "chose" the school or school system) and an example of people's propensity to like the specific case ("my Congressman") more than the general institution ("the Congress"). But it is important to add that defenders of public school orthodoxy frequently cite these "satisfaction" data as evidence that all is well from the customers' standpoint. We suggest only that "satisfaction" among charter customers ought not be discounted more steeply than satisfaction among consumers of the conventional product.

[18] See Chester E. Finn, Jr., Bruno V. Manno, Louann A. Bierlein, and Gregg Vanourek, *Charter Schools in Action: Final Report* (Washington, D.C.: Hudson Institute, July 1997), especially Part I.

of answers — "computers and technology" (36 percent), "nice people running the school" (35 percent), "teacher's attention" (34 percent), "class size" (34 percent), and "curriculum" (33 percent) — mostly had to do with educational practices as well.

By contrast, three of the four most common student "dislikes" concerned non-academic matters and the fourth involved a classic pupil gripe: "poor sports program" (29 percent), "not enough other activities" (29 percent), "food" (29 percent), and "too much homework" (29 percent). Table A-1 in the Appendix shows that three-fifths of charter students also report that their teachers are better than the teachers in their previous schools — just 5 percent say their new instructors are worse — while half report being more interested in their school work, compared to 8 percent who are less interested.

Are Charter Schools Good Enough for My Child?

It is one thing for charter schools to be liked by children, but how are they viewed by parents who have suddenly become empowered education consumers?

Survey data make clear that these schools are extremely popular with parents. At least two-thirds say the charter school is better than their child's previous school with respect to class size, school size, attention from teachers, quality of instruction, and curriculum — compared to just 2–3 percent who believe the new school is worse. Over three-fifths of parents say their charter school is better with respect to parental involvement, extra help for students, academic standards, accessibility, and discipline.

Families seek out charter schools for many reasons, but most of the reasons are educational.[19] (See Table 4–4.) As one Michigan parent puts it, "The individual teachers display a real commitment to excellence and fostering growth and development in the students. This is a breath of fresh air after our experience with the mainstream schools."

Perhaps most encouraging is that achievement gains reported by students were confirmed by parents. Among charter parents who said their children did "below average" work at their previous school, 32 percent indicate that their children are now doing "excellent" or "above average" work, and 55 percent indicate "average" work. Of those whose children performed "poorly" at their previous school, 45 percent now report "excellent" or "above average" work, and 37 percent report "average" work. In Massachusetts, almost two-thirds of charter parents believe their child is

---

[19] Caroline M. Hoxby argues that this is generally true of school choice situations. See the essay "When Parents Can Choose, What Do They Choose?" in *Earning and Learning: How Schools Matter*, eds. Susan Mayer and Paul Peterson (Washington D.C.: The Brookings Institution Press, 1999).

TABLE 4–4. Reasons Parents Chose Charter School (by Income)[a]

	Lower Income[b] (< $30,000)	Middle Income ($30–59,999)	Upper Income (>$60,000)	Total
Small size of charter school	52.5%	54.2%	57.6%	53.0%
Higher standards at charter school	44.2%	47.9%	50.6%	45.9%
Program closer to my educational philosophy	37.2%	48.2%	59.7%	44.0%
Greater opportunity for parent involvement	45.5%	45.7%	37.9%	43.0%
Better teachers at charter school	45.3%	39.3%	40.3%	41.9%
Unhappy with curriculum/teachers at previous school	29.8%	39.2%	42.2%	34.5%
My child wanted to come here	34.9%	27.3%	25.2%	30.3%
Location of charter school more convenient	41.9%	20.6%	13.4%	29.5%
Charter school offers before/after school programs	33.2%	18.9%	13.3%	24.3%
People told me this is a better school	27.5%	19.0%	11.7%	21.8%
Previous school was unsafe	25.9%	18.5%	10.8%	20.1%
My child's special needs not met at previous school	20.3%	22.4%	17.8%	19.9%
Prefer private school but could not afford	21.5%	17.9%	15.2%	18.7%
My child was doing badly in regular school	20.4%	16.6%	9.5%	16.9%
Other	7.1%	14.4%	15.2%	11.0%

[a] "Sample B" parent survey respondents from 30 charter schools across 9 states; N = 2,978 (February 1997); percentages may not add to 100 due to invalid and non-responses.

[b] $30,000 was our "lower-income" threshold because it captures all families (with four or fewer children) who are eligible for the federal free and reduced-price lunch programs.

doing better academically as a result of switching schools.[20] In Arizona, 55 percent of charter parents report that their child is doing "a lot better" than in his or her previous school, and another 24 percent say "a little better."[21]

Karen J. Holden (Parent, Renaissance School, Douglas County, Colorado)

Karen Holden, a manager at a private firm that administers millions of dollars of Air Force environmental contracts, is the mother of two teenagers, the younger of whom is in the middle school program at Renaissance. Holden explains that her daughter "was actually receiving an okay education in public elementary school. But I was looking ahead to middle school, concerned. My older daughter suffered through middle school and high school. My younger daughter is extra bright and I didn't want her to get lost in the large public school."

Holden is a member of the charter board and has been active in the school since its inception. "The difference here," she says, "is the absolute love of learning. My daughter gets up every day happy to go to school. In three years, she has never said 'I don't want to go to school today.'"

She especially values the school's small size and family atmosphere. "My older daughter was lost in a huge school system and I never knew it was happening. Here I will know the second any issue arises. Everyone from the education director to the teachers and students all know my daughter and me well. This extended family provides other people who care about your child's growth."

The school isn't perfect. Holden worries that its academics may not be rigorous enough to "stretch the bright students" and acknowledges that the board has not been effective enough in communicating with parents. Her biggest worry? How to find her daughter "a high school this wonderful, so she doesn't lose all that she has gained." Her biggest wish: for the school systems to treat charter schools "as a solid choice, not a slap in the face. They should be helping the charters become partners in public education."

CHARTER TEACHERS: REINVENTING THE PROFESSION

According to Hudson Institute survey data, over 90 percent of charter teachers are "very" or "somewhat" satisfied with their school's educa-

[20] Pioneer Institute for Public Policy Research, "Poll Finds Higher Satisfaction Rate Among Charter School Parents," *Policy Directions*, June 1998, 2.

[21] Mulholland, *Arizona Charter School Progress Evaluation*, 11.

tional philosophy, size, fellow teachers, and students; more than three-quarters are content with their school's administrators, level of teacher decision-making, and the challenge of starting a new school. Fewer than 3 percent say they hope to be elsewhere next year. A 1998 study by the University of Minnesota reports that 81 percent of that state's charter teachers are satisfied with their work experience, compared to just 6 percent who say they are dissatisfied.[22] The National Education Association (NEA) reports that 72 percent of the charter teachers whom it surveyed, if they had it to do over again, would still teach in a charter school. (Just ten percent said they would not; eighteen percent were undecided.)[23] A survey of Arizona charter teachers concludes that they "are quite satisfied."[24]

Like parents, teachers are gravitating to charter schools primarily for educational reasons. When we asked why they opted for charters, teachers gave these top reasons: the school's educational philosophy (77 percent), wanting a new school (65 percent), like-minded colleagues (63 percent), good administrators (55 percent), and class size (54 percent). Least commonly cited by charter teachers as a "big factor" in their decisions were convenient location (28 percent), reduced union influence (24 percent), safety (15 percent), attractive compensation (10 percent), and difficulty finding other employment (9 percent).

The NEA's 1998 charter teacher survey yielded similar results. Eighty percent cited "freedom from district rules and regulations" as a reason they chose charter schools and 61 percent cited "freedom to teach the way I want." (Seventeen percent said they chose the school because it was free from union involvement!)[25] Charter teachers also appear to enjoy the challenge of starting a school from scratch and designing new education programs. A California teacher summed it up well: "I feel like I'm a sponge. I'm always soaking up something new, something interesting, something challenging. I really feel free to use my professional judgment in a way that's never happened before this school."

Charter schools may be creating a new breed of teacher with more responsibility, enhanced incentives for success, greater autonomy, longer hours, and heightened accountability. They seem to be doing for their teachers what excellent independent schools and exemplary public schools have long managed to do for their professional staffs.

Teachers' pay, on average, is about the same in charter schools as in neighboring public school systems, but their job security is less. (Few char-

[22] Center for Applied Research and Educational Improvement, *Minnesota Charter Schools Evaluation: Final Report* (College of Education and Human Development, University of Minnesota, 1998), iv.

[23] Julia E. Koppich et al., *New Rules, New Roles? The Professional Work Lives of Charter School Teachers* (Washington, D.C., National Education Association, 1998), 132.

[24] Mulholland, *Arizona Charter School Progress Evaluation*, 42.

[25] Koppich et al., *New Rules, New Roles?* 129–31.

ter schools confer tenure; jobs depend on performance, enrollments, etc.)[26] According to a charter teacher in Colorado who receives less money than her public-school counterparts, "We'd all prefer pay parity with the district, of course, but there are trade-offs, like smaller classes, smaller schools, and greater job satisfaction."

A Massachusetts charter teacher says, "I finally know what it means to be an 'empowered teacher.' I can set high expectations for my kids, design my own curriculum, pick out my own texts. . . . I'd be crazy not to want to work here." At City On A Hill Charter School in Boston (see chapter 3), Sarah Kass set out to empower and invest in her teachers:

> [A] school's excellence can only be sustained if we sustain those teachers and diversify what their career path is at our school. Presently we are launching an investment fund for teacher entrepreneurship to invest in our teachers' ideas. Over time we look to pay for teachers' research time, sabbatical time, course work, and university teaching (with our partner, Northeastern University), so that our teachers will stay sustained and refreshed and our students will benefit from their continued growth and development.

The biggest plus for charter teachers is professional empowerment. Many teachers are strongly committed to the education and welfare of children but find themselves stifled by "the system." Some have been around long enough to feel the pinch of control-crazed superintendents, politicized school boards, sluggish administrators, heavy-handed state regulations, low-performing schools, apathetic kids, and burned-out colleagues. Some give up. Others develop their own vision — and yearning — to do it differently and better. Charter schools afford teachers the opportunity to reinvent their jobs, take on new challenges, and work "outside the box."

INTERVIEW

Keith Grauman (Teacher, Guajome Park Academy, Vista, California)

As a founding faculty member of Guajome Park Academy — a charter middle and high school north of San Diego that opened in 1994 — Keith Grauman brought with him 23 years of teaching experience in history and social sciences, all but four of them in public education. He holds a master's degree in history from San Diego State University.

---

[26] The 1998 NEA survey found 30 percent of charter teachers reporting higher salaries than at their previous school; 50 percent reporting salaries "about the same"; and 20 percent reporting lower salaries. The 1997 Hudson survey yielded almost identical results. As for job security, the NEA found 34 percent of charter teachers with tenure. Thirty percent also gave affirmative answers to the question "I do not have tenure but I do have job security." It is not clear to what extent those two subgroups overlap. Ibid., 106.

He and his fellow founders created a "dream team" to design what they called "our new secondary school of choice."

What was your greatest hope for this charter school? I wanted to take "regular" kids, get them engaged in "irregular" learning, and have them produce beyond the prevailing standards of student achievement found in most districts.

How is teaching at this charter school different? I've never worked harder—ten hours at school and four hours (sometimes six) at home each day. More on weekends. . . . I'm not sure we've mastered what it takes to have a sustainable work environment! But the small classes and the computer and technological support are to die for.

What is the hardest thing about teaching in this school? The most satisfying? Hardest is not being able to rest or reflect on what we've done. Often, our celebrations occur when we're least able to appreciate them. We're physically drained. Most satisfying is getting to know the kids, which is a lot easier due to our smaller classes. We can get inside their heads and their lives. If there were one thing I could change I would have each staff member accountable for only a few things (not everything!). But overall, I believe the school is working well.

What troubles you most about teaching in a charter school? Sometimes parents think we are a business that can change or repair parts in an appliance, not a school that needs to nurture and guide.

SCHOOL INNOVATION

The promise of charter schools does not begin and end with pupil achievement or constituent satisfaction. Schools of choice are also meant to innovate. According to the federal study of charter schools (a multiyear evaluation called *A Study of Charter Schools*, commissioned by the U.S. Department of Education), "realiz[ing] an alternative vision for schooling" was most often cited by charter founders as the primary reason for starting their schools (cited by 58.9 percent of respondents).[27]

Today, many charter schools are fonts of educational and organizational creativity. A California study found that 78 percent of that state's charters were experimenting with new instructional practices, compared to 3 percent of comparison public schools; 72 percent of charters were implement-

[27] RPP International, *The State of Charter Schools: Third-Year Report*, 42. However, it is worth noting that this varies widely by school type: 67.5 percent of the founders of newly created schools cited this as their most important reason for founding the school, compared to 40 percent for the founders of preexisting public schools and 34.5 percent for the founders of preexisting private schools.

ing site-based governance, compared with 16 percent of conventional schools; and two-thirds of charters had adopted increased parent participation practices, compared with 14 percent of conventional schools.[28] A Massachusetts study found that Bay State charters were engaged in innovative practices while also implementing "good old-fashioned education practices," which the report termed "retrovations."[29]

Some observers view charter schools as R&D centers where new education models are devised and tested. Indeed, some school systems are availing themselves of the charter opportunity for this purpose. (We return to this topic in chapter 9.) But most charter schools have a more immediate reason to innovate: to provide students and parents with attractive alternatives.

That does not always mean plowing virgin soil. One Michigan charter founder wryly remarks that "Giving good, solid, traditional education is innovative today." Much that we have found in charter schools is also done in some conventional schools. Many charter schools draw upon practices proven over decades of research and experience. Their "innovation" may lie in their rejection of fads and their embrace of the tried-and-true.

School innovation is also situational and relative to the context. It is scant consolation to disgruntled parents and struggling students in inner-city Detroit that a school in rural California has a terrific independent study program. It might as well be on the moon. The fact that many charter schools simply offer a curriculum, program, or philosophy that differs from the norm in their particular locale should not be discounted. Offering a back-to-basics curriculum is novel indeed in a district that favors hands-on, child-centered learning. And where old-fashioned ways are the reigning orthodoxy, progressivism may be a breath of fresh air for some. The job of charter schools is to satisfy their customers, not to demonstrate to outside analysts that they have devised something never before observed in this galaxy.

Not all innovations are academic. Changes in organizational and institutional arrangements may well prove more significant. We have seen distinctive grade clusters, unconventional grade combinations, multiyear instructional teams, multisite schools, and several schools that replace principals with committees of teachers.

The Charter School of San Diego, which opened in 1994 and serves grades 6–12, encompasses 18 sites around the city and covers about 250 square miles. The school has a year-round calendar, eschews traditional grade levels, and targets at-risk urban youth. It offers a host of support services, including health care, counseling, and job placement. Students can earn a standard diploma, prepare for the General Education Develop-

---

[28] R. G. Corwin and J. Flaherty, *Freedom and Innovation in California's Charter Schools* (Los Alamitos, Calif.: SWRL, 1995).

[29] Rosenblum Brigham Associates, *Innovation and Massachusetts Charter Schools* (Boston: Massachusetts Department of Education, 1998), 6.

ment (GED) certificate, or take the California High School Proficiency Exams to graduate. A recent evaluation by the San Diego school district commented, "The school has been successful in reversing the downward spiral of failure in student achievement."[30]

Charter schools have also devised unconventional approaches to governance, staffing, scheduling, and financing. "The difference is the autonomy and governance structure," says a Minnesota charter principal, "not necessarily the curriculum and instructional practices." In October 1998, the Reeves Elementary School, a Miami charter school operated by the Edison Project, became the first school in America to invite its staff to acquire shares of the private management company that runs it. Under this pioneering arrangement, everyone—from custodian to principal—can become eligible for stock options and would be able to sell their stock after Edison becomes a publicly traded company. This innovation is also creating strong incentives for educators to want their schools to succeed. The American Federation of Teachers has blessed the arrangement. Edison intends to offer this option in all its schools.[31]

Some of the most powerful alterations we have witnessed have to do with technology. Particularly striking are a handful of "virtual" charter schools that exist primarily in cyberspace. The Choice 2000 On-Line Charter School in California is "open" twenty-four hours a day, and its students (drawn from all over the state) mostly attend via computer.[32]

Some charters begin afresh with whole-school transformations based on original designs. In Fort Devens, Massachusetts, several parents founded the Francis W. Parker Charter School, which incorporates the nine principles of Theodore Sizer's Coalition of Essential Schools. (Sizer and his wife Nancy spent the 1998–99 year as the Parker school's acting co-principals.) Boston Renaissance School employs the Edison model, which includes a set of standards, curriculum, tests, and instructional methods that group students for three years in "houses" staffed by differentiated teaching teams. The parent-initiated Chelmsford Public Charter School in Massachusetts is based upon the "systems thinking" of Massachusetts Institute of Technology professor Jay Forrester, emphasizing problem-solving skills via an interdisciplinary curriculum. The school is organized into two multigrade "houses" and managed by Beacon Education Management, a for-profit company.

---

[30] San Diego City Schools, *The Charter School of San Diego: First-Year Evaluation* (San Diego: San Diego City Schools, 1996), ii.

[31] "Stakeholder Teachers; Charter Schools Educators Offered Stock Incentives," *Worcester Telegram and Gazette*, 7 November 1998, A12; and Analisa Nazareno, "Employees Vote to Buy Stock in Edison Project," *Miami Herald*, 22 October 1998.

[32] Matt Richtel, "California District Puts Public School Online," *New York Times*, 23 August 1997.

PARENTS AS PARTNERS

If charter schools can declare any clear-cut victory today, it is in the battle against adult disengagement. One of the secrets of these schools' success is their knack for tapping vast reservoirs of parental involvement. Some of this can be attributed to the fact that these are schools of choice; engagement begins with seeking out the school and registering one's child. Yet that is true of a wide array of "magnet" programs and specialty schools that do not necessarily achieve the sustained involvement we have observed in most charter schools.

According to a Massachusetts parent who founded a charter school, "The school system basically told parents: 'Be good parents and bake your cookies for our fundraisers, but we don't want your advice on anything important.' That's what pushed us to start this charter school." It is common for charter schools to insist that parents sign "learning contracts" for their children and not unusual to require that they volunteer a certain number of hours per week.[33] Some also offer special adult classes and services. "In this school," says a Michigan charter teacher, "we welcome and accept parent involvement. In my previous public school, we really didn't want parents to be involved . . . and I think that parents knew it."

Colorado's Renaissance Charter School expects twenty hours per semester from parents or other family members, and a volunteer coordinator has the job of leveraging this people power. The Colin Powell Academy in Detroit requires a minimum of ten hours of "sweat equity" per parent per year; options for honoring that commitment include a parent-run after-school program and parent-supervised lunch periods (so teachers can take a break).

In Massachusetts, charter parents report twice as many meetings with their child's teacher as do district school parents, as well as more phone conversations, and almost twice as many written communications from school. Education researchers have long known the value of parent involvement, yet many schools have trouble getting parents through the door. Charter schools seem to be reversing that trend.

Many charters go beyond parent "involvement" and include parents in institutional governance. A recent California study found that 88 percent of that state's charter schools included parents on their governing bodies. Twenty-one percent of teachers surveyed by the NEA say their charter schools were initiated and developed mainly by parents — and 24 percent point to a "collaborative of teachers and parents."

---

[33] Strictly speaking, these are not enforceable requirements for a public school, but charter schools are able to bring a lot of moral suasion and peer pressure to bear — as well as coming up with extraordinarily imaginative volunteer options.

Such patterns are not unusual among private schools, but they are far from the norm in U.S. public education. And they are not without their difficulties, as parents with little experience in organizational governance sometimes let their passion (or concern for their own progeny) trump their judgment. Nor is it clear whether parents will prove able and willing to sustain these high levels of school engagement. A few charter schools have observed some diminution of parent involvement in the third or fourth year. Still, we are seeing a reconnection of parents with schools that is uncommon enough in public education as fairly to be termed a significant accomplishment of the charter movement.

Bang for the Buck

Many charter-friendly legislators say that they support this strategy because they expect these new schools to yield "more bang for the buck," demonstrating superior productivity and enhanced efficiency, not least by being able to devote all their resources to education rather than overhead and bureaucracy. At the same time, most charters have skimpier funding than conventional schools. According to a 1998 study from the Massachusetts Charter School Resource Center, "In the aggregate, charter schools receive less money per student to operate and house themselves than do regular public schools. In all states in which they now operate, charter schools receive from 50 percent to 100 percent of the annual average funding per student allocated to school operations by the local school districts in which they are situated. Unlike regular public schools, they receive no capital funds in addition to their operating funds."[34]

Thus, improvements that charter schools are able to produce are often examples of heightened efficiency. But in visiting charter schools, we were also reminded of the old tale of the farmer who fed his horse a bit less each day while remarking on how well the horse kept performing its tasks and how much its efficiency was improving. Eventually, of course, the horse dropped dead. We sense that a better test of charter schools is not doing more with less but being challenged to do more (and better) with the same resources that conventional schools have.

Still, we have encountered encouraging examples of charter efficiency. At California's Vaughn Street Learning Center, principal Yvonne Chan

---

[34] John Dolan, Douglas Murray, and Gregory Walsh, *Charter School Facility Financing: Constraints and Options* (Boston: Pioneer Institute, February 1998), 1. In California, where charters are granted by district boards, there are funding disparities not only from one district to another but even within the same district. See Amy Stuart Wells, *Beyond the Rhetoric of Charter School Reform: A Study of Ten California School Districts* (Los Angeles: University of California at Los Angeles, 1998), 33–35. While this finding is one that corroborates our own field work in California, we disagree with the author's conclusion that "charter schools can [not] be successful organizations without some form of subsidy from the private sector."

thought it was ridiculous that it took the local school district a year to purchase classroom computers. She did it in six days — and for less money. Besides saving the charter school time and money, this also had a "ripple effect" on the local school district. After *Sixty Minutes* ran a story on Vaughn Street, the Los Angeles Unified School District (L.A.U.S.D.) revised its purchasing system. Vaughn Street also worked out with the Agriculture Department a more efficient way of administering the federal school lunch program, saving thousands of dollars. L.A.U.S.D. soon followed suit.

The Boston Public Schools (B.P.S.) receive 27 percent more public money per pupil than City On A Hill Charter School.[35] Despite aggressive private fundraising, City On A Hill still spends 3 percent less than B.P.S. per pupil. Yet its pupils have outperformed their B.P.S. counterparts by wide margins in reading and math.

The co-director of a promising new charter in Newark notes that "Charter schools do more with less. In our first year, North Star received an average of $7,480 in basic government aid for each of its students, roughly 83 percent of what was spent on their Newark peers." Still, it managed to have a 96 percent attendance rate, benefit from a "Tocquevillian outbreak of parent involvement," cut class size to 18, extend the school day and year, partner with local civic organizations, build a state-of-the-art computer network, and offer an outdoor education program.[36]

How do some charters do more with less? There are no systematic data, but we have some clues. We have witnessed first-hand at least four areas where these schools often realize savings or create efficiencies:

- First, they are better than most district schools at using parental "sweat equity" and leveraging other non-monetary resources to supplement their budgets. Many parents are happy to lend a hand, and many charter starters take an entrepreneurial view toward community partnerships and fundraising.
- Second, many charter schools pare their administrative personnel to a bare minimum. Often they accomplish this by having teachers perform "double duty" — perhaps serving as a coach as well as an English teacher, or counselor as well as math instructor. Sometimes board members shoulder administrative functions.
- Third, charter schools tend to eschew the extras that regular schools normally offer. Many get by without non-academic programs like sports and drama. (Parents looking for lots of alternatives and amenities for their children will, in general, be better off turning elsewhere.)

[35] This calculation includes capital funding and competitive grants that the Boston Public Schools receive.

[36] Norman Atkins, "Charter Schools Are Public Schools," *New York Times Magazine*, 14 June 1998, 49.

- Fourth, many charter schools "outsource" some of the school's functions to external providers. According to the federal study, 41 percent of charter schools contract out for payroll, 48 percent for insurance, 50 percent for legal services, and 41 percent for social services.[37]

The Demand for Choice

Surely one indicator of the efficacy of charters is the demand for these schools of choice. This demand takes two forms. First, more would-be operators are seeking charters than can be awarded under whatever numerical cap the state has placed on their numbers. For example, Central Michigan University has received over 200 requests for charter licenses in 1999, though it can only grant a maximum of 75. The week after the Colorado charter law took effect in 1993, the state department of education received more than 350 calls from people wanting to know how to start a charter school.[38]

Second, most charter schools have waiting lists. The federal charter study found 70 percent of charter schools with more applicants than they had room for, concluding that "If success is judged by parents and students voting with their feet, charter schools are in demand."[39] In Massachusetts, enrollment has nearly quadrupled since the first charters opened in 1995, and 5,660 students linger on waiting lists.[40] The marketplace appears to be signaling that the charter movement has strong appeal—and is poised to grow faster where permitted.[41]

We also see an appetite for charter schools (or their like) abroad. England and Wales have some 1,175 schools that resemble U.S. charters. These are attended by about a fifth of all secondary pupils and until recently were known as "grant-maintained" schools because, under the Tory governments, they received their funding directly from London and were fully independent of their local education authority.[42] Although Tony Blair's Labor government, pressed by the teachers' unions, has taken steps to place them back under local control and limit their spread, the schools already in existence will continue to enjoy substantial autonomy. (Such a

[37] RPP International, *The State of Charter Schools: Third-Year Report*, 49.

[38] David Hill, "Charter Champion," *Education Week*, 4 October 1995, 27.

[39] RPP International, *The State of Charter Schools: Third-Year Report*, 10. The quote comes from RPP International, *A Study of Charter Schools: Second-Year Report* (1998), 97.

[40] *The Massachusetts Charter School Initiative: Expanding the Possibilities of Public Education*, Massachusetts Department of Education, 1998, 13.

[41] Of course, demand for charter schools is sometimes problematic. In some communities, there is an ill-conceived demand for a school that turns out to be a flop (or a ruse). For example, before their scandals came to pass, Citizen 2000 in Arizona and Marcus Garvey Charter School in Washington, D.C. did not lack for students (see chapter 6).

[42] Sue-Ann Levy, "A Smarter Approach to Learning," *Toronto Sun*, 5 October 1996, 13.

reining in of charter-like schools in the aftermath of a government change lends credence to the concern of some U.S. charter critics that this reform strategy remains vulnerable to shifting political winds.)

New Zealand, by contrast, is liberalizing its approach. In 1989, all of the country's two thousand-plus public schools were converted to charter-like status, though their freedom was constrained by a nationwide curriculum and teacher contract. At that time, the government completely abolished local school boards and gave every school its own "governing school council."[43] Parents were also given the opportunity to choose their child's school.[44]

Part of the point was to introduce greater efficiency and effectiveness in the education system. Part, though, was to tailor instruction more precisely to student needs. According to Dr. Judith Aitken of New Zealand's Education Review Office, these self-governing schools cater to a "mass market of one." She points out that "Very few public education systems anywhere are highly regarded for their ability to think in terms of individual students, and supply individually-geared programmes, treating their students not as groups, cohorts, classes, or demographically-defined populations, but as unique service customers."[45] More recently, the government of New Zealand has moved to "block fund" some of its schools, giving them markedly greater control of budgets and personnel. Some 14 percent of the country's schools now operate in that mode.

In neighboring Australia, the state of Victoria in 1998 established a category of "self-governing" public schools. In a school obtaining this status, the school council will have the power to employ staff, own real estate, invest the school's money, and enter into all sorts of partnerships and joint ventures. Its five-year agreement with the state contains provisions akin to those of a U.S. charter. Explained Education Minister Phil Gude, "What this initiative is about is 'empowerment.' Empowering local school communities to be their best and to offer an exemplary education to our young people. . . . What it is, is an acknowledgment that not all schools are the same and that one size does not fit all."[46]

In Canada, too, we find ten charter schools operating in the province of Alberta in early 1999 and similar legislation under consideration in other provinces. The first in-depth study of Alberta's charters found—in terms familiar to U.S. charter watchers—that

[43] Levy, "A Smarter Approach to Learning," 13.

[44] New Zealand Ministry of Education, "Schooling in New Zealand: A Guide," February 1999, http://www.minedu.govt.nz/Schools/Guide/guide.htm.

[45] Judith Aitken, "Increasing Flexibility of Secondary Schools: Getting to Grips with the Notion of a Mass Market of One," address to an International Symposium on Secondary Education, Toronto, Ontario, 12–14 November 1998.

[46] News Release from the Office of the Minister for Education, 8 April 1998; from http://www.vic.gov.au.

There is a wide diversity in educational programs being offered; half focused on the needs of under-served students and half offer a particular methodology or approach to learning. School size ranges from 70 to over 300, class sizes are small, enrollment is increasing and retention is high. Satisfaction rates for parents and teachers involved in charter schools are strong and appear to be based on sound educational reasons. Governance issues, isolation, and the lack of facilities funding and clear accountability guidelines are the most common challenges experienced by the schools.[47]

In famously centralized Japan, the ruling party is studying the charter concept and a group is seeking to establish that nation's first charter school. There are charter schools up and running in a suburb of Santiago, Chile, and rumblings of interest in Argentina. Even in Pakistan, some communities are creating their own charter-like schools in response to the government's failure to provide suitable schools for the children.[48]

THIS KID'S GOT POTENTIAL

Imagine a five year-old boy running about, trying everything, exploring and getting into trouble. He is growing fast, not very self-disciplined, and beginning to show his own (temperamental) personality, but scarcely ready to be judged as a fully developed person. What one says about a five-year-old is not "He turned out well" but, rather, "He's still a little kid but he's off to a terrific start."

That is how we view the charter movement. Yet policymakers and school reformers have an overwhelming tendency to judge education reforms prematurely. The charter idea shouldn't be victimized in that way. It is too busy growing up and fending off bullies.

Meanwhile, an immense machinery of research and evaluation has cranked up to appraise the efficacy of these new schools. Hefty studies are underway at the U.S. Department of Education and many of its state counterparts. That is all to the good. Somewhat more troubling are signs that charter schools are being held to a different standard than regular schools. We would be among the last to argue against demanding standards for all schools, but we have been around education policy debates long enough to be suspicious of double standards and wary of foes of change masquerading as analysts.

For now, the surest conclusion we can reach is that, while charter

[47] Society for the Advancement of Excellence in Education, "News Release: Study of Canada's First Charter Schools Released," 24 November 1998, http://www.saee.bc.ca. See Beverly Lynn Bosetti, *Canada's Charter Schools: Initial Report*, Society for the Advancement of Excellence in Education, SAEE Research Series No. 3, British Columbia, October 1998.

[48] Barbara Crossette, "Third World Fills a Void as Villagers Run Schools," *New York Times*, 10 May 1998.

schools are unquestionably a dynamic force for change in education and indisputably popular with those who know them best, the jury is still out regarding their effectiveness in boosting student achievement. At the end of the day, the verdict may well hinge on how well these schools are able to overcome their start-up problems, to which we turn next.

5

TRIALS BY FIRE

Deborah Springpeace didn't realize it, but in July 1996 she was beginning the wildest ride of her life. She had agreed to launch the Seven Hills Charter School (an Edison Project school) in a depressed section of Worcester, Massachusetts. Fortunately, this was not her first time on the education speedway. Certified in three states, Springpeace had taught English in a big inner-city high school, at a halfway house for juvenile offenders, at a Catholic school, and in suburban public schools. She had also been an assistant superintendent for curriculum and instruction and served as a middle school principal for a decade. But nothing quite prepared her for Seven Hills.

The most pressing problem was opening the school three months before its building was ready. That meant spending the first quarter year in two temporary (and substandard) sites, while an ambitious $4.7 million renovation project proceeded at the school's permanent location, an abandoned, century-old school building. Organizational homelessness brought many woes, especially in student discipline, aggravating the fact that the school was flooded by children with special needs. To this day, parents insist that nearby schools waged a quiet campaign to "dump problem kids" on Seven Hills, even filling out charter applications for some troublesome youngsters to offload them. Meanwhile, the local district took its time in forwarding records of special-education children. (The day one of us visited Seven Hills in May 1998, the charter school received one child's "individual education plan," requested the previous September.)

Combine an inadequate facility and a lot of youngsters with severe behavior problems and disabilities and you have a real challenge. At first, Seven Hills teachers struggled just to maintain order. Children fought, bit, and kicked. Suspensions were many. This was not the oasis of learning that the school's founders had envisioned—and had promised the community.

Many lessons can be drawn from the birth trauma of Seven Hills, above all the fact that launching a charter school isn't easy. Yet Seven Hills was luckier than some. It is now thriving. Other charter schools have been stymied, stalled, and stranded by their start-up struggles. Some remain locked in life-and-death battles. As one Colorado school head remarked to us, "In retrospect, I was probably crazy to take the job."

Why is it so difficult to launch a charter school? What can be done to ease these problems? This chapter describes the most common challenges and some ways that charter schools are meeting them. Both elements are important, for charter schools are vulnerable to the "abstract virtues/concrete vices" phenomenon. That is, many of the strengths of the charter movement—such as enhanced education choice and accountability—are general and distant, while many of its challenges—such as political ambushes and lack of start-up funding—are concrete and immediate.

START-UP PROBLEMS

In other entrepreneurial ventures, we expect start-up calamities and high failure rates. But we seldom view schools that way. Yet charter schools resemble small businesses as well as educational institutions. The skills needed to succeed with them include financial acumen, political shrewdness, Herculean stamina, and tolerance for trial and error, as well as educational vision. According to a California teacher, "Trying something as major as starting a charter school, you're unlikely to get it all right. We had to reconfigure what we were doing, especially in the way we organized and used the time of the teachers."

Every charter school is distinctive, and each encounters singular challenges. Yet after visiting nearly a hundred charter schools and interviewing thousands of their occupants, we find that many sing similar tunes. We have compiled a charter blues album with seven songs of woe. The first three problems arise from external causes; the other four are largely self-imposed.

Policy Dilemmas

1. STATE CHARTER LAWS.

Every charter school enters the world inscribed with the provisions of its state's charter law. Some jurisdictions have strong statutes, hospitable to the creation of many vigorous schools, while others enact measures so weak that it is scarcely worthwhile seeking a charter. In some states with exceptionally limp charter laws, such as Arkansas and Wyoming, there aren't any actual charter schools in operation (as of September 1999). Opponents of charter schools have deduced that keeping a statute weak can undermine the entire concept, leaving the state with the appearance but not the reality of a charter program. Here are five common features of weak charter laws:

- Eligibility for schools is defined narrowly. For example, existing schools may "convert" to charter status, but new schools may not be started.
- Tight limits are placed on how many charters may be issued or how many students may enroll in them.
- Charter approval is confined to local school boards, with no effective means for appealing adverse decisions. In other words, the entity that many charter founders are keenest to escape has the absolute power to bar the exit door.
- Constraints are placed on school operations akin to those that burden conventional schools — e.g., teacher certification requirements, uniform salary schedules, and collective-bargaining agreements.
- Charter schools receive less than full per-pupil funding, with no allowance for facilities and other capital expenses.

Table 2–1 dissects the nation's weakest charter law.

Strong charter laws are altogether different in many ways that matter to people starting schools. Not surprisingly, the states with strong statutes have the lion's share of charter schools. The two states with the strongest laws — Arizona and Michigan — had a third of the nation's charters in 1998–99, while many jurisdictions with weak laws had few or none (see Table 2–1).[1] Here are ten characteristic features of a strong charter law:

- Almost anyone may submit a charter proposal — a group of teachers or parents, a nonprofit organization, a commercial firm, even a former private school.
- Multiple sponsors can grant charters, and/or a workable appeals process is in place so that adverse decisions by local boards can be reconsidered elsewhere.
- Waivers are automatically granted from most state and local regulations.
- The school has effective control of its budget, personnel, curriculum, and other essentials.
- The state places no limits on the number of charter schools or their enrollment.
- The school may hire whom it likes (including people without conventional certification).
- Operating funds (per pupil) are equivalent to regular public schools.
- Schools have access to start-up and capital dollars.
- Schools are exempt from collective-bargaining agreements.
- A sound statewide charter accountability system is in place.

[1] As can be seen in Table 2–1, the 24 states with relatively strong laws had 1,627 charter schools up and running as of September 1999, while in the 11 jurisdictions with relatively weak statutes the total number of charter schools in operation was just 54. (Two states were unranked.)

TABLE 5–1. Mississippi's Charter Law: Weakest in the Nation
(as of September 1999)[a]

GENERAL STATISTICS:	
Number of Schools Allowed	Six.
Number of Schools Operating	One.
APPROVAL PROCESS:	
Eligible Chartering Authorities	State board of education. (Petition must first be approved by local school board.)
Eligible Applicants	Existing public schools.
Types of Charter Schools	Converted public schools only.
Appeals Process	None.
Formal Evidence of Local Support Required	Yes.
Term of Initial Charter	Four years.
Automatic Waiver	Yes (except as specified in the law).
Legal Autonomy	No.
Facilities Assistance	No.
FUNDING:	
Amount	Basic funding not addressed. No additional funds appropriated.
Path	From district to charter school.
Fiscal Autonomy	No.
Start-Up Funds	None.
TEACHERS:	
Collective Bargaining/District Work Rules	Charter teachers remain employees of district.
Retirement Benefits	Yes.
STUDENTS:	
Eligible Students	Students of local district and children of school staff.
Mandated Assessments	Same as district: meet state education goals and take state-mandated tests.

[a]Source: Center for Education Reform http://edreform.com.

The strong-weak distinction helps illumine the legal framework within which charters operate, but life in the real world of policy is not static. Charter laws are dynamic: circumstances change; experience counts; trial and error are inevitable. No legislature enacts the perfect charter statute for all time. It is important for these laws, and the programs they authorize, to be refreshed as lessons are learned, new problems arise, and priorities evolve. *Adaptive* charter laws are at least as necessary as strong ones, provided, of course, that the adaptations lead to program improvements rather than policy backsliding.

Consider Arizona, famed for the boldness of its charter law — and the vigor of its charter program — but now also for its handful of well-publicized abuses and failures. Amid dozens of fine charter schools, some opportunistic people (and school districts) were able to exploit the program for financial gain, with educational quality occasionally taking a backseat. A few schools collapsed. Today, there are demands from many quarters that the legislature put a brake on its freewheeling charter law. The hard part will be to resist going too far in the opposite direction and crippling a vibrant program. But laws that are too strong are rare. Most adapting has happened when states that initially enacted feeble statutes realized that they must energize them. Important amendments have followed in such states as Georgia, Minnesota, and California. For example, in 1998 the Georgia legislature agreed to allow start-up charters in addition to conversion schools.

Even the U.S. Congress has discerned the advantages of strong charter laws. In reauthorizing the $100 million program of federal start-up aid, the Charter School Expansion Act of 1998 established priorities for distributing money that favor states which add to their number of charter schools, allow multiple authorizers, and confer real fiscal autonomy.

2. FINANCES.

Fiscal obstacles are the greatest barriers for many new charter schools. These include lack of capital financing, especially for facilities; little or no start-up money; inadequate per-pupil operating funds; and uneven cash flow.

The absence of capital is a huge handicap, since the greatest initial cost for any new school is a usable facility. A 1999 study of charter facilities financing reports that "It is not uncommon for facilities costs to amount to 20–25 percent of a charter school's costs."[2]

Conversion schools can usually avoid this pitfall, but start-ups seldom have ready access to a facility. As a result, infant charter schools often find themselves in places that do not look like conventional schools — "portables," strip malls, former churches, lofts and warehouses, converted restaurants, or abandoned parochial schools. This is not necessarily catastrophic, but it may invite trouble. And some charters with fine education plans never open their doors because they cannot locate any doors to open. The absence of capital funding is thus apt to tip the charter movement in favor of relatively prosperous communities and big corporate operators, at the expense of "mom and pop," inner-city, and rural schools.

[2] Bryan Hassel, "Paying for the Charter Schoolhouse: A Policy Agenda for Charter School Facilities Financing," Charter Friends National Network, January 1999, http://www.charterfriends.org/facilities.html.

Schools normally also need desks, chairs, computers, textbooks, playground equipment, and so forth. Lacking bonding authority and other sources of tax-financed capital, charter founders must either raise private funds or obtain credit somewhere — and then pay off the loans from their operating budget, slicing into funds meant for teacher salaries, phone bills, and field trips. But credit is hard to come by for most charter schools, since they have brief (or nonexistent) track records, a novel legal status, rarely more than five years of assured cash flow, and few assets to offer as collateral. When borrowing is possible, the price is often high. One Colorado school that was fortunate enough to assemble financing to construct its own building is paying an estimated $800–900 per child per year — almost a fifth of its budget — just to cover the mortgage.

As for start-up funds, the 1998 federal study of charter schools comments that their absence "was the most frequently cited difficulty" facing new schools.[3] The authors cited the director of a start-up charter who "reported that she had to put her farm up as collateral to purchase portable units in order to open the school." Such economic hurdles are especially daunting for low-income people and grass-roots charter schools.

Tables 5–2 and 5–3 depict the start-up costs of two charter schools as a percentage of their first-year budgets. The first, Boston's Academy of the Pacific Rim (toured in chapter 2), was quite successful in raising outside funds. It was able to sustain its whopping start-up costs not because the state paid extra but because an entrepreneurial institution with a dynamic leader went out and rustled up the difference. In charter schools that are less adept at supplemental fundraising, however, the start-up costs may cannibalize the operating budget: The Texas Academy of Excellence in Austin shows how initial expenses can eat into operating funds during the first year for schools that are unable to raise additional money for their launch.

Once opened, charter schools face plentiful financial pressures. Few receive as much money per pupil as their district school counterparts (see Table 5–4). Few states turn on the cash spigot until the first students walk through the door. This defies logic when it comes to an institution that must hire and train its teachers before it can educate children. But it is standard operating procedure under many state charter laws.[4]

Some states allot funds irregularly during the school year, leaving

---

[3] RPP International, *A Study of Charter Schools: Second-Year Report* (Washington, D.C.: U.S. Department of Education, 1998), 105.

[4] Solving it isn't easy, either. Arizona's attempt to provide start-up funds for charter schools, and to front-load their annual payments from the state, has been implicated in a large fraction of Arizona's highly publicized charter debacles, as errant operators have, in effect, pocketed the extra dollars (or the assets purchased with them) when their schools closed down. As we write, "reform" in the Arizona context means *slowing down* the flow of state dollars reaching new charter schools.

TABLE 5–2. Financial Profile: Academy of the Pacific Rim[a]
(Start-up Costs and First-Year Operating Costs, 1997–98)

Budget Category	Operating Budget	Start-Up Costs	Total First-Year Costs	Start-Up Costs as % of Total
Academic Program (teacher compensation and supplies)	$322,728	$ 44,038	$ 366,766	12%
Staff Compensation	128,500	—	128,500	—
Facilities and Utilities	96,350	14,333	110,683	13%
Special Education and Tutors	83,500	—	83,500	—
Technology	47,000	108,000	155,000	70%
Administrative Costs	42,900	18,458	61,358	30%
Art, Music, P.E., and "Healthy Habits"	35,400	—	35,400	—
Transportation	11,900	—	11,900	—
Teacher Professionalism	11,300	—	11,300	—
Stakeholder Communication	10,200	—	10,200	—
Parent and Community Partnerships	3,500	—	3,500	—
Summer Program (teachers, food service, curriculum, transportation)	—	65,992	65,992	100%
Furnishings	—	52,000	52,000	100%
Start-Up Management	—	20,813	20,813	100%
Renovations	—	18,500	18,500	100%
Teacher Recruitment	—	3,099	3,099	100%
Total Cost	$793,278	$345,233	$1,138,511	30%

[a]Source: Personal communication with the authors.

schools hard-pressed to meet payroll. Some apportion money based on the prior year's enrollment, a huge problem for fast-growing schools. Others wait until late in the year to adjust allotments based on enrollment fluctuations after "count day" in October. Though the Colin Powell Academy opened in early September 1996 in the poorest ZIP code of Detroit (see chapter 10), it didn't receive any money until October 20th. The school's founder himself borrowed $10,000 to get it launched.

3. POLITICAL OPPOSITION.

According to the federal charter study, 21 percent of charter schools reported "difficulties in implementing their charters" arising from state or local board opposition — not to mention district resistance or regulations (20 percent), state education department hostility or regulations (14 per-

TABLE 5–3. Financial Profile: Texas Academy of Excellence[a]
(Start-Up Costs and First-Year Operating Costs, 1996–97)

Budget Category	Operating Budget	Start-Up Costs	Total First-Year Costs	Start-Up Costs as % of Total
Instruction:				
Payroll Costs	$181,362	—	$ 181,362	—
Professional and Contracted Services	55,557	—	55,557	—
Supplies and Materials	10,504	13,100	23,604	55%
Other Operating Costs	2,512	—	2,512	—
Subtotal	*249,935*	*13,100*	*263,035*	*5%*
General Administration:				
Payroll Costs	41,082	6,000	47,082	13%
Professional and Contracted Services	9,196	—	9,196	—
Supplies and Materials	3,569	—	3,569	—
Other Operating Costs	11,017	—	11,017	—
Subtotal	*64,864*	*6,000*	*70,864*	*8.5%*
Plant Maintenance and Operations[b]:				
Professional and Contracted Services	64,905	85,000	149,905	57%
Supplies and Materials	2,967	—	2,967	—
Other Operating Costs	3,963	—	3,963	—
Subtotal	*71,835*	*85,000*	*156,835*	*54%*
Data Processing Services	126	—	126	—
Curriculum and Instructional Staff Development	9,565	—	9,565	—
Community Services	100	—	100	—
School Leadership	55,142	—	55,142	—
Interest on Debt	1,338	—	1,338	—
Total Cost	$452,905	$104,100	$ 557,005	18.7%

[a]Source: Personal communication with the authors. The school expected to have 96 children in its first year but enrolled only 58. The state funding system was based on estimated enrollments, so the school received extra funding in its first year. (It also received a sizable federal grant and managed to raise about $7,000 on its own.) In the second year, the state disbursed money based on actual enrollments during the first part of the school year, and the school had about 90 students.

[b]The school moved into the Texas State Loan Building, which it leased at market value (reflected in the school's operating budget). The $85,000 start-up cost associated with "Plant Maintenance and Operations" refers to structural changes, outdoor work, and temporary buildings.

TABLE 5–4. Illustrative Shortfalls in Charter School Operating Funds

State	Charter Funding Scheme
Colorado	Guarantee 80% of per-pupil operating revenue: the remaining 20% is negotiated between school and district. (Under amendments adopted in 1999, virtually full funding will begin in 2000–2001.)
Florida	District can take up to 5% for administrative services.
Georgia	Funding negotiated with sponsoring district.
Minnesota	State per-pupil revenue is provided, but local portion remains with district.
New Jersey	90% of funds are provided to charter schools.
Texas	District-approved charter schools must negotiate with sponsoring district.

cent), difficulty with unions (10 percent) or bargaining agreements (7 percent), and trouble with federal regulations (6 percent).[5] This surely understates the problem, for the researchers could only survey those schools that made it through this minefield alive, not those that perished along the way.

Political and bureaucratic resistance to charter schools comes in two variants. The "macro" version takes the form of onerous application procedures, absurd timetables, and meager funding formulae, as well as weak charter statutes and other elements of a charter-hostile environment. The "micro" version entails attacks on specific schools in particular places: applications denied or delayed, hostile votes from the local teachers union, sneak attacks from zoning boards and fire inspectors, and so on. For example, in Tucson, Arizona, charter schools are prohibited from locating in residential areas, while in Flagstaff, they are charged rental and sales taxes.[6] (We look at additional examples in chapter 8.)

School-Level Dilemmas

4. LACK OF BUSINESS ACUMEN.

Charter founders are often education visionaries but less often veterans of meeting payrolls, balancing budgets, negotiating contracts, following due-process rules, and filling out voluminous federal forms. Yet someone must be competent in all those areas and more.[7] According to a California charter board member, "Though we had a well-intentioned group of parents and staff, no one ever anticipated how much work this would be. We've

---

[5] RPP International, *The State of Charter Schools: Third-Year Report* (Washington, D.C.: U.S. Department of Education, 1999), 44. It is worth noting here that conversion schools reported more political opposition than start-ups.

[6] Kelly Pearce, "Charters Ask Level Playing Field," *Arizona Republic*, 11 July 1998.

[7] Sometimes the problem is reversed: schools launched by worldly people with ample business experience but few (or vague or dreamy) education ideas.

had a lot of enthusiasm but we've come up short on fortitude." A Massachusetts charter founder adds, "Starting this school reminded me a lot of starting my own business. A lot of time went into mundane things. I underestimated the amount of time I'd need to devote to things like furniture and computers and supplies."

While conventional public schools often seem top-heavy with administrators, some charters are under-administered. So long as the director is also buying the copier toner and the governing board chair is answering the phone, there is not likely to be anyone to focus on next year's budget or the arcana of obtaining federal Title I funding. Tiny schools find these problems especially acute. Non-bureaucratic operation, though almost always an educational blessing, can be an organizational curse. According to Harry Fair of the Renaissance School (see interview below), "The school started with a tremendous amount of good intentions and with great plans for what to do with kids but without the discipline of a business."

5. GOVERNANCE TIFFS AND MANAGEMENT FRAILTIES.

Founders of charter schools are not always well suited to run them. Some educators are better at creation than execution. Zealous parents often have difficulty yielding the reins to professional educators. Nervous, type-A charter boards tend to micromanage. In several states, the foremost problems among new charter schools, once their doors open, concern inexperienced management, personality clashes, and intramural political woes. The modal problem arises from conflict between board and principal, but other common problems involve teachers versus administrators, staff versus parents, or parents (or teachers) splitting into factions. The most common symptom of governance trouble is the abrupt replacement of the principal during the school's first year or two.

In Massachusetts, six of the fifteen charter schools that opened in 1995 changed principals after their initial year, and three of the seven that opened the following year had new leadership by mid-1998.[8] At the International Studies Academy in San Francisco, turnover on the governance council led to profound conflicts. One student concluded that "[T]he adults have acted just like a bunch of kids who don't know how to get along with each other." After five years of operation, the local board of education decided in 1998 not to renew the school's charter.

According to Dr. Richard O'Connell, superintendent of the Douglas County Public Schools in Colorado (see profile in chapter 9), "Charter boards and directors are having a really tough time. The boards are micromanaging. I'm really concerned about the future of charter schools if this trend continues." (All six Douglas County charters replaced their principals in 1998, and three did so again in 1999.)

[8] Muriel Cohen, "Charter School Changes," *Boston Globe*, 26 July 1998.

Some school operators appear to have little awareness of how successful governing boards work. Seeking to reverse what they see as autocratic rule by "experts" in a typical school system, some charter boards are too democratic (deferring to every parent in the school, for example), resulting in a leadership vacuum or factionalism. Others wind up themselves being heavy-handed and autocratic in their quest for efficiency and accountability or because they don't trust others to sustain the founders' education vision.

6. FRANTIC STARTS.

Most charter schools get off to a late, rushed, and hectic start. Many open their doors to children without adequate preparation, sometimes neglecting such necessities as training staff and completing the curriculum. Such schools almost always limp at the beginning — and would have been better served had six additional months been available. "We opened too fast," lamented one Texas school head. "The first semester was awful."

Sometimes this problem is within the school's power to solve. But often the frenetic scramble is triggered by an ill-planned state (or local) application review cycle that doesn't deliver formal charter contracts until, say, June, giving the successful applicants just two or three months to create schools from scratch.

Several jurisdictions have figured this out and have accelerated their decision cycles. For example, Texas, Arizona, Ohio, Massachusetts, and the District of Columbia all now make it possible to obtain charters well before (in some cases, as much as a year before) the schools actually open.[9] New York's new law requires final decisions by January for schools opening in September.

7. ENROLLMENT PROBLEMS AND SURPRISES.

A charter school might have a top-notch curriculum, a great staff, and be ready to roll, yet be blind-sided by the children who turn up (or fail to). Enrollment troubles take three forms: not enough total students (with attendant budget and staffing hardships); too many children of one kind (age, gender, grade level, etc.) and not enough of others; and a surfeit of kids with needs and challenges different from those the school expected. Some charters face all three. In this domain, charter schools closely resemble business start-ups, only some of which readily find customers and clients. Americans are accustomed to a high mortality rate among new restaurants, for example, when the "market" doesn't match the founders'

[9] The downside is that charter founders who gain extra time to launch their schools frequently find themselves in yet another resource bind. For example, some funding is necessary to pay key people during the planning and training phase. An equity issue lurks here, too. A longer lead time *sans* start-up funding is apt to favor schools initiated by prosperous individuals and organizations and to work against low-income groups and grass-roots organizations.

TABLE 5–5. Barriers Facing Charter Schools (Federal Sample, 1996–98)[a]

Barriers	Estimated Percentage of Schools Reporting Difficulties in Implementing Their Charters
Lack of start-up funds	54.7%
Inadequate operating funds	41.4%
Lack of planning time	37.4%
Inadequate facilities	35.8%
State or local board opposition	20.7%
District resistance or regulations	19.9%
Internal processes or conflicts	14.2%
State department of education resistance	13.5%
Health/safety regulations	11.3%
Union or bargaining unit resistance	9.8%
Accountability requirements	8.9%
Hiring staff	8.8%
Collective-bargaining agreements	7.0%
Community opposition	6.0%
Federal regulations	5.6%
Teacher certification requirements	4.9%

[a]RPP International, *The State of Charter Schools: Third-Year Report* (Washington, D.C.: U.S. Department of Education, 1999), 44. The responses represent a range of 571 to 601 schools.

dreams, or the operator can't respond flexibly to the market that actually emerges. But we do not think this way about schools.

Our own observations about charter start-up problems were generally corroborated by researchers working for the U.S. Department of Education (see Table 5–5). Their survey found that insufficient start-up and operating funds, lack of planning time, and inadequate facilities are the greatest barriers faced by charter schools.

INTERVIEW

Harry Fair (Board Member, Renaissance Charter School, Douglas County, Colorado)

Harry Fair runs a holding company that is involved with start-up ventures in the computer industry, where Mr. Fair has worked for more than twenty years. He is treasurer of the alumni board of directors of the University of Denver, chairs the CEO Exchange Program of the Denver Metro Chamber of Commerce, and chairs the board of directors of the Renaissance School. In his spare time, he collects and races motorcycles.

Why did you become involved with Renaissance School, considering that you don't have kids there? I believe that a person needs to give back to the community — and I'm not at all satisfied with how school systems work. As it happens, when the school began I was a neighbor in the office park where it was first located. The school's charter promised a representative of the business community on the board. When they approached me, I was ready.

What has been your greatest disappointment? The operational component of the school; it's still not working as well as it should. And I'm not overly proud of the quality of education that everybody is getting. We can do better.

What lessons do you draw from the Renaissance experience?

- First, when you're doing something this different you should expect turnover in teachers and administrators. Kids, too. Turnover does not represent failure.
- Second, facilities turned out to be a much bigger issue than we appreciated. The "trailers" turned out to be very detrimental, although better than nothing.
- Third, we should have done a better job of marketing, of public relations, of letting people really understand what this school is about.
- Fourth, I would highly recommend that there be a stronger business component in the creation of a charter school. These schools are founded by emotionally involved parents. They need checks and balances — a business sanity check. The board is the level where this should come together.
- Fifth, understand that when you're starting it you're in an entrepreneurial mode; then you need to run it, which calls for a very different mindset.

What have been the school's most aggravating start-up problems? Facilities, of course. Then operations. Then classrooms. We had situations where the teachers didn't get along with each other.

Did Renaissance experience governance problems? The way a lot of companies and schools start up is very entrepreneurial, a person or group with a great idea and fantastic amount of energy to get it done. It's executed through brute force and tenacity. Everyone's hands are in every nook and cranny. That works well in creating an entity but it reaches the point where the entity needs to shift into a more sophisticated organizational structure, more of a logical division of labor in which everyone does his own job. The transition from the entrepreneurial to the organizational is very difficult.

What qualities or skills are most important for successful participation in a charter board? The single most difficult thing to find is the visionary person who can understand what is trying to be accomplished over the long run and can break that down into its tactical sub-elements. The most damaging thing I've seen on charter boards is the parent community being involved in the board with everyone having his own opinion of what the school should be, never able to settle on a clear direction for the school. You need a board with a single focus of understanding. It's fine to elect a board, but not fine to have two hundred people in there telling them what to do.

What has been the greatest friction between your charter school and its district? From my standpoint, the biggest issue has been the general lack of desire on the district school board's part for charter schools to be successful. Douglas County could do a lot more to support charter schools if they chose to.

The Life Cycle of Charter Schools

Charter schools are dynamic institutions with a life cycle of their own. Generally, the second year brings fewer problems than the first, and the third and fourth bring fewer still. One need only walk into a second- or third-year charter school to sense the difference. The place feels calmer. People are more surefooted, not as frazzled, with less of a "deer in the headlights" look. Staffers are more seasoned, routines are set, the student and parent bodies are stabilized by a cadre of veterans, and unexpected developments are less likely to induce panic. A California school head adds, "We've learned a lot over the first few years. Running this place now is just instinct. I know how to do it."

Table 5–6 shows how start-up concerns diminish over time. Comparing first-year problems in the Hudson sample schools to the incidence of those same problems in 1996–97, we can observe that—in every case—the problem eased with time.

Still, the second year (and beyond) is no stroll in the park for many charter schools. It may be more orderly, but it frequently calls forth woes of its own. Some are variations on the start-up difficulties described above, or the emergence in more acute form of concerns that had initially been swept under the rug. Recurring problems include mounting frustration with meager facilities; continuing friction with local officials; fresh governance conflicts; curriculum adjustments and staff turnover; a continuing stream of kids with problems; and lingering financial stress. Meanwhile, *new* problems also arise in veteran charter schools. We observed three:

- Staff burnout
- Worrisome test scores
- Pressure to imitate conventional schools

TABLE 5-6. Charter School Start-Up Issues[a]

	Schools that Began 94–95 or Earlier (n=13)		Schools that Began 95–96 (n=14)		Schools that Began 96–97 (n=10)	Total Start-Up Schools (N=37)	
	School's 1st Year	1996–97	School's 1st Year	1996–97	School's 1st Year	School's 1st Year	1996–97
Governance							
No/few concerns	46%	77%	50%	57%	60%	51%	67%
Some concerns	15%	15%	43%	36%	30%	30%	26%
Grave concerns	38%	8%	7%	7%	10%	19%	7%
Funding							
No/few concerns	0%	23%	29%	43%	30%	19%	33%
Some concerns	31%	54%	50%	50%	50%	43%	52%
Grave concerns	69%	23%	21%	7%	20%	38%	15%
Students							
No/few concerns	54%	69%	43%	57%	50%	48%	63%
Some concerns	38%	31%	50%	43%	30%	51%	37%
Grave concerns	8%	0%	7%	0%	20%	11%	0%
Staffing							
No/few concerns	54%	85%	57%	86%	40%	51%	85%
Some concerns	23%	15%	36%	14%	40%	32%	15%
Grave concerns	23%	0%	7%	0%	20%	16%	0%
Facility							
Very good	0%	15%	36%	36%	10%	16%	26%
Fair/adequate	85%	77%	36%	43%	60%	59%	59%
Inadequate	15%	8%	29%	21%	30%	24%	15%

[a]As observed by Hudson researchers and/or noted by those interviewed during 1995–96 and 1996–97.

STAFF BURNOUT.

It is hard to sustain the breakneck pace that characterizes many new schools. In the blunt words of an Arizona teacher, "I'm busting my ass here." At the Minnesota New Country School in LeSueur, a progressive, year-round charter school with plenty of technology and self-directed learning, teachers must contend with the demands of school management, participatory governance, financial planning, and the design and application of new education methods and systems of accountability—all this while teaching! As one instructor observed: "It's a real question. Can a school like this survive and be successful only with a heroic level of energy, dedication, and even self-sacrifice?"[10]

At the typical new charter school, the first year is grueling. The following summer is full of last-minute student recruitment, teacher hiring, book buying, building cleaning, and haggling with the district. (And that's even without such common second-year challenges as adding grades or moving to a new site.) A further price is exacted if the principal, teachers, and governing board members had little opportunity to catch their breaths, look after the shreds of their personal lives, or engage in any serious long-range planning. Though the high rate of turnover among charter principals results chiefly from fractious governance arrangements, some of it is attributable to burnout. Charter critic Richard Rothstein warns that "In an initial burst of enthusiasm, teachers and parent volunteers in many charter schools will be willing to work 80 hours a week, clean bathrooms, and give up weekends and vacations to realize a vision of what schools can be. But this can get tiresome."[11]

WORRISOME TEST SCORES.

It is common for schools to administer state or district achievement tests in the spring. That means the initial results probably arrive early in year two. For some charters, these scores bring good news. For others, though, the test results do not match the founders' and parents' expectations and may not furnish the positive evidence that is needed to get the charter renewed, to attract additional students, etc.

The Vaughn Next Century Charter School (which has won California's "Distinguished School" award) was faced with a dilemma when test scores fell after the school obtained its charter. Much of the reason for the decline was that, before going charter, the school did not test children with learning disabilities or those who had recently emerged from the bilingual program. The new results were more honest. Yet they placed the school in an

---

[10] Ross Corson, "Le Sueur-Henderson: Minnesota New Country School," *The American Prospect*, July/August 1998, 56–57.

[11] Richard Rothstein, "Charter Conundrum," *The American Prospect*, July/August 1998, 59.

awkward spot, since the community was expecting clear achievement gains.[12]

Since 1992, Sacramento's Bowling Green Elementary School has risen from among the district's worst achieving to one of its average schools, though it enrolls many low-income and minority children. Yet even those encouraging results do not meet the lofty goals inscribed in the school's charter document. According to the principal, "We came to the realization that we couldn't do it all." Furthermore, the district switched its testing instruments three times in six years, so obtaining clear, comparable achievement data was nearly impossible. In the end, the school board renewed Bowling Green's charter in 1996, but the school had to recalibrate its goals and do some soul-searching about its mission, obstacles, and limitations.[13]

Like many district schools, charters frequently struggle with their assessment tools. Tricky situations arise where tests imposed by the state or district are built on curricular assumptions at odds with the school's education strategy. Some charter educators don't believe in standardized tests, favoring portfolios of student work instead. Some school teams earnestly insist on designing their own assessment systems. Some states and districts (and schools) switch tests, effectively wiping out the baseline. Meanwhile, journalists eager for a juicy story may play fast and loose with test data, ignoring the school's time horizon or neglecting to compare its performance to baseline data. And there is no dearth of charter foes eager to trumpet questionable findings or draw misleading conclusions.

PRESSURE TO IMITATE CONVENTIONAL SCHOOLS.

Schooling in America resembles a giant rubber band: it can be stretched and twisted into novel forms but has an uncanny tendency, whenever the tension eases, to resume its previous shape. Team sports, bus transportation, after-school programs, oboe lessons, talent shows, proms, and driving classes are part and parcel of most children's educational experiences. Charter schools tend to focus more on core academics and to abjure other programs and activities. Their philosophies — and tight budgets — mean they must stick to their knitting. Although students and parents may welcome the distinctive features of their charter school, they also may not want to forego the bells and whistles of conventional schools. Rothstein asserts that "Americans are unlikely to abandon their long-held conviction that well-rounded schooling includes physical education, art, and music, as well as math and reading. . . . [A]s charter schools face the same problems

---

[12] Rothstein, "Charter Conundrum," 48.

[13] See Rothstein and Susanna Cooper, "Sacramento: Bowling Green Elementary," *The American Prospect*, July/August 1998.

regular schools confront, they will find themselves, perhaps to their own astonishment, developing remarkably similar solutions."[14]

FIRE-FIGHTING: SOLUTIONS TO START-UP PROBLEMS

Charter schools face plenty of obstacles, yet about 1,700 of them have managed to start — and for the most part thrive — despite all the perils and pitfalls. Here we examine some factors that contribute to successful charter launches. We have grouped them in two categories: favorable environmental conditions and steps that schools themselves can take.

Environmental Conditions

Waiving regulations and introducing school choice do not, in and of themselves, assure charter success. The environment in which these schools are born needs to supply certain nutriments if they are to thrive. Especially important are a strong, flexible law, a decent relationship between school and sponsor, and access to capital and technical assistance.

1. A STRONG, ADAPTIVE CHARTER LAW.

A well-crafted statute (described earlier in this chapter) goes a long way toward lowering barriers to entry for new charter schools. It can free the school from stifling regulations, create opportunities for fresh organizational designs, and fence off a wide enough zone of freedom for parents and teachers to innovate. In states with weak laws, prospective school founders start the race with leaden shoes. Considering the barriers that charter schools face, states that seriously want to try this education reform strategy should pass strong laws — and those with limp statutes should dose themselves with the legislative equivalent of Viagra.

2. A CIVIL RELATIONSHIP BETWEEN SCHOOL AND SPONSOR.

The charter itself is a legal contract and, as with any contract, it has two parties. As we have seen, states allow for different kinds of sponsors. In Alaska, Kansas, and New Hampshire, only local school boards can grant charters (subject to state approval). In Michigan, charters may be authorized by local school boards, intermediate school boards, community colleges, and state universities. In Arizona and Texas, charters can come from either the local board or the state. In Massachusetts, they come only from the state.

What are the sponsor's obligations? It is no easy thing to balance accountability with flexibility, and most education agencies are strangers to this dilemma. Some sponsors did not really want the charter school in the first place and have scant interest in helping it succeed. This is especially

[14] Rothstein, "Charter Conundrum," 60.

visible in Colorado, where many schools won charters only because the state board of education reversed denials by local boards, which then found themselves in the role of unwilling sponsors. Schools in Illinois have recently faced the same dilemma.

Acrimony often colors relations between charter schools and their districts, and sometimes it is serious enough to damage the education being provided. However, according to the 1998 federal charter study, "Our fieldwork suggests that political resistance declines somewhat over time as charter schools and districts learn to coexist"[15]—an impression corroborated by the authors' research in numerous states. District leaders are usually pragmatists, accommodating to changes even if they did not want them. The fact that most charter founders are intrepid and tireless, even relentless, may spark conflict early on but has proven to be an asset over time.

3. ACCESS TO TECHNICAL ASSISTANCE AND SOURCES OF CAPITAL.

In many states, infant charter schools are not left to sink or swim on their own. Help can be obtained from resource centers, sometimes supplied by the state itself, sometimes by private organizations. The assistance they provide ranges from legal aid to math curricula, from obtaining federal dollars to publicity.

Such resource centers can make the difference between a robust charter program and a feeble one. Since many educators lack experience managing a staff and board (not to mention purchasing textbooks, making payroll, and drafting annual reports), the right kinds of help can add tremendous value to charter programs.

For example, the Pioneer Institute assists Massachusetts charters by identifying potential school founders, developing leaders, building and sharing a knowledge base of proven practices and common pitfalls, publishing research, securing funding for start-up costs and facilities, matching outstanding teachers with charter schools, boosting public awareness, and advising charter-minded policymakers. Pioneer has been instrumental in enhancing the quality of the charter movement in Massachusetts.

INTERVIEW

Linda Brown (Pioneer Institute, Boston)

Linda Brown directs the Massachusetts Charter School Resource Center at Boston's Pioneer Institute for Public Policy Research. She served for 22 years as associate head and business manager of an independent school in Cambridge. Pioneer's resource center has been replicated in almost every state with a strong charter law. Brown is com-

---

[15] RPP International, *A Study of Charter Schools: Second-Year Report*, 116.

mitted to increasing student achievement and views charter schools as the "engine driving all schools to higher standards."

Why did you become involved with the charter school movement? After lamenting for over 22 years that it was a shame that I couldn't do for public schools what I was able to accomplish for students in an independent school, I decided to put my mouth where my mouth was! The phrase "independently managed public schools" was too seductive for me to resist.

What has frustrated you most about the charter movement? The differences in quality from state to state. States in which the movement is about quantity and not quality tend to taint other states. The quality of charter schools is critical to their success.

Charter schools are difficult to launch. Is there an adequate supply of intrepid reformers? Massachusetts doesn't have an infinite supply of school reformers ready to go for charter status. Fortitude and risk are not the issue. Capacity is. In Massachusetts, it seems right to have a limited number of charter schools and to insist on their high quality and sterling accountability.

What are the most common problems that charter schools face? Early problems: buildings and bucks. Later problems: governance and leadership. Ongoing problems: buildings and leadership.

What qualities are most essential for charter school success? Expanding the impact of charter schools will depend on four things: (1) improving academic performance; (2) increasing the quality of charter schools, especially in urban areas; (3) enhancing the schools' long-term stability; and (4) replicating charter school successes in other schools. While producing superlative achievement is ultimately a function of good teaching and sound curriculum, it is first and foremost a product of effective school leadership.

The private sector can also assist infant charter schools. Indeed, a new industry is emerging, comprised of providers of services that charter schools need but may not be able (or wise) to handle directly. In some locales, we can find commercial service providers working closely with a state-based charter school assistance office and a nonprofit technical support center. (See Table 5–7 for examples.) The District of Columbia, whose charter program really took off in 1998, already has three nonprofit technical assistance providers: Friends of Choice in Urban Schools, the D.C. Charter School Resource Center, and the Apple Tree Institute for Education Innovation, as well as assistance provided by the D.C. Public Charter School Board. Yet another outfit—the Charter School Development Corporation—is working to secure capital for facilities.

In jurisdictions with strong charter statutes, government sometimes lends a hand, too. As of February 1999, five jurisdictions were providing

TABLE 5–7. Charter School Allies—Public, Private, and Nonprofit[a]

Organization	Illustrative Activity
California Network of Education Charters	Its annual conference draws attendees from across the country (and beyond).
Center for Education Reform (D.C.)	A national clearinghouse and support organization for charters. Conducts research, evaluates state charter laws, maintains a school database, and publishes a workbook for school founders.
Center for Market-Based Education (Ariz.)	This arm of the Goldwater Institute conducts research, compiles report cards on Arizona charters, and hosts forums and conferences.
Charter Friends National Network (Minn.)	Publishes research on charter schools, conducts planning workshops, distributes updates on federal policies, and runs seminars on facilities funding and school designs.
Colorado League of Charter Schools	Educates policymakers; provides technical assistance, networking, and advocacy; evaluates schools statewide; and conducts conferences and workshops.
Florida Department of Education	Has a technical assistance unit that conducts workshops and town meetings around the state regarding developments in the charter world.
Michigan Association of Public School Academies	Advocacy, technical assistance, and information clearinghouse for the state's charter schools. Lobbies the legislatures and weighs in on court battles.
North Carolina Education Reform Foundation	Watchdog for charter interests. Has battled caps on the number of schools, helped charter employees participate in the state retirement system, and simplified audit requirements affecting charter schools.
Pioneer Institute (Mass.)	Charter School Resource Center identifies principals and teachers, researches best practices, secures funding, and works with policymakers.
Thomas B. Fordham Foundation[b] (D.C.)	Collects and disseminates information on charter start-up problems, performance, innovation, and accountability. Provides policy analysis of the charter movement.
U.S. Department of Education	Researches many aspects of the charter movement.

[a]This list is illustrative, not exhaustive. Several dozen more organizations also provide help to charter schools. For a helpful listing, see http://www.charterfriends.org/contacts.html.
[b]One of the authors is president of the foundation, and one is a trustee.

TABLE 5–8. Per-Pupil Facilities Funding for Charters (as of January 1999)[a]

State	Amount Per Pupil	Source	Flexibility
Arizona	$900–$1,200	State appropriation	Schools may spend funds for any legitimate purpose.
District of Columbia	$600	Federal appropriation	Schools may spend funds for any legitimate purpose.
Florida	$387–$587	State appropriation	Schools may use funds to pay for capital-related expenses only.
Massachusetts[b]	$260	State appropriation	Schools may spend funds for any legitimate purpose.
Minnesota	Up to $465 in building lease aid, plus $168 in other funds	State appropriation	Schools may only spend funds for lease payments.

[a]Bryan Hassel, "Paying for the Charter Schoolhouse: A Policy Agenda for Charter School Facilities Financing," Charter Friends National Network, January 1999, http://www.charterfriends.org/facilities.html. Amounts are approximate.
[b]Massachusetts's funding was a one-time appropriation in 1998–99.

some sort of capital funding (or the equivalent) to charters, over and above their regular operating budgets, though these programs were limited and the amounts modest. (See Table 5–8.) In addition, Colorado permits a state authority to issue bonds on behalf of charter schools and, beginning in 2000, will supply charters with their share of the district's "capital reserve."[16]

Philanthropists and civic entrepreneurs can also assist, particularly in lowering barriers to entry and safeguarding schools' freedom.[17] For starters, they can help with acquisition of facilities, equipment, and materials. For example, the Fenton Avenue Charter School (see chapter 2) received assistance with its technology program from the Riordan Foundation, the Mattel Foundation, Educational Management Group, and General Telephone and Electronics.

Charters can also benefit from use of public or private financial authorities to build or renovate facilities. Such an outfit may provide schools with

[16] "States Address Funding Issue for Charter Facilities," Charter Schools Development Corporation, Washington, D.C., Charter Schools Bulletin, 2, no. 2 (Summer 1998): 1.
[17] For an example of what we mean by a civic entrepreneur, see Giving Better, Giving Smarter: Renewing Philanthropy in America, Washington, D.C.: The National Commission on Philanthropy and Civic Renewal, 1997.

access to bond financing on favorable terms, pool loans to several schools to reduce the lender risk, or furnish a revolving fund of privately raised dollars. Civic entrepreneurs can themselves donate or lease facilities at low cost. For example, Carole Little and her business partner, Leonard Rabinowitz, donated a $6.8 million building to the Accelerated Charter School in Los Angeles. A group that includes Rabinowitz has also promised to undertake a whopping $50 million fundraising effort for the school as it expands.[18]

In Denver, philanthropists and business groups contributed some $4 million to rehabilitate an historic school building to house a charter school run by the Edison Project. Through their family foundation, Donald and Doris Fisher of San Francisco (founders of The Gap clothing chain) are giving $25 million in start-up assistance to California school districts that convert low-performing schools into charter schools managed by the Edison Project.

Civic entrepreneurs can also help to fend off political attacks by supporting the growing network of charter watchdog, advocacy, and "friends" groups. Such organizations blow the whistle when legislative or regulatory assaults loom.

What Schools Must Do for Themselves

Outsiders can only do so much. For a successful launch, charter planners must strive to locate solid leadership, carve out adequate planning time, and obtain a serviceable building.

4. EFFECTIVE LEADERSHIP.

Many analysts believe that low educational achievement in America is inseparable from the problem of weak school leadership. Do those in charge of a school nurture a culture of achievement and professionalism? How are parents, students, and staff treated? Are challenges and crises met directly or deferred for another day?

Effective leadership can go a long way toward overcoming typical charter barriers. With steadfast leadership, a well-crafted governance arrangement, smart staffing, and advice from charter veterans, many problems can be averted.

School founders must, for example, take pains to hire a crackerjack principal and then delegate sufficient authority to that person. Ardent parents may continue to shape the school's policy but should not meddle in its management. Charters can learn from success stories among pri-

---

[18] Accelerated School began as a K-7 school. Its plans call for expanding the school to pre-K-12 for 1200 students. That will require major enlargement of both education programs and facilities, the latter to include a gymnasium, outdoor athletic field, etc. Hence the ambitious $50 million capital campaign.

vate schools and colleges, many of which have long histories of successful governance.

Political opposition can sometimes be mitigated by anticipating turf wars and engaging potential foes in early dialogue. Foresighted charter founders anticipate that districts will get defensive about disappearing pupils and dwindling budgets, and are sometimes able to minimize the political fallout.

Since many founders lack business acumen, it is wise to structure the full staff and board so as to assemble the whole spectrum of needed expertise. This could mean hiring a veteran business manager (or outsourcing the school's management), dividing the top job between two people (as Fenton Avenue School in Los Angeles has done), or building the necessary knowhow into the school's governing board (as Colorado's Renaissance School has done).

5. ADEQUATE PLANNING TIME.

Time can be a new charter school's most precious asset. Launching a school brings a million things to do—from obtaining a building to selecting a curriculum; from hiring and training teachers to arranging for transportation and janitorial services; from getting a fire inspection to networking the computers. Most of these activities take time, which means they get neglected when staff are racing the clock. By building in months or even a year of prep time, charter founders can circumnavigate many shoals.

As a Massachusetts school founder remarks, "Our decision to spend a year planning and preparing for the opening of the school was the best idea we had." Fenton Avenue's Joe Lucente reports, "The five-month lead time between the approval of our charter and our date of operation was invaluable. It allowed us to hit the road running."

Frantic starts can be made more manageable by doing a trial run with a summer program. The SEED Public Charter School in inner-city Washington, D.C.—a boarding school for at-risk kids—had 40 students attend summer camp before it opened in the fall of 1998. Part of the reason was to give the staff a trial run before the school actually launched, but part was to expose youngsters to the unique atmosphere of a boarding school to determine whether such an environment would work for them.

PROFILE

Mark Kushner (Leadership High, San Francisco)

Mark Kushner, former English teacher, tennis coach, and lawyer, wanted to create San Francisco's first "start from scratch" charter high school. He says, "I wanted urban kids in San Francisco to have the same opportunity I had to get the best public education possible."

In 1994–95, he spent a year at Harvard, designing the school.

While there, he founded a charter school research group and explored leadership development, the new school's central theme. He received a $10,000 grant from a San Francisco foundation to pursue the project.

In July 1995 — two full years before his school opened — Kushner returned to San Francisco to begin creating it. He talked with families and community leaders. Their message was clear: "They wanted a small school that would provide a college-prep program for urban minority kids just like, as one parent told me, 'rich kids have in private schools.'"

During the summer of 1996, he pilot-tested the instructional program with 24 middle-school youngsters. In the morning, they received rigorous academics salted with leadership skills. The afternoon was devoted to paid service projects that resembled real jobs. San Francisco school board members and parents were invited to visit. In retrospect, Kushner says, this stage was "critical to the school's success."

Finally, Kushner and his colleagues made their case to the school board. He knew it would be a tough sell. While two charter schools were already operating in San Francisco, the board had rejected the last three proposals to come before it. Kushner recalls, "I saw the application process as a political campaign. I created a board of trustees and another advisory board to rally the political support I would need to get the charter approved. I also met with each member of the school board to discuss with them what I wanted to do." The charter was granted by the school board in December 1996 and okayed by the state in April 1997.

Next, he needed a facility. After several frustrating attempts, Kushner arranged a lease with Golden Gate University, in which the school would use the fifth and sixth floors of the law school building and have access to the library, computer labs, and other facilities.

After a four-day retreat for students, Leadership High opened in the fall of 1997, serving its first class of 100 ninth graders from almost every ZIP code in town (about 75 percent are minorities, and 10 percent were previously enrolled in private schools). The school will add a grade level each year until it tops out at grades 9–12 with 400 students.

Leadership High gives its students 320 minutes of instruction per week in core subjects, about 25 percent more than regular San Francisco high schools. The school has excursions and field trips, clubs and sports teams, physical education, and mandatory uniforms.

Kushner's advice to those who want to open a charter school is simple: "Take your time and think through what you want to do. Get plenty of input from the community. The process is tedious and time-consuming but worth it. And never take no for an answer."

6. FINDING A SERVICEABLE FACILITY.

The best staff and curriculum in the world are of little avail if they have nowhere to work. Conversion charters generally bring their buildings with them, but most start-ups must scrounge for a facility. Some are able to lease a mothballed parochial school or community center that is unused before 3 P.M. Others settle for converted office space in a strip mall, a former warehouse, church basement, or those dreaded portables.

Sometimes charters get a helping hand. The Guajome Park Academy in Vista, California faced a facility problem when it added high school grades, so it joined forces with several organizations to build a new learning center.[19] The school would never have been able to finance this $2 million investment on its own. The Medical Center Charter School in Houston shares a facility with the St. Nicholas II private school, which arranged for the building's construction. The charter school pays rent to St. Nicholas and purchases other services (including food) from the private school.

The Massachusetts Finance Development Agency has helped several schools gain access on favorable terms to disused state or federal facilities. The Chicago Public Schools provided $2 million to the Illinois Facilities Fund to create a revolving fund for charter facilities and equipment.

SEVEN HILLS, SEVEN MONTHS LATER

As we saw at the beginning of this chapter, the Seven Hills Charter School was initially shell-shocked by its facility woes and enrollment surprises. Children were being suspended for violent behavior, some families pulled out, and a few teachers grew disillusioned. Yet the school weathered its storms.

Once the building renovations were completed and the teachers — at an epic staff meeting — decided on a new code of conduct, the school gradually, painstakingly, began to transform itself. Discipline problems waned. Kids began learning. The school developed a fine music program and one of the best technology packages we have seen, complete with a computer for each family, an impressive technology staff, state-of-the-art multimedia classrooms, and a thriving school-to-parent communication system.

Much of this was due to the influence of the Edison model, which Deborah Springpeace calls "brilliantly conceived": "I had spent my middle school career trying to turn the Queen Mary around," she recalls. "When I saw the Edison model, it was all there."

But building-level leadership made a big difference, too. When all was

---

[19] The Vista Redevelopment Commission is serving as a guarantor for five years, at which point the facility will be owned by Guajome.

said and done — after the staff had been battered and drained, then revived and renewed — Springpeace asked her colleagues to choose one word to describe the school's first year. Words like "desperation," "pain," "exhaustion," "mayhem," and "shell-shock" must have crossed their minds. But in the end they all agreed with the teacher who called it "spiritual" — because they were not just educating kids — they were saving lives.

What advice does Springpeace have for people thinking about launching a charter school?

> First, don't pass up the opportunity. My whole career was preparation for this. I'm so glad I challenged myself to one last great adventure. Dream. Next, take time in the design phase to figure out what you want the school to look and be like. Take six months of staff development. Last, remember that charter schools are not built in a day. Tell parents that. There will be problems. It's like the wagons going West. There's treasure ahead, but dangers along the way. It's been the adventure of a lifetime.

Launching a charter school is no picnic. It should not be undertaken by the squeamish, timid, or irresolute. That it can be done, however, is evident from a thousand cases. Deborah Springpeace did it at Seven Hills. Mark Kushner did it at Leadership High. Their schools are thriving, as are others all across America.

But one high hurdle remains to be cleared by virtually every charter school in the land, as well as by every state's charter program. Indeed, it may be the make-or-break issue for the charter movement as a whole. In the next chapter, we try to assemble the accountability puzzle.

6

THE ACCOUNTABILITY PUZZLE

[U]nclear laws and lax implementation in many states cloud charter schools' relationships with government and threaten to replace performance with compliance as the basis of charter school accountability.

Paul T. Hill, Lawrence C. Pierce, and Robin Lake, How Are Public Charter Schools Held Accountable?

SOME VIEW accountability as the third rail of the charter movement, others as the holy grail. Some fear it will lead to the demise of charter schools. Others see it as a desirable but unrealistic goal. In this chapter, we examine the puzzle of charter accountability and suggest a way of piecing it together that has large implications for U.S. public education.

The chief aim of accountability is to find and sustain good schools while weeding out or repairing bad ones. In the case of conventional public schooling, the main accountability mechanism relies on bureaucratic control from higher levels within "the system." In charter schools, by contrast, accountability is propelled mostly by public marketplaces in which a school's clients and stakeholders reward its successes, punish its failures, and send it signals about what needs to change. The main function of such a system is to furnish parents, policymakers, taxpayers, and others with information about the school's working and its effectiveness. The assumption is that an ample supply of such information will equip them to take actions that will lead to good schools flourishing and bad ones disappearing—or mending their ways. The traditional top-down system of bureaucratic regulation can then recede.

Unfortunately, the needed information—and the new accountability strategy that hinges on it—is scarce in U.S. education. The charter movement must break new ground. Today it is painfully difficult to find out what schools are doing and how well they are working. One reason for America's widespread angst about its schools is that getting solid information about them is like breaking into a bank vault. Yes, a determined citizen can hound system administrators for test scores, obtain records from board meetings, file Freedom of Information Act claims for some data, and navigate the corridors of the state department of education to obtain more. But most of the vast quantities of information about individual schools might as well reside in the vaults of Fort Knox. And much of what is "out there" is obsolete or incomprehensible.

Why? One explanation is the scale, complexity, and sluggishness of any large bureaucracy. But another has to do with secretiveness about performance and skittishness about blame. With happy exceptions, the U.S. school establishment is wary of releasing (even obtaining) comparative data on academic performance. There is nothing akin to the independent audit that corporations (and universities, private schools, pension funds, etc.) receive — and transmit to their stockholders, investors, customers, and employees. "Transparent" is one of the last adjectives one would use to describe schooling in America today. With opacity, however, comes mistrust. With secrecy comes suspicion — and the impulse to clamp down with more regulations from on high.

Thus today's typical form of school accountability depends on rules and compliance: make schools follow plenty of regulations, micromanage what they do and how they use their resources, and ensure that plentiful enforcers and bureaucratic controls are in place to keep anyone from doing anything untoward. No graduating without two years of social studies. No classes with more than 27 pupils. No after-hours tutoring by teachers unless they receive additional compensation. Nobody in the building before 7:37. No less than 35 minutes of math instruction per day. No teachers without state licenses. And when something goes awry, another regulation, checkpoint, or enforcer is put in place to ensure that it never happens again.

The language of accountability-via-regulation is the only one that many school systems speak, and it is the one that many people have in mind for charter schools as well. But that approach will only make charter schools more and more like conventional schools, crippling their potential to be different.

We envision a different approach to accountability, designed to help charters present bona fide education alternatives. We call it accountability-via-transparency. That means a regimen in which so much is known about each school that its various watchers and constituents (including families, staff, board members, sponsor, the press, and rival schools) can and routinely do "regulate" it through market-style mechanisms rather than command-and-control structures. If flaky people are operating a dubious school with a weird curriculum, classrooms are out of control, money is being squandered (or pocketed by the school head), or test scores are sagging, this will be no secret to its community. Either the school changes its ways or it finds itself without students (or without its charter renewal). Conversely, a school that works well will find people beating a path to its doors.

Such an approach to accountability should guide the relationship between charters and their sponsors and should inform the statewide charter program (and in time, we hope, the whole enterprise of public education). The latter part of this chapter offers an extended description of how a "transparent" charter accountability system would work tomorrow. Before getting there, we review the more familiar approaches to accountability in today's charter world.

CHARTER SCHOOL ACCOUNTABILITY: ARIZONA AND MASSACHUSETTS

Arizona has been called the "Wild West" of the charter movement because of its aggressive, "go for broke" approach. Applicants can obtain charters from multiple sources. Charters are granted for 15 years (three times the usual length) to converted public, converted private, and start-up schools. Many for-profit firms are operating Arizona charter schools, and there is no cap on the number that can be sponsored by local school boards (and generous caps on those granted by the two statewide boards).

Massachusetts, in contrast, has been termed the "Harvard" of charter authorizers due to its deliberate pace and selectivity. In the Bay State, only the state board of education can grant "Commonwealth charters," though the local school committee and teachers' union must sign off on "Horace Mann" schools. The cap was raised in 1998 from 25 schools to 50. Massachusetts is widely known for having the most meticulous charter accountability system in the country.

ACCOUNTABILITY ARIZONA-STYLE

(as told by Lisa Graham Keegan, State Superintendent
of Public Instruction)

How will you know whether charter schools are more effective than regular schools? I don't seek to prove that all charter schools are more effective or efficient than traditional schools. I would like to have data for all public schools that tells the public what student performance is, as judged against a predetermined standard, and how much money is being spent in what ways at the school site. Only then could we even compare any school with another.

How do you like it when Arizona is called the "Wild West" of education reform? I don't see it as harsh criticism, simply amazement! Although many people talk about wanting to introduce market forces into public education, few are comfortable with the degree of change that will bring.

What is your view of the adequacy of Arizona's current arrangements for "policing" its charter schools without overregulating them? I fear a reversion to the comforts of regulation. My responsibility as superintendent is over all public schools and I see much more fraud and misuse in the traditional system than in charter schools. When we do discover fraud, the story is seen as an indictment of the individual when it is a district school, but an indictment of the system when it is a charter school.

I also fear the cries for more "monitoring," which too often translate into unproductive regulatory schemes. The best "monitoring" program is a strenuous application process. As schools are forced out into the private financial markets to obtain financing, I believe that initial vetting will be strengthened. I also support changes in Arizona's charter law to ensure that no school board which is in financial trouble can start charter schools.

Most importantly, I seek to monitor schools on the basis of academic achievement. We have struggled to create and employ very high quality academic standards in Arizona. I truly believe that much of the process-heavy monitoring we do is borne of having little to no real information about the learning taking place in a school. I hope our standards and testing will begin to resolve what I consider this crisis of ignorance.

Other thoughts? Let the schools teach us what is possible rather than requiring of them what we believe would be best. All the front page stories about school struggles will soon be old news, but permanent changes and improvements will come from our focus on allowing the marketplace to develop in the presence of strong public accountability. We aren't there yet. But I think that, for the first time in our history, we know what it will take to do this right: student-centered funding, clear standards and testing, and the willingness to allow school operators into the marketplace to provide their services. I truly believe we will get this right to the great benefit of our children.

ACCOUNTABILITY MASSACHUSETTS-STYLE

(as told by Scott W. Hamilton, former Associate Commissioner
for Charter Schools)[1]

What are the key elements of the state's system of "monitoring" its charter schools? Three simple questions: Is the school's academic program a success? Is it a viable organization? And, is it faithful to the terms of its charter? Each school must develop an accountability contract that describes the school's objectives as well as the measures it will use to document progress toward those objectives, including credible student assessment tools. Charter schools must

---

[1] This interview was conducted in 1998, when Hamilton was the senior official responsible for charter schools in the Massachusetts Department of Education. He has since taken a position with a private foundation. Mr. Hamilton is also a former colleague of the authors.

publish an annual report and obtain an independent financial audit. In addition, charter schools are subject to an annual day-long site visit conducted by a small group of Massachusetts citizens who are not involved in the school. The most important duty in this process is to keep the focus of evaluation on educational results and to guard against the inclination of government to focus instead on school inputs.

What types of interventions has the state made in sub-par charter schools? Have these been sufficient? Several schools have had problems in terms of educational quality or governance that were so significant that we placed them on probationary status. When this happens, we work with the school to develop a remedial plan to remedy the problems. In some cases, the problems have been rectified. In others, it is too soon to tell. In one case, a charter school voluntarily returned its charter hours before the State Board of Education was going to vote to revoke it.

How does the Commonwealth judge which schools deserve to have their charters renewed? A charter school must submit a renewal application that offers credible responses to our three evaluation questions. Following receipt of a renewal application, an independent evaluation team conducts a 4–5 day "inspection." Inspired more by the British school inspection model than by the typical accreditation model, this site visit focuses on the school's academic results. We then review the renewal application, the inspection team's report, past annual reports, and financial audits, and then make a recommendation to the Board of Education.

Massachusetts has grown its charter movement relatively slowly compared with some other states. Why? Mere numbers and speed of expansion won't do any good if the "product" is shoddy. For us, this enterprise is about creating better, not just more, public schools. We have been very choosy in our application process, knowing that it is easier to prevent a bad school from being chartered than to close one down once it opens. As a result, charter schools are associated with high quality and are a more compelling and durable reform.

ACCOUNTABILITY IN ACTION

As noted in the federal charter study, states presently tackle the charter accountability challenge in very different ways. Some have adopted a centralized, state-run approach, others a market-based strategy, and still others a district-managed framework that relies on local accountability augmented by statewide tests. Nearly nine in ten charter schools are having their finances monitored, seven in ten have their student achievement and attendance reviewed, and six in ten are checked for compliance with regulations and instructional practices. A third or fewer are monitored for governance arrangements, pupil behavior, and school completion rates. Charter schools use various types of assessment methods to report on student achievement, with 86 percent using standardized tests and 75 percent using state tests. Many also use student portfolios (79 percent) and performance assessments (70 percent) to augment test scores.[2]

What do these varying approaches look like in practice? In 1998, the Chicago School Reform Board of Trustees approved a new charter accountability policy. Under it, the city's charter schools are evaluated annually based on test scores, attendance, financial stability, and compliance with laws (e.g., open-meeting rules and fire regulations).[3] This is mostly a compliance-style system, but Chicago has so many energized civic groups and zealous education reformers that every bit of data is bound to be scrutinized in the marketplace as well as by the Trustees.

The District of Columbia Public Charter School Board requires each of its schools to develop an accountability plan that specifies the school's academic, nonacademic, and organizational goals and its plan for complying with unwaived regulations. A multi-school self-help group called the D.C. Charter League for Accountable Schools (DC CLAS) contracts with consultants to provide participating schools with technical assistance as they develop these plans and work to achieve their goals.

Texas is nationally known for its comprehensive public school accountability system, based on academic standards and statewide tests. For the most part, the Lone Star State has applied that system to its charter schools, too. Among the seventeen "first generation" charters for which two years of data were available in mid-1998, ten took part in the state's "regular" accountability system while seven opted for an alternative arrangement meant for schools that serve student populations "outside the norm" (e.g., dropouts, newly arrived immigrants, etc.). Of the ten schools in the regular system, one was "recognized" for strong performance while two were classified as "low performing."[4] Of the seven charters in the alternative program, however, six were deemed to "need peer review" — that is, to have posted unsatisfactory results. Some of these schools had set their performance targets extremely high. Perversely, the accountability system that found them falling short of those ambitious goals will tempt them to set lower sights in the future. Educational accountability, it turns out, is indeed complicated.

---

[2] RPP International, *The State of Charter Schools: Third-Year Report* (Washington, D.C.: U.S. Department of Education, 1999), 3, 50–56.

[3] "Charter Schools and Accountability," *Chicago Tribune* (editorial), 8 September 1998.

[4] According to a state official, one of these schools has so few third graders taking the test that the data was a fluke, while the other is a dropout recovery program that probably should have put itself in the "alternative accountability" program.

In Arizona, besides the state's "Wild West" accountability system (out-lined above by Keegan) — and in response to political threats of heavier-handed regulation — charter leaders launched their own new self-policing and quality control body in late 1998. Dubbed the Association for Perfor-mance-Based Accreditation (APBA), its transparency-minded mission state-ment says:

> Market-based systems work most effectively when consumers and other stake-holders have ready access to meaningful, accurate, and timely information. The mission of the Association for Performance-Based Accreditation (APBA) is to provide such information for parents, students, schools, governing boards, sponsoring entities, and other interested parties to assist them in eval-uating schools.

APBA intends to publish information about the goals and progress of each charter school that it accredits, including students' Stanford 9 scores, pupil performance on the new Arizona state tests, academic gains on other assessments, the school's annual report, and an annual parent survey. But APBA is new and does not yet have a record of accomplishment. Today, probably the best data source in Arizona is the Goldwater Institute's web site, which contains a great deal of information on each of the state's char-ter schools.[5]

In addition to state- and district-wide charter accountability systems, remarkable developments are bubbling up from the schools themselves. The most promising approach we have seen uses a sophisticated perfor-mance management system at the building level. (It could be used district-wide, as well.) Similar systems have helped huge corporations and small businesses boost efficiency, drive innovation, improve service, and reen-gineer processes. Many hospitals, museums, and other nonprofit organiza-tions also use such systems, though few schools do.

The virtue of this approach is that it drives accountability from the bot-tom up (through voluntary information disclosure) instead of from the top (via regulatory compliance). With more conventional systems, state offi-cials pull performance information out of schools, whereas with the per-formance management approach, teachers and schools leaders *push* infor-mation out to their many constituencies.

Performance information is not the same as old-fashioned "management information": how many note pads and staplers an office has, how much is being spent on what, and so on. While those things are worth knowing, they are not the soul of education accountability. Performance information for schools focuses on key academic indicators and results (homework completion, mastery of standards, graduation rates, and test scores). If

---

[5] Kelley Pearce, "Web Site Tracks Charters," *The Arizona Republic*, 10 February 1999. See http://www.cmbe.org.

well executed, such systems can boost transparency and create more professional, client-responsive schools.

Several versions are being developed. For example, New American
Schools has supported the work of design teams that have created standards-based management information systems. One of these, the Modern
Red Schoolhouse Institute, has linked all its standards to interdisciplinary
curriculum units, and has an information system capable of generating
reports on student achievement that closely match the standards to those
units.[6] Another system is called ACHIEVE, piloted in a dozen charter
schools (and four conventional public schools) in 1998–99. By January
2000 it will be in about 100 schools in 9 states. With this system, schools
can track not only what academic standards have been taught, but also
which have been *mastered* by which pupils. Schools then communicate this
progress to parents, teachers, and the community.

PROFILE

ACHIEVE — A School-Based "Performance Information System"

ACHIEVE, based in San Francisco, selected sixteen schools in five urban areas in 1998–99, after a competitive bidding process in which
100 schools expressed interest in trying the system. Its second phase
will involve rolling the system out to many more schools and districts.
ACHIEVE deploys advanced technology to do four things:

1) enable adults in the school to share information about students;
2) help teachers share information about curriculum, pedagogy, and
   students, thereby boosting their professional development, knowledge base, and effectiveness;
3) arm parents with information about their children's progress and
   problems; and
4) increase the flow of information between teachers and administrators.

Schools are giant repositories of information. Few organizations
generate more data each day. Teachers are awash in information
about students, yet this is rarely shared, infrequently analyzed, and
seldom saved in ways that maximize its utility.

ACHIEVE captures and uses this information. At year's end, there
are notes from every week of a pupil's time at school: grades, interac-
tions with other students, conversations with parents, strategies employed with (or without) success, etc. A new teacher encountering a
struggling student can, with a click of her desktop mouse, learn what
worked best with that child last semester. All teachers have access to a
database of proven strategies on how to maximize each student's
learning. This reduces the frustration that many teachers feel. Schools
can also pinpoint concerns: specific content and skills that a student

---

[6] Two of the authors were once associated with the Modern Red Schoolhouse project.

has not yet mastered, homework completion rates, and more. Besides the student-related information, ACHIEVE's database archives lessons and curricula developed within the school. With this tool, teachers can build on the knowledge and skills that students have mastered. For example, an 11th grade teacher can search the database for all references to Shakespeare in 6th through 10th grade, then build lessons on the Shakespeare topics that students have already covered.

The system also helps set the school's agenda by spotting trends and delivering hard information instead of hunch and anxiety. A chart showing homework grades plummeting in all 6th-grade classes, for example, can shift the conversation at staff meetings from vague impressions and the question of *whether* the quality of students' homework has dropped to *how* the school can get those falling scores to rise.

Finally, the system arms parents with information. Every week, they receive a listing of skills and content covered in each of their child's classes and a summary of his progress in learning them. They also get comments about their child's classroom performance and suggestions for reinforcing learning at home. Such progress reports are far superior to the minimal feedback given by report cards and can serve as early warning signals to parents when problems first loom. When parents contact the school, they find people who know a great deal about their particular student. The principal, for example, can log onto the ACHIEVE system and have a full set of information to share with a concerned parent. She can even access lesson plans so as to tell the parent about missed homework and assignments due the next day.

These examples illustrate promising steps on the accountability path. Unfortunately, today's charter world has too few of them. Instead, accountability typically means a half-baked version of the top-down regulation-and-compliance system that the state or community applies to its conventional public schools, usually accompanied by a raging debate about whether more or fewer of the usual rules should apply to charter schools. Often, too, discussions of charter accountability focus obsessively on the narrow question of whether schools will have their charters renewed or be closed down by their sponsors. Some media accounts are so transfixed by school "failures" and "survivals" as to resemble articles about intensive care wards or gladiator contests.

CHARTER CLOSURES: SIGN OF FAILURE OR ACCOUNTABILITY AT WORK?

According to the federal charter study, "By the beginning of the 1998–99 school year, thirty-two charter schools had closed. This represents about 3 percent of the charter schools that had opened since 1992."[7]

---

[7] RPP International, *The State of Charter Schools: Third-Year Report,* 10; for details on

Why do charter schools close? Reasons vary widely. The Center for Economics and Law Charter School in Philadelphia voluntarily shut its doors in late October 1998 when its fire alarm and sprinkler systems failed to work. (State officials had also cited the school for discipline and staffing problems.) The Arizona Career and Technology High School, a vocational charter school in Mesa, was closed in January 1998 due to management problems, including safety concerns and the filing of inflated enrollment figures. The Marcus Garvey Charter School in Washington, D.C. was closed in the spring of 1998 after a saga of scandal that included the conviction of the principal for assaulting a newspaper reporter and two police officers and charges that the school had displayed a pattern of mismanagement.[8]

The Johnson/Urban League Charter in San Diego was shut in 1996 based on the recommendation of the local superintendent, due to a recondite dispute over whether the school was operating within its authority when it hired its own lawyers and declared itself a legal entity. Although test scores had risen, there were long-simmering governance disputes at the school and considerable community dissension over its existence. Indeed, this school's demise seems to have had more to do with power struggles than academic performance or fiscal integrity.[9]

Also in San Diego, Windows Charter School had its charter revoked in 1996 (barely two months after it was granted) for safety violations and failure to meet enrollment goals. (Windows eventually became a satellite school of Guajome Charter School in Vista.) The well-functioning Clayton Charter School in Denver, Colorado was voluntarily shut down by the Clayton Foundation, primarily due to competition from other charter schools.

We are aware of just a few examples of closures due to educational inadequacy. Georgia's Midway Elementary School did not get its charter renewed in part because of its lack of educational innovation. Michigan's Turtle Island school failed to attain its educational goals. Dakota Open, a K-12 charter program for at-risk Native American students in Minnesota, had its high school program terminated by state officials after the school failed to produce satisfactory results and incurred high absenteeism. Teacher and school organizer Tim Ellis complained, "The whole area of Indian education for 200 years has been a failure, and yet we're supposed to cure all those problems within three years."[10] Inadequate enrollment,

---

these closings see Center for Education Reform, *Charter Schools: A Progress Report—The Closures*, Washington, D.C., 1999, http://www.edreform.com/pubs/CharterClosures99.htm.

[8] Valerie Strauss, "School Board Revokes Marcus Garvey Charter," *Washington Post*, 19 May 1998, B1.

[9] Susan Gembrowski, "Trustees Revoke Charter of School in Emerald Hills," *San Diego Union-Tribune*, 27 November 1996. See also: Eric Premack, "California Charter News 27 November 1996," Charter Schools Project, California State University, Sacramento.

[10] Maureen M. Smith, "Charter School for American Indians Is Partly Closed," *Star Tribune*, 10 June 1997.

which may or may not be related to low educational quality, is another cause of charter failure, accounting for half a dozen of the closures reported by the Center for Education Reform.

The most common reasons for school closings have been organizational chaos, management meltdown, and fiscal shenanigans. Edutrain in Los Angeles was the first charter school to be shut down. The school was at least $1 million in debt when its charter was revoked—and the principal was leasing a $39,000 sports car and paid $7,000 for a secret retreat for selected staff members.[11]

At Arizona's now-defunct Citizen 2000 Charter School, the director, Dr. Lawndia White Venerable, wrote school checks for her mother's mortgage, her home renovations, her divorce attorney's fees, jewelry, flowers, and swimming pool supplies. Venerable asserted that she was just paying herself back, since she had loaned the school a lot of start-up money. But she failed to separate her own finances from the school's. (Arizona law prohibits such commingling.) Citizen 2000 also exaggerated its enrollment figures to get $250,000 more in state funding than it was due. In 1996, the school closed its doors and filed for bankruptcy—minutes before a state hearing to determine whether its charter should be revoked.[12]

Naturally, there is pain and hardship when a school shuts down. Students must find and enroll in other schools, and the transition surely throws a spanner into their learning for the year. Teachers must locate new jobs. Districts must recalculate enrollments and re-program funds. Still, it is noteworthy that so few charter schools—under three percent—have actually shut down. Compared with other start-up ventures, that looks pretty good.

School closures can also be construed as achievements for the charter movement—and we suspect that a few more such "achievements" are warranted. Terminating a charter school for cause demonstrates that accountability has teeth in this corner of American public education. This essential feature of charter schools helps distinguish them from the vast majority of school reforms. When this one doesn't work, it has a built-in override mechanism—a "panic switch" that allows concerned public officials to terminate any school that is failing its students or ripping off taxpayers. Thus, charter schools have what economists term "option value": they allow reform to evolve gradually while maintaining a degree of reversibility. If a few charter schools falter, the charter strategy nonetheless endures. Meanwhile, the charter movement buries its dead, while the regular public school system tends to keep them on life-support long after all brain function has ceased. According to former Arizona state senator Tom Patter-

---

[11] Carol Innerst, "Loss of Mandate Rare Among Charter Schools," *Washington Times*, 19 December 1996.

[12] Hal Mattern, "Citizen 2000 Charter School Closes," *Arizona Republic*, 19 November 1996. See also Steve Stecklow, "Arizona Takes the Lead in Charter Schools—for Better or Worse," *Wall Street Journal*, 24 December 1996.

son (see chapter 11), "It's important to allow for failure, it really is. Public schools never fail. They just keep graduating kids that can't read or write."

With about 1,700 charter schools now operating, there are bound to be some bad apples. The question is whether that signals a spoiled barrel or a few troublesome worms. The answer, we believe, is the latter. Still, wormy apples eventually taint the whole barrel. The charter movement must be vigilant in chucking them out, in policing itself through hard-nosed accountability and a laser-like focus on the educational bottom line.

It is important to distinguish, though, between bad schools and weird schools. The charter universe contains some eccentric stars that some people would like to dim due to their eccentric curricula, unproven methods, new-age practices, and other disconcerting signs. But just how bizarre must a school be to justify its elimination? We have also seen some peculiar lessons within America's "regular" public and private school systems. In a diverse country that is devoted to freedom and tolerance and stumbling toward a philosophy of educational choice, we should not hasten to stamp out schools on grounds of otherness. Unless children are in peril, we are wise to avoid overregulation of schools that people want to attend. In schools of choice, at least, they are not there against their will. So long as the school accepts all comers and doesn't advocate the superiority of one race or group over another, so long as families and other constituents have ample information, and so long as the school's sponsor is monitoring its performance vis-à-vis its claims, the fact that it strikes some observers as weird ought not be reason to shut it.

Note, too, that total meltdown is not the only sign of institutional trouble, nor is closure of a school the only solution to its problems. We have seen ailing charter schools as well as dead ones. They sicken for various reasons. Some recover. Others don't. Some would benefit from intervention, technical assistance, monitoring, perhaps even a penalty, but they don't deserve the electric chair. Indeed, the death sentence might be imposed less often if states and communities (and the charter movement itself) were better supplied with rehabilitation options.

Looking across the present charter accountability landscape, we observe some good examples of imaginative strategies and sound systems. But we also see an unhealthy preoccupation with school closures and a strong tendency to revert to public education's familiar pattern of command-and-control. If the charter movement is to succeed in the long run, we believe it needs a different and subtler concept of accountability.

GENERALLY ACCEPTED ACCOUNTABILITY PRINCIPLES FOR EDUCATION (GAAPE)

Charter schools in particular and public education in general would benefit from something akin to the Generally Accepted Accounting Principles

(GAAP) by which private-sector firms (and many nonprofit organizations) report their activities and results using standardized formats and independent audits that embody uniform definitions and common information categories. This could be termed "Generally Accepted *Accountability* Principles for Education" (GAAPE). It borrows the central premises and best attributes of the accounting principles while recognizing key differences between schools and private firms and going well beyond financial matters.

Charter accountability can be thought of as a system of checks and balances that maintains public oversight and authority, maximizes the virtues of market forces, and minimizes the vices of bureaucratic regulatory systems. In a lightly regulated education environment, ample information is essential for securing trust, both from clients and from sponsors. The idea behind GAAPE is that, even as individual schools have wide-ranging freedom to govern themselves, they also remain accountable via the market-place — and to sponsors and policymakers — thanks to their transparency. GAAPE affords everyone concerned with a school the means through which to see what is actually happening there and how well it is working. Instead of a brick wall around such information, the school is surrounded by glass.

The business world provides a partial model. Its accounting standards are meant to ensure the financial transparency and comparability of individual firms.[13] GAAP undergirds nearly every element of a company's financial record-keeping and accounting: its daily bookkeeping, its quarterly and annual reports to shareholders, its independent audits, its filings with various government agencies, the representations it makes to lenders, vendors, and investors, and much more. It is ubiquitous. It is what enables marketplaces to work, by giving buyers and sellers reason to believe that the information they are basing their decisions on is reliable for the firm to which it applies, and comparable to similar sorts of information from other firms and other years. It creates trust by supplying reliable and intelligible data.

Two notable points about business accounting standards have parallels in the world of educational accountability-via-transparency. First, these are not government regulations, nor are they concerned with the nature of the firms to which they apply or with the inputs and activities of those firms,

---

[13] GAAP principles are organized under seven objectives for financial reporting that aim to provide information about how to assess: 1) rational investment and credit decisions; 2) the amount, timing, and uncertainty of future cash flows; 3) the economic resources of a firm and the claims on those resources; 4) a firm's operating performance during a period; 5) the way an enterprise obtains and uses cash; 6) how management has discharged its stewardship responsibility to owners; and 7) explanations and interpretations that help users understand the financial information provided. The 133 specific "statements" that are part of GAAP include such matters as "earnings per share," "accounting for derivative instruments and hedging activities," "accounting for stock-based compensation," "employers' accounting for pensions," "accounting for sales of real estate," "disclosure of longterm obligations," and so forth.

much less with their plans, dreams, or philosophies. Rather, they are consensus statements developed in the private sector (by the Financial Accounting Standards Board), concerned chiefly with making available — to all who want it — immense amounts of accurate, reasonably intelligible, comparable information about a firm's performance. They take for granted that, while this information will be useful to government regulators (the Securities and Exchange Commission, say, or Federal Trade Commission), it is meant primarily for use by customers, suppliers, shareholders, managers, and others in the private sector who have reason to appraise the performance of particular firms.

Second, these principles apply both to businesses themselves *and* to the accounting firms that audit and report on their financial condition. Moreover, they apply universally (albeit with specialized provisions for different sorts of organizations, such as for-profit and nonprofit). It doesn't really matter whether one's firm makes bricks, burritos, or bank loans, whether it is a hospital, a taxi company, Yale University, Mario's Pizzeria, or Microsoft. The same basic accounting principles apply to all and, at some level, all these dissimilar entities can be compared with one another — by an investor or banker — according to the conventions and norms that the principles mandate.

The GAAP principles and the accounting system they inspire are taken for granted, but they have been a tremendous asset to the U.S. economy and the success of American-style democratic capitalism (and they have been imitated by much of the world). They also protect consumers, investors, and others. By making the workings of financial markets and individual firms visible to all, weaknesses are more likely to be exposed and successes made known rapidly. With free and open information, resources can travel quickly to more productive uses.

Here is how we see the education parallel. If vital information is made available about individual schools, in formats that are clear and useful to multiple constituencies and comparable from one school to the next, genuine accountability becomes possible. Accountability-via-transparency is a systematic approach to providing parents, educators, policymakers, taxpayers, and others with information that shows whether the charter approach is working. Such information is not just the responsibility of individual schools, but also the obligation of their sponsors and monitors, both to obtain, analyze, and use in their capacities as stewards and then to amass, distill, and report to the public. Reporting it is more than inscribing it on a government form and putting it in a file, or disclosing it when someone asks a question. We mean voluntarily, energetically, and regularly pumping the information out into view, such as by newspaper notices and web-site postings.

As in the world of arms control, the credo of such an accountability system should be "trust but verify." That is, the system is designed to give schools plenty of freedom and implies confidence in what they will do with their freedom. But such trust is inseparable from people's confidence that the school is telling the truth and doing what it says. Trust must be backed up with hard evidence and reliable information.

With schools, as with private firms, there is a bottom line to the information system. But with schools it's a bit tricky. In the commercial sector, everyone's primary interest is profitability. In education, student achievement is paramount, but it is not the only product of a good school — consider also the fostering of citizenship and character — and it is not the same in all schools. A school working with disabled youngsters or former dropouts, say, may actually be more successful than an advanced "science/math" school, even though its test scores are lower. Thus the "bottom line" isn't as easy to track, report, and compare in education as in the private sector. All the more reason, we believe, for maximum feasible transparency.

As shown in Table 6–1 and elaborated in the paragraphs that follow, we visualize GAAPE functioning at three levels: the individual school, the charter sponsor, and the state.

Level I. The school routinely and systematically discloses complete and accurate information about its program, performance, organization, and finances.

Though statewide systems are often the focus of accountability discussions in education, it is essential that individual charter schools plan carefully for their own accountability needs. An accountable school habitually produces timely, valid, and reliable information about its progress toward its goals, thereby ensuring that parents and staff, governing board and chartering authority, and other constituents and audiences know what value they are receiving. A good school-based accountability system yields four kinds of information, all tied to the school's mission. The mission, of course, must underlie all. What challenges does this particular school seek to meet and what needs will it serve? What does it intend to accomplish? Schools that cannot answer such questions with precision have no business enrolling children.

I-A. Educational achievement. The school makes public its academic (and other) objectives, the indicators that it uses to track its progress toward those goals, and information regarding its progress to date. It includes its standards for students, its curriculum, its instructional methods, and the results of its pupil assessments, revealing enough information about those assessments that readers can easily compare this school's achievement with other schools. Achievement is reported in *absolute* terms (how students are performing vis-à-vis the school's standards), in *value-added* terms (how much more they know at the end of a month or year

TABLE 6–1. Accountability in the Financial and Education Sectors

Accountability in the Financial Sector (GAAP)	Accountability in the Education Sector (GAAPE)
LEVEL I: FIRM. The firm has internal controls and provides all necessary information to its auditor(s), including an annual report to stockholders. Its financial statements are prepared using Generally Accepted Accounting Principles (GAAP).	LEVEL 1: CHARTER SCHOOL. The school must have internal controls and a transparent operating system so that its clients and constituents (parents, sponsors, community members, journalists, policymakers, etc.) can hold it accountable for its performance.
LEVEL II: AUDITOR. The auditor obtains the requisite information from the firm and makes sure that the financial records accord with GAAP. The auditor reviews and "signs off" on the firm's financial statements, signaling to the market that the firm's books are in good order and contain reliable information.	LEVEL II: CHARTER SPONSOR. The sponsor grants the charter, enters into an accountability agreement with the school, monitors its performance (such as by examining test scores and making site visits), and decides whether to renew the charter after applying its own (publicly disclosed) criteria.
LEVEL III: FASB. The Financial Accounting Standards Board sets the Generally Accepted Accounting Principles, with advice from firms, accountants, regulators, and policymakers.	LEVEL III: THE STATE. The legislature crafts the charter law, outlining the accountability provisions for individual schools and the standards and tests that bind all schools. The state also arranges for audits and evaluations of its entire charter program.

than at the beginning), and in *comparative* terms (in relation to district, state, or national norms or standards or the performance of other schools and students). These reports are broken down by relevant demographic categories (e.g., gender, ethnicity, and family income).

I-B. Fiscal soundness. The school undergoes an annual financial audit by a qualified firm, using generally accepted accounting principles, and makes public the results. This audit will produce data that are vital for appraising the school's immediate and long-term solvency and for informing its constituents about how it spends its money.

I-C. Organizational viability. The school provides public information on its governance system, the demand for its services (e.g., number of applicants, number accepted, waiting list), student and staff turnover, discipline issues, and other indicators of constituent satisfaction or dissatisfaction. It holds regular, open board meetings, making public (in advance) their time, place, and agenda. The school also makes available to all who want it (e.g., via the Internet) detailed information on the composition, tenure, by-laws, modes of (s)election, duties, and powers of its governing board. It makes available the minutes of its board meetings (save for personnel or other confidential matters) and all nonconfidential portions of its contracts with staff members together with information about their education and prior experience.

I-D. Compliance with the law. The school publishes aggregate information about the gender, age, race/ethnicity, English language proficiency, and disabilities of its students. To the extent that laws and regulations have not been waived, the charter school shows how it is complying with them, including but not limited to local health and safety codes as well as federal and state anti-discrimination norms.

Commentary: Charters and their sponsors should agree to the general contours of an accountability plan *before* a school opens its doors. This agreement should include the general academic and nonacademic goals that the school seeks to attain and a timetable for establishing the indicators by which progress toward those goals will be gauged. (Benchmarks should be attuned to the baseline performance levels of students attending the school.) The plan should also include evidence that the school is both efficient and ethical. Accountability means more than test scores. Top-notch charter schools lay all their cards on the table—deuces as well as queens—in order to keep parents, the community, and sponsors informed about what is happening. This is the essence of transparency.

Once the school is up and running, its accountability mechanisms should include timely and regular disclosure of essential information to pertinent audiences. At minimum, an annual report is called for, but good schools do more. Virtually all the information suggested here could appear on a well-tended web site. One charter school that we know provides parents with weekly progress reports and sends its annual report to a thousand people, including legislators and community members. The best charter schools achieve a level of candor about themselves that may be painful in the short run, when awkward situations arise, but that serves them well in the long term.

Level II. Charter sponsors routinely and systematically disclose complete and accurate information about their criteria and procedures for school approval, monitoring, intervention, and renewal, and supply comparable information about each school for which they are responsible.

II-A. Charter approval process. The sponsor discloses its procedures, criteria, and timetables for reviewing charter proposals. It makes public all questions that it requires applicants to answer, as well as any fees they must pay, materials they must supply, and other conventions of its review process. It describes its means of verifying the fiscal soundness, good character, and crime-free records of key individuals associated with proposed charter schools. It describes its process for reviewing charter applications. It invites public comment when reviewing an application and makes the application available for public inspection, together with all nonconfidential supporting materials. If the sponsor rejects a charter application, it provides applicants with a written explanation of its reasons. If it gives conditional approval, it makes public the terms and conditions that the school must meet before gaining final approval. If the sponsor approves an application, all subsequent documents, including the charter or contract itself, are made public.

II-B. Monitoring charter schools. The sponsor arranges at least annually for site visits to each of its charter schools, and obtains a written report from that visit, to which report the school has reasonable opportunity to reply. The composition and mandate of the site-visit team are disclosed, as are all nonconfidential portions of the written report and the school's response. The sponsor will obtain from each charter school, and make public, an annual report that contains at least the information outlined above in Level I.

II-C. Schools in difficulty. The charter sponsor has well-formulated criteria and procedures for monitoring its schools and, when appropriate, intervening in the event that a school fails to demonstrate satisfactory progress toward its goals or shows signs of severe educational, organizational, or financial malfunction.

II-D. Charter renewal process. The sponsor has a well-formulated procedure for considering the renewal of its charter schools. The process occurs in clearly delineated stages and includes opportunities for public comment. The sponsor discloses its timetable, procedures, and renewal criteria, including an appeals process in the event of disagreement. All elements of the review process are public (except any that involve confidential personnel matters). The sponsor will, at minimum, faithfully apply all accountability requirements found in the state's charter law. Whatever process is used should result in a recommendation for renewal, conditional renewal, or non-renewal, which recommendation (and the reasons for it) will be presented in timely fashion to the charter school for its comments. A final decision is made at least six months prior to the expiration of the charter.

Commentary: Some charter sponsors do exemplary work. Others have vague, sloppy, or erratic procedures for school approval, renewal, and (especially) monitoring and intervention. Most view their only options as either letting the school do what it likes or killing it outright.

A strong and careful application process is the crucial first step in establishing the conditions for charter school success. Next, a sound monitoring plan includes means for picking up warning signals of schools in distress. Once it spots a malfunctioning school, the sponsor should have a menu of possible remedies that may include (1) warning the school, placing it on probation, and insisting that it rectify the problems within a specified period, either on its own or using technical assistance from some provider; (2) intervening to change the school's leadership; (3) inviting a successful charter school to assume responsibility for the troubled school; (4) reclaiming the charter of a school that has failed to open after a specified period; and (5) closing the school and arranging the timely transfer of its students to other schools.

When it is time to renew a charter, typical criteria include satisfactory progress in meeting academic and other school goals, fiscal probity, and compliance with applicable laws. A special panel may be helpful in reviewing school renewal requests and advising the sponsor, perhaps a panel that includes respected community members. Outside reviewers are especially useful where the charter is reviewed by an agency that was forced against its will to grant the charter in the first place — e.g., a hostile local board that was overruled "on appeal."

Level III. The state routinely discloses complete and accurate information about its charter program, and obtains regular audits and evaluations of that program.

III-A. Program data. The state annually makes public at least the following information about its charter schools:

- The number and age of charter schools, their origins (e.g., new school, former public school), the duration of their charters, and the identities of their sponsors and operators.
- Numbers and characteristics of students enrolled in charter schools.
- The academic achievement of charter students with respect to state standards (as measured on state tests or other assessments).
- All state funds expended on charter schools.
- Laws and regulations that charter schools must obey, information about compliance with them, and all waivers granted to charter schools.
- Data on student and staff attendance (including attrition and turnover) and discipline.
- Data on charter applications and renewals submitted, approved, and denied by all charter sponsors.
- Information on all actions by charter sponsors concerning schools in difficulty.

III-B. Audits. The state arranges for timely audits of this information by individuals or organizations with no stake in the success or failure of the state's charter program and no role in its management. The state publishes the results of such audits.

III-C. Evaluations. The state also arranges for independent evaluations of the quality, efficacy, efficiency, and impacts of its charter program, and publishes the findings of all such evaluations. Questions to be addressed by evaluators include at least the following:

- How the academic achievement of the state's charter schools compares with that of its regular public (and, where possible, private) schools.
- The organizational viability, governance, and fiscal soundness of the state's charter schools.
- Compliance by charter schools with pertinent state and federal laws and regulations.
- Efficacy of the state's management of its charter school program, including soundness (and transparency) of the state's accountability processes.
- A classification of the organizational and educational characteristics of the state's charter schools.
- An appraisal of the charter schools' handling of at-risk children, including admissions, services provided, and evidence of results.
- An appraisal of the nature and extent to which charter schools are affecting "regular" public and private schools.

Commentary: States should systematically gather, compile, and make public an array of information about their charter schools and charter program. But independent audits and evaluations are even more important to a successful accountability system built on the principle of transparency. Professional accounting firms, working with experts on education data, can satisfactorily handle the audit duties. When it comes to evaluations, it is best to commission more than one, and to look to state or regional think tanks and university policy centers for talent. But it is also important to include enough out-of-state experts to counter any in-state biases and enough laymen to offset any educator biases.

Solving the Puzzle

In this chapter, we have examined charter school accountability in theory, accountability in action, and the mixed signals sent by charter closures. We have also outlined "GAAPE," a new way for schools, sponsors, and states to assemble the accountability puzzle. To us, the key to accountability is transparency. This means bulldozing the walls that surround vital information about school performance and sharing that information with the world; pushing information out, not making people tug. To be sure, there is some risk of data overload, but this is a lesser danger than suffocating from lack of information or falling back on command-and-control strategies.

Much remains to be done on the accountability front throughout U.S. education. But the country stands to learn from the charter experience what education accountability can actually mean, why it matters, and how — besides regulatory compliance — it can be achieved in public education. If the charter movement accomplishes only that, it will have been a worthwhile undertaking.

Part II

RENEWING PUBLIC
EDUCATION

7

THE CASE AGAINST CHARTER SCHOOLS: A TEN-COUNT INDICTMENT

In Part I, we peered into specific charter schools, surveying their accomplishments and problems. But we are only half done. The charter phenomenon reaches well beyond individual schools and the people they touch directly. It also raises a host of big-picture questions, figures in tough political struggles, alters the practices of entire school districts, bolsters communities, and leaves tracks on American education as a whole. Part II considers these issues.

The present chapter weighs the case *against* charter schools. Any bold reform strategy inevitably gives rise to doubts and objections. Opponents, critics, and anxious interest groups will naturally emerge. Though some charter doubters pose meretricious and self-serving objections, others are sincerely concerned with the well-being of children and the soul of public education.

Ten Allegations

We have identified ten weighty charges against charter schools. Some are legitimate, others specious. Most lie somewhere in between. Some of these points are discussed fully here; others recap explanations made elsewhere in these pages and are given in brief. Here are the indictments:

1. Charter schools rob funds—and students—from regular public schools.
2. Charter schools are too risky.
3. Charter schools are not truly accountable.
4. Charter schools are not really different from regular schools.
5. Charter schools "cream" the most fortunate kids and leave the neediest behind.
6. Charter schools don't adequately serve disabled youngsters.

7. Charter schools balkanize American society and weaken the principal institution that knits us together.
8. Charter schools invite profiteering from public education.
9. Charter schools are a stalking horse for vouchers.
10. Charter schools do not go far enough.

Allegation # 1
Charter schools rob funds — and students — from regular public schools. While they may benefit a few youngsters, they hurt many more by biting into district budgets.

While it is true that charter funds are typically subtracted from district revenues, that is because their students are subtracted from district rolls. The fundamental concept of any education choice regimen is that money follows children to the schools their families select. Public dollars are meant to be spent for the education of a particular *student*. They are not entitlements for *school systems*.

Moreover, most charter schools are underfunded (as we saw in chapter 5). Though funding formulae and amounts vary by state, on average, charter schools receive about four-fifths of the dollars per pupil that conventional public schools receive, according to estimates by the Center for Education Reform.[1] In Minnesota, only the "state share" of the student dollar reaches the charter school, leaving the district with all its locally generated revenue — and fewer students to educate. In some states (e.g., California, Colorado, New Jersey, Arizona, and Florida), local school systems may profit from charter schools via overhead charges and licensing fees. In other jurisdictions (e.g., Georgia, Illinois, Wisconsin, and Wyoming), charter budgets must be locally negotiated.

Furthermore, charter schools sometimes bring new money into a district by drawing onto district rolls (and into the state funding formulae) children who would not otherwise be there: dropouts, home-schoolers, private school pupils, and youngsters who live outside the district but choose to enroll in its charter schools.[2] In Wisconsin and Massachusetts, school systems continue receiving state money for youngsters who leave for charter schools. To mollify opponents and ease districts' fiscal upsets, Bay State legislators opted to continue paying districts (on a diminishing basis) for funds "lost" when students transfer to charters.[3]

---

[1] Center for Education Reform, Washington, D.C., June 1998. Estimates were obtained from state officials. The aggregate average figure is a simple average of all the charter states, regardless of population or student enrollment.

[2] From the perspective of a state budget director or municipal government, this development is no "bargain." They may well look askance at being asked to support youngsters in charter schools who would not otherwise appear in their budgets. But from the standpoint of school systems, additional enrollment is a source of additional revenue.

[3] This reimbursement process is complicated: in year one, the district receives 100 percent of any increase in money deducted from its budget and sent to a charter school; in year two,

Ultimately, this allegation boils down to the question: whose youngsters (and dollars) are these, anyway? School funds are appropriated to provide the best possible education for a community's youngsters, not to fill institutional coffers or keep failing schools in the black. The surest way to keep students from leaving district schools is to run schools that nobody wants to leave — not by barring the exit. There is also some evidence that competition from charters is healthy for regular schools, even when it is a medicine they don't like to swallow. (See chapter 9.)

Allegation # 2
Charter schools are too risky. They gamble with children's lives and taxpayers' hard-earned dollars.

Denver school board member Lynn Coleman told charter applicant Cordia Booth, "I have a problem with you taking public dollars to experiment." Leonard Fox, president of the Denver Classroom Teachers Association, echoed that sentiment: "We think a lot of charter schools are just experiments. We shouldn't be supporting experiments at the expense of the other students."[4]

This sentiment gained credence in the 1997 Public Broadcasting System report, "Education's Big Gamble: Charter Schools." After touring several schools, correspondent John Merrow concluded by asking, "Are charter schools gambling with our tax dollars and our children? Yes, some of them are. Do charter schools represent an educational revolution? Absolutely. . . . All we can say for certain right now is that the name 'charter school' is no guarantee of anything. Whatever you do, read the fine print."

Indeed, risks accompany charter schools, as with any major organizational innovation. But the vast majority of today's charters are thriving. Their clients are mostly satisfied. They display promising signs of achievement and productivity gains, as well as positive effects on the larger education system. Moreover, some risk is justified when the alternative leaves children in unsafe and failing schools. One should beware of the double standard that holds charter schools to a level of perfection while many district schools get away with educational malpractice because they are parts of "the system."

When critics allege that charters are gambling with children's lives, they often cite the fact that many charter schools employ uncertified teachers.[5] What they miss is that strong charter laws welcome educators from diverse

the district receives a 60 percent reimbursement; in year three, 40 percent; and in years four and beyond, the reimbursement ceases.

[4] David Hill, "Charter Champion," *Education Week*, 4 October 1995, 23. Fox did go on to support Booth's proposed charter school, though.

[5] This charge is commonly overblown. According to Hudson Institute survey data, some 72 percent of charter teachers are certified by the state in which they are teaching and an additional 17 percent are working toward such certification. Many of the remainder are certified in other states.

backgrounds precisely because state certification programs often fail to ensure teacher quality and because policymakers are eager to draw more
individuals with talent and energy into the state's classrooms.

In Michigan, this issue heated up when the State Board of Education
threatened to crack down on charter schools that employ uncredentialed
teachers. Political tempers flared as Democrats initiated the investigation
and Republicans claimed they were not consulted. (The board was evenly
split on party lines.) After the media reported that a state audit failed to
find credentials for 132 teachers in schools chartered by Central Michigan
University, the issue threatened to explode. In the end, though, it was a
false alarm. A *Detroit News* editorial commented, "A records check has
been conducted . . . and the findings strongly suggest the whole thing is a
non-issue. . . . [A] spokesman in the superintendent's office told us that
'every one of the teachers in question is there legally.' Most had the credentials from the very start, but trifling glitches — last names changed by
marriage, missing Social Security numbers and the like — made it hard to
match up teachers' records."[6] Meanwhile, the *Detroit Free Press* reported
in 1997 that over a thousand teachers in that city's public school system
lacked proper credentials. (In 1999, the Michigan legislature assigned control of this dysfunctional system to the city's reformist mayor.)

What about the fear that extremist groups will start schools? Some charter advocates consign this risk to the marketplace, trusting parents to
know what is best for their children. We don't much like public dollars
and implicit public approval being given to crackpot schools. But in a
democracy, people are trusted with many choices. What they need is ample
information about their options. We are also mindful that some of today's
conventional public schools have curricula that are plenty eccentric. (For
example, at El Puente Academy for Peace and Justice in New York City, a
course called Hip-Hop 101 teaches students how to rap, break-dance,
deejay at parties, and write graffiti.)[7] They get away with it because they
are part of "the system."

The surest way to contain this risk for charter schools has three elements:

1. *Vigilant sponsors.* No school should be awarded a charter unless
    its sponsor is satisfied that it will produce good citizens according
    to a publicly defensible conception of citizenship. This should in-
    clude a clear sense of the pluralistic nature of American society
    rather than a particularistic infatuation with any one class, race, or
    group. These are public schools, after all.
2. *Transparent schools with ample consumer information.* If a school
    imparts divisive ideas, hateful attitudes, or bizarre lessons to its

[6] *Detroit News*, 13 April 1998.
[7] Heather MacDonald, "An F for Hip-Hop 101," *City Journal*, Summer 1998, 56.

pupils, this should be visible to parents, the media, the community, and the school's sponsor. Ample public information about what particular schools actually teach will enable the marketplace to function better.

3. *A coherent academic core required of every school in the state (or district) and measured by regular assessments.* A solid basic curriculum for all schools, charters included, will limit the opportunity for educational mischief (and, admittedly, for unbridled curricular diversity) to the portion of the academic program that lies beyond the common core. Today, regrettably, few states have satisfactory standards in place, much less the assessments and accountability arrangements that cause schools to take them seriously.

Allegation # 3
Charter schools are not truly accountable. Only when they become notorious does anything happen to them. Practically none actually get closed down for academic malfeasance.

This is a serious concern. Writing in *The American Prospect*, Richard Rothstein states that "The premise on which charter schools are based — that we can hold schools accountable for results — is a myth. . . . [T]here is no consensus about how to assess educational outcomes objectively. . . . Yet almost all supporters of charter schools agree that accountability will be the fulcrum of their success."[8]

Promising accountability systems for charter schools are still few and far between. In some states, the necessary standards and assessments are not in place; the cognizant boards and bureaucracies do not know how — or don't much want — to monitor their charter schools; or the law is muddy as to whether anyone has authority to do anything about weak performance by charter schools.[9] There are only the earliest stirrings of serious self-policing by the charter movement itself. And we have seen several troubling instances of political pressure by charter operators seeking to ensure that the bar isn't set too high, or pressure to exempt them from sanctions that would otherwise apply to a failing school. (The

---

[8] Richard Rothstein, "Charter Conundrum," *The American Prospect*, July–August 1998, 46.

[9] California illustrates several of these problems. It has changed its state assessment system three times since the charter law was passed in 1992. For a useful but incomplete analysis of the California charter school accountability situation, see Amy Stuart Wells, *Beyond the Rhetoric of Charter School Reform: A Study of Ten California School Districts* (Los Angeles: University of California at Los Angeles, 1998), 19–27. For a careful analysis of how Los Angeles charter schools are held accountable and the extent to which they are reaching the goals found in their charters, see WestEd Regional Laboratory, *Los Angeles Charter District Charter School Evaluation* (Los Angeles: Unified School District, 1998).

argument is usually that "We can trust the marketplace to handle account-ability.")

In Ohio, as of spring 1999, the State Board of Education had approved virtually every charter petition that reached it. It also made the chief academic criterion for charter success (and renewal) test scores at least equal to those of surrounding communities. The problem is that the sur-rounding communities are places like Cleveland and Dayton, school sys-tems with lamentably low test scores. To say that charter schools need only match that sorry performance sets a low bar indeed. That, regretta-bly, seems to have been precisely what some Buckeye State charter opera-tors intended.

One must not, therefore, assume virtue on the part of charter opera-tors. That is why a sophisticated accountability system (such as we out-line in chapter 6) and a well-functioning marketplace are essential for a successful charter program. Here we note that, in states where the "not accountable" allegation turns out to have legs, the charter movement is apt to be in serious trouble over time. And it won't find us among its defenders.

Allegation # 4
Charter schools are not really different from regular schools. They are
trendy and get plenty of hype but do little that is not already being done
by other schools.

How innovative are charter schools? How different from the "conven-tional" public and private schools of their communities? The answers vary, since there is no single charter model. They are more like artisan creations than assembly-line products. When critics suggest that little is happening in charter schools that is not found elsewhere in U.S. education, they are partly correct. Many charter programs are variations on familiar curricular and pedagogical themes. Some represent thoughtful returns to proven but neglected strategies.

In their contexts, however, virtually all charter schools are innovative (see chapter 4). Education arrangements familiar to cosmopolitans can ap-pear revolutionary to locals who never before had access to anything of the sort. Yes, the possibility exists that corporate-style charter chains will resemble cookie cutters, delivering the same program in Worcester as in Wichita. If it is a solid program, however, and if its like is not available to children and families in Worcester (or Wichita), it may be plenty innova-tive in the eyes of its clients.

It is ironic that some critics who allege that charter schools are not very different from conventional schools are the same people who charge that these are eccentric places run by kooks. It appears they want schools that are both different and the same.

Allegation # 5
Charter schools "cream" the most fortunate kids and leave the neediest
behind. They are elitist academies with subtle (and not-so-subtle) screening
mechanisms to discourage the enrollment of children they deem
undesirable, such as low-achievers and discipline problems.

This is a legitimate concern in a few charter schools. But the weight of
evidence pushes toward the opposite conclusion: many charters are consci-
entiously serving more than their "share" of difficult-to-educate children.
Far from "creaming," they are often the recipients of numerous troubled
and at-risk youth, sometimes pointed in their direction by regular schools.

As we saw in chapter 4, the proportion of children served by charter
schools who are eligible for the federal school lunch program, who are
disabled, and who have limited English proficiency is comparable to the
proportion served by regular schools. And charter schools serve a higher
percentage of minority youngsters than regular schools. Yes, some charter
schools are attended mostly by white, upper-middle-class youngsters, just
as many conventional public (and private) schools are. But this is far more
apt to result from the location of the schools and the thrust of their education programs than from discriminatory admissions procedures. Yes, many
charters are serious about academic standards and behavioral norms,
which may lead them to "counsel out," suspend, or expel youngsters who
cannot or will not comply. But that is precisely the same impulse that is
leading more public school systems to steer disruptive students into "alternative" programs — many of which turn out to be charter schools or close
facsimiles. Finally, some 26 percent of U.S. charters report that "serving a
special population" was one of the primary reasons for founding a charter
school, with one-fifth of these schools saying that was their most important motivation.[10] Surely this is the opposite of "creaming."

Allegation # 6
Charter schools don't adequately serve disabled children. Some disregard
federal and state special education statutes. Some do not have the staff or
resources to operate a quality special education program. Others attempt
to deter the disabled from enrolling.

We have visited some charter schools that seem not to know how to
handle disabled students, and some that are ill-prepared for youngsters
with severe handicaps or unusual needs. Undoubtedly, some schools have
hinted to families that their disabled children might be better served elsewhere. But this is surely true. Just as parents of non-disabled youngsters
must be clear-eyed about what a particular charter school will and will not
do for their child — it might not, for example, allow him to play varsity

---

[10] RPP International, *The State of Charter Schools: Third-Year Report*, 42.

football or learn Japanese — so too should parents of disabled children be careful school shoppers. If they want the full panoply of government-imposed procedures and services, they may be happier elsewhere. If their child has a disability that requires a particular treatment, a given school — charter or otherwise — may or may not be the best place to obtain it.

Some charter schools fill particular niches for disabled youngsters. The Metro Deaf Charter School in Minnesota enrolls only deaf students in grades K–6 and is nationally regarded as a model for the education of hearing-impaired pupils. American Sign Language is taught as the primary language and English as a second language. In Lawrence, Massachusetts, Community Day Charter School offers all of its students an "inclusive educational program" with no tracks or government-style "individual education plans" (IEPs). After pupil evaluations, parents are told their legal rights and then invited to waive conventional IEPs in favor of the school's ubiquitous "student services agreement." The school thus offers a unique education program to every child. Disabled youngsters are not labeled or made to feel different.

Charter schools are popular with those parents of disabled youngsters who have sought them out, often because such families want something distinct from the cumbersome procedures of conventional "special" education. In the 1997 Hudson Institute survey, among the parents who indicated that their children have disabilities or other special needs, two-thirds reported that their charter school's curriculum and teaching are better than those of the school their child would otherwise be attending.

The federal charter study reports that "In most states, the percentage of students with disabilities in charter schools was similar to the percentage of students with disabilities in all public schools" in those states.[11] And a 1999 report on special education commissioned by the U.S. Department of Education says, "In contrast to concern expressed by disability advocates that charter schools may exclude students with disabilities, students with disabilities are not greatly under-enrolled in charter schools. In fact, rather than excluding students with disabilities, many charter schools specifically targeted these students."[12]

Yet some persist in their claim that charters neglect the disabled. In 1997 testimony before a Congressional committee, Tim Sindelar (an attorney with the Disability Law Center in Boston) alleged "a pattern, in Massachusetts, of significant problems with admissions to charter schools and in delivery of appropriate services for children who are admitted."[13] Charter

[11] RPP International, *The State of Charter Schools: Third-Year Report*, 36.

[12] Thomas A. Fiore, Sandra H. Warren, and Erin R. Cashman, *Charter Schools and Students with Disabilities* (Washington, D.C.: U.S. Department of Education, 1999), 15. See also Thomas A. Fiore and Erin R. Cashman, *Review of Charter School Legislation Provisions Related to Students with Disabilities* (Washington, D.C.: U.S. Department of Education, 1999).

[13] Statement of Tim Sindelar before the Committee on Education and the Workforce, U.S. House of Representatives, Hearing on Charter Schools, 9 April 1997.

critic Richard Rothstein argues that "Special education presents another 'creaming' danger. . . . [A] charter school could effectively limit special education obligations by recruitment and counseling policies that might formally meet requirements but effectively discourage special education enrollment."[14] Nancy Zollers of Boston College's School of Education alleges that for-profit charter schools in Massachusetts "have done a decent job of including students with mild disabilities, [but] . . . have engaged in a pattern of disregard and often blatant hostility toward students with more complicated behavioral and cognitive disabilities. The source of this pattern is . . . the profit motive." According to many of those on the front lines of the charter effort in Massachusetts, the allegations by Zollers and her coauthor were a canard. As one wrote in rejoinder, "The facts about our school were contorted, distorted, stretched, twisted, and, in some cases, simply fabricated."[15]

We acknowledge that some charter schools do not meet all their students' special needs. Part of the reason may be stinginess, malfeasance, or insensitivity, but mostly it is due to lack of experience, expertise, or resources. That this situation needs fixing does not, however, mean that greater regulatory zeal is the proper remedy. A better solution is to make sure *before* issuing a charter that the school has addressed this issue in a reasonable way — it has the staff it needs to do what it says it will do and no one is denied admission because of disability. That does not mean every charter school must accommodate every need of every disabled child. Regular public schools don't do that, either; they may well send a youngster with particular disabilities to a school across town that is better suited to that child's needs.

This allegation goes both ways: many district schools do not adequately serve children with disabilities. For example, the *Washington Post* reported in July 1998 that the District of Columbia's special education program is "in disarray," with thousands of disabled children on long (and illegal) waiting lists, backlogs for hearings reaching almost a thousand youngsters, many special education students being sent to private schools, and soaring program costs.[16] Boston College's Zollers also concedes that "public schools have not had a good track record with children with behavioral needs."[17]

---

[14] Richard Rothstein, "Charter Conundrum," *American Prospect*, July/August 1998, 55.

[15] Zollers's views are presented in Nancy J. Zollers and Arun K. Ramanathan, "For-Profit Charter Schools and Students with Disabilities: The Sordid Side of the Business of Schooling," *Phi Delta Kappan*, December 1998, 298. See also "Massachusetts Charters Assailed for Excluding Disabled," *Education Daily*, 8 December 1998. The *Kappan* published a collection of letters to the editor disputing the claims made in the Zollers and Ramanathan article, with responses by the authors. See "Backtalk," *Phi Delta Kappan*, April 1999, 626–40.

[16] Doug Struck and Valerie Strauss, "D.C. Special Ed System Still in Disarray, Report Says," *Washington Post*, 20 July 1998, B1. See also Doug Struck and Valerie Strauss, "FBI Probes Special-Ed School Used by D.C.," *Washington Post*, 29 July 1998, B1.

[17] Zollers and Ramanathan, "For-Profit Charter Schools," 302.

The real special education issue is not whether charters are adequately serving disabled youngsters but whether they are able to serve them *differently* than conventional schools. Washington's answer is a resounding no. Even as one unit of the U.S. Department of Education sponsors studies showing that disabled children are well represented and satisfactorily served by today's diverse charter schools, another branch seeks to standardize them. According to new federal regulations issued in March 1999, charter schools must serve children with disabilities in the same manner as conventional schools (regardless of whether the charter receives the requisite funds).[18]

It seems to us that charter schools are *meant* to be different, even in special education. To insist that they model themselves on conventional schools in their treatment of disabled youngsters is akin to saying that every hospital must perform every operation in exactly the same way. If so, there is not much point in having charter schools, at least not for youngsters with disabilities.

Allegation # 7
Charter schools balkanize American society and weaken the principal institution that knits us together.

Paul Gillis, president of the Virginia NAACP, said this of charter schools: "We're not going to sit idly by and see our school systems wrecked. From all that we can see . . . these charter schools are hell-bent on taking us back to the 1950s and '60s and beyond." Speaking to Old Dominion legislators just before they voted on a charter bill, Gillis warned, "We're going to watch your vote. If you vote against us, we're going to come after you."[19] (The bill passed the third time, though Virginia has one of the country's weaker charter laws.)

Do charter schools invite segregation? Most, if oversubscribed, are required to use a lottery or other random method to admit students, but the nature of some schools and neighborhoods is such that they attract members of specific ethnic or affinity groups. When a school's founders are Hispanic community activists, the surrounding community is almost entirely Hispanic, and the school's mission stresses bilingual education, is it surprising that 95 percent of its applicants are Hispanic?

When does specialization become balkanization? This is an enduring issue in discussions about the rise and future of the "common school," which Boston University's Charles Glenn has called "the most powerful

[18] U.S. Department of Education, "I.D.E.A. '97 (Part B Final Regulations)," Washington, D.C., March 1999.

[19] Jan Cienski, "Charter Schools Criticized," *Free Lance Star*, 21 January 1997. That bill, as well as the one that later passed, did contain antidiscrimination provisions.

TABLE 7–1. Estimated Percentages of Enrollment in Charter Schools (1997–98) and All Public Schools in the Twenty-four Charter States (1996–97) by Racial/Ethnic Category[a]

Racial Categories	Students Enrolled in Charter School Sample (1997–98)	Students Enrolled in All Public Schools in 24 Charter States (1996–97)
White, not of Hispanic origin	51.8%	58.7%
Black, not of Hispanic origin	19.0%	16.8%
Hispanic	20.6%	19.3%
Asian or Pacific Islander	3.7%	4.2%
American Indian or Alaska Native	3.8%	1.0%
Other	1.1%	N/A

[a]RPP International, *The State of Charter Schools: Third-Year Report* (Washington, D.C.: U.S. Department of Education, 1999), 30.

possible means of forming the attitudes, loyalties, and beliefs of the next generation and thus of 'molding citizens' to a common pattern."[20]

Consider Sankofa Shule, one of Michigan's several Afro-centric charter schools. This unconventional institution observes African Independence Day and Malcolm X Remembrance Day instead of traditional holidays, and its daily "affirmation" (recited by the entire school) begins, "I pledge to my African nation. . . ."[21] The District of Columbia's much-publicized Marcus Garvey Charter School, before it was closed in 1998, enrolled only black children — surely a result of its unabashed Afro-centrism. The faculty, board, and students at the A.G.B.U. Alex and Marie Manoogian Charter School in Southfield, Michigan are almost all Armenian. (It was a private Armenian church school before it received a charter.)[22] The N.F.L.-Y.E.T. Academy in South Phoenix is almost completely Hispanic, as is the Raul Yzaguirre Charter School in Houston. We have also encountered Native American charter schools, schools attended primarily by Mormons, a school comprised largely of Iraqi/Muslim farmers, even an Amish charter in Kansas.

When it comes to race, however, charter schools as a group are at least as well integrated as regular public schools. (See Table 7–1.)

State data vary. Charters in Connecticut, Massachusetts, Michigan, Minnesota, Florida, and Texas enroll a much lower percentage of white

[20] Charles Glenn, *The Myth of the Common School* (Amherst, Mass.: The University of Massachusetts Press, 1988), 236.
[21] Thomas Toch, "The New Education Bazaar," *U.S. News and World Report*, 27 April 1998.
[22] Toch, 46.

students than their public school counterparts, while Connecticut, Massachusetts, and Texas charters enroll higher percentages of Hispanic students. In Alaska, California, Colorado, and Georgia, the fraction of charter students who are white is larger than in the state's public school system as a whole. The federal study also found that 72 percent of charter schools are not "racially distinct" from their surrounding school district, that 16 percent have a much higher percentage of non-white students than their surrounding district, and that only 12 percent of charter schools have a much lower percentage of non-white students than the district. The federal analysts found "no evidence that charter schools disproportionately serve white and economically advantaged students. . . . [C]harter schools generally mirror the state's racial composition" of students in all public schools.[23]

The involvement of clergy and religious organizations in charter schools brings another balkanization controversy. Church officials in Chicago, New York, and Detroit have proposed closing parochial schools and opening public charters in their place. Others hope to create charter schools alongside continuing parochial schools in order to serve more low-income youngsters. Religious leaders in Grand Rapids, Newark, and Tallahassee have already been instrumental in opening charters while striving to maintain a clear separation between church and state.

A New Jersey federal judge has ruled that the operation of a charter school in a church facility does not violate the First Amendment.[24] In an attempt to deal with this issue proactively, the New York State Charter School Resource Center has issued guidelines on the "role that religious institutions can play in expanding educational opportunities through the state's charter law."[25] According to the Resource Center's legal advisors— mindful of New York State's stringent constitutional provisions as well as the federal Bill of Rights—careful precautions must be taken and various "bright lines" drawn in order to maximize these educational opportunities while minimizing wrongful entanglements.

Rev. R. B. Holmes, Jr., who is pastor of a Baptist church in Tallahassee, says of the charter school whose board he chairs, "It's truly a public school. There's a role for a community of faith in the public education system. You can't use tax dollars to perpetuate your religious beliefs. But you can use tax dollars to make sure every child gets a good education and parents have some options."[26]

[23] RPP International, *The State of Charter Schools: Third-Year Report*, 2, 30–32.

[24] E. E. Mazier, "Establishment Clause was not Bar to Running Charter School in Space Leased from Church," *New Jersey Lawyer*, 18 October 1998.

[25] William H. Mellor, Clint Bolick, Dana Berliner, and Matthew Barry, "Questions and Answers about the Involvement of Religious Organizations and Individuals in Charter Schools," Washington, D.C., Institute for Justice, 17 February 1999.

[26] Lynn Schnaiberg, "Buildings in Hand, Church Leaders Float Charter Ideas," *Education Week*, 10 February 1999.

The "balkanization" charge must also contend with the fact that some charter schools are designed for specific groups of children. The Chicago Preparatory High School serves youngsters who struggle with substance abuse. The Lowell Middlesex Academy in Massachusetts specializes in educating high school dropouts. There are also charters focused on teaching the arts, technology, the environment, automotive engineering, and other specialties, both mainstream and offbeat. Each tends to attract a distinctive clientele, self-selected to be sure, but invariably less "diverse" than a random cross-section of the local population.

Is this good or bad? One's conclusion must hinge on whether one is more taken with schools that have internal coherence of program and community combined with fairly homogeneous demographics, or with schools that boast a rainbow of students but do not engage any particular community or feature a coherent education plan. Sure, the occasional school manages to do both. But if one must pick, which approach does the country more good?

The chartering process contains some built-in safeguards against divisive schools. First is the requirement that the school admit anyone who applies (or, if oversubscribed, use random selection) and not discriminate on such grounds as race, ethnicity, or religion. Another is the due diligence that responsible sponsors perform before issuing (or renewing) a charter. Public money should not flow to schools that preach segregation, racial superiority, or hatred, even if there is a "market" for such things.

For those unsatisfied by these inherent mechanisms, additional steps can be taken to enlist charter schools in the quest for racial diversity. But these typically cause problems of their own. North Carolina charters are under attack for enrolling *too many* minority children. The state requires that charter schools reflect the "racial and ethnic composition" of their communities. Healthy Start Academy in Durham does not. Under the rules, it is supposed to have 55 percent white students, but in reality only two of its 168 pupils were white at the end of year one. Yet its kindergartners boosted their scores from the 42nd to the 99th percentile on the Iowa Test of Basic Skills. Its second graders lifted their scores from the 34th percentile to the 75th. Should this school be punished because it has attracted mostly African-American students?

Indeed, North Carolina's minority families have flocked to charter schools. Over half (53.1 percent) of the students enrolled in North Carolina charter schools are black, compared to 30.8 percent in district schools,[27] with 13 of the 34 charter schools operating in 1997–98 having enrollments more than 85 percent black. Thus, thriving schools like Healthy Start may be in danger of being shut down. But Vernon Robinson (see profile in chapter 9) notes that this school neither discriminates in its ad-

---

[27] RPP International, *The State of Charter Schools: Third-Year Report*, 33.

missions nor teaches Afro-centrism in its classrooms, and that it has adver-
tised in churches and newspapers in white areas. He asserts: "We must
decide whether the desire of parents and children to learn should take
precedence over the experts and their quest for diversity. . . . At some
point, we must let our people go to the schools they want to attend rather
than where someone else wants them to go."[28]

Instead of government-style enforcement of racial balance, a market-
based alternative such as Robinson advocates would leave it to people's
good judgment to set checks and balances on charter schools. This approach, most evident in Arizona, assumes that there won't be much demand for separatist schools. An effective way to help such a marketplace
police itself is to make it more transparent, providing maximum information to consumers. When people see that a given school is divisive, most
will shun it.

Today we find a hodgepodge of approaches: (1) a few charter laws that
seek to enforce "acceptable" demographics; (2) some sponsors that are
conscientious about ensuring equity and diversity in charter schools; and
(3) some locations where charters are freely given and the antidote to balkanization is the marketplace. We believe that the second and third options
are preferable. The marketplace will usually do a decent job, but charter
sponsors should also be vigilant. By setting "boundary conditions" for
schools before approving them, sponsors can go a long way toward
achieving both excellence and equity. Here are six criteria that sponsors
might use when determining which charter applications to approve:

1. Charter schools must not discriminate against students (or others)
   on the basis of race, ethnicity, gender, age, or disability.
2. Charter applications that portend racial, religious, or ethnic conflict or division shall not be approved.
3. Charter schools must not teach or practice religion.
4. Charter schools will instruct students on the meaning of the U.S.
   Constitution and the values that underlie it (e.g., freedom, equality,
   justice, and the rule of law).
5. Charter schools will respect each person's rights, including freedom
   of speech.
6. As public schools, charter schools will take seriously their responsibilities toward the well-being of their communities.

So long as boundary conditions such as these are in place before charters
are granted—and are then responsibly monitored—the chips should be
allowed to fall where they may.

[28] "Closing Charters," *Wall Street Journal* (editorial), 6 July 1998, A14.

Allegation # 8
Charter schools invite profiteering from public education. Many people are out to make a quick buck, and charter schools allow them to stuff their pockets with taxpayer dollars while shortchanging kids.

Writing in *U.S. News and World Report*, Tom Toch alleged that many of Arizona's charter high schools were designed by corporate operators to exploit the fact that the state only requires secondary students to attend four hours a day, with the firms running the schools pocketing the difference. Some save additional dollars by substituting self-paced computer instruction for real teachers.[29] What Toch failed to mention is that the four-hour law is also used aggressively by district-based alternative high schools in Arizona, and that many of the charter schools that employ this approach enroll a high percentage of drop-outs, at-risk youngsters, and children of migrant workers who would not otherwise be in school at all.

Yes, charter schools can cause dollar signs to light up in people's eyes. A couple in Grand Blanc, Michigan turned a private school they owned into a charter school in 1996 and began charging it $200,000 a year in rent—thrice the rate paid by nearby schools. Some charter heads pay themselves generously. Some contract with their own firms or their relatives to furnish instructional or management services. But the profit motive runs in multiple directions. Some local sponsors use the charter law to pad their budgets. For example, several Arizona districts have sponsored charter schools far across the state. This "long-distance chartering" brings revenues into districts that commandeer a share of the schools' per-pupil allotment (sometimes up to 10 percent, more often 2 or 3 percent). Arizona is the best-known locus of long-distance chartering, but not the only one. California has several examples, particularly its "cyber schools."[30]

The most controversial charter proposals involve for-profit firms seeking to operate the school itself.[31] In 1998, opponents mounted a full-scale attack on this practice in Massachusetts. When the state granted charters to several schools run by private companies, the public school establishment

[29] Thomas Toch, "The New Education Bazaar," *U.S. News and World Report*, 27 April 1998.

[30] As we write, steps are underway in Arizona to curb several of the easiest paths to profit via charter schools by, for example, limiting what districts can "charge" charter schools that they sponsor and by curbing various forms of "up-front" funding for the charter schools themselves. Of course this is apt to make it harder for "mom and pop" schools to be launched—and to favor the charter operators with deep pockets and established credit. No good deed goes unpunished. In 1999, California cracked down on cyber-charters serving home-schooled children who live far from the school site.

[31] One example of a critique of the for-profit motive in education can be seen in Alex Molnar, *Giving Kids the Business: The Commercialization of America's Schools* (Boulder, Colo.: Westview Press, 1996).

and its legislative allies erupted. "We're talking about profiteering here," charged Senator Marc Pacheco, a Democrat from Taunton. "Money is being taken from our public schools and being handed to for-profits." John Silber, then chairman of the State Board of Education, soberly noted that the companies are not yet making any money, and if they "do not outperform the public schools, they will be discredited."[32] Furthermore, he added, "The evidence now is that it [granting charters to schools managed by private companies] works." According to Governor Paul Cellucci, "Whether or not charter schools are privately managed is irrelevant as long as they provide a quality education."[33]

Another dust-up occurred in Dayton, Ohio in early 1998, when then-superintendent James A. Williams boldly proposed that five of the city's worst-performing schools be "reconstituted" as charters run by the Edison Project. The Dayton Education Association balked, and its president insisted that her union would not stand for a "corporate takeover by a New York company."[34] But the tiff had more than local implications. According to the *Dayton Daily News*, "Because Dayton apparently is the only district in Ohio looking to Edison, that makes the community a battleground. What happens here takes on statewide significance. [Superintendent] Williams doesn't just have to persuade the local teachers' union about Edison's appeal; he has to persuade the OEA."[35]

The Ohio Education Association proved implacable. It rolled heavy artillery down the interstate to Dayton, insisting that for-profit school management firms gain no beachhead in the Buckeye State and threatening to contest any contract with the Edison Project.[36] The union managed to stymie the superintendent's proposal. But Edison's allies obtained a charter from the state board of education, enabling them to bypass the union and the politics of the local school board.[37] The school opened in September 1999.

The threat of profiteering, like that of balkanization, is real but limited. Private firms have made money from public education for years by, for example, selling textbooks, computers, and chalk to school systems. Most

---

[32] Jordana Hart and Jill Zuckerman, "For-Profit Firms Get Four of Eight Charters for Schools," *Boston Globe*, 26 February 1998, B1.

[33] Adrian Walker and Scot Lehigh, "Campaign 98: On Charter Schools, A Split Down Party Lines," *Boston Globe*, 30 March 1998.

[34] Lynn Hulsey, "Teachers Union Blasts For-Profits," *Dayton Daily News*, 10 February 1998, 2B.

[35] Ellen Belcher, "Charter-School Debate Stalls Because There's No Trust," *Dayton Daily News*, 15 January 1998, 10A.

[36] Ellen Belcher, "Dayton Is Charter Battleground," *Dayton Daily News*, 5 February 1998, 14A.

[37] Chester E. Finn, Jr. is the president of the Thomas B. Fordham Foundation; Bruno V. Manno is a trustee of the Foundation; and Gregg Vanourek is a former employee of the Foundation, which promotes education reform in Dayton, Ohio and has been active with the charter school debate mentioned here.

profit-seeking charter operators work closely with grassroots groups, and (at least outside Arizona) typically devise a structure in which the local group holds the charter — and is accountable for the school's results — while outsourcing the school's day-to-day work to the private firm. In all these arrangements, the public's most important safeguard is the fact that nobody can profit for long from a bad school. The only way to make money from charter schools over time is for them to attract and retain customers by providing an effective education.

Allegation # 9
Charter schools are a stalking horse for vouchers. The "agenda behind the agenda" is to accustom people to a partial education marketplace and then surprise them with the full Monty.

In the *Phi Delta Kappan*, Anne C. Lewis likens charter schools to vouchers, with all their dangers and pitfalls:

> [W]ithout more reflective policy making and greater understanding of the potential effect of charter schools on public education, the eventual impact of the movement could be as great as that of vouchers. Many in our society want to break up the public school system by treating education as a commodity and making it totally subject to consumer choice. Most parents and citizens find that goal objectionable, but they could find themselves, like a frog put in a pot of cold water that is heated slowly, unable to notice a change until it is too late.[38]

Though the enactment of charter legislation can be entangled with the politics of vouchers, it is also the case that some charter advocates support vouchers while others are opposed. (And some voucher proponents favor charter schools, while others do not.)[39] The charter idea transcends party and ideology. It reflects no single agenda. A recent report finds as many as twelve discrete purposes embodied in charter laws: providing a better education to needy youngsters, developing innovative practices, running schools according to new education visions, operating more efficiently, injecting choice and competition, making education more accountable, and on and on.[40] Some would add vouchers to that list of hoped-for charter consequences. Others abhor the prospect.

---

[38] Anne C. Lewis, "Politicians, Research Findings, and School Choice," *Phi Delta Kappan*, June 1998, 723.

[39] For example, Bryan C. Hassel supports charter schools but not vouchers. See his chapter, "The Case for Charter Schools," in *Learning from School Choice*, eds. Paul E. Peterson and Bryan C. Hassel (Washington, D.C.: The Brookings Institution, 1998), 33. And renowned economist Milton Friedman supports vouchers but is not enamored with charter schools (see chapter 8).

[40] Paul Hill, Larry Pierce, Robin Lake, and Paul Herdman, *Charter Schools: Accountability for Results* (Seattle: University of Washington Center for Reinventing Public Education, 1998), 21.

Charters and vouchers both introduce customer choice and competition into education. But the differences between the two strategies are at least as great as the similarities. The central distinction, of course, is that children armed with vouchers can attend private schools, ordinarily including church-affiliated schools. By contrast, charter schools remain *public* schools, open to all who choose to attend and accountable to public authorities for their continued existence.

Allegation # 10
Charter schools do not go far enough. There will never be enough of them. They are hard to replicate. They function more like a pressure-release valve for dissidents than as a fundamental structural change.

This charge—alone among those in this chapter—is often heard from critics on the right as well as from the school "establishment." From the school establishment, it is voiced by "systemic" reformers eager to change the whole of public education for all children. From the right, it is brought by people convinced that charters do not produce the needed revolution.

These critics could be prescient. Charters could remain a marginal reform, either because the barriers to entry are so high or because they don't appeal to many families. Meanwhile, they run a considerable risk of being re-regulated into clones of conventional schools. Later chapters are devoted to an exploration of these issues. For now, we simply applaud the fact that charters aren't the only significant reform underway in U.S. education. With various forms of "systemic" reform flanking them on one side, and all manner of school choice strategies on the other, the country will have ample opportunity to compare the effectiveness of charters with different approaches to education improvement.

In this chapter, we have examined a double handful of charges leveled by critics against charter schools. Next, we enter the political arena to see what their opponents actually do to fight them.

8

POLITICAL BATTLEGROUNDS

> For those who seem to be intimidated or afraid of educational reform, we would like to offer a challenge: put politics, money, and special interests aside momentarily and spend a day at [the charter school my children attend], observing and interacting with the kids, then join our family for dinner afterwards. Ask questions, listen to the kids' answers, then make your decisions.
>
> *Michigan parent*

JIM AND FAWN SPADY don't look like warriors. An attractive, successful, and energetic young couple living near Seattle, they became deeply frustrated with the local public schools. As Fawn recalls, "When I tried to get involved, one principal said he was happy to have me do bake sales, but nothing that involved academics."[1] They reluctantly opted for private school for their children, but refused to give up on public schools. Jim explains, "OK, we've taken care of our kids. But so many people have no choice; they're left behind."[2]

In 1995, after the lower house of the state legislature passed a strong charter law that died in the Senate, the Spadys drafted an initiative to allow for "independent public schools" launched by certified teachers. The state's major teachers' union, the Washington Education Association (WEA), and the Democratic Party opposed it.

The Spadys failed to get the necessary 180,000 signatures for the November ballot, but tried again the next year. This time they obtained over 195,000 signatures.[3] They also modified their proposal into a strong charter plan that was more parent- than teacher-centered.

---

[1] Carol Innerst, "Pair Let Voters Rule on Charter Schools," *Washington Times*, 23 October 1996.

[2] Barbara D. Phillips, "Parents Take the Initiative," *Wall Street Journal*, 10 October 1995, A20.

[3] In Washington, citizens can place measures before the electorate on the statewide ballot—called a direct initiative—or can place before the legislature initiatives that, unless enacted by

Alongside the Spadys' charter initiative (I-177), the 1996 ballot included an even more controversial voucher measure. By October, more than $2 million had been spent for and against these measures, including over $200,000 of the Spadys' own money. Besides the two teachers' unions, opponents this time included the PTA, the state's business leadership, the League of Women Voters, the Anti-Defamation League, and the Northwest AIDS Foundation. The Spadys were branded right-wing ideologues (they were staunch Democrats) whose risky scheme "would drain money from the public schools, skim rich white kids, and abandon all manner of accountability to parents and educators."[4]

I-177 was defeated, 64–36 percent, at the polls, but foul play was involved. The state's Public Disclosure Commission found numerous violations of law by WEA, including failure to disclose more than $400,000 in secret NEA donations (among the most serious campaign violations in Washington's history), illegal transfers of money, and formation of an unregistered political action committee. In early 1998, WEA and NEA officials settled with the state, paying a fine of $430,000, acknowledging that they had broken the law, though claiming it was unintentional. According to a *Tacoma News Tribune* editorial, "Washingtonians cast their ballots that year [1996] without ever learning that the anti-charter campaign was being bankrolled from the deep pockets of a national union with a vested interest in the educational status quo."[5]

In 1997 and 1998, the Spadys tried yet again. Although Democratic Governor Gary Locke and the legislature passed a budget that included $5 million for charter schools, and a charter bill cleared the House, that bill did not reach the Senate floor for a third consecutive year — and then a fourth. WEA used its considerable political muscle to persuade every Democrat on the Ways and Means Committee to oppose the measure. Goliath again prevailed.

From Hostility to Wary Embrace

The more the charter movement spreads, the more enemies it attracts. Yet there is also some evidence that opposition diminishes over time. We have identified four stages in the evolution of the education establishment's re-

---

the legislature without amendment, then go on the ballot. The Spadys shifted from the former approach to the latter, partly to avail themselves of the extra six months that this gave them to gather signatures. Faced again with strong union opposition, the House passed an alternative bill but the Senate was only willing to adopt a weak charter law with tight caps on the number of schools, severe funding disadvantages, and a feeble appeal system. The Spadys and their allies rejected that Faustian bargain, which meant the question would go to the voters.

[4] Michelle Malkin, "Washington State's Chance for Choice," *Wall Street Journal*, 4 November 1996.

[5] "No Excusing WEA Election Violations," *Tacoma News Tribune*, 3 March 1998, A8.

action to charters. These are most evident at the local level, but they have counterparts in state capitals, even on the banks of the Potomac.

1. Stop them cold: prevent any charter schools from opening.
2. Keep them few and weak: burden them with so many limits and regulations that their numbers remain small and those that start have scant autonomy.
3. Out-do them: compete with them in order to minimize the number of children leaving district schools for charter schools.
4. Accept them: put the charter idea to work for the system's own purposes, as R&D sites or as a framework for innovations that are hard to effect under the usual rules.

Here we look at the first two responses. In the next chapter, we examine the third and fourth.

Efforts to block charters entirely are manifest both in moves to derail enabling legislation (as happened in Washington State) and (less often) via judicial strategies. Constitutional challenges have been mounted in California, Massachusetts, Michigan, Colorado, and Wisconsin.[6] Locally, there are innumerable instances of school districts rejecting charter applications, sometimes on grounds of merit but more often out of petty politics or jealous determination to cling to "their" pupils and revenues.

Once legislation is enacted and the first charters appear, their foes do not go gently into the night. They criticize the schools for chaotic beginnings, unconventional buildings, hiring uncertified teachers, rejecting or expelling children, contracting with private firms, and so on. If they cannot stop the charter movement altogether, they tackle the schools one by one and weigh them down with restrictions like those that burden regular public schools: union contracts, uniform pay scales, limited curricular or fiscal independence, and similar handicaps.

According to charter watcher Joe Nathan, who recently studied nine states, over 90 percent of respondents reported that teachers' unions and school board associations strove to keep charter sponsorship exclusively in the hands of local boards (rather than state boards, public universities, etc.).[7] "For all practical purposes," says a California school head, "making the district the only charter-granting entity restricts what a charter proposer can do. The person who has the chalk draws the line."

Weak charter laws usually result from legislative compromise. According to a Massachusetts policymaker, "The cap on the number of charters that we could have was nothing more than an artificial compromise to get the charter legislation passed." Bay State lawmakers also had to agree to

---

[6] The charter laws in Massachusetts, Michigan, and Colorado were upheld. In California, the suit is still making its way through the courts.

[7] Joe Nathan, "Heat and Light in the Charter Movement," *Phi Delta Kappan*, March 1998, 504.

reimburse school districts for funds lost when students leave for charters. Such compromises are more the norm than the exception. Researcher Bryan Hassel points out that "Legislatures across the country have departed substantially from the 'charter school idea' in the charter laws they have adopted."[8]

The hamstringing does not cease when a charter law is signed. Opponents then seek to wrap the resulting schools in red tape through further legislation, executive order, or judicial fiat, sometimes via zoning, limited access to retirement systems, and plain harassment. In early 1999, the California legislature was almost persuaded by the teachers' union to mandate collective bargaining for all the state's charter schools, while the Ohio legislature capped the number of such schools in the Buckeye State. New Jersey flirted with restricting the number of pupils who could attend charters. The Massachusetts legislature briefly slapped charter schools with a requirement that board members submit detailed data on personal income, investments, debts, and property holdings, even though superintendents and district school committee members were under no such obligation.[9]

North Carolina's charter program was nearly undone by the issue of whether charter employees could participate in the Teachers' and State Employees' Retirement System. The legislature intended to include them, but the state treasurer raised technical and financial concerns. One solution suggested was to place charter schools under local school systems, empowering the districts to appoint and remove members of their governing boards. (The issue was settled by the legislature in October 1998 by offering each charter school a one-time opportunity to join the state retirement system.)[10]

When asked about features of North Carolina's charter law that he would change, Vernon Robinson (see profile in chapter 9) answered, "The supply of charter seats is limited by restrictions on enrollment increases,

---

[8] Bryan C. Hassel, "Charter Schools: Politics and Practice in Four States," in *Learning from School Choice*, eds. Paul E. Peterson and Bryan C. Hassel (Washington, D.C.: Brookings Institution Press, 1998), 250.

[9] "An Onerous Rule for Charter Schools," *Boston Globe* (editorial), 3 March 1998, A10. (This requirement has since been greatly relaxed.)

[10] Almost immediately after this issue was resolved, another one emerged. The North Carolina charter law requires that 75 percent of the teachers in grades K-5 and 50 percent of those teaching grades 6–12 be licensed. In mid-November 1998, a newspaper article published state department of education teacher data for charter schools purporting to show that 23 of the 34 charters in operation in 1997 were in violation of this requirement. (See Tim Simmons, "Most Charters Fall Short of Teacher Standards," *Raleigh News and Observer*, 13 November 1998.) After several days of exchanging charges back and forth, the state records were shown to be mostly inaccurate. For example, charter teachers who are certified out of state show up as unlicensed in North Carolina. State Board of Education Chairman Phil Kirk commented, "I regret that the department put into writing information that is of questionable accuracy." See Tim Simmons, "School's Fury Gives State Pause," *Raleigh News and Observer*, 24 November 1998.

caps on the number of schools per district per year, and a state cap of 100 schools. These restrictions must go." But a Tarheel legislator takes a different tack: "The bureaucracy," he insists, "through its rules and regulations, subverted the intent of the legislature and made its own policy about charter schools."

During the summer of 1998, the District of Columbia was preparing to greet its first large batch of charter schools. (Three had opened earlier.) As the number of new charters rose, local politicians and the school system began to signal alarm. D.C. Council member Jack Evans (then a candidate for mayor) described "the whole [charter] movement [as] very troubling" and urged a moratorium on the issuance of charters. Other candidates sought to cap the maximum number of such schools. (The mayoral winner, Anthony Williams, is an unabashed proponent of school competition in general and charter schools in particular.) On several occasions, Superintendent Arlene Ackerman has voiced misgivings about charter schools and recommended a go-slow approach to their creation. Yet in fall 1999, the District of Columbia found itself with 27 charter schools enrolling some 7,000 youngsters—nearly 10 percent of the city's public school population. Upwards of $61 million followed these children. A veteran observer of D.C. education politics commented that "charter schools may be perceived as a threat or enemy of traditional schools. And this could be the beginning of some very difficult times."[11]

As we noted in the previous chapter, the "financial drain" argument assumes that all revenues associated with a child's education somehow belong to the *system* rather than to the school the child actually attends. It also takes for granted the perpetuation of traditional district budget practices, whereby practically all spending decisions get made in the superintendent's office. The fiscal impact of charter schools would be quite different if districts (or states) moved to pupil-based funding, where money follows children and individual schools make their own budget choices. That might not end financial strife, but it would stop central offices from protecting favorite programs at schools' expense, put all schools (including charters) on equal footing, and encourage them to find creative ways of sharing resources and squeezing the most from available funds.

CHARTER OPPONENTS

We observe continuing—and ever more sophisticated—hostility toward the charter idea from several directions, especially from teachers' unions, school boards, and superintendents. Yet not all charter critics are moved by blind devotion to the status quo. We also see plenty of anxiety concern-

---

[11] Valerie Strauss, "Charter School Movement Growing in D.C. amid Questions, Concerns," *Washington Post*, 8 September 1998, C1, C10. These numbers are preliminary estimates.

ing legitimate issues such as jobs, accountability, and the future of public education.

Teachers' Unions: A Changing Tune?

The initial reaction to charter schools by national, state, and most local teachers' unions was defiance. When the first charter proposal appeared in Minnesota in 1991, the unions, recognizing the fundamental power shift that it entailed, rose up in protest. The Minnesota Education Association called the proposal "a costly hoax," predicted that charter schools "may turn out to be the biggest boondoggle since New Coke," and asserted that they "are just plain bad public policy."[12]

The Michigan Education Association (MEA) was pivotal in getting Michigan's first charter law declared unconstitutional in 1994, effectively halting the flow of funds to the state's newborn charter schools. According to a Michigan teacher, "As a 25-year public school veteran and former union member, I was shocked at MEA's all-out attack on our charter school law. They were effective in killing our initial law and almost shutting down this charter school. They obviously have lost any focus they might have had on teaching and learning."[13]

But the union had other arrows for its bow besides legislative and courtroom activity. An MEA officer threatened a state university president that union members would refuse to accept his students as teacher trainees, would not donate money, and would decline to participate in university training programs if that institution chartered schools that did not meet the MEA's standards, which included adherence to collective bargaining agreements.[14]

In July 1998, days before the Milwaukee Common Council was to approve the first city-sponsored charter schools in the country, the Milwaukee Teachers' Education Association (MTEA) filed a lawsuit arguing that the charter measure is unconstitutional. MTEA President Paulette Copeland said, "This is just one more step in dismantling Milwaukee's public schools," charging that the charter program's "injurious payment scheme" will force them to cut programs and lay off teachers. Taking issue with the union's stand, State Senator Alberta Darling (R-River Hills) said

[12] Joe Nathan, *Charter Schools: Creating Hope and Opportunity for American Education* (San Francisco: Jossey-Bass Publishers, 1996), 99.

[13] The court deemed the law unconstitutional because charter schools were not deemed to be public schools as defined under the state constitution. This led to enactment of another charter law. The original 1993 measure was, however, eventually upheld by Michigan's Supreme Court, which found that charter schools are indeed "under the ultimate and immediate control of the state and its agents," that charters can be revoked by public authorities, and that the public maintains control of the schools through these authorizing bodies.

[14] Joan Richardson, "Union Pressures State University over Charter Schools," *Detroit Free Press*, 4 June 1994, cited in Peterson and Hassel, 261.

its action "shows the disconnect between the union and the rest of the community. . . . The public will see this as being against reform."[15] School board member John Gardner voiced a blunter view: "The MTEA has one agenda with the choice and charter schools: It's . . . to kill them." John Matthews, chief of staff to Governor Tommy Thompson, lamented, "Once again, there are students caught up in union politics."[16]

As mentioned above, the California Teachers Association (CTA) launched a missile at the state's charter program in early 1999. The original California charter legislation designated the staff of charter schools as employees of the school rather than the district and exempted all charter staff from existing collective-bargaining agreements. The CTA's top legislative priority for 1999 became overturning this provision in the charter law (though about half the schools had their own collective-bargaining agreements). A bill to accomplish this end was introduced by Carol Magden, Democratic assemblywoman from San Francisco.

Eric Premack, director of the Charter Schools Development Center in Sacramento, said this bill "would take away probably the most important freedom that charter schools have. It would not only force them to bargain collectively, but to bargain as part of the existing bargaining units." The measure passed the Assembly's Democrat-controlled Education Committee, though two Democrats and all the Republicans voted nay. After vociferous opposition from charter supporters, business leaders, and other Assembly members — and a big rally on the capitol steps — a compromise was struck. It recognizes that charter employees have the right to organize themselves if they wish and to choose their own union representation.

Such battles occur in many places. The San Diego Teachers' Association circulated rumors, leaked documents, and rigged elections in an attempt to undermine a charter school for inner-city youth.[17] A Los Angeles union leader asserts that "Charter schools . . . will do little more than take money away from the traditional public school system. There really is no need for such schools since things are generally fine as they are."

The national unions' response had the same tenor at first. In 1992, a senior National Education Association (NEA) official wrote members of Congress that the NEA was "unalterably opposed" to using federal funds to help create charter schools.[18] In 1996, American Federation of Teachers

---

[15] Daniel Bice and Joe Williams, "As City Vote Nears, Teachers Union Files Suit over Charter Schools," *Milwaukee Journal Sentinel*, 22 July 1998.

[16] Joe Williams, "Teachers Union Blamed after Talks Fail with Private Bruce Guadalupe School," *Milwaukee Journal Sentinel*, 1 October 1998.

[17] K.L. Billingsley and Pamela Riley, *The Empire Strikes Back: How California's Educational Establishment Is Hindering the Growth of Charter Schools* (San Francisco: Pacific Research Institute for Public Policy, 1995), 8–10.

[18] Joe Nathan, "Heat and Light in the Charter Movement," *Phi Delta Kappan*, March 1998, 504.

(AFT) spokeswoman Donna Fowler said, "There is a sense that charter schools could be harmful to public schools. . . . They may work for a few while siphoning resources from other schools."[19]

In time the national unions modified their tunes. But their newfound tolerance for the charter concept is enveloped in conditions and limitations. The AFT insists that charters have local school board approval; that their employees must be covered by the district bargaining agreement; that they hire only certified teachers; and that private schools not be allowed to convert to charter status. The NEA has made similar demands. Adding such conditions to a charter program is like announcing that one favors airplanes so long as they don't have pilots, propellers, or wings. The essence of the concept is diluted, and chances dim that any significant number of charter schools will come into existence.

Yet both unions have also launched pilot charter projects of their own. The NEA has initiated schools in Colorado, Connecticut, Hawaii, Arizona, and California.[20] The AFT has worked through some of its local affiliates to create partnerships with charter schools in Texas and California. Explains Gayle Fallon, president of the Houston Federation of Teachers, "[T]he AFT is flexible. They say 'This is the national position, but if it doesn't work for you, you don't have to follow it.' The attitude is that if the local is happy and it's working, it's okay."

She describes her own view, and the stance of the Houston union, in these terms:

> I've been relatively supportive of charter schools, with a couple of conditions. It has to have a reason for existing, a strong accountability system, and a good educational plan. I've been very critical of some weak programs that have come up. We have a lot of ownership of the Raul Yzaguirre Charter School; I sit on the board of the Tejano Center, which runs it. The AFT flew in a staff member to help write the charter application. As for Wesley [another inner-city Houston charter school led by celebrated principal Thaddeus Lott], we have a long history. I sent my godson there. When they wanted to become a charter it was for all the right reasons. They had a good program and wanted to be left alone. There are some others that we've worked with. There are a lot of things they don't know how to do. On the whole, we have a pretty decent working relationship with most of the charters.

According to Mark Knapp, president of the NEA's San Diego chapter, by launching their own charter schools the unions hope to show that collective bargaining agreements need not hinder education quality or reform. Moreover, union officials can scarcely avoid noticing that teachers across

---

[19] Carol Innerst, "Charter Schools Get Mixed Reports," *Washington Times*, 4 August 1996.

[20] The project is being independently evaluated (via site visits and case studies) by a team of researchers from the University of California, Los Angeles.

the country are drawn to charter schools. Andrea DiLorenzo of the NEA's Center for the Advancement of Public Education remarked that "This is not just politically savvy—there are members we know who want to do this."[21] Another union official has observed that the charter movement is like a train, and if the NEA tries to stop it, "It's going to run us over."[22] A Minnesota teacher echoed that sentiment: "[J]ust once, I would like to see our union get in front of an issue like charter schools that have much to offer. . . . Wake up!"[23] A California teacher remarked, "The union tried to set up a lot of confrontations as we were organizing this school. I don't understand why they opposed this school. This is something the parents wanted to do. The union really has to change its outlook if it's going to try to get people like me involved in it again."

A 1998 NEA study of charter teachers reveals overall satisfaction and "reasonably high" morale.[24] By a three-to-one margin, they would choose to teach in a charter school again. The most frequent response they gave when queried as to why they chose a charter school is "Freedom to teach the way I want."[25]

What are we to make of the national unions' professed interest in charter schools even as many of their state and local affiliates remain on the warpath? It's a complicated picture. We have met thoughtful teacher unionists who are attuned to the long-term well-being of children, not to mention their own professional and organizational survival. Some now embrace charter schools or close facsimiles. This attests to their judgment, to the power of the charter idea, or to the urgency of the education problems that the country faces.

Houston's Fallon is one such. So is her colleague to the north, Adam Urbanski, president of the Rochester [New York] Teachers Association and AFT vice president. Urbanski has produced his own compelling vision of a transformed system of public education that closely resembles the charter concept—and contemplates a profound rethinking of the role of unions in school reform:

> Instead of giving up on public schools altogether . . . why not make public schools more like private? . . . [T]he way to make public schools more effective is to emulate some of the desirable features of private schools: small size of schools and smaller class size; less bureaucracy and fewer layers of adminis-

[21] Lynn Schnaiberg, "In Midst of Skepticism and Scrutiny, NEA's Five Charter Schools Push On," *Education Week*, 11 March 1998.
[22] "Teachers' Unions Joining Experiment with Charter Schools," *New York Times*, 22 September 1996.
[23] Quoted in Joe Nathan, *Charter Schools*, 113.
[24] Julia E. Koppich, Patricia Holmes, and Margaret L. Plecki, *New Rules, New Roles? The Professional Work Lives of Charter School Teachers* (Washington, D.C.: National Education Association, 1998), iv.
[25] Ibid., iv, 23. More than one response was possible.

tration; more choice and more market dynamics; and, most importantly, the right to set and enforce high standards of conduct and academic rigor.[26]

Urbanski heads a new organization called the Teacher Union Reform Network (TURN), whose mission is to craft a vision of unions attuned to student achievement and teacher professionalism. Meanwhile, NEA President Bob Chase talks of a "new unionism" in much the same language.

We have been around education politics long enough to take such proclamations with a spoon of salt. But we also see promising signs of adaptation to a changing environment. It is clear that the public favors bold school reform. It is also clear that the unions must ultimately be responsive to their members—the teachers themselves—the vast majority of whom care deeply about education quality and children's welfare, are understandably nervous about job security, and worry about reversing the country's hard-won commitments to education equity. Every year, more teachers express interest in the charter option, the good it can do for children, and the professional opportunities it affords educators. Their organizations are well aware of this—and aware, too, that they have all but marginalized themselves in the eyes of charter teachers.

The NEA study points out that 68 percent of charter teachers say that there is no local union involvement in their schools, with this number mushrooming to 89 percent in start-up charters. Seventeen percent admit—on a union-sponsored survey—that "no teacher union association or involvement" was one of their reasons for choosing to teach in a charter school.[27]

It is not too surprising, under the circumstances, that the NEA and AFT would rethink their stance toward such schools. Yet the lion's share of their interaction with charters remains confrontational at the state and local levels. On a few occasions, this has led to organizational schizophrenia. For example, when Joan Heffernan, a veteran teacher in Norwich, Connecticut, decided to launch a charter school after her district quashed the expansion of a program she had created, she was recruited to join the NEA's charter initiative and help start a school in Norwich. What they didn't bank on was opposition from the NEA's local affiliate and the local school board. Even union charter schools, it seems, may encounter union opposition! (Eventually, the Norwich school obtained its charter from the state board of education.)[28]

---

[26] Adam Urbanski, "Make Public Schools More Like Private," *Education Week*, 31 January 1996, 31. Urbanski's vision recalls Albert Shanker's 1988 speech outlining the charter school idea.

[27] Koppich et al., *New Rules, New Roles?* 23, 31.

[28] Schnaiberg, "NEA's Five Charter Schools Push On."

School Boards and Superintendents

If the teachers' unions resemble battleships steaming into statewide combat against strong charter laws, then local boards and administrators are more like tanks shooting at individual schools. In Colorado, where local boards have much sway over charter schools, the Adams 12 School District is famously hostile to the idea (except for a gifted-and-talented school launched by a board member). It was the only district in the state to file an *amicus* brief on Denver's side when that city's school board denied a charter to the Thurgood Marshall Middle School. District 12 has also been enmeshed in interminable hostilities with the Academy of Charter Schools, a Core Knowledge school that is also Colorado's largest charter. The district gave this school the lowest per-pupil operating revenue (80 percent of the district's own figure) of any charter school in the state—and then offered to boost it to 89 percent if the growth-minded school agreed to cap its enrollment. (This Faustian bargain was speedily rejected by the charter board.)

Several hundred miles to the west, on the flank of the spectacular Sangre de Cristo mountains, little Crestone Charter School was inundated with district-generated paperwork (including having to report its attendance *twice* a day). It was also hampered by a locally imposed fiscal straitjacket, kept on a year-at-a-time charter, and plagued by student and staff attrition as a result of ceaseless tiffs with the school district, which resents the charter school drawing as many as a quarter of the small community's student population.

Examining the Massachusetts scene, researchers Tom Loveless and Claudia Jasin witnessed angry school system reactions to the emergence of charter proposals. Typically, they report, a local district forecasts huge financial losses due to charter-induced pupil flight, then threatens "the elimination of art and advanced placement classes, possible teacher layoffs, reductions in sports programs, the closing of after-school services, and an end to tutoring programs."

Loveless and Jasin say this tactic has paid off:

Community reaction was swift and dramatic. Local newspapers ran editorials against the new schools and their founders. One editorial cartoon showed a charter founder in a trench coat, lewdly beckoning to shocked passersby. Town meetings were convened at which speaker after speaker condemned the charters, proclaiming that they took money away from public schools. In one town, rumors spread that disciplinary action would be taken against teachers who had any contact with charter officials. . . . In still another town, a charter school founder reported that students calling her a "charter whore" baited her children into fights. When one of her children started having nightmares, she pulled him out of school. When the harassment continued, she ended her relationship with the charter school, sold her house, and moved away, leaving the town that had been home for 16 years.[29]

In New York City, school system chancellor Rudy Crew teamed up with Randi Weingarten, head of the powerful United Federation of Teachers, to oppose Governor George Pataki's 1998 charter bill. The Governor played hardball, however, threatening to veto a juicy pay raise for legislators if they did not pass this legislation. Even then, the well-organized opponents forced significant concessions, including a cap of 100 schools for the entire state, half of them to be sponsored (if at all) by the charter-averse Board of Regents.

Other Foes

Sparring with teachers' unions and school boards would seem to be fist-icuffs enough, but round three in the charter boxing match entails jabs from other vested education interests, including teacher colleges, school administrators, disability advocacy groups, competition-wary private schools, and assorted critics.

Although the legislature authorized the University of North Carolina to sponsor charter schools, the university president advised his campuses not to get involved. When the faculty of the University of California at San Diego voted against basing a college-prep charter school for low-income students at their campus, the provost of the university's Thurgood Marshall College nearly resigned in dismay, creating a furor on campus.[30]

When then-Senator Gary Hart introduced charter legislation in the California legislature in January 1992, the education reform battles were raging in the Golden State. Not only had Assembly member Delaine Eastin (who was later elected state superintendent of public instruction) introduced a separate charter bill, but there was also a voucher initiative on the table. In retrospect, the charter legislation probably would have failed in California (and Arizona and several other states) without the threat of vouchers to soften the opposition.[31]

Even in those circumstances, however, established interests strove to keep the charter law weak: the union wanted local contract provisions to apply; the state PTA sought prescriptive language concerning parent involvement; and the state credentialing commission wanted all charter teachers to be licensed. (The school boards association generally supported

---

[29] Tom Loveless and Claudia Jasin, "Starting from Scratch: Political and Organizational Challenges Facing Charter Schools," *Educational Administration Quarterly*, vol. 34 (February 1998).

[30] Preuss Charter School did open in September 1999.

[31] A number of legislators and political observers report this phenomenon: the specter of vouchers making charters more palatable to established interests that otherwise would have fought them. On the other hand, as we saw in Washington State, it is also possible for the animus triggered by a voucher proposal to help sink a charter measure.

the proposal as a way to boost local control of education.) Both Hart's and Eastin's bills made it through their respective chambers, but reconciling them in conference proved nearly hopeless. Only through a series of parliamentary maneuvers did the senate bill get passed on the last night of the session and signed by Governor Pete Wilson.[32]

As noted above, the Democratic sweep of the statehouse in 1998 brought new threats to charter schools and new hope to the teachers' union. A legislator close to the union moved to subject all California charters to local teacher contracts, a change that would sorely weaken their freedom in the personnel area. Only when former governor Jerry Brown, now mayor of Oakland, a city eager to start new charters, intervened to oppose this bill (and to help persuade Governor Grey Davis to threaten to veto it), did the sponsor withdraw the proposal. It was a close call, and a reminder to education reformers that election day can bring setbacks as well as gains for the charter movement.

Numerous criticisms of charter schools have appeared in the media. In 1998, *U.S. News and World Report* featured a cover story called "The New Education Bazaar." Focusing on two states with fast-growing charter programs, editor Thomas Toch painted a picture of profiteering, nepotism, high staff turnover, and church-state conflicts, reporting that "[I]n scores of charters in Arizona and Michigan, curricula and teaching are weak, buildings are substandard, and financial abuses are surprisingly prevalent."[33] An article in *The New York Times Magazine* cited similar concerns. Its subtitle conveyed the essential message: "With the growing popularity of school choice, yet another treasured public institution falls into the hands of the free market—for better and for worse."[34]

The local press is often fierce in calling attention to every blemish on the charter body while disregarding the positives. For example, the summer of 1998 brought a week-long critical appraisal of the charter scene in Arizona by a suburban paper.[35] It exposed some problems, exaggerated others, poked a lot of people in the eye, and overturned a few charter applecarts.

While it is valuable to have any reform strategy scrutinized by careful journalists and thoughtful analysts, many charter critiques are obsessed with the handful of bad apples in the barrel and inattentive to the far larger number of successful schools and satisfied clients.

Some observers also exaggerate their claims and their evidence. Based on very little data, for example, Yale psychology professor Seymour B. Sarason, a longtime critic of contemporary school reforms, concludes that

[32] Gary K. Hart and Sue Burr, "The Story of California's Charter School Legislation," *Phi Delta Kappan*, September 1996, 37–40.

[33] Thomas Toch, "The Education Bazaar," *U.S. News and World Report*, 27 April 1998, 36–37.

[34] Michael Winerip, "Schools for Sale," *The New York Times Magazine*, 14 June 1998, 42.

[35] "Guinea Kids," *The Tribune*, Mesa, Arizona, 23 August 1998, A1–A11.

"[C]harter schools . . . will be another well-intentioned, very flawed effort at school reform."[36] A report by veteran charter critic Amy Stuart Wells was billed as "the most in-depth study of charter schools ever conducted," though it only presented case studies of 17 charter schools in a single state (California) and included interviews at just 22 regular public schools. Its sweeping—and unwarranted—conclusion was that "The charter school reform movement, as least in California, has failed to live up to many of the claims put forth by its proponents."[37]

Most attacks on charter schools come from the left—featuring charges of elitism, inattention to diversity, neglect of the disabled, and other equity issues—but some critics can be found on the right. They contend that, whatever its merits, the charter movement deflects the needed revolution by stealing the thunder from vouchers and other truly free-market alternatives. Nobel laureate economist Milton Friedman, for example, has this to say about charters:

> I believe that charter schools are at best an unstable halfway house on the road to effective parental choice. They do provide a wider range of alternatives to some parents and in this way introduce some competition on the demand side. But they remain government institutions subject to control by the educational establishment. . . . [T]he charter school can compete for students only in narrowly specified dimensions. And this is true whether the charter school is run by a non-profit group or by a for-profit entity like Edison. When Edison sets up a private school, its customers are parents and children; when it competes to run a charter school, its customer is the board of the charter school, not individual parents and children. . . . Despite this analysis, I have not opposed and do not oppose charter schools. The drive for them is a welcome sign of a reaction against our unsatisfactory educational system and I believe in as much experimentation as possible. In Mao's words, let a hundred flowers bloom and let the market do the weeding.[38]

[36] Seymour B. Sarason, *Charter Schools: Another Flawed Educational Reform?* (New York: Teachers College Press, 1998). This book appears to be more a reprise of his previous work, *The Creation of Settings and the Future Societies* (San Francisco: Jossey-Bass, 1972), than an in-depth look at the charter phenomenon.

[37] Amy Stuart Wells, *Beyond the Rhetoric of Charter School Reform: A Study of Ten California School Districts* (Los Angeles: University of California at Los Angeles, 1998), 7, 14–15. See also UCLA Charter School Study Press Release, December 3, 1998, 1. For a response, see Gary Hart quoted in Nick Anderson, "Study Doubts Charter School Success Claims," *Los Angeles Times*, 4 December 1998; a memorandum from Eric Premack, UCLA Charter Study (Sacramento: Institute for School Reform, December 4, 1998); and "Give Them a Chance: Study Condemns Charter Schools Too Soon," *San Diego Union-Tribune* (editorial), 7 December 1998, which questions the study's "sweeping generalizations" and concludes: "We are all for a fair evaluation of charter schools once they have had time to demonstrate their worth. This preemptive strike in the guise of a study hardly qualifies."

[38] Personal correspondence with the authors, 25 November 1998.

Fair-Weather Friends

Besides critics, skeptics, and enemies, charter schools also have their share of "fair-weather friends": people and groups that appear cordial when the sea is calm but turn their back on the charter movement when the water around it gets choppy.

The national teachers' unions can now be viewed in this light. Even as they launch their own charter pilot projects and laud these schools as laboratories of innovation, they press for the rejection or weakening of charter bills in one state after another. They seem to have concluded that it is imprudent to fight the charter idea itself—far better to claim to support it while working assiduously to confine it.

President Clinton, himself, is something of a fair-weather friend, singing the praises of charter schools while declining to battle on their behalf with his own bureaucracy or with established education interests. His words are always friendly, even gushy. He had this to say, for example, during a September 1997 visit to California's San Carlos Charter Learning Center:

> Pretty soon—and if all the states will join in—we'll have well over 3,000, perhaps even over 4,000 [charter schools] by the year 2000, which is enough to have a seismic echo effect in all the public school systems of America. . . . [T]he only way public schools can survive . . . is if all our schools eventually—and, hopefully, sooner rather than later—are run like these charter schools.[39]

And yet, as *The Economist* noted in 1997, the Administration's charter "policy points in the right direction, but it is sadly timid," presumably due to anxiety about offending key allies and supporters.[40] Indeed, the federal government's stance toward charters can fairly be termed schizophrenic. On the one hand, all manner of senior officials—from the president and secretary of education on down—routinely take to the bully pulpit to proclaim their love for charter schools, citing them as examples of educational excellence, innovation, and accountability. The U.S. Department of Education has also awarded nearly $200 million in school start-up grants and has commissioned excellent studies that probe the nooks and crannies of the charter world.

On the other hand, Washington does not give charter schools their "share" of aid from the major federal education programs, such as Title I (compensatory help for disadvantaged youngsters), I.D.E.A. (for disabled pupils), and "Porter-Obey" funding for schools installing new education designs. The formulas that distribute these dollars were all written for

---

[39] Remarks of the President and Mrs. Clinton, San Carlos Charter Learning Center, 29 September 1997, available on http://scclc.sancarlos.k12.ca.us.

[40] "Schools at the Top of the Hill," *The Economist*, 22 February 1997, 27–8.

school districts and remain oblivious to charter schools, meaning that, in most places, a charter seeking such funding for its poor or handicapped pupils must go on bended knee to request it from the district. The red tape involved is enormous, the local politics are often ferocious, and few charter schools have the kind of administrative staff needed to obtain, manage, and account for categorical dollars from Washington.

The federal government has also placed charters in the same regulatory straitjackets it uses for conventional schools. In special education, particularly, Washington's enforcers seem bent on ensuring that charter schools do not deviate from the myriad requirements of this top-heavy program, effectively curbing their ability to innovate in this arena (as we saw in chapter 7).

A troublesome precedent was set in 1997, when the federal Office for Civil Rights handed down two rulings against the Boston Renaissance Charter School in response to a disability discrimination complaint, charging that a family was forced to withdraw its son after a teacher transferred him out of her classroom without notifying them. The school had made some procedural errors and originally did not have enough special education teachers to accommodate its unexpectedly large population of disabled pupils. However, the Boston public schools had delayed sending over student records for months after the charter school started, and many parents concealed their children's learning disabilities in the hope of giving them a fresh start.[41]

Still, Boston Renaissance had bent over backwards to cope with the challenging and sometimes disruptive behavior of the young boy on whose behalf the complaint was filed by the Massachusetts Advocacy Center. When the principal decided that his school day would end at noon, his parents agreed. Apparently their older son was thriving at Renaissance, and the mother was committed to do "whatever it takes to stay in this school."[42] (Indeed, after the suit was resolved, his parents sent him back to the school.)[43] But federal enforcers were on a mission. They pressed Boston Renaissance into a "resolution agreement" whose sixteen provisions gave federal officials effective oversight over the school's entire special-education program.[44]

Besides special education, race has caught the attention of Washington

---

[41] Peggy Farber, "The Edison Project Scores—And Stumbles—in Boston," *Phi Delta Kappan*, March 1998, 506–11. For a response to Farber's accusations, see John E. Chubb, "Edison Scores and Scores Again in Boston," *Phi Delta Kappan*, November 1998, 205–12.

[42] Ibid.

[43] In addition, the disability rights attorney who previously sued the school now calls Boston Renaissance a "model" for other charter schools. Chubb, "Edison Scores," 208.

[44] This resolution agreement also pertained to an allegation of a racially motivated transfer of another student, which was found to be without evidence. See Bruno V. Manno and Gregg Vanourek, "Norma Cantu Strikes Again," *The Weekly Standard*, 27 October 1997, 14.

enforcers. The Justice Department recently went to court in South Carolina and Louisiana, citing forty-year-old school desegregation orders to prevent the launch (or conversion) of charter schools—including several designed for at-risk and minority youngsters—and demanding racial composition data in advance of a school's opening as a condition for its approval. Since schools cannot know the ethnicity of their staff and students until they arrive, this creates a Catch-22 requirement that could choke off all charter activity.[45]

Despite all the fine speeches and radio addresses, it seems clear that Washington does not accept the fact that charter schools are meant to be autonomous and idiosyncratic. They do not fit neatly into the regimen of regulations and formulas designed for large district bureaucracies. Applying for federal aid, for example, is usually the job of a full-time administrator who combs through hundreds of pages of paperwork to generate the requisite funding for a whole group of schools. Most charter schools are forced to take on this burden themselves, even though they are often underadministered and the forms they must complete were designed for entire districts.

We encountered a charter school in North Carolina that was undergoing a surprise I.D.E.A. compliance audit. Because the pre-audit paperwork was not written for individual schools, the staff spent days poring through the material when, in the end, only a dozen pages were relevant to its situation. The result is that charter schools lose valuable staff time, feel harassed, and sacrifice sizable amounts of federal aid.

In Arizona, the new Title I allocation requirements will send all federal dollars directly to charter-averse local districts, entirely bypassing the charter-friendly state education department. One troubling result, according to a senior Arizona official, is that charter schools will not receive funds on the basis of "current year" enrollments. (Districts receive Title I dollars based on their previous year's enrollments.) This is a hardship for fast-growing schools, as many charters are. In the past, the state could hold some Title I dollars in reserve to deal with this contingency, but with the new federal requirements this will no longer be workable.

Fair-weather charter friends can also be found on Capitol Hill. In mid-1998, a bill was proposed in the Senate that would channel federal start-up funds to states in proportion to the number of charter schools that get started. Senators from states without charter laws wanted other "innovative" schools to receive these dollars, too, even though few such schools are schools of choice, truly free from regulations, or held to account for their results. (Oregon managed to obtain several million federal charter dollars before even enacting a charter law.) Fortunately, the proposed

[45] Clint Bolick, "Bill Lann Lee's War on Charter Schools," *The Wall Street Journal*, 22 March 1999, A-23.

amendments were rebuffed and the Charter School Expansion Act of 1998 gave states additional monetary incentives to strengthen their charter programs by boosting the number of schools, allowing multiple sponsors, and giving schools greater autonomy.

<hr>

INTERVIEW

Mary Hartley (Arizona State Senator)

Mary Hartley is serving her third term in the Arizona State Senate, where she is the ranking Democrat on the Education Committee. A mother of three (and grandmother of one), she previously served on the school board of the Alhambra Elementary District. Senator Hartley is the best known critic of Arizona's freewheeling charter program. In this interview, she tells how, in her view, the state's charter law ought to be amended.

Why did you become active in the charter school debates? I served on the Arizona School Boards Association's Legislation and Resolutions Committee. While sitting on this committee, the seeds of the charter school movement were planted. The school district I represented had had a charter-like school for some time. At the urging of a parent group, we had created a traditional "back to basics" school, so I understood the benefits of the charter concept and supported the creation of charter schools then. I am disappointed, however, in the way they have been instituted and implemented in Arizona.

Why is that? In Arizona, charter schools were a compromise for a very politically conservative legislature which really wanted (and still wants) vouchers. Thus, the charter school debate is surrounded by the tension and politics of the private school choice debate. Furthermore, the charter school law itself is inadequate because it does not address many of the complex issues public schools face. I hope to move past the polarizing politics and make changes to the charter school law which will make the program stronger and more accountable.

What are your principal objections to charter schools as they have developed in Arizona? We have moved far too rapidly in the proliferation of these schools and we have sacrificed quality for quantity. There is not an adequate system of oversight and evaluation in place and no one — not the charter school sponsors, the Department of Education, or the State Legislature — is willing to say that they are ultimately accountable for a charter school that fails or goes bankrupt. The lack of accurate information available to parents and the limited input and due process that parents have at some charter schools are also concerns.

Has the charter movement responded to your criticisms? To a limited extent. The state Attorney General has issued opinions which support my position on what public school statutes should apply to charter schools. I have also been successful with a number of amendments to the charter program. But I have met with limited success in dealing with my fundamental concerns: (1) the need to limit the number of new schools, (2) requiring a comprehensive, independent evaluation of the charter program, (3) increasing the responsibility of the Department of Education in charter school oversight to enhance accountability, (4) requiring full disclosure to parents of their rights to be involved in the governance of their charter school, and (5) codifying the requirement that charter schools comply with the open meeting, public records, procurement, and anti-nepotism laws that other public agencies must adhere to.

What alternatives would you suggest for improving America's schools? One of the most promising ideas on the horizon is complete open enrollment among standard school districts. Secondly, a system needs to be instituted that would give local governing boards and county school superintendents the sole ability to charter schools. I also feel that legislation passed in the State of Pennsylvania would serve as a good model for charter school legislation because it is proactive in addressing many of Arizona's oversight issues.

What do you think will happen with the charter school movement in Arizona over the next five years? If no measures are put in place to assist parents in making informed decisions and provide more oversight and accountability, I believe Arizona will continue to have the "charter school scandal of the month" as it has over the past couple of years. When parents can access accurate information and make informed decisions, the number of new charter schools will most likely level off and charter schools will serve the niche populations that are not achieving success in their standard public schools.

Arizona's "bad" charter schools have been much in the news, but isn't it the case that many more schools are succeeding? The jury is still out. Without a comprehensive, independent evaluation, it is impossible to measure the impact of charter schools in Arizona. What is success? What is failure? A school that stays financially afloat with a 40 percent turnover rate is not successful in my book. A converted private school that serves a homogeneous population of students with high test scores and enthusiastic parents is not necessarily a success either. We need data that go beyond simple newspaper articles to know what is really happening in their classrooms and we need research to know if any of the good things that are happening in charter schools — which are truly new, unique and innovative — can be incorporated into standard public school curricula.

Can you describe something about Arizona charter schools that you applaud? I have been very impressed by the charter schools that target their efforts to at-risk students, especially in the upper grades, youngsters who have had social-behavioral problems or failed in the traditional school setting. Some of the alternative education and job skill-focused charter schools have turned these students' lives around.

Other thoughts on charter schools? I continue to remind myself and others that the idea behind charter schools was *public* school reform. Charter schools are public schools and they need to stay that way, meaning they need to be accountable to the public and to parents. In Arizona, the politics of school vouchers and an anti–public education legislature seem to have eclipsed the public school reform debate and, sadly, charter schools have become victims of that controversy.

INTERVIEW

Lisa Graham Keegan (Arizona State Superintendent of Public Instruction)

First elected to her present post in 1994, Lisa Graham Keegan had previously spent four years in the Arizona House of Representatives, including two as chair of that chamber's Education Committee. Trained as a speech pathologist, this mother of two is also a tough-minded strategist and visionary reformer. Her commitment to charter schools is strong, as is her clarity about the reform principles that they embody.

What's been your greatest accomplishment as a public official? Your biggest disappointment? As a legislator, I was proudest of helping write the law for Arizona charter schools, especially the provision that disconnects new charter schools from having to ask permission for their existence from a local governing board.

My greatest frustration was solved when we created a new funding basis for public education in Arizona in the summer of 1998. Funding has been disconnected from local school district boards and instead is calculated and received on a per-pupil basis.

Many of us did not want to see Arizona attempt to solve the inequalities inherent in district taxing systems merely by tinkering with the flawed premise of most public school funding systems. These systems typically base education funding on the property wealth of an area rather than on a child's presence in a classroom. That's bad tax policy, unfair social policy, and antithetical to an education marketplace. The money available for public schooling should be strapped to the back of a child and only released to the school of choice.

Arizona's new laws have created such a system for charter schools, and a slightly more complex — but still student-centered — formula for traditional public schools. I believe this child-centered funding represents the best answer to the dozens of school finance lawsuits which remain unresolved in the country today.

How did Arizona jump so far ahead of the charter bandwagon? We jumped ahead because we created a welcoming law. The single most important provision is allowing schools to apply directly for their existence to an independent board.

What have been the main pluses of this rapid growth? Keep in mind that we don't *create* this rapid growth. It is a sign of demand. All we did was allow the creation of these schools in situations where people wanted them. The most important plus is that this has made for more choices in public schooling. Many of us believe the demand is not only present but growing. Also, as the number of charter schools grows, the impact on the rest of the system increases.

Is it correct to say that Arizona would not likely have the strong charter law it now has if there hadn't been a credible "threat" of vouchers? Yes. We definitely owe our charter law to the threat of vouchers. How ironic that we had proposed only 2,000 vouchers for low-income children, amounting to $1,500 per pupil. By November 1998, we had almost 30,000 students in charter schools at an annual cost to the state of nearly $142 million.

How do you like it when Arizona is called the "Wild West" of education reform? I don't see it as harsh criticism, simply amazement! Although many people talk about wanting to introduce the forces of the market into public education, few are comfortable with the degree of change that will bring.

AGAINST THE ODDS

Considering the opposition they face, it is remarkable that so many charter schools are operating today. What has enabled them to proliferate? We find four main reasons.

First, they enjoy bipartisan support and, at least for now, more influential friends than enemies.

Second, for the most part, charters are still flying below the radar, not yet so numerous or disruptive that their foes have trained all the heavy artillery on them. As they become a larger threat to established interests, they will doubtless get more attention. Indeed, early efforts to "roll back" charter gains are already visible in California, New Jersey, Ohio, and several other states.

Third, charter schools solve an astonishing array of different problems.

Americans are inventive — and this movement is marvelously adaptable. Some people seek charters to protect their children from dreadful inner-city schools. Others launch charters to undo consolidation moves that closed community-anchoring rural schools. Some charter clients yearn for a more traditional education for their kids, others for the exact opposite. And on and on.

Finally, the people who set out to start their own charter schools are among the most stubborn men and women in America. Many won't take no for an answer. Yet despite the charter movement's growth, it is important to recall that "no" has frequently been the only answer. Many would-be charter founders have been overpowered by their opponents. An unknowable number of charter schools were never born.

This chapter opened on the front lines of a tough, statewide political battle, with Jim and Fawn Spady defying the mighty teachers' unions. Similar dramas have played out in dozens of communities around the country. Some of today's hottest battles are raging in middle-class suburbs that like to think their public schools are fine. There are revolts in such upscale communities as Princeton, Cape Cod, Martha's Vineyard, Vail, Aspen, and Palisades, New Jersey. In Princeton, the appearance of a single charter school polarized the town. Writing in the *New Jersey Monthly*, English teacher Brian Hanson-Harding asked:

> Why, then, would there be a charter school in a place like Princeton, where the public schools are generally looked on as being exceptional? This well-kept and largely well-heeled burgh has the kind of schools that many people pick up and move for. Per-pupil spending hovers around $10,000, and immaculate elementary schools with state-of-the-art computer technology feed into a high school that regularly garners awards and recognition.[46]

Yet some Princeton parents were dismayed by the system's smugness, its lack of a clear mission, and its emphasis on esteem-building and trendy methods at the expense of solid academic content. So charter schools became the arena for a clash between progressives and traditionalists. Former district Superintendent Marcia Bossart reflects, "Ten years ago, perhaps, a district like Princeton didn't need to pay attention to market share. We do now."[47]

THE SCHOOL WITH FIFTEEN LIVES

The most contentious suburban charter battle we have seen has raged for several years in the affluent northwestern suburbs of Chicago. Marilyn Keller Rittmeyer is on the front lines. A public school educator (sixth grade), wife, doctoral candidate, and mother of five, she joined a group of other suburban moms who started meeting in each others' homes in 1995.

[46] Brian Hanson-Harding, "Brave New School," *New Jersey Monthly*, September 1997.
[47] Ibid.

They were outraged that the public schools in their communities had been seduced by whole-language reading, fuzzy math, multi-age instruction, "literature circles," student-developed curricula, and other progressive approaches. They dreamed of launching a more traditional K–8 school based on E.D. Hirsch's "Core Knowledge" sequence. When Illinois passed a charter law in 1996, they realized that they could turn their dream into reality. The school would be named for Thomas Jefferson, and they set out to write their own "declaration of independence."

The small, 6,500-student Community Consolidated School District #59 would not let them secede. It rejected the group's 1996 charter application, citing concerns about facilities and special education. Members of the Thomas Jefferson board took their charter proposal to other nearby school boards over three years but were rejected fifteen times.[48] (The founders chose to seek a charter from every district in which they intended to solicit students. Such "multiple district charter schools" are allowed by Illinois law.)

Rittmeyer and company decided to appeal to the State Board of Education. The state board also said no at first, but in June 1998 it overturned District 59's rejection of the charter petition. Immediately, the teachers' unions cried foul. Bob Haisman, president of the Illinois Education Association, deplored the action as "a political railroad job that totally ignores the cherished elements of local control of education." District 59, with funding for legal expenses offered by some neighboring boards, decided to take both charter school and state board to court, arguing that the latter "has no authority to expropriate local tax dollars to fund a school which is chartered by the state board." In September, a circuit court judge rejected that suit and upheld the state board's approval of the charter.

Time will tell what happens to Rittmeyer and her compatriots — District 59 has already taken its suit to the next judicial level — and to hundreds of other charter advocates battling in America's school reform trenches.[49] For in this war, no clear winner is in sight. A charter board member in Michigan described how the outcome may hinge on one or two strong political leaders: "The charter school situation in this state is still somewhat tenuous. If [John] Engler is no longer governor, or if leadership changes in the legislature occur, those opposed may win the battle."[50] Yet the charter movement has also gained considerable momentum and may now be beyond the capacity of opponents to stop. American education is already beginning to show signs of its impact. In the next chapter, we examine some of these signs.

[48] "District 59 to Sue State over Charter School," *Chicago Sun Times*, 15 July 1998. See also Becky Beaupre, "Schools of Thought at Odds," *Chicago Sun Times*, 1 April 1999.

[49] The judge denied the District's request for a "stay," which would have essentially stopped all progress on the school. Apparently, District 59 has vowed to fight to the bitter end. Still, Thomas Jefferson Charter School struggled into operation in fall 1999.

[50] Bryan Hassel said much the same about Massachusetts: "One remarkable aspect of the Massachusetts law, then, is that the *realized* placement of authority is highly contingent on the orientation of the Secretary of Education." See Hassel quoted in Loveless and Jasin, "Starting from Scratch," 23.

9

BEYOND THE SCHOOLHOUSE DOOR: CHANGING SYSTEMS

> The effects . . . reach beyond the schools themselves. Tradi-
> tional public schools have had to respond to the presence of
> charter schools as students leave one system for another.
>
> *Lisa Graham Keegan, Arizona State Superintendent of*
> *Public Instruction, Senate testimony, March 1998,*
> *Washington, D.C.*

WE HAVE identified four stages in the traditional education system's typical reaction to charters. The first ("stop them cold") and second ("keep
them few and weak") of these were the subject of the previous chapter.
Now we turn to stages three and four:

- Outdo them: successfully compete with them so as to minimize the
  number of children leaving district schools for charter schools; and
- Accept them: embrace the charter idea and use it for the system's
  own purposes.

We first visit two districts powerfully affected by the charter movement.
Douglas County, Colorado is home to six charter schools enrolling 5 percent of its students. It illustrates a "stage three" response. Kingsburg, California is one of a few "charter districts" in the nation and demonstrates
how the charter idea can be used by a district to do things differently (a
"stage four" response).

Douglas County, Colorado: From Sideshow to Friendly Rival
1998–99 DISTRICT ENROLLMENT: 30,000
FIRST CHARTER SCHOOL: 1993–94

Douglas County is one of the fastest growing places in America, a vast
tract of prairie south of Denver that is rapidly turning into a sprawling
upper-middle-class suburb.

The Douglas County Public Schools (DCPS) are scrambling to keep up, opening half a dozen new schools almost every year. As enrollments rise by several thousand youngsters annually, nearly all its elementary schools operate year-round.

DCPS is forward-looking. Its management team, captained by veteran superintendent Rick O'Connell, is top-notch. (See profile below.) Its school board is stable, careful, and responsible. It negotiated a rare, performance-based contract with its teachers' union. It recently opened a dazzling new campus with a technology focus that combines middle school, high school, and college under one gigantic roof. It has studied new education designs, curricula, and assessment systems and has steadily modified its own practices to take advantage of other people's ideas and successes. The superintendent believes that school choice is good for public education.

DCPS is the sort of school system in which most parents are happy to enroll their kids. Indeed, good public schools are part of the county's allure and a contributor to its amazing growth. Most Douglas County residents are content, as shown by the successful passage of recent bond issues. Most, but not all. Some families drive their children long distances to private schools. And a full 5 percent of the student population has made its way into the county's charter schools — a sizable fraction in a state where the charter enrollment exceeds 2.5 percent.

CHARTER SCHOOLS REACH DOUGLAS COUNTY

The first two such schools were launched in 1993–94, Colorado's maiden year as a charter state. Both are "Core Knowledge" schools, embracing the knowledge-centered, grade-delineated curriculum sequence developed by E. D. Hirsch. Renaissance School joined them in 1995–96 and is almost their opposite — an experiential, child-centered, "progressive" institution with multi-age groupings, traces of Montessori methods, and no grades.

Parents dissatisfied with the offerings of the regular system founded all three schools. For some, DCPS was too progressive, while for others the system's standard curriculum and school design were too stodgy. Colorado's charter law provided education escape valves for both sets of dissidents.

This pattern has persisted. The three newest Douglas County charters (which opened in 1997–98) are also parent-initiated. Again, they are a mixed lot in terms of philosophy and curriculum. One is the county's third Core Knowledge school. Another is a full-fledged Montessori school. And one — the Colorado Visionary Academy — is an education hodgepodge claiming to blend "high academic standards . . . traditional skills [and] exploration and application," along with Socratic teaching methods.

DCPS gained an early reputation as a charter-friendly district. Its officials addressed national conferences and Congressional hearings on how to work with charter schools. There were no pitched battles. The schools received both the full per-pupil operating revenue (PPOR) and also the "capital reserve," a more generous fiscal arrangement than most Colorado charters enjoyed. And DCPS adopted a businesslike approach to its charter schools. The charters were obliged to buy only a few services (such as liability insurance and fiscal audits) from the system; the rest were displayed on a menu with a dozen and a half items priced on a per-student basis, from intra-district mail service for $2.62 per pupil per annum to special education at $355.

Douglas County's approach to special education was (and is) striking. If the charter school contracts with the district — all initially opted to do so — it gets both direct services for its disabled pupils and what amounts to an insurance policy. Should the proverbial "$50,000 student" turn up at the charter, needing a full-time attendant and special transportation, these costs would be absorbed by DCPS rather than by the charter budget. On the other hand, that "insurance" costs the charter school nearly 10 percent of its total budget, and in 1998–99 several Douglas County charters shifted to a private provider of special education services. The aggrieved school system, now in a less permissive mode, has demanded that they resume the district-based arrangement.

DCPS leaders take pride in their charter-friendly stance. They are genuinely open to new ideas and promising alternatives. Moreover, the district's remarkable growth made it easy to absorb charter schools, which simply meant that the system did not have as many additional students of its own each year, a far different situation than is faced by districts where charters subtract kids and resources.

A rare crossover from charter to system occurred in 1997 when one of Renaissance School's founding parents, Jacqueline Killian, successfully ran for a seat on the DCPS board. This may deepen the amicable relationship over time. But strains are also appearing.

Bumps along the Road

The first significant dust-up in Douglas County involved facilities. Because of its enrollment growth, DCPS has no spare buildings. The issue was whether it would help its charter schools build, lease, or otherwise acquire their own facilities. The answer turned out to be no more than the absolute minimum sort of help. Most important, DCPS would not promise a landlord or finance company that, if the charter school closed, it would use the property. Thus, besides making the charters pay rent from their operating budgets, the system declined to co-sign the documents that would turn the charters into reasonable commercial risks as long-term tenants or borrowers.[1] Explains Superintendent O'Connell: "We don't want to be on the

---

[1] Colorado's constitution bars any government unit from entering into multi-year contrac-

hook for a building built to charter specifications and inherit it if the charter school goes out of business. Our rationale has been that we're providing space for these kids anyhow and would have to if the charter school goes under."

Douglas County evidently viewed its first three charter schools as a sideshow, an acceptable escape valve for obstreperous parents, but essentially irrelevant to the booming district. They provided mildly eccentric programs in scruffy facilities—O'Connell's distaste for the "portable" units is almost palpable—and consumed more than their share of the attention of central office administrators. One could sense pride in being in the education vanguard vying with exasperation over the bother caused by charter schools—and the mild rebuke to the system that their existence implied.

In the spring of 1997, this ambivalence turned more negative when the second trio of charters was approved. Two of these were okayed by the DCPS board, but the third was imposed by the State Board of Education, reversing a negative decision by the district. This came as a shock to DCPS, which had been conscientious in its review of charter applications and had turned down the Visionary Academy due to what district leaders saw as serious inadequacies in its design. The school board "lost it" vis-à-vis charter schools, recalls a prominent county resident, when the sixth school was forced on them. Suddenly, it seemed as if the system was not in control of its charter program.

That program, moreover, had grown too large for Assistant Superintendent Pat Grippe to oversee. "When there were just three of them," he recalls, "I could ad hoc it with them and tailor it." But six was a lot, and Grippe is also responsible for "learning services" throughout the sprawling system and for much of the planning of new schools. DCPS devised a structural solution: a new position in Grippe's office, a half-time "charter school liaison." Although the capable woman placed in that post—a former DCPS principal named Laura Harmon—was generally viewed as charter-friendly, her appointment rankled. The system had hinted that the charter schools would be consulted about this selection, but they were not. Moreover, the liaison's salary was added to the charters' "mandatory buy-backs," meaning their budgets were paying for an administrator they had neither sought nor chosen. At Platte River Charter School, a board member can rattle off the precise sum—$11,645 in 1997–98—coming out of his school's budget to support her position. And with Harmon's appointment came a sense of creeping bureaucratization: charter schools were now viewed as a "program" by the system and kicked a rung down the organizational ladder.

---

tual obligations, but school systems are known to be stable, permanent entities, whilst charter schools are institutional novelties with no track record, uncertain life expectancies, no taxing or bonding authority, and few tangible assets. From the perspective of a banker, say, a single charter school is not a very good candidate for a long-term mortgage.

A Widening Gap

As DCPS began its annual budget review in early 1998, the disquiet among charter advocates deepened. Under Colorado's charter law, these schools are funded from district revenues — but adverse decisions can be appealed to the charter-friendly State Board of Education. Tensions are inherent in this setup. In Douglas County, the new budget suggested that the district had indeed come to see charter schools as a special program rather than an enrollment-driven entitlement. Though DCPS per-pupil revenues were actually rising, inflation and teacher salaries were escalating faster and so reductions had to be made somewhere. The superintendent set out to whittle $2.37 million from a budget of $155 million. The charters bridled at the prospect that they might have to absorb some of the cost of what they viewed as spendthrift practices by the "regular" schools.

But absorb they did. When the board was finished crafting the 1998–99 budget, the charters were trimmed by some $37 per pupil from the amount they would have received under the statewide formula if the entire DCPS budget had been parceled out on the basis of enrollments. The pinch was not severe — charters still enjoyed an increase over the previous year — and the regular district schools took a heavier hit. But the decision set a precedent: charter schools as "program," not entitlement. Their "reduction" would have been greater — O'Connell had proposed twice as deep a cut — if they had not banded together to make a noisy public fuss. That signaled another coming-of-age in the charters' relationship with the system, now more openly confrontational. As recalled by DCPS charter coordinator Laura Harmon, "The tenor of that meeting was really adversarial and aggressive. I think they could have accomplished the same thing with less acrimony."

The mounting friction between Douglas County and its charters has other elements. The first three schools had enjoyed fairly lenient contracts concerning such matters as when, during the year, enrollments would be tallied for budgeting purposes. Now the district wanted more advance notice, both from the new schools and — as charters came up for renewal — from the older ones. DCPS insisted, for example, that by February 15 each charter would project its enrollment for the following year and actually identify every student. Inasmuch as most charter schools have unpredictable enrollments, frequently including youngsters whose families "school shop" at the last minute, such requirements struck them as more than bureaucratic — more like a straitjacket. They were also irked by a line in the new contract stating that, in a dispute between a charter school and DCPS, the district, rather than a mediator, would have the last word. More recently has come the system's refusal to let its charters outsource their special education programs.

The system has grown more persnickety about the schools' academic performance, too. O'Connell remarks that "Our charter kids are not doing quite as well as the regular school kids. Their test scores are the same or a bit less." Though two of the charters bested the district-wide average in 1998, the "progressive" Renaissance school lagged behind, particularly in math. Concurrently, Renaissance was applying for its charter renewal. Rather than simply approving the renewal, the DCPS administration insisted that the school develop a "student achievement improvement plan." This precipitated a leadership change at Renaissance, where education director Paula Keller, who had been with the school from its founding, was encouraged to seek employment elsewhere. Indeed, she became the fifth charter director to quit or get fired at the end of the 1997–98 school year—and before summer's end the sixth was gone as well—suggesting that upscale places like Douglas County are not immune to acute charter governance problems, even (in Renaissance's case) as late as the third year of operation. As Keller puts it, "The board wants a more recipe-driven approach in all classrooms. I have a bias toward program diversity." This leadership turnover concerns O'Connell. "You can't run a business or a school," he comments, "if you're changing leaders every year. You can't get a vision and stick with it if you're constantly spending time on new leadership."

Nor did tensions over facilities vanish. When Renaissance opened in "portables" on a dirt field within a new office park, the school's founders thought they had an agreement with the park's developer to construct a school building for them to lease. Because of Colorado's prohibition on multiyear commitments and the district's refusal to backstop the obligation, the developer got cold feet. After two years in portables, families were restive and the school sought other options. It found a finance company willing to create a package that permitted construction of a new building, and the school moved into its handsome (though simple) built-to-order facility during summer 1998. The problem is the 10.5 percent interest rate attached to such a high-risk (from the lender's standpoint) venture, a rate that everyone said could have been lowered had DCPS guaranteed the lease. This entails a huge drain on Renaissance's budget.

INTENSIFYING COMPETITION

O'Connell and his colleagues are changing their view of charter schools. Despite the county's continuing growth—and the fact that all six charters combined would barely fill a normal-sized high school—one detects growing wariness toward this innovation and a mounting sense that the district should work harder to respond to impulses that lead families down the charter path.

Exhibit A is the saga of Golden Trails, a would-be charter school for gifted youngsters that was planned by parents who felt that DCPS did not do right by their talented offspring. Instead of granting the charter, the DCPS response was to co-opt the concept. O'Connell explains that they had known for some time that the district was not adequately serving its gifted pupils, and the Golden Trails initiative crystallized their resolve to act. "There's no question about it," he acknowledges. "The charter proposal was a catalyst for something we should have done twenty years earlier."

He counter-proposed to the parents that DCPS would create a new multisite "magnet" program for gifted and talented students. Though a few parents wanted the charter, most of the Golden Trails planning team agreed to O'Connell's offer. Late in 1998, three gifted and talented programs opened as district-run schools-within-schools.

INTERVIEW

Dr. Richard O'Connell (Superintendent, Douglas County School District, Colorado)

Rick O'Connell has been the Douglas County superintendent since 1981 — the second person to fill that position. He grew up and attended college in New Jersey, where he also taught fifth grade. He moved to Colorado in 1969 and has lived there since, his work including stints as principal and assistant superintendent. He holds a doctorate in school administration and is an ardent fisherman, both in the Rocky Mountains and off the reefs of Central America.

How has your view of charter schools changed as they have grown in Douglas County? Initially, I was curious and basically positive about the idea; I just felt the whole choice factor was going to benefit all parties involved. I agree with the view that public schools have been — I hate to say a "monopoly" — a "one-choice business" until recently. I felt that everyone would benefit from more of a business-customer model with more options for the customer. As a consumer, I can pick and choose what I want in any other walk of life. I think that education consumers should have that opportunity, too. It's been amazing to me how forceful the aspect of choice is with parents. The power of this idea is a very big driving force. It sometimes seems incongruous to me that they would choose a charter school over one of our schools, but they do.

Do you see charter schools as a challenge to public education, a preview of the future, or an interesting sideshow? All of the above. Sideshow is not the best term; more like an interesting alternative. My hunch is that in Colorado, at least in Douglas County, charters won't attract more than about 10 percent of the student population. We're at 5 or 6 percent right now. If we got to 20 or 30 percent, I'd have major problems.

What has been the impact of charter schools within your district? The whole awareness of choice and competition is healthy. It moves some dissatisfied customers out, away from our principals and teachers. Overall, it's had a real positive impact. I also think it's brought a much higher level of awareness to charter parents and boards about just how tough it is to run a school.

What have charter schools been able to do that you can't as easily do? Smaller classes are their greatest achievement. I don't think personnel flexibility has been that much of a bonus. They've made some mistakes by not checking people out carefully enough. They end up getting the people we don't hire.

Can you characterize the people who are going to charter schools in Douglas County? They're the same types of people we have in the regular schools. They're not weirdos or outcasts. They're regular people who have concerns about their kids and, in some cases, the perception that their kids were poorly served by the regular schools.

What advice would you offer to your colleagues faced with the charter phenomenon? Realize and understand that the whole choice issue is a very compelling phenomenon for parents and customers. Be an advocate for charter schools and assist in every way possible. Take a positive attitude. Their kids are just as important. Help the kids succeed. Be pleased a year or two down the road when the charter parents realize how tough it is. Nobody is going to say thanks. Don't say, "I told you so."

Kingsburg, California: "Taking Back Our Schools"
1998–99 DISTRICT ENROLLMENT: 2,006
FIRST YEAR AS A CHARTER DISTRICT: 1996

Kingsburg is located in a lush agricultural area about twenty-five minutes south of Fresno. There are nearly 8,500 residents in the town, which has a strong and durable Swedish heritage. The district serves grades K–8 only, enrolling over 2,000 students in 1998–99 (up nearly 180 students since it went charter). After eighth grade, students typically attend Kingsburg High School, a separate district.

Kingsburg had wearied of the state telling it how to run its schools, a situation that former Superintendent Ron Allvin says was brought on by passage of Proposition 13 in the early 1970s and by the ensuing cut in local property taxes that made the state the chief funder of California's public schools. Along with the additional state money came more control from Sacramento. A lot of Kingsburg residents agree with Allvin, who says, "Many of the laws passed by the California state assembly are promulgated by the bureaucracy for districts like Los Angeles, not ones like ours." The community wanted out from under the state's thumb and also wanted parents more involved in their kids' education.

Enter Allvin, a maverick, not least for his belief that "Giving parents more choices in public education is the only way that public education will survive." He suggested to his board that Kingsburg become a charter district. He once reflected:

> I've been in public education for over 35 years. Two of the things that have done most to take power away from local community control of schools have been the increasing state role in telling us what to do and the growth of the unions and collective bargaining agreements. This had led to a loss not only of community control but also of parent involvement and accountability. Parents don't think people at the school want to hear from them or can do much about what they tell them because bureaucrats outside the district control so much of what schools do. I saw the district charter as a way of taking back our schools and making them real community institutions.

The board agreed to pursue Allvin's idea. Rather than settle for the 50 percent teacher approval level that California requires for a district conversion, Allvin set the threshold at 70 percent. He assembled a volunteer group of teachers to write the charter. In time, despite some opposition, 70 percent of the teachers did support the proposal and the board approved it (4 to 1) in early 1996. Kingsburg received its go-ahead from the state in May.

Since the school district already existed, there were few start-up problems. The elected school board remains the governing body, each school continues to have a teacher advisory council, and there was no need to create a new special education program. But seemingly minor points produced unexpected problems. As one principal recalls, "Over the course of a four-month period, one person in our district office spent over 150 hours negotiating with the state over how our attendance forms and teacher credential forms would look. What a waste of time."

OFFERING FAMILIES MORE CHOICES

Kingsburg uses its charter as a permit to offer a menu of education options from which parents can choose. Allvin and his colleagues viewed this as a major benefit of the charter approach (and the reason enrollments have risen). All parents are invited to sign a four-page parent/school/student compact that asks them to select one of six programs for their children. These range from typical schools to home schooling and include an alternative program for youngsters with discipline and behavior problems.

The compact states that, "Should the parents or student . . . consistently fail to support the development of responsibility and respect in the students of this Charter District, the school reserves the right to dismiss the student from the District." A due-process procedure exists for doing this. It has yet to be invoked.

This options *cum* contract approach has helped the district get parents to shoulder greater responsibility for their children's education. In several instances, the school has called in parents and students to tell them that they are violating the compact and must shape up. This has led to a turn-around in the attitude of many previously disengaged parents and trouble-some students.

DOING THINGS DIFFERENTLY

The Kingsburg Community Assistance Program (KCAP) is a nonprofit organization that works closely with the schools to assist parents and students. It does everything from providing tutors and mentors to finding volunteers to repair the cars of single parents so they can keep doctors' appointments. The executive director is a dynamo who says, "Every needy child has a needy parent and we try to match parents and kids with people who can help them so that the kids succeed."

With the advent of the charter, money-handling has changed somewhat. Previously, each school had a small discretionary budget for materials. These amounts have now grown, though the district continues to handle payroll and major purchases. (Kingsburg has a budget of about $10 million.)

The charter has had other interesting effects. There is less absenteeism by teachers and students. More homework is being completed. Parent participation in report card conferences often reaches 99 percent. The district has greater flexibility in hiring substitute teachers. It was able to take quick action under a statewide class-size reduction initiative and can now purchase teaching materials (e.g., phonics-based reading texts) that are not on state lists.

Several groups have asked Kingsburg if they could come under its charter umbrella. The district responded positively to parents from Hume Lake (about 90 minutes away) who sought approval for a satellite home-schooling campus. A high school in nearby Exeter has also expressed interest in coming under the charter, which would give Kingsburg its own high school. The school board likes the proposal, but some believe that state law does not allow an elementary district like Kingsburg to provide a high school education without changing its legal status.

Allvin retired in July 1998. His last three years were "the most exciting professional years of my life. More than anything else, the charter has allowed us to restore community control of our schools. . . . I can't imagine why other districts haven't taken advantage of this opportunity to re-write the play book on how we do public education." His successor, Dr. Jim Haslip, was attracted to the position because of the district charter arrangement. He has pledged to "move full-speed ahead with the charter approach."

IMPACTS ON DISTRICTS

Not everyone in the charter movement believes that these schools are meant to change the system. For some, their school is an exception, a haven, even a fortress, intended only to serve a particular population of children for whom conventional schools are not working. In this view, each charter has its own "niche" market: children with special needs, the progeny of fussy parents, or youngsters who have left (or been expelled by) conventional schools. Says the director of Arizona Career Academy, "We're here to pick up the individuals who just don't fit." He doesn't see his school competing with the regular system but filling a lamentable gap in its services.[2] This is a benefit to public education itself as well as to those directly affected. But it is not the same as viewing charters as change agents within the larger enterprise of schooling. Indeed, niche schools may even retard such change by easing the local demand for it and giving the noisiest dissidents a pressure-release valve. In the words of economist Albert O. Hirschman, "There are many . . . cases where competition does not restrain monopoly as it is supposed to, but *comforts and bolsters* it by unburdening it of some of its more troublesome customers."[3]

Those who view charter schools as havens are more like refugees than pioneers. The Douglas County charter experience began that way as discontented parents started new schools to gain options for their kids. Across the mountains in tiny Crestone, the charter law enabled disgruntled parents to escape from a stodgy, authoritarian school system. In Lake George-Guffey, also in the Colorado high country, gaining a charter meant retrieving control of two little rural schools from a distant school board — and fending off the threat that one might be closed.

This "refugee" spirit is also manifest when a few teachers unite to create their own alternative to spirit-dulling schools. As we saw in chapters 2 and 3, that is why Joe Lucente and his colleagues extricated Fenton Avenue from the bureaucratic toils of the lumbering Los Angeles system and why Sarah Kass and Ann Tolkoff founded Boston's City On A Hill Charter School. Sometimes would-be pioneers get cold feet and settle for refugee status. Vernon Robinson, President of the North Carolina Education Reform Foundation (see interview, this chapter), finds such reversals deeply frustrating. He told us, "My biggest disappointment has been to watch what happens when charter founders get their approval. Most lose interest in building a movement for change."

[2] Kelly Pearce, "Niche for Square Pegs," *The Arizona Republic*, 7 March 1999.
[3] Albert O. Hirschman, *Exit, Voice, and Loyalty: Response to Decline in Firms, Organizations, and States* (Cambridge: Harvard University Press, 1970), 59. Emphasis in original.

Both views—charters as catalysts for systemic change and charters as havens—are legitimate. It is not wrong for parents to care mostly about their own children's education or for teachers to be passionate mainly about what happens in their classrooms. "Locals" as well as "cosmopolitans" have an honorable place in the charter movement. Charter analyst Ted Kolderie says, "For the teachers who found them and the students who enroll in them, . . . it is the schools that are important. But for others, . . . 'charter schools' has been about system-reform . . . a way for the state to cause the district system to improve."[4] Even as we honor that duality, however, we confess to keener interest in the "spillover," "multiplier," and "pioneer" effects of charter schools in a country wrestling with acute and widespread education problems. In the remainder of this chapter, we review some clues that charter schools' effects do reach beyond the populations they serve directly.

So far, anecdotes supply most of the evidence. Few American communities have any charters today and in most that do, these schools remain a marginal presence, all but imperceptible to people not involved with them. We are not sure what a "critical mass" will be, but we have seen it in a few places—most often in small or mid-sized communities where a single new school can loom like an iceberg in a pond. In Crestone, Colorado, for example, the charter school—with less than 40 pupils—enrolls more than a quarter of the town's children.

Some analysts judge that the political compromises and constraints adopted in order to secure passage of charter legislation—the "weak" laws described in chapter 5—so emasculate this reform strategy that its system-changing effects are severely limited from the outset.[5] But where strong laws lead to viable new schools, the impact may be perceptible even where the charter presence is small. We have been to communities where the appearance of one or two charters catalyzes beneficial effects from competition, heightened entrepreneurship among the "regular" schools, a scramble to find efficiencies, even "copycat" schools that borrow a curriculum, disciplinary strategy, or extra service from the charter school.

These district-level effects are what most education reformers hope will result from the charter movement. We classify them in two ways. First, there is straightforward competition—a tug of war over pupils and resources. This we term a "stage three response," and we observed it in Douglas County. An editorial in the *Boston Globe* spotted it in the Bay

---

[4] Ted Kolderie, "A Major Education Reform—The Charter Idea: Update and Prospects" (Minneapolis, Minn.: City Innovation, 1995), 8. See also Bryan C. Hassel, *The Charter School Challenge: Avoiding the Pitfalls, Fulfilling the Promise* (Washington, D.C.: Brookings Institution Press, 1999), 128–43.

[5] Bryan C. Hassel, "Charter Schools: Politics and Practice in Four States," in *Learning from School Choice*, eds. Paul E. Peterson and Bryan C. Hassel (Washington, D.C.: Brookings Institution Press, 1998), 249–71.

State as well: "Right now, at least, the real competition [with charter schools] is over students. . . . The unions and public administrators have plenty of cause to worry—and to improve. That's one of the best reasons for charter schools to exist."[6] According to a Michigan charter principal: "We're on the ground floor of changing education. . . . Other schools are now trying harder because we're here." A Massachusetts parent and charter founder remarked: "We're a threat to the district. I love it."

A friendlier response—call it "stage four"—has the district embracing the charter idea as a way to achieve its own ends. One version of this creates schools that function as R&D sites or labs that experiment with novel practices that can then be moved into other schools. One California superintendent noted, "Innovative practices used in the charter school have been stolen and implemented in other district schools. No one in those schools wants to admit it, but everyone knows where they came from." Another version is the district's complete embrace of the charter model as its own *modus operandi*, a way of recasting relationships with the state or promoting reforms that regulatory or collective-bargaining constraints forbid. The Kingsburg district illustrates this approach. As one principal there commented, "I was a charter skeptic. But I now see how it's helped us do things that we could never have done under the umbrella of the conventional district system."[7]

The Virtues of Competition

Federal Express and other commercial delivery services emerged because the U.S. Postal Service could not be counted upon to get a letter to its destination the next day. As these private firms began to cut into the Postal Service's revenue base, this legendary government monopoly reinvented itself to survive. Its overnight mail is a welcome product of that reinvention process—and a consequence of competition.

A similar phenomenon can be observed in public education in some communities, thanks to charter schools (and other forms of school choice). Competition busts monopolies and triggers change. It does this by changing the reward system. Ted Kolderie comments:

> In the charter strategy, incentives are central. [Charter opponents] do not want the pressures this would bring on them—to change and improve their own programs or to see students leave. . . . The state's interest, on the other hand, is precisely in creating these incentives for the districts to act . . . these

---

[6] "Good Scores for Charter Schools," *The Boston Globe*, 19 July 1996.

[7] Hassel ("Charter Schools," p. 250) presents a similar perspective, suggesting that "Charter schools might make an impact on the school system through three mechanisms. First, they might serve as laboratories. . . . Second, charter schools might serve as competitors to school districts. Third, charter schools might, over time, simply replace district schools as the primary purveyors of public education."

pressures to be responsive, innovative and careful about their costs. Without the dynamics that make performance necessary, the system will remain inert, unable to generate internally the will to do the hard things that excellence requires.[8]

In Holland, Michigan, the public school system lost about 100 students to charter schools in the fall of 1996—a palpable shift, though less than 2 percent of the district's enrollment. The new schools filled quickly. As a result, the superintendent wrote a letter to every family that left for charter schools: "Although I do not know why you decided to leave Holland Public Schools, I want you to know you are missed. If for any reason you find the educational experience your child is having does not meet your expectation, we'd like to extend an opportunity for you to come back to Holland Public Schools."

Lansing has seen a handful of charter schools open in recent years, initially losing 1,000 of its 19,500 students (though some have since returned). In response, the district undertook an aggressive marketing plan that included television ads during the 1998 winter Olympics.[9] The Mesa, Arizona school system has been advertising its own education options in movie theaters and the Yellow Pages. One elementary school principal uses a videotape and glossy brochure to attract pupils to his school.

The most notable district responses to competition go well beyond ads. "In order to survive," comments former Flagstaff superintendent Kent Matheson, "we had to quit our whining and do a better job ourselves." His system added full-day kindergarten and several magnet schools. His successor is trying to woo an award-winning charter school back under the system's roof.[10]

Other charter-impacted districts are also developing new options for "customers" who might otherwise defect to charter schools. Douglas County did this with its gifted and talented program. So did Battle Creek, Michigan, which created two new schools in 1998 in partnership with the Edison Project, in response to three charters that also opened that year. (Edison had been wooing district officials for several years, but the advent of charter schools led to consummation of this otherwise controversial relationship.) Superintendent Mike Bitar acknowledges that the charters put the district "in a different kind of position right now. We do have to be more assertive about marketing our schools."[11]

In Jackson, Michigan, the school system lost 365 pupils to charter schools in 1997. Mary Lou Konkle, president of the Jackson Education

---

[8] Kolderie, "A Major Education Reform," 3, 5.

[9] Liz Wyatt, "Schools Compete for Pupils, Funding," *Battle Creek Enquirer*, 28 June 1998, 4A.

[10] Kelly Pearce, "Charters' Growth Shows No Sign of Slowing," *The Arizona Republic*, 7 March 1999.

[11] Wyatt, "Schools Compete for Pupils, Funding," 1A, 4A.

Association, declared, "We can't afford to lose any more students." A committee of teachers was formed to stem the exodus. Its recommendations included magnet schools for math and science, fine arts, and languages and an accelerated school for at-risk kids. The most radical suggestions proposed an overhaul of the district's early childhood program (nearly 100 of the students lost to the charter schools were kindergartners). According to superintendent Gregg Mowen, these ideas helped "jumpstart the [district's planning] process for how to respond to the coming of charter schools."[12]

Nor is it unknown for district leadership to be changed in response to competition. After little Queen Creek, Arizona lost a third of its elementary pupils in 1996 to a new basics-centered charter school, it fired its superintendent and began infusing more phonics into its reading curriculum.

PROFILE

Vernon Robinson (Director, North Carolina Education Reform Foundation)

A graduate of the Air Force Academy, Vernon Robinson served as a SAC missile crew commander and later as an intelligence officer. He is known as North Carolina's foremost proponent of charter schools. His support of the charter concept from 1991 to 1996 paid off when landmark charter legislation was passed by the General Assembly in 1996 and amended in 1997.

Where did the charter movement in North Carolina come from, what types of opposition did it encounter, and what was involved in surmounting that opposition? I was the first individual in North Carolina to call for charter schools in 1991. Several opponents of school choice who had scoffed at charter schools became born-again believers in 1994 at 10 P.M. election night when the Republicans took control of the state legislature and vouchers had the first shot of passing. Because there were a number of wimpy Republicans in the House and Senate, I adopted a strategy that the full school choice bills — vouchers and tax credits — could be used to force a compromise on charter schools. The plan worked like a charm, getting the support of many different groups, including the business community and the teachers' union.

What made you decide to become an advocate for charter schools? I thought they were more likely to quickly liberate children, parents, and teachers than vouchers because it would be easier to pass

---

[12] Sara Scott, "Teachers Seek Ways to Stem Flight of Students," *Jackson Citizen Patriot*, 20 November 1997.

strong charter legislation. From the perspective of one who is concerned with African-American kids, any choice is better than the one most black parents have today.

In North Carolina charter schools, are the neediest kids getting access and being well served? Yes. My favorite story about this is from the Rocky Mount Charter School. Several CEOs whose children attended private school were founders of that charter school. One day I got a call from one of their wives with the happy news that her maid's grandson had won the lottery and would attend the charter school. Charter schools create opportunities for all children, even the maid's grandson. While the state's school age population is 24.9 percent black, the charter school enrollment is 50.1 percent black.

What do you expect the charter movement in North Carolina to look like in five years? If the charter movement falls prey to the appeasement siren song of gutless charter school founders who attempt to curry favor with the state education establishment in the hopes that their school will be left alone, the movement will be co-opted and crushed. If it is vigilant, there will be 300–400 schools statewide, and school districts will begin conversions en masse to meet the competitive threat. It is a 50–50 proposition.

What would you like your educational legacy to be? For hundreds of thousands of children, Vernon Robinson of North Carolina was the conductor on the freedom train to educational opportunity.

An Arizona analysis suggests that competition has made a positive difference for district schools in the state with America's liveliest charter program. The study sorts district responses into the low-cost kind (e.g., using flyers and other marketing tools to explain their own services to parents) and costlier moves that actually change the available services (e.g., starting a full-day kindergarten program). While the mere whisper of charters may trigger the former, the authors contend that "only direct competition from charter schools pushes districts to adopt high cost reforms. Further, positive achievement results are most apparent in the sub-performing districts. This is in sharp contrast to the fears of many school choice opponents, who believe that competition will harm poorly performing schools."[13]

Not every reaction is coherent, though, much less positive. "I saw a lot of chaos, a lot of confusion and a lot of controversy" in Arizona, comments charter scholar Eric Rofes, "but I also saw districts that were responding."[14]

[13] Robert Maranto, Scott Milliman, and Frederick Hess, "Does Public Sector Competition Stimulate Innovation? The Competitive Impacts of Arizona Charter Schools on Traditional Public Schools," unpublished paper. For anecdotal information on Queen Creek, Arizona (where a third of the district's elementary school students left) and Mesa, see "Resistance Is Futile," *The Bellwether* (Phoenix, Ariz.: Goldwater Institute, 8 September 1998).

[14] Pearce, "Charters' Growth Shows No Sign of Slowing."

Rising customer-consciousness is also palpable in Massachusetts. When one charter offered all-day kindergarten, the local school committee set out to do the same thing. Recalling the district's strong opposition to the original charter request, a parent remarked on the irony: "We wanted all-day kindergarten for our kids, so we made that request a part of our charter petition to the state. We even added extended day care. Now the district has decided to have all-day kindergarten. If this charter school is so bad for the district—as all their bureaucrats told us time and again—why is the district now copying what we did?" The Williamsburg School Department initiated a low-cost after-school childcare program for elementary parents to help offset the loss of students to the Hilltown Charter School. When the Cape Cod Lighthouse Charter School opened its doors, the Nauset regional school district began a specialized school-within-a-school to compete with it. Coincidences?

Even Boston took notice when five of the state's first fifteen charter schools were located there. Within months, the district and its teachers union launched a "pilot schools" project, by which regulations and contract provisions can be waived. This opportunity led staff members at Fenway Middle College High School to return their newly granted state charter and become a Boston pilot school instead.[15] Ten such schools were operating in Boston by 1998, with more on the drawing boards. Superintendent Thomas Payzant acknowledges that this would not have happened without the spur of charter schools.

Rochester, New York agreed in 1999 to allow its public schools to convert from district-run institutions to independently chartered sites. Adam Urbanski, head of the Rochester teachers' union, predicts that the Rochester board will contract with groups to run the schools, keep those schools accountable, and "do nothing in between" except coordinate various support services.[16]

Halfway across the country, in Rochester, Minnesota, a Montessori school sought a charter, but the board instead moved to create its own Montessori school. Later, it inaugurated a "back to basics" school in response to parents who were dissatisfied with the choices that they had. In Duluth, the school board had rejected several charter proposals. But when a local university began flirting with a charter approval (public colleges can sponsor charter schools in Minnesota), a board member decided to get serious about charter schools because "We don't want to be in a situation

[15] Larry Myatt and Linda Nathan, "One School's Journey in the Age of Reform," *Phi Delta Kappan*, September 1996, 24–25.

[16] June Kronholz, "School Boards' Role Shifts with New Education Choices," *Wall Street Journal*, 7 June 1999.

where this is foisted on us. If we're viewed as standing in the way, some-
body will eventually go around us."[17]

We saw how Douglas County fended off a seventh charter school by
launching its own "gifted and talented" program. These districts *are* behaving
differently in a world of education choice. Some are rising to the challenge.
This is especially true in smaller or mid-sized districts, where the system is
often more nimble and the impact of a few charter schools is more readily felt.
But a handful of the country's larger school systems are responding, too, as we
can see in Boston, Minneapolis, St. Paul, Chicago, and Denver.

Harvard economist Caroline Hoxby finds that competition makes a difference in public school systems. She argues that one of America's traditional—if rarely acknowledged—forms of school choice is parents' ability
to make decisions about where to live, thereby choosing among school
districts. This analysis bears on the charter phenomenon, since autonomous charter schools have many of the characteristics of a public school
district. Hoxby says:

> An increase of one standard deviation in the degree of choice among districts
> causes a small (and statistically significant) improvement in student achieve-
> ment. Students' reading and math scores improve by about 2 percentile
> points. . . . However, an increase of one standard deviation in choice among
> districts causes a large improvement in schools' efficiency. . . . [In short:] An
> increase in choice improves student achievement even while accomplishing
> substantial cost savings. The implications for schools' productivity (the ratio
> of student achievement to dollars spent) are powerful.[18]

There is little doubt that charter schools *can* have such an impact in
communities where there are enough of them to be felt. As Hoxby has
observed, not everyone needs to exercise choice for it to have an impact on
the former monopoly. Markets can be transformed when ten or twenty
percent of consumers shift from one product to another. Today, there is no
way to know how many American communities will be affected in this
way by the charter movement. But it is unmistakably happening in Mesa,
Arizona. According to a *Wall Street Journal* account, Mesa "is wooing
parents with ardor uncommon in a public service. All school employees,
from bus drivers to principals, now take customer-service workshops. Two
percent of their pay depends on whether they live up to customer-satisfac-
tion and performance goals that range from returning phone calls to
boosting reading scores."[19]

[17] Joe Nathan, *Charter Schools: Creating Hope and Opportunity for American Education*
(San Francisco: Jossey-Bass, 1996), 91.

[18] Caroline M. Hoxby, "Analyzing School Choice Reforms That Use America's Traditional
Forms of Parental Choice," in Peterson and Hassel, *Learning from School Choice*, 133–55.

[19] June Kronholz, "Charter Schools Begin to Prod Public Schools Toward Competition,"
Wall Street Journal, 12 February 1999.

Dr. James Zaharis (Superintendent, Mesa Public Schools, Arizona)

Jim Zaharis has been in Mesa for 33 years, 14 as superintendent. Previously, he taught high school psychology, English, and history. He began his career in industry but "was bored — and was a young idealist who loved teaching."

What was your view of charter schools prior to their arrival in Mesa? Has it changed? Before there were charters, Mesa started its own "new initiative" schools, really its own charters. I believed from the beginning that the charter movement could be healthy for education, serving as a gadfly to cause the system to improve. Unfortunately, the charter movement in Arizona has become politicized. Now we see religious fervor and politics driving maybe ten percent of these schools. I predicted we'd have some great charters and some people in jail. That's exactly what we're getting.

Do you view charter schools as a challenge to public education, a preview of the future, or an interesting sideshow? I'm a little schizophrenic on this one. I'm 56 years old and believe in public education, especially the way it's been done in the West. I worry that in a nation that is desperately seeking common roots, we will separate into different philosophical camps when it comes to educating the young and will become balkanized. I think education should serve the common good. On the other hand, I value competition and choice. Now we're seeing some of the fruits — and some of the rancor — coming from this.

How are charter schools affecting your school system? We're getting about a 20 percent return rate from charters to the public system. I think we're seeing a bit of cresting of the charter movement here, which is three years ahead of the rest of the country. Still, if you lose 3,000 kids, you have much less money flowing into the system. Charters are a challenge, but we're up to it.

How is the school system responding to that challenge? I have to be a pragmatist and live in the world we occupy, which is now a world of choice. I also believe in judo, taking the energy that's coming at you, grabbing it, and using it to your advantage. That's what we're doing with the energy shown by the charter movement. It's stimulating us to innovate. We have charter-like schools in the system and are creating more of them. The money follows the child to the school. Our view is that if this school can't serve you, we've got one down the street that can. We have three "fundamental" schools now, an arts school, and a Montessori program functioning as a school-within-a-school. For the Montessori program, the school board used the charter law to gain additional personnel flexibility. We're now in discussions about using an old downtown high school building that could become an educational mall with a series of charter-like niche schools — and also serve as a catalyst for urban redevelopment.

What do you see ahead? The good charter schools will grow, the bad ones will fall away. Enrollments may max at five percent. I don't think I'm being naïve. I just hope that the rhetoric can tone down from the acrimony into really looking at benefits for children and not destroying communities.

What advice would you give to superintendents in other communities who are faced with the possibility of charter schools on their doorstep? If the law is as liberal as Arizona's, you need to get out in front of the parade and lead it, take advantage of the energy that's there, use it to help children. If the law is more stringent, I might be a lot more careful and engage in a lot more negotiation. The law dictates the legal and political environment.

CHARTER SCHOOLS AS DISTRICT ASSETS

Districts can also achieve their own purposes with the help of charter schools, creating schools not possible under the usual ground rules, using them as labs to test innovations, and employing them as part of a broader reform strategy. Mesa's new Montessori school would have been difficult to staff due to state certification requirements, but the charter law enabled the district to snip that red tape. Houston contracted with Thaddeus Lott, director of the pathbreaking Wesley Elementary school, to operate Wesley and several nearby schools as a charter cluster, partly to liberate him from the district's own bureaucratic burdens. Lott now reports directly to the Houston superintendent. He says that the charter "allows us to feel like we're not committing a crime by doing things differently."[20]

The San Carlos Charter Learning Center, California's first charter school, was created by the district board and superintendent "as a research and development site for the San Carlos School District [whose] successful innovations will be transferable to other schools in the district." In her 1997 visit to the school, First Lady Hillary Rodham Clinton aptly compared the San Carlos approach to "test kitchens . . . [that help us] learn from each other and . . . get to scale in the sense that we know what works [and can then spread these ideas] to every school."[21]

---

[20] Tyce Palmaffy, "No Excuses," *Policy Review*, January/February 1998, 19.

[21] Remarks of the President and Mrs. Clinton, San Carlos Charter Learning Center, 29 September 1997, available on http://scclc.sancarlos.k12.ca.us.

Some of the charter innovations first cooked on the San Carlos stove are now part of the district menu — e.g., use of personalized learning plans, thematic instructional units, multi-age classrooms, and technology-based instruction. The charter also brought new flexibility to district hiring policies and the ability to outsource some education services. For example, one school now contracts with the city's recreation department for physical education services. Nearly all district schools have begun to seek grant money from foundations, a strategy pioneered by the charter school. Superintendent Don Shalvey commented, "No doubt about it. The charter school was the spark for much of the instructional innovation that has gone on in the district." Adds school board member Beth Hunkapillar, "The innovations undertaken by the charter school are like viral infections in the body of the district, spreading themselves around."

Sometimes a charter school that was not intended for R&D ends up serving that purpose. This happened in Lowell, Massachusetts, where Lowell Middlesex Academy had been an alternative program for high school dropouts run in conjunction with the local community college. After enactment of charter legislation, the college converted it to an autonomous charter high school. Karen Moore, the school's executive director, says that the school is "seen as a place with a strong track record of getting kids that no one else in the school district could work with to complete school and go on to college or work." This success led the district to contract with the community college to start an alternative program for middle school youngsters with major discipline problems — a sort of in-district charter modeled on the Academy. The new alternative now serves 25 troublesome kids, and the college receives about $300,000 from the district for operating it.

In nearby Lawrence, all students at the Family Development Charter School are taught and tested in both English and Spanish. The District is sending its teachers to the charter school to learn about this innovative "two-way" language program. Yet another example can be found in Boston. Sarah Kass (see interview in chapter 10), cofounder of City On A Hill, describes her school's warming relationship with the district that surrounds it:

> We have found the Boston Public Schools increasingly open to collaboration, and . . . have launched several important teacher-driven collaborations. . . . Most significantly, our federally funded Urban Calculus Initiative is a . . . collaboration exploring how we can prepare more urban youth to study calculus in high school. We believe that collaboration with the public school system will be most beneficial to the students of Boston and to the long-term professional development of teachers.

Denver, too, is innovating. At first, the board and superintendent wanted nothing to do with charters and were accused by some of "stonewalling."

Today, however, Denver hosts two autonomous charter schools; and a third, the Pioneer Charter School, is a joint venture by the district and the University of Denver, demonstrating that it is possible to run a successful urban school if one is willing to do things differently. (More jaundiced observers argue that both superintendent and school board were stung by criticism of their anti-charter stance, and that the end of busing, deepening dislike of the teachers' union, and a couple of new faces on the school board created an opportunity to reposition themselves.) Located in a Hispanic neighborhood, the school is pre-K through 5 and uses the district curriculum with an extra emphasis on literacy. Its main innovations involve differentiated staffing and outsourced services. It operates at 80 percent of per-pupil operating revenues, but the district provides a building and the school's founders have raised private dollars. Denver school board president Sue Edwards comments, "The more variety we can provide within public schools, the better. We're striving to meet the needs of each and every student."[22]

We saw in chapter 7 how former Dayton superintendent James Williams sought to "outsource" five of his low-performing district schools to the Edison Project, using Ohio's new charter law. When this was foiled by a hostile teachers' union, business leaders and Edison went directly to the state board of education to obtain a charter for a new school in Dayton (which opened in 1999). Meantime, other Daytonians sought state charters; one small school opened in September 1998, and four more such schools were operating by September 1999). This flurry of charter activity induced the teachers union in spring 1999 to compromise and work with Williams and a local school reform group to develop Ohio's first "conversion" charter in one of the city's least successful elementary schools.

The union is learning from the charter experience in Houston, too. Observes Houston Federation of Teachers president Gayle Fallon, "We've learned that sometimes small is better, something we need to look at in structuring our schools. You can carve a large school into small units that work a lot better for a lot of kids. I've also learned [that] if you give people who are normally disenfranchised an opportunity for input into a program, they'll not only design a good one, they'll also work harder than anyone can imagine to make it work. Saturdays, too. As long as we're careful not to do charters for the sake of charters, we can get positive results."

Chicago is making substantial use of the charter option as a way of piloting innovation while also serving children. By 1998, the "reform board" (answerable directly to Mayor Richard Daley) had awarded all fifteen charters that the legislature authorized for the city, nearly all of them to new schools. Charter contracts include strict accountability re-

---

[22] Carlos Illescas, "Two Schools Prepare to Chart a New Course," *Denver Post*, 24 August 1998, 1B, 3B.

quirements focused on improved student performance, with wide operational latitude given to individual schools to produce these results. Board
President Gerry Chico terms the charters "a laboratory in which new ideas
about organization, structure, curriculum and instruction can be tried and
tested. When these charters demonstrate new approaches to education that
prove effective, we will be applying these ideas to other schools in
Chicago."[23]

The charter-as-test-kitchen approach has clear limits. It assumes that the
basic structures and power relationships of the familiar school system will
remain intact, not be transformed by the charter phenomenon. Instead, it
allows a small number of charter schools to operate on the side, in their
own little realm, but not changing the ground rules — "charters in a box."

Occasionally a district's use of the charter opportunity is purely util-
itarian. After a bond issue failed, the Nacogdoches, Texas district and
Stephen F. Austin University devised a way to use the state's charter law to
add a much needed elementary school by converting the privately operated
campus lab school to a charter. Down on the coast, one of Texas's most
successful charter schools will join the Corpus Christi district, serving families on an offshore island that the system had long refused to provide with
its own school. After island residents took matters into their own hands
and created a charter school (including construction of three buildings),
the new district superintendent invited them to reaffiliate.

But traffic flows in two directions. Gayle Fallon notes that a Texas district may play the charter card to ease the threat that a school will go
directly to the state and thereby subtract pupils and dollars from the district. She observed that some of Houston's "regular" public schools "are
turning into charters, especially at the elementary level. We had nineteen
'internal' charters last year [1996–97] and more now. But they don't always work well. The bureaucracy tends to revert to business as usual."

As in Kingsburg, the little town of Cartersville, Georgia has become a
charter district. Superintendent Harold Barnett comments: "I was hoping
we'd release a burst of energy from our educators, improve academic performance, and increase parent involvement. We've been able to do all three
things. And the culture of parent involvement we've created has helped the
schools be much more responsive to the public we serve."

GAINING MOMENTUM

Initial studies suggest that, more often that not, charter schools are having
an impact on their surrounding districts. The University of California's

---

[23] Leadership for Quality Education, *Chicago Charter Schools — Portraits: Year One 1997–
1998* (Chicago: Leadership for Quality Education, 1998), 1. On the Chicago reform effort
see Anthony S. Bryk, Penny Bender Sebring, David Kerbow, Sharon Rollow, and John Q.
Easton, *Charting Chicago School Reform: Democratic Localism as a Lever for Change* (Boulder, Colorado: Westview Press, 1998).

Eric Rofes has studied their effects in 25 communities.[24] Two-thirds reported mild to strong effects on the school system, with such responses as these:

- Opening schools organized around a specific philosophy or theme.
- Creating "add-on" programs such as after-school programs or all-day kindergartens.
- Offering more diverse activities or curricular resources.
- Outsourcing services through contracts with private providers.
- Public-relations and marketing campaigns to attract new parents or win old ones back.

Change comes slowly, though. A 1998 Massachusetts study examined how charter operators and district-based educators view the sharing of innovations. Most charter people believe it is the "mindset" of charter schools that should be replicated — e.g., designing programs for every child to succeed, the commitment of the entire community to the school — rather than specific school practices. But most non-charter educators see structural and attitudinal barriers to replicating what charter schools do. These range from financial and organizational constraints facing district schools to the anger that accompanies the loss of revenues to charter schools and the perception that charters have polarized communities. Attitudinal barriers are the hardest to overcome.[25] Still, based on the Massachusetts experience so far, the researchers concluded that "Overall, the educational effects of charter schools on district schools have been positive or neutral."[26]

How will this turn out? We are fairly bullish. The evidence in hand suggests that it is as true in education as in other domains that, when competition enters a monopoly situation, change follows, but other observers are more cautious. Bryan C. Hassel, for example, writes that "As they are now constituted, charter school programs will have difficulty achieving the system-changing impact their proponents envision. In part they are limited by legislative compromises that diminish charter schools' ability to act as effective laboratories, competitors, or replacements for existing district schools."[27]

[24] Eric Rofes, *How Are School Districts Responding to Charter Laws and Charter Schools?* (Berkeley, Calif.: Policy Analysis for California Education, 1998).

[25] A study of California charter schools arrived at similar findings. It found that there are seldom "mechanisms in place for charter schools and regular schools to learn from each other" and that "educators' belief that charter schools have an unfair advantage inhibits competition that would, in theory, force improvements." But the author concludes — incorrectly, we believe — that "competition and cooperation . . . are at odds with each other . . . [and] that choice and competition often lead to greater stratification." See Amy Stuart Wells, *Beyond the Rhetoric of Charter School Reform: A Study of Ten California School Districts* (Los Angeles: University of California at Los Angeles, 1998), 54–58.

[26] Rosenblum Brigham Associates, *Innovation and Massachusetts Charter Schools* (Boston: Massachusetts Department of Education, 1998), 26.

[27] Hassel, "Charter Schools," 266.

STATE-LEVEL EFFECTS

Doubts notwithstanding, charters are beginning to change the education reform debate at the state level. Though these schools are barely a radar blip in most states in terms of raw numbers, they have disproportionate symbolic and political importance. William Windler, senior consultant with the Colorado Department of Education, has documented the ways in which his state's charter movement "has benefited the state's entire public education system."[28] Windler says, "Many districts are now viewing charter schools, and in a broader sense, all schools of choice as a key tool to implementing Colorado's Standards Based Education initiative. . . . Most charter schools are becoming a real asset to public education."[29]

According to the Pennsylvania Department of Education, "Charter schools are exciting and innovative initiatives that will change and improve the educational landscape in Pennsylvania and across America. . . . Six charter public schools serving nearly 1,000 students opened in the Commonwealth within ten weeks of the passage of Act 22 of 1997, Pennsylvania's charter school law."[30] Thirty-one charter schools were open by 1998. Building on the success of the state's charter program, Governor Tom Ridge has proposed charter districts. He said: "Take what's good about charter schools — the flexibility, the empowerment, the community control — and enlarge the scope. Make the charter apply not just to one school, but to the entire district. Give communities the opportunities to make decisions about how all their kids will learn, not just a few."[31]

After the Texas State Board of Education awarded 41 "open-enrollment" charters to schools in early 1998 (in addition to the 19 that were already open), then–board chairman Jack Christie said, "This is a large step in the bold experiment to create competition and excellence in the [Texas] public school system." An even larger step was taken in September 1998 when the Board okayed an additional 85 open-enrollment charters.

In Massachusetts, which had 34 charter schools open in 1998–99, enrolling more than 10,000 youngsters from 180 districts, the state Department of Education reports, "Perhaps the most revolutionary innovation of charter schools, often overlooked or taken for granted, is the concept itself: extraordinary freedom at the school level and genuine accountability for results. . . . With charter schools leading the way, perhaps the day is

---

[28] William Windler, "Colorado's Charter Schools: A Spark for Change and a Catalyst for Reform," *Phi Delta Kappan*, September 1996, 66–69.

[29] From the state department of education's *Colorado Charter School Information Packet and Handbook*, http://www.cde.state.co.us/chintro.htm.

[30] Pennsylvania Department of Education, "Charter Schools: Questions and Answers," December 1998; see http://www.cas.psu.edu/docs/pde/charfaq.html.

[31] Radio Address by Governor Tom Ridge, "Charter School Districts," 30 September 1998.

not far off when all public schools will be given the latitude charter schools enjoy in exchange for real accountability for results."[32]

Charter schools help illumine other education policy issues. For example, states currently face an acute dilemma concerning school finance: should money continue to be directed through categorical programs (e.g., anti-drug campaigns) and special groups or populations (e.g., children with limited English proficiency), traveling from one bureaucracy to the next, with each jurisdiction peeling off overhead and adding rules? Or should money flow from state authorities to families, following students to the schools of their choice? The charter movement pushes in the latter direction. In Massachusetts and most of Arizona, for example, state money for charter pupils follows them directly to their schools, with no intervening agent. This led one state policymaker to comment, "If we can do that for charters, we can have money follow kids to any school." Arizona's charter schools played a key role in that state's move to child-centered capital funding for all schools. In early 1999, the California State Board of Education approved a plan to provide direct funding from the state to its charter schools for most operational expenses, without the dollars having to pass through district bureaucracies.

Meanwhile, the charter laws themselves are also changing. Texas raised from 20 to 120 the number of "open enrollment" charters that the state board of education could issue. (It may also issue an unlimited number of charters for "at-risk" youngsters.) In California, the legislature was confronted with 1.2 million signatures to place an initiative on the ballot that would greatly liberalize the state's charter law. It bowed to the inevitable and amended the law itself, lifting the cap on the number of charters allowed, authorizing state and county boards of education to grant charters denied by local school boards, and requiring districts to make empty facilities available to charter operators.[33]

NATIONAL EFFECTS

Echoes from the charter movement are also audible in Washington. Senior federal officials — and candidates — often talk about charters these days, usually in warmly positive terms. U.S. Secretary of Education Richard Riley says, "The charter school movement represents what is best about American education — a willingness to change, to be impatient, to demand excellence, and, at the same time, a deep, abiding commitment to the democratic principles that define public education."[34]

[32] *The Massachusetts Charter School Initiative: 1998 Report* (Boston: Massachusetts Department of Education, 1998), 6–7.

[33] Robert C. Johnson, "California Reaches 'Historic' Charter Schools Agreement," *Education Week*, 6 May 1998.

[34] Remarks by Richard W. Riley, U.S. Secretary of Education, 1997 National Charter

Senator John Kerry (D-MA), once described in *The Boston Globe* as "clueless about charter schools,"[35] eagerly enlisted in the charter movement two years later. After describing the "chaos in governance" faced by U.S. public schools, he proposed "a bold answer: Let's make every public school in this country essentially a charter school . . . with decentralized control, site-based management, parental engagement, and high levels of volunteerism."[36]

Charter schools now have their own small federal program, too. In 1994, Congress authorized a new Public Charter School Program. By 1999, its appropriation exceeded $100 million and it had bipartisan support in Congress.[37] (These funds are used mainly for school planning and start-up expenses.)

Charters have even begun to figure in debates about the major federal education aid programs, all of which were designed to serve school systems rather than individual schools (much less individual students). It has not gone unnoticed that—as we saw in the previous chapter—charters tend not to get their "fair share" of these aid dollars. Both the General Accounting Office and the Congressional Research Service have attested to this problem, and some members of Congress would like to solve it. At this writing, it is far from certain that this will happen—it could mean a wholesale restructuring of complex formulas and eligibility rules—but charter schools are at least causing consideration of the possibility.

They attract ample media attention, too. Throughout this book, we have cited articles—often cover stories—from major national newspapers and magazines, as well as local publications. Television programs like "Sixty Minutes" and PBS's "Merrow Report" have also featured charter schools, blemishes and all. All this attention has helped the charter idea gain attention from lawmakers, philanthropists, business leaders, and pundits. It should be no surprise, therefore, that a 1997 poll by the Democratic Leadership Council showed the popularity of charter schools: 67 percent of Americans support them, while only 26 percent are opposed. And more than half of those surveyed say that "our educational system will only improve through more choice and competition among schools."[38]

School Conference: "Strengthening Education Through Innovation and Public School Choice," Washington, D.C., 4 November 1997.

[35] Jon Keller, "Kerry Is Clueless about Charter Schools," *The Boston Globe*, 26 August 1996.

[36] Press release, Office of Senator John Kerry, Northeastern University, 16 June 1998, 5–6.

[37] In October 1998, President Clinton signed new charter school legislation that gives priority to states with "strong" charter laws, ensures that charters get their fair share of federal funds, allows states to reserve 10 percent of their grant funds to support dissemination activities, and authorizes another federal charter study.

[38] Marc Penn, *The New Democratic Electorate: Survey Results November 1997* (Washington, D.C.: Democratic Leadership Council, 1997), 16; see also Laureen Lazarovici, "New Poll: Charter Schools, National Standards Popular," *Education Daily*, 13 August 1997, 1–2.

We judge that charter schools today are more influential than their numbers suggest. They are at the epicenter of America's most powerful education reform earthquake, and their rumblings don't just affect school systems. They are also transforming communities, the subject of our next chapter.

10

BEYOND THE SCHOOLHOUSE DOOR: BUILDING COMMUNITIES

> We expected to open a school. We didn't expect to gain a community.
>
> *Parent-founder, Platte River Charter School, Douglas County, Colorado*

A WATER PIPE burst days before Colin Powell Academy was scheduled to open in the poorest ZIP code of Detroit, flooding the entire building. It was a charter founder's worst nightmare. Launching the school would be hard enough — hiring and training teachers, completing the paperwork, and attending to thousands of other details — without such a disaster. But everyone pitched in to rescue the school. The flooding prompted an extraordinary round-the-clock community effort to pump and mop and paint. The crisis engaged parents, students, and others from the neighborhood, including youngsters who had been in trouble with the law. Some say the local homeless folks guarded the school from vandals while it was being refurbished. If the community had not mustered mops, buckets, sweat, and toil, Colin Powell Academy would not have opened in August 1996. But open it did.

Today, this charter school enrolls about 220 young African-American children from a neighborhood rife with liquor stores, bars, graffiti, and drug dealers. Housed in an abandoned Catholic high school leased from the Archdiocese for a dollar a year, Colin Powell Academy emphasizes character development, curricular basics, and community leadership. Plans call for it to add a grade a year — it is now K-7 perhaps all the way through high school.

This school was the dream of Pastor Ellis Smith of the Jubilee Christian Church, who envisioned a neighborhood school "rising out of the ashes and becoming a pillar of strength in a downtrodden community." Pastor Smith has "a passion for children [and saw] a dire need for a new educational paradigm that was more student-focused and less focused on finances, politics, and bureaucracy." (See interview below.) So he joined with others in the community and obtained a charter in April 1996 from Central Michigan University.

Smith was elated by the strong response to the flood, for it showed him that the community had already embraced this charter school. He remarks that such schools are important because "they empower communities." By giving families and educators the opportunity to create a school with which they choose to affiliate, charter schools impart a sense of control to people, give them status, and make them members of a community that embodies their values and transmits these norms to a new generation.

INTERVIEW

Rev. Ellis L. Smith (Founder, Colin Powell Academy)

Why did you go out on a limb and launch a charter school? I could hear the apathy and despair from parents who were not satisfied with our traditional public schools, but were not in a position financially to send their child to a private school. To me, this is a "calling": to make a significant impact on the academic development of urban youth.

What is your greatest source of personal satisfaction with this school? Your greatest disappointment? I was quite pleased when I learned that our fourth grade students made a dramatic 57-point turnaround on the state math test. There was also a 22-point increase on the reading test. My two major disappointments are the lack of state-certified African-American male teachers and the fact that we have to turn away hundreds of parents who wish to enroll their children at Colin Powell Academy.

What is your greatest hope for the school's future? My greatest hope is to be in a position to facilitate college scholarships for every student who graduates from Colin Powell Academy.

How important are charter schools as an education reform strategy for America? Charter schools are an essential component of educational choice and reform, primarily because they empower communities. Their greatest potential impact is in economically disadvantaged communities. These parents don't have the financial capacity to enroll their children in private schools. In most of these communities, the most stabilizing institution is the church. I'm pleased to see more religious leaders getting involved in establishing charter schools. The only caution would be maintaining a separation of church and state and being cognizant of the applicable laws.

This chapter contends that charter schools are not only education institutions; they are also examples — and wellsprings — of community rebirth.

They are instruments of civil society as well as places of teaching and learning. We have seen the experience of Colin Powell Academy repeated across the land. The exercise of founding and sustaining a charter school can breathe new life into ailing communities as well as faltering education systems.

If Alexis de Tocqueville — celebrated chronicler of *Democracy in America* — were to visit these shores today as he did in 1831, he would surely regard charter schools as vibrant contemporary examples of Americans' enduring zest to form new organizations to meet human needs. As a middle path between the impersonal agencies of government and the private affairs of individuals and families, charter schools are precisely the sort of mediating institution that forges healthy communities.[1] They bring people together to tackle common problems, to strive toward shared objectives, and to create a moral order in which to raise their children. In the next few pages, we discuss the shaky condition of civil society in public education and see how charter schools strengthen it.

CIVIL SOCIETY AND PUBLIC EDUCATION

By "civil society," we mean the web of non-governmental institutions and organizations through which people advance common goals and pursue shared interests.[2] These range from groups like the Knights of Columbus and B'nai B'rith to the American Red Cross and the Girl Scouts. From this organic process of coming together to work toward mutual objectives arises "social capital," which the eminent sociologist James Coleman defined in this way:

> If physical capital is wholly tangible, being embodied in observable material form, and human capital is less tangible, being embodied in the skills and knowledge acquired by an individual, social capital is less tangible yet, for it exists in the *relations* between persons. Just as physical capital and human capital facilitate productive activity, social capital does as well.[3]

[1] In British political circles, the search for a "third way" between what John Kay calls "benign socialism" and "benign Thatcherism" has evoked much discussion. Kay comments that "Education is about shared values in communities, and is undermined by the polarisation of authority between individuals and the state. That is why neither marketisation nor central political control work: the most successful education institutions are rarely found within such contexts. Around the world, the most successful educational institutions are, almost invariably, strongly embedded in communities. Education reform requires the creation, or recreation, of these communities." See John Kay, "Evolutionary Politics," *Prospect* (July 1998): 31–35.

[2] David Brooks, "Civil Society and Its Discontents," *The Weekly Standard*, 5 February 1996, 18–21; Gertrude Himmelfarb, "Second Thoughts on Civil Society," *The Weekly Standard*, 9 September 1996, 21–24.

[3] James S. Coleman and Thomas Hoffer, *Public, and Private High Schools: The Impact of Communities* (New York: Basic Books, 1987).

A school's social capital is born of the relations among the children who attend it and the adults involved with it. A school lacking social capital is not likely to be a productive learning environment—nor much of a community asset.

Tocqueville was the first of many observers to see Americans' lively civic participation as a defining characteristic of our society. Yet over the past century, public education has witnessed—and contributed to—a serious erosion of the qualities that impressed Tocqueville. Ironically, this erosion results in part from efforts that were styled education "reforms" by their promoters. Three are worth noting.

First is the rise of the expert professional and the decline of local lay control over what happens in school. While these reforms did move education policy largely beyond the reach of party bosses and patronage machines, they also set in motion a process that today has put public schools beyond the self-correcting reach of community politics. David Mathews, Kettering Foundation President and former U.S. Secretary of Health, Education, and Welfare, describes this culture of professionalism:

[T]he public as a real force in the life of the schools was deliberately and systematically rooted out. Citizens were replaced with a new group of professionals, true guardians of the public interest, there to do what it was assumed citizens couldn't or shouldn't do.[4]

"Local control" is still the mantra chanted on behalf of the present governance arrangements, but the phrase masks a system of bureaucratic and interest-group politics that, in most places, is walled off from the needs and priorities of those whose interests it nominally serves. "Experts" have come to dominate most education decisions, and government has become their chosen mechanism for retaining control. Outside of small towns and special circumstances, education's version of civil society suffers grave damage from this situation.

A second well-meant reform that weakened the social capital of public education is what Diane Ravitch terms the "crusade for efficiency."[5] This movement incorporated into schooling the principles of mass production and scientific management described by Frederick Winslow Taylor and his followers. It led to a heightened emphasis on credentialed expertise, orderly management, uniform operations, and large-scale organizations. In the words of Francis Fukuyama, "Taylorism, as scientific management came to be known, epitomized the carrying of the low-trust, rule-based

[4] David Mathews, "Public-Government/Public-Schools," *National Civic Review* 85, no. 3 (Fall 1996): 15.

[5] Diane Ravitch, *The Great School Wars: A History of the New York City Public Schools* (New York: Basic Books, 1974), 189–230; David B. Tyack, *The One Best System: A History of American Urban Education* (Cambridge: Harvard University Press, 1974), 126–98.

factory system to its logical conclusion."[6] In education, it led to a quest for efficient operations, amongst which an especially noteworthy — and dubious — accomplishment was the consolidation of thousands of small schools and school systems into larger units. Fewer villages and towns retained their own schools and, when they did, the schools were often run by officials sitting miles away in the office of the "regional" or "consolidated" school district. As vast "comprehensive" high schools became the norm, the one-room schoolhouse became a faint memory.[7] Local control and community engagement eroded further. Industrial-style labor unions arose to combat industrial-style management. And the school's capacity to produce social capital and nurture civil society was further diminished.

Third, public education became an arm of government rather than a creature of its diverse communities. This pattern originated in the early nineteenth century with the "common school reformers" for whom, in the words of Boston University professor Charles Glenn, "[T]he state was conceived as ultimate guardian and guarantor of a social order in which individuals would be liberated from intermediate traditions and loyalties, in the interest of progress, enlightenment, and national integration."[8]

The state's role in education grew exponentially in the 1960s with the proliferation of new government programs targeted at special needs (e.g., "at-risk" kids) and interests.[9] Each program brought new money — but also fresh mandates, regulations, and pressure groups, all tending to pull schools in multiple directions and deflect them from their core academic duties. The judiciary, too, became more deeply involved in education governance, particularly via racial desegregation. In a thoughtful analysis of this contentious issue, David Armor argues that school desegregation levied huge social, political, and economic costs, including malign effects on community and neighborhood life.[10] How can one's school be a pillar of civil society if it is located in someone else's community? How can it strengthen ties among neighbors if neighborhoods are ignored by school assignment maps and fractured by hours-long bus rides? Today, not sur-

---

[6] Francis Fukuyama, *Trust: The Social Virtues and the Creation of Prosperity* (New York: Free Press, 1995), 226.

[7] We pointed out in chapter 3 how, in 1930, the U.S. still had more than 127,000 separate school districts and 262,000 separate public schools. Today, there are but 15,000 districts and 85,000 schools, even though total enrollments have doubled.

[8] Charles Glenn, *The Myth of the Common School* (Amherst, Mass.: University of Massachusetts Press, 1988), 236.

[9] On the relationship between education and the government between 1965 and 1980, see Diane Ravitch, *The Troubled Crusade: American Education 1945–1980* (New York: Basic Books, 1983), 267–320.

[10] David Armor, *Forced Justice* (New York: Oxford University Press, 1995); see also Michael Heise, "Assessing the Efficacy of School Desegregation," *Syracuse Law Review* 46, no. 3 (1996): 1093–1117; Diane Ravitch, *The Schools We Deserve: Reflections on the Educational Crises of Our Time* (New York: Basic Books, 1985), 182–259.

prisingly, we hear a growing chorus (including many minority leaders) seeking to end court-ordered busing in such cities as Denver, Cleveland, Boston, Seattle, Philadelphia, and Minneapolis.[11] Meanwhile, the public schools in such places are not much help as community-builders.

While something was doubtless gained from these efforts to profession-alize the schools, boost their efficiency, and use government to expand access to them, something has also been lost: the singular place of the school as a creature of its own community and the responsibility of those who inhabit that community. Even while chanting "local control," re-formers have severed the roots that once anchored schools to their neigh-borhoods and towns. The result is "one best system" of public education that is remote from citizens and losing its legitimacy in their eyes. Tocque-ville foresaw the effect of such a system when he wrote of the

> despotism [that] democratic nations have to fear: . . . a network of small com-plicated rules, minute and uniform, through which the most original minds and the most energetic characters cannot penetrate. . . . [S]uch a power does not destroy, but it prevents existence; it does not tyrannize, but it compresses, enervates, extinguishes, and stupefies a people.[12]

Tocqueville penned those words in 1840, just as Horace Mann and his colleagues were working to establish the "common school" under govern-ment auspices and laying the foundation for the system whose enervating effects Tocqueville anticipated.

The "Silent Revolution"

In recent years, America has enjoyed a lively debate about its civic health. In 1977, Peter L. Berger and Richard John Neuhaus argued that our civic infrastructure — neighborhoods, families, churches, and voluntary associa-tions — was badly frayed.[13] Today, the best known variation on that theme holds that Americans are retreating from civic engagement, a view promi-nently associated with Harvard political scientist Robert Putnam, whose evocative image, "bowling alone," suggests his concern with "the strange disappearance of social capital and civic engagement in America."[14]

---

[11] Peter Applebome, "A Wave of Suits Seeks a Reversal of School Busing," *New York Times*, 26 September 1995, A1, 21; James S. Kunen, "The End of Integration," *Time*, 29 April 1996, 39–46; "Rethinking School Integration," *CQ Researcher*, 18 October 1996.

[12] Alexis de Tocqueville, *Democracy in America*, ed. Richard Hefner (New York: New American Library, 1956), 303–4.

[13] The original Berger and Neuhaus essay has been published along with a collection of current commentaries in Michael Novak, ed., *To Empower People: From the State to Civil Society* (Washington, D.C.: American Enterprise Institute Press, 1996). The essay spawned a mediating structures project, one of which was on education. For the volume on education see David S. Seeley, *Education Through Partnership: Mediating Structures and Education* (Cambridge, Mass.: Ballenger Publishing Company, 1981).

[14] Robert Putnam, "The Strange Disappearance of Civic America," *The American Prospect*, Winter 1996, 34.

Another prominent political scientist and public opinion expert, Everett Carll Ladd, advances a contrary proposition. While acknowledging that some forms of civic participation are declining, he believes that citizen engagement on the whole is rising and manifesting itself in new forms and groups, a shift that he terms the "silent revolution."[15]

This debate about the health of civil society will likely continue, but it has been clear for years that many people would like to foster greater community and intimacy within education and to reconnect the public with its schools. For example, in New York City in the 1960s, the "community control" movement led to massive decentralization of the school governance system. (Here, the outcome was divisiveness and racial strife more than empowerment.) This effort to reestablish links between the public and its schools has had many voices and versions — radical, liberal, and conservative — as reformers began to criticize the "one best system" and to call instead for "open schools," "free schools," "alternative schools," "schools of choice," even for "deschooling" society. These critics held that schools should do more to value individuals, tend to the needs of each student, and foster community.[16]

Some of this was romantic nonsense, but much of it contained an important truth: schools can afford to be different, need to be responsive, and work best when the people involved with them have a sense of ownership. This impulse remains visible in such education reforms as the Coalition of Essential Schools (in which each school reinvents itself), in the proliferation of "alternative" schools, and in mini-schools, magnet schools, and "schools within schools." Chicago for a time placed a "local school council," consisting primarily of teachers and parents, in charge of running each of the city's public schools. (A vestige of that arrangement persists today.)

National attention to the condition of civil society has brought a flurry of studies and reports, many of which emphasize the role that K-12 education can play in helping America meet the challenge of civic renewal. Many argue that the effort to improve teaching and learning includes giving families more choices among schools, and they often laud the charter school strategy.[17] For example, the bipartisan National Commission on Civic Renewal recommended in 1998 that

---

[15] Everett Carrll Ladd, *The Ladd Report on Civic America* (New York: The Free Press, 1999). See also Ladd, "The Data Just Don't Show Erosion of America's 'Social Capital,'" *The Public Perspective*, June/July 1996, 1–5.

[16] Diane Ravitch, *The Great School Wars*, 251–378; Ravitch, *The Troubled Crusade*, 228–66.

[17] The National Commission on Civic Renewal, *A Nation of Spectators: How Civic Disengagement Weakens America and What We Can Do About It* (College Park, Md.: The National Commission on Civic Renewal, 1998); The Council on Civil Society, *A Call to Civil*

The federal government, states, and localities should cooperate to increase parental choice through such measures as open enrollment and public school choice within districts (and even beyond). Within five years, every state should enact meaningful charter school legislation, and the federal government should dramatically increase its support for charter schools.[18]

CHARTER SCHOOLS AS COMMUNITIES

Schools have always been institutions around which communities bond. It is obvious in small towns — and visible in the panic that consumes them when a school district consolidation threatens the loss of the little school that helps give a hamlet its identity. Today, as small town life gives way to the metropolis, as once-stable residential patterns grow more mobile, as families scatter across the landscape (and sometimes fragment), and as other community-anchoring institutions such as churches, cafes, and shops become destinations for car journeys rather than for short strolls around the corner, schools are asked even more often to fill that role.

Charter schools display most of the elements that sociologist Robert Nisbet deemed essential to community, including a high degree of personal intimacy, social cohesion, and moral commitment.[19] Nisbet seemed to be anticipating them when he wrote that "Community is the product of people working together on problems, of autonomous and collective fulfillment of internal objectives, and of the experience of living under codes of authority which have been set in large degree by the persons involved."[20]

Creating a charter school presents those involved with the opportunity to build their own education community. We are accustomed to this in private education but it happens less often in the public sector. A 1998 Massachusetts report points to "a strong sense of community among administrators, staff, parents, and students" as a leading characteristic of charter schools.[21] We have identified five attributes that characterize charter schools as learning communities.

Society: Why Democracy Needs Moral Truths (New York: Institute for American Values, 1998); The National Commission on Philanthropy and Civic Renewal, *Giving Better, Giving Smarter: Renewing Philanthropy in America* (Washington, D.C.: The National Commission on Philanthropy and Civic Renewal, 1997).

[18] National Commission on Civic Renewal, *A Nation of Spectators*, 16.

[19] Robert Nisbet, *The Social Philosophers: Community and Conflict in Western Thought* (New York: Thomas Y. Crowell Company, 1973), 1.

[20] Robert Nisbet, *The Quest for Community: A Study on the Ethics of Order and Freedom* (San Francisco: Institute for Contemporary Studies, 1990), report 1953, xxix.

[21] Rosenblum Brigham Associates, *Innovation and Massachusetts Charter Schools* (Boston: Massachusetts Department of Education, 1998), 7.

1. A SELF-GOVERNING, MISSION-DRIVEN INSTITUTION.

At the heart of the charter idea is the designation of the individual *school* rather than the *system* as the essential "unit" of public education. Viewed this way, each school needs the operational, programmatic, and financial autonomy to run its own affairs as it sees fit. This school-specific approach turns the familiar structure of public education on its head.

Treating schools as autonomous units means that each is a distinct organization with a unique mission aligned with its philosophy and values. This mission guides school-based decisions about which activities, people, and budget priorities will best achieve the desired ends.[22] Charter schools also strive to keep their mission front and center in everyone's mind. Parents may be required to read the mission statement and sign a note attesting to their agreement with it. Mission statements are posted in hallways and shorthand versions are inscribed on mugs and uniforms. Distinctiveness, coherence, and focus are the result. Though some charter schools are housed in shopping malls, most are the antithesis of "shopping mall schools" that try to be all things to all students.

Charter schools illustrate the principle of "subsidiarity," which states that problems should be solved as close to home as possible, preferably by a community for itself, rather than by a distant government. In so doing, charter schools restore true local control to public education. In an era when so much of our lives has been metropolitanized, this is a major plus.

2. A VOLUNTARY COMMUNITY.

Charter schools are schools of choice. People create them because they perceive a need or spot an opportunity. Nobody is forced to start, attend, or work in them. The fact that individuals choose to create or enter these education communities has its own power. It is rare for people to want to play active roles in their community when they have no choice over which community it is.

Although charters are *public* entities, they are not government institutions. This vital distinction runs counter to what James Ceasar and Patrick McGuinn see as the modern tendency to equate "public" and "common" matters with those that are "governmentally or publicly run."[23] In the charter universe, "public" does not mean "governmentally run." These schools are voluntary communities.

They also leverage consumer power to break down the government's monopoly. Control is wrested from experts and bureaucracies and turned over to parents and citizens, including poor and previously disempowered

---

[22] Paul Hill and Mary Beth Celio call a school's ability to focus its work around a coherent instructional program "integrative capital." Hill and Celio, *Fixing Urban Schools* (Washington, D.C.: Brookings Institution Press, 1998), 72–74.

[23] James W. Ceaser and Patrick J. McGuinn, "Civic Education Reconsidered," *The Public Interest* (Fall 1998): 94.

people. People who once thought themselves *victims* of the system suddenly become *owners* of their school. As a parent and founder of one California charter told us, "We began to think we could do better for our kids than the district was doing. Sure as hell we couldn't do any worse. If we go belly up, at least we tried."

Nina Lewin (Parent, Chelmsford Public Charter School, Massachusetts)

Nina Lewin is the mother of three children, ages ten to fifteen. Her middle child has been enrolled for two years in the Chelmsford Public Charter School Middle School, a grade 5–8 school that opened in 1996 with 154 students. The school is managed by a for-profit firm named Beacon Education Management. Nina holds a B.A. degree in chemistry and, with her husband, has started two small businesses that deal with industrial water treatment.

Her family sought "a school that had a philosophy of education that was compatible with ours—one that took an interdisciplinary approach to subjects, that saw all subject matter as related, and that saw knowledge as having a practical application and a practical dimension. Our middle child is gifted and wasn't growing academically in her public school. She needed more challenges and flexibility than the school could offer." They couldn't find a conventional public school that suited them so they joined with like-minded parents to start a charter school. After three months of "fierce planning, the group developed a working model for the school."

Lewin calls her experience as a charter founder "a family affair. We all were involved in planning for it and in working to open it—everything from serving on the planning committee, to finding a company to help with the management of the school, to cleaning up the building and painting the walls. It's been an intense experience. It takes an extremely dedicated group to collaborate and create a charter school."

---

3. INTIMACY, SCALE, AND INVOLVEMENT.

Most charter schools are small. The federal charter study estimates their median enrollment at 132 students, less than a third of the 486-pupil public school average in 24 charter school states. Almost two-thirds (65 percent) of the charters enroll fewer than 200 students. (About 17 percent of regular public schools are that small.)[24] With small scale comes intimacy, familiarity, and safety that are often missing from the larger and more

[24] RPP International, *The State of Charter Schools: Third-Year Report* (Washington, D.C.: U.S. Department of Education, 1999), 20–21.

anonymous institutions of American public education. One of the cherished attributes of many charter schools is that everyone in the school knows everyone else — children and staff alike — by name.

When, as occasionally happens, a charter school's enrollment is larger (see, for example, the profile of Sequoia School in chapter 2), it is not unusual for it to create family-style sub-units called "houses," "academies," or "castles." Sometimes the teacher stays with the same children for several years, adding constancy to these important relationships. Classes of children frequently remain together, too, even when teachers change. These family-like qualities may be reinforced by the wider than usual age span in many charters, which are more apt to cover the entire K-12 range or to combine the elementary and middle or middle and high school years.[25]

In this smaller and more stable environment, the school can focus on the needs of individual children rather than batch-processing them. Before- and after-school tutoring and individualized learning plans and contracts are widely used to tailor instruction and help everyone succeed.[26] One student in California mused, "I feel like the teachers at this school are like bloodhounds, always tracking me down, always right on my rear."

Intimacy and familiarity are also fostered through parent involvement, beginning with selecting the school itself. In investigating the effects of public school choice, political scientist Mark Schneider and colleagues conclude that "the act of school choice seems to stimulate parents to become more involved in a wide range of school-related activities that build social capital."[27] Once chosen, charter schools have many ways to engage parents and community members. Some are self-evident, such as including parents on governing boards. Others are less obvious, such as using parents as instructors, or using the school as a family education center. Many charters ask parents to sign contracts specifying how many hours they will volunteer. Almost every charter prides itself on its open-door policy, in contrast to conventional public schools that are more apt to welcome Mom and Dad only for stated events like open houses and parent-teacher conferences.

The West Michigan Academy for Environmental Sciences has a unique way of engaging parents. It is located on a sixty-acre rural site and offers a school "farming" project in which parents (and other community members) can buy shares, and in return, receive their portion of the fresh vege-

<hr/>

[25] RPP International, *The State of Charter Schools: Third-Year Report*, 22–23.

[26] On the use of personal education plans for all students and the use of parent participation agreements in Massachusetts charter schools and how this fosters a sense of community, see Rosenblum Brigham, *Innovation and Massachusetts Charter Schools*, 15–16.

[27] Mark Schneider et al., "Institutional Arrangements and the Creation of Social Capital: The Effects of Public School Choice," *American Political Science Review* 91, no. 1 (March 1997): 91.

tables and fruits. But more is usually entailed than celery and radishes. In a recent survey of charter teachers conducted for the National Education Association, 71 percent report that "parents are significantly involved in making educational decisions at their schools."[28] In conventional public schools, by contrast, fewer than one-fifth of parents participate in major school decisions.[29]

4. A PROFESSIONAL COMMUNITY.

Charter schools represent a marvelous opportunity for educators to form their own professional communities. In the words of Sarah Kass, they offer teachers the opportunity "to see themselves as educational entrepreneurs with a stake in the visioning of a school" (see interview below). As we saw in chapter 4, they afford educators the chance to reinvent their own careers. One Minnesota teacher told us that "Freedom to dream and not be constrained by laws and rules . . . this is one joy of working at this charter school."

Since charter schools confront less red tape, teachers can deploy their professional judgments, set their own instructional priorities, pick their materials, and engage their students in projects and activities that inspire them. They can write their own curriculum or adapt one to fit their pupils' needs. Teachers are included on governing boards of most charter schools.[30] Perhaps even more important is that they *chose* to work there. All this helps forge a professional community in which staff feel a sense of collective responsibility. As one California teacher told us, "There's not a lot of time wasted in extraneous things here. People know what they're about, why they go to meetings, and what we want to accomplish. I feel free to use my professional judgment in a way that's never happened before."

This is not only the occasional anecdote. The recent survey of charter teachers by the National Education Association (NEA) reports that:

- 61 percent of teachers agree or strongly agree that they have substantial authority over curriculum.
- 64 percent say teachers have authority over the selection of instructional materials.
- 54 percent say that teachers control student discipline policy.
- 48 percent say that teachers have substantial authority over teacher hiring.[31]

---

[28] Julia E. Koppich et al., *New Rules, New Roles? The Professional Work Lives of Charter School Teachers* (Washington, D.C., National Education Association, 1998), 35.

[29] Steve Farkas et al., *Playing Their Parts: Parents and Teachers Talk About Parental Involvement in Public Schools* (New York, Public Agenda, 1999), 13.

[30] Koppich et al., *New Rules, New Roles?*, 117.

[31] Koppich et al., *New Rules, New Roles?*, 32–34.

A California charter study stated that "Many teachers noted they were more satisfied with these schools because they had more control over their own classrooms. These teachers thought they were better able to meet the needs of their students, many of whom had fallen though the cracks in the regular public school system."[32]

Charter schools also provide teachers with such desiderata as small classes and professional development opportunities.[33] The NEA reports that 42 percent of charter teachers have classes of 16 to 20 pupils and another 36 percent have classes of 21 to 30. Upwards of 85 percent report that their schools set aside time and money for professional development — and 81 percent say the teachers decide what kinds of professional development they need.[34] In short, charters offer teachers entrepreneurial opportunities and more chances to be involved with school policymaking and planning — important elements of any professional community.

5. MANY KINDS OF NEIGHBORHOOD.

While some charters function as neighborhood schools in the old-fashioned sense, others reflect different sorts of neighborhoods. Today's charter communities transcend contiguous geographic space to include parents' workplaces, curricular philosophies, values, etc. A school's community may consist primarily of people with a shared outlook, interests, needs, or circumstances. Some charter schools are found in ethnic or racial enclaves, others in "values communities."

The Medical Center Charter School in Houston sits at the edge of the 50,000-employee, 675-acre Texas Medical Center. It was created to teach the children of people who work there. As one parent observed about the arrangement, "Having my daughter close by makes me a lot less nervous."

In Southeast Reno City, Kansas, the Yoder Community Resource Center operates the 55-student Yoder Charter School. The community is rural, the population is conservative, and over half the students are Amish. The school has a waiver from the state's sex education requirements and an explicit mission to practice and reinforce "the values taught at home, including responsibility, compassion, honesty, and strong work ethics." In chapter 2, we saw another example of a values community in Michigan's Excel Charter Academy. According to Julie Veeneman, the parent of an Excel eighth grader, "Traditionally, American schools are based on geographic, economic, or religious communities. This school is different — struggling to make a community where none previously existed. The academic and moral focus of this school are what define this community."

[32] SRI International, *Evaluation of Charter School Effectiveness* (Menlo Park, Calif.: SRI International, 1997), IV-3.

[33] Steve Farkas and Jean Johnson, *Given the Circumstances: Teachers Talk About Public Education Today* (New York: Public Agenda, 1996), 14–17.

[34] Koppich et al., *New Rules, New Roles?*, 30, 112–115.

Religious communities can also intersect with the charter movement. Although, as we noted in chapter 7, there are lines that must not be crossed, it is also a fact that religion plays a significant role in American communal life. If churches and religious groups are willing to form (secular) charter schools that provide a great education and revitalize neighborhoods, we should welcome them with open arms.

PROFILE

Sarah Kass (City On A Hill Charter School, Boston)

Sarah Kass is cofounder and president of City On A Hill. She helped raise over $2 million to start the school and launch its Fund for Teacher Entrepreneurship. A graduate of the Chicago public schools, she holds a B.A. in history from Yale and an M.A. in English from Oxford, where she was a Rhodes Scholar. Kass has taught in public schools in New Haven, Chicago, and Chelsea, Massachusetts. When asked what it was about the existing system that impelled her to launch a charter school, she said, "I found that students were regularly graduated who could not read. I found that decisions were made without consulting teachers. And I found that there was little possibility for the community to play a real role in the school, and for the students to get to understand what it would mean to be effectively participating citizens."

In discussing the impact her school has had on the local community, she commented that

City On A Hill enjoys numerous school-community partnerships. We collaborate with the YMCA in which we are housed, the Museum of Science, the Gardner Museum, Boston's Jeremiah E. Burke High School, Northeastern University, the New England Conservatory, and over 60 agencies that host our students as winter interns. Through this work, City On A Hill has engaged many adults in the education of our students and the professional development of our faculty. And as many of these institutions had not had habits of working with urban youth, we have made them attuned to our students and given our students access. As some of the agencies that host our students as interns are politicians' offices and newspapers, we have found new allies politically. Our openness to community collaboration and our invitation to engage the public in our year-end assessment process (over 100 community members serve each June as jurors) have, I think, demystified charter schools for many people, and made citizens aware of the realities of City On A Hill.

Kass also notes some of the ways the school itself functions as a community: "We hold ourselves to common practices, expectations, and daily/ weekly habits. We refer to ourselves as a community, and define expectations in terms of community. We are a learning community for students as well as teachers. We insist that we improve our program regularly based on what teachers are learning in their classrooms. I think teachers would say we are a professional community. The longer we exist, the more salient is our school culture. The true civic test for us is whether our graduates will be engaged in our greater American civic community — will they vote? will they run for office? will they get involved in their neighborhoods or jobs beyond the call of duty? This only time will tell."

CHARTER SCHOOLS AND THE CIVIC COMMUNITY

Charter schools are not gated communities. They interact with the places where they operate. Some play roles in purposive civic efforts to transform those places. That is abundantly clear at NFL/YET in South Phoenix, where the charter school is the jewel in the crown of an ambitious Hispanic community renewal effort. It is also true a few miles away where, as part of a multifaceted effort to revitalize a gang- and drug-infested neighborhood, the Mesa Arts Academy worked to open a police substation on campus and helped residents form "Citizens on Patrol" groups with fast access to police officers. (It has a solid arts program, too!)

Charter schools channel new energy into public education by giving organizations that would not ordinarily be much involved the opportunity to launch schools of their own. Groups such as chambers of commerce, youth organizations, and colleges are now creating and operating charter schools. In Milwaukee, a Common (i.e., City) Council committee approved four existing nonsectarian private schools in 1998 to become the first city-sponsored charter schools in the nation.[35] This will eventually bring nearly 800 students under the umbrella of public education and is contributing to a boom in school facility construction — just five years after voters rejected a school building referendum — without a tax increase for Milwaukee residents.[36]

In Lawrence, Massachusetts, the nonprofit Community Day Care wanted to start a school so that children and their families could continue to receive educational and social services through middle school. Before the charter law was passed, the day care center had worked with community activists to create a private school. The charter law presented executive director Sheila Balboni with "the opportunity to open a public school. The result is that several parents have told us that the only reason they've decided to stay in Lawrence is that they've found this charter school for their child to attend. If it wasn't for this school, they'd be enrolled in

[35] One school decided not to open as a charter school for the 1998 school year because the state department of public instruction has refused to give these schools full per-pupil funding that includes special education services, arguing that the city has contracted with private schools rather than creating new charter schools.

[36] Joe Williams, "Classroom Boom May Be on Horizon," *Milwaukee Journal Sentinel*, 6 December 1998, 1.

Catholic schools or be gone to a district with safe, clean schools that meet the needs of their kids and teach the basics." Community Day Charter School kept residents in the city *and* in public schools.

Charters are sometimes faulted for dividing rather than uniting communities. (See our discussion of "balkanization" in chapter 7.) People bringing such charges, however, are usually cosmopolitans with little appreciation of what makes neighborhoods and communities tick. It is worth recalling what Charles Glenn terms the "mistake made by Horace Mann and his followers . . . their ungenerosity toward the stubborn particularities of loyalty and conviction, the 'mediating structures' and world views, by which people actually live."[37]

Charter schools are sensitive to such "stubborn particularities." While the "one best system" of public education would have everyone pass through standardized institutions and similar experiences, a different vision of public education regards it as a decentralized array of self-governing, results-oriented schools run by all sorts of different providers. James Ceasar and Patrick McGuinn argue that "the real threat to American unity lies not in the existence of multiple civic ideals — even when they are engaged in energetic and rancorous debate — but in the absence of civic engagement or in the standardization of the civic idea."[38] Charter schools are, to borrow from Peter Drucker, "not the collectivism of organized governmental action from above . . . [but] the collectivism of voluntary group action from below."[39] They lie at the intersection of civil society and public education.

FEW Americans are better attuned to the importance of community action and civic strength than General Colin Powell, former chairman of the Joint Chiefs of Staff. He was born in Harlem to immigrant parents from Jamaica, struggled with school in the Bronx, was wounded in Vietnam, became a battalion commander in Korea, and masterminded the Desert

---

[37] Glenn, *The Myth of the Common School*, XI.

[38] Ceasar and McGuinn, "Civic Education Reconsidered," 90, 103. On the role of government and American pluralism, see Diane Ravitch, "The Future of American Pluralism," in Lamar Alexander and Chester E. Finn, Jr., *The New Promise of American Life* (Indianapolis, Ind.: Hudson Institute, 1995), 72–87. On how distinctive schools with specialized objectives or student bodies can be legitimate public schools, see: Diane Ravitch, "Schools that Specialize: Are They Democratic? Do They Work?" *The Washington Post Education Review*, 28 July 1998, 1, 28–30; Christian Smith and David Sikkink, "Is Private Schooling Privatizing?" *First Things* (April 1999): 16–20. The pluralist nature of American society — especially as it relates to education and concerns the relation of religious schools to public authority — is eloquently discussed in John Courtney Murray, *We Hold These Truths: Catholic Reflections on the American Proposition* (New York: Sheed and Ward, 1960, 1988). Murray's insights are as relevant today as they were in 1960.

[39] Peter Drucker, *The Ecological Vision: Reflections on the American Condition* (New Brunswick, N.J.: Transaction Publishers, 1993), 9.

Storm war effort before ascending to the highest military position in the land.

Upon retirement, though, his true passions — for inner-city youth and community building — emerged in full force. That is why Pastor Smith was thrilled when General Powell agreed to let his name be attached to this start-up charter school in inner-city Detroit. When the general visited the school in September 1997, he electrified students and teachers with these words: "I've been privileged to be knighted by the Queen of England, I've been privileged to receive Medals of Freedom from two Presidents of the United States, Presidents Bush and Clinton. All those awards mean nothing to me compared with having my name associated with this school."

Perhaps General Powell could see what this one school was beginning to do for its students, families, and community. If America is to make charter schools such as Colin Powell Academy widely available to its families, however, we must resolve a host of major issues that the charter movement faces today. Those issues are the subject of the next chapter.

11

THE GREAT ISSUES

T HE CHARTER MOVEMENT, as we have seen, is spreading fast. Yet for all the attention showered on them, charter schools are dwarfed by the behemoth of American public education. They educate fewer than one percent of U.S. schoolchildren. Today they are more like scattered specialty shops than ubiquitous convenience stores. Still, they are mostly doing well by those who attend them and are beginning to influence the broader education system that surrounds them. This leads us to wonder about the millions of families whose children are not yet being well educated by the "regular" schools. Will charters evolve into options for them, too? The answer to that question hinges in part on the political battles we reported in chapter 8. But it depends also on how the charter movement addresses the great dilemmas that it faces. We have spotted eight of these long-term issues that will shape the future of charter schools in America.

It is easier to spot them, of course, than to forecast their outcome with confidence. Since our crystal ball is not especially clear, we also sought the views of three of the country's keenest observers (and most influential shapers) of the charter scene. To each, we posed the eight issues and asked for a prediction or recommendation: "Tell us how you think this issue is apt to unfold or what you think is most apt to yield a happy result."

Louann Bierlein is education policy advisor to Louisiana Governor Mike Foster, in which capacity she has played a lead role in upgrading that state's charter law. Bierlein is considered one of the earliest and keenest policy players in the national charter movement; her initial work depicting key components of a strong charter law was used as a bible by many charter proponents as their statutes were being crafted.

Gary K. Hart is now Secretary of Education in the administration of California Governor Grey Davis. At the time he responded to our questions, he was codirector of the California State University Institute for Education Reform. From 1974 to 1994, he served in the state legislature, including twelve years chairing the Senate Education Committee. In that capacity, he was principal author of California's charter law. He has also been a high school history teacher. He is a Democrat.

Until 1999, Dr. Thomas C. Patterson served as a senior member of the Arizona Senate, including a term as majority leader. He was instrumental in enacting—and protecting—the Arizona charter law. He is a physician and a Republican.

The remainder of this chapter consists of the eight issues we posed, the responses of these guest commentators, and our own reflections.

Will charter schools furnish compelling evidence that they provide superior education?

If and when it becomes clear that charters yield stronger student achievement, we are confident that more people will want their children to benefit—and more policymakers will stare down the opposition and let these schools proliferate. Today, we have only early returns.

BIERLEIN: I firmly believe that charter schools will produce the types of compelling evidence not often found in traditional systems. While some charter folks (especially those focused on experiential learning, etc.) view conventional testing programs with disdain, most are committed to the concept of accountability and the necessity of data. Indeed, none of Louisiana's six charter schools operating in 1997–98 voiced concern when the state asked them to pre- and post-test all their students using a normed instrument. My biggest concern is not whether charter schools are collecting necessary results-based data, but the fact that much of this information is school-specific, making aggregation very difficult. This is not the fault of charter schools, but of states that need better results-based accountability measures for all their public schools.

HART: Is it the right (and a fair) question to ask charter schools to provide "compelling evidence that they provide superior education"? I don't think so. Did we pledge that they would be better? No. What we asserted is that we would provide meaningful alternative choices for parents and students based on articulated outcomes—a breath of fresh air in a system that too often can't seem to think outside a very confining box. The irony is that it is usually opponents of charter schools within the educational establishment who suggest that, unless charter schools demonstrate that they are superior, they should not be allowed to grow—or even continue to exist. The temptation to make charter schools the magic bullet for an ossified education system is great, but if we succumb to that temptation we risk falling into the trap of making unrealistic assertions. Charter schools are off to a good start—but let's neither promise more than we can deliver nor hold ourselves to a much higher standard than other public schools.

PATTERSON: Charter schools in Arizona were born in an era in which assessments were in total chaos. Additionally, many are niche schools for underachievers. Charter schools ultimately can justify their existence *only* by driving improved educational achievement. Early results are mixed. However, good assessment tools are now being developed, more excellence-oriented schools are being attracted to the market, and parents are becoming more aware of academic performance issues. Charters must soon "fish or cut bait." They should do fine.

THE AUTHORS: Will charter schools provide a superior education? Superior to *what*? Superior to all other schools in America? Superior to the state's average test scores? Or superior to the schools that their pupils would otherwise be attending? Gary Hart has reframed the question nicely. The results proposed in a school's charter must be based on a realistic appraisal of the situation of the youngsters enrolled in that particular school. Of course, we should hold all students (and schools) accountable to high standards. Still, it is folly to view charters as a miracle cure. This reform strategy will do more good if we view it as an example of a different approach rather than an end in itself.

Will accountability prove to be a ticking bomb for charter schools?

Besides test scores, these schools are legitimately held to account by their sponsors for the other promises they make in their applications, for responsibly tending the youngsters in their care, for handling public dollars with integrity, and for complying with whatever regulations have not been waived. Yet many of the essential gauges and performance indicators remain to be developed. Only a few states and communities have devised solid charter accountability systems.

BIERLEIN: In the traditional education world, the terms "hard evidence" and "school success" are never thought of simultaneously. Many educators have successfully fought efforts to collect and use test-based achievement information. Therefore, most states, districts, and the professional education community do not have well-developed tools for the gathering of non-anecdotal information and only a few have begun to use such information for accountability purposes. Charter schools should not be expected suddenly to invent wonderful assessment tools, when the traditional education community has failed to do this after two decades.

HART: All meaningful charter laws have at their core an important trade-off: freedom from state laws and bureaucratic constraints in exchange for concentration on education results and customer satisfaction. So accountability concerns must be given close attention by charter advocates. However, we are dependent to a significant extent on either local or state assessment systems that must apply to all public schools, including charter schools. Given the controversial and complicated nature of assessment, this will continue to be a rocky road. We must insist that charter schools are not held to a high assessment standard while other public schools get a free ride.

PATTERSON: Education bureaucrats often equate "accountability" to a massive paperwork exercise designed to ensure compliance. Charter schools define accountability in terms of satisfying market demands, which can be tricky for publicly funded institutions. Some early charter school operators did stimulate unrealistic expectations. However, charter schools must encourage their own accountability *for results* or they will be forever vulnerable to re-regulation. We are in a race for time as charters try to convince the educational culture that freedom works while their foes work tirelessly to turn them into regular public schools with an alternate funding mechanism. I'm worried.

THE AUTHORS: Accountability ought to be a ticking bomb for *every* school in America — not just charters. Today, unfortunately, accountability remains the "third world" of American education — underdeveloped and in grave need of massive amounts of aid and technical assistance. Perhaps the legacy of charter schools will be their service as test pilots for new and improved accountability systems. (We discuss in chapter 6 how that might work.)

Will the barriers to entry be eased or eliminated?

Chapter 5 discussed how risky, costly, and arduous it is to launch a charter school. The higher the barriers to entry, the fewer will be the number of people intrepid (or foolhardy) enough to make the effort. We don't yet know how copious is the supply of tireless individuals willing to take this risk. Clearly, there are hundreds of them, but are there tens of thousands? Moreover, we glimpse early signs of "burnout" among charter leaders (and sometimes teachers) who work round-the-clock and often round-the-calendar to make their schools succeed. Where will their successors come from?

BIERLEIN: I am concerned with the burnout factor and whether there will be a never-ending cadre of folks ready to take on the charter challenge. Successfully educating at-risk students (which is what many charter schools are attempting to do) is difficult enough, but doing so with resources significantly less (in most cases) than the traditional schools is almost impossible. For many it is one battle after another. For example, after many months of work, a group of black community leaders finally obtained charter approval from the state board in Louisiana (after being turned down by the local board), only to have the U.S. Justice Department and the federal courts become involved because of desegregation oversight issues. These folks — many of whom are educators — want to serve students living in downtown housing projects, almost all of whom are slated to become dropouts unless something different happens for them. Yet the cards are stacked against them. My hope is that the opposition will continue to subside and many legal barriers will be weakened. New leaders will come from minority communities and churches — individuals who often strongly opposed charter schools a few years ago but now view them as a means to save their communities. There are lots of people who care out there.

HART: The largest barrier to entry in California is lack of capital funding and technical expertise on budgeting, legal, and management issues. However, as charter schools continue to generate political support and media attention, I believe these resource issues can, and will, be successfully addressed. For example, our own Charter Schools Development Center continues to expand its technical assistance base, and states such as Minnesota have developed innovative lease-aid arrangements for charter school capital support.

PATTERSON: Charter schools in Arizona will receive over $1,000 per student in lieu of capital funding. While more is always better, lack of capital funding is not the most vexing barrier at this time. The increased regulatory burden is becoming significant, as friends and foes alike demand more data collection, more administrative complexity, and more spent on legal and accounting fees. Another concern is that some city councils (e.g., Tucson) have been co-opted by teachers' unions and have used their zoning powers malignantly, such as requiring a five-acre minimum for charter schools.

THE AUTHORS: The supply of charter schools is a far more serious issue than the demand, because the barriers to entry (weak charter laws, dogged political foes, trigger-happy regulators, funding shortfalls, etc.) are mountainous. If they remain so, charter schools will not be able to serve all those who crave them, much less attain the critical mass needed to reinvent public education. The massif is daunting, yet we see more and more intrepid climbers picking new paths up and around it. In chapter 5, we enumerated a number of creative solutions to charter start-up problems. Policymakers can help, too, by passing strong, adaptive charter laws.

Are charter schools temporary or permanent?

Should such a school, once created, be expected to last forever (so long as it keeps getting its charter renewed), or is it a specific response to a particular education need that may pass or be met in a few years? Is a charter school more like a stone building or an igloo? What happens when the founders graduate or grow weary? Will a different school serve the next group?

We do not think of schools as temporary entities that need to be disposed of or recycled after a time. But perhaps charters will cause us to consider that possibility. This may be more relevant for "mom and pop" schools led by a few zealous individuals than for "franchise" operations that run several dozen schools in various places. Will the former tend to vanish while the latter endure? If so, the charter movement could evolve from a variegated cornucopia of chef-owned restaurants into chains of Pizza Huts and Olive Gardens.

BIERLEIN: In theory, the concept of a charter school should no longer be necessary fifteen to twenty years down the line. By that point, each and every existing school in this nation could be operated under the charter principles of school-based control and accountability. In reality, it will take many decades until societal and economic pressures can move the traditional system to this point. In the meantime, charter schools will continue to grow. Many individual schools will become "permanent" entities (as many private schools have over the years). Some will close because of failures, while others will disappear because they will have served their purpose of educating a certain group of kids.

HART: Charter schools ought never to be static and they certainly are not entitled to legal permanence—such entitlements are exactly the problem confronting the existing public education system. I have always been partial to the image of charter school advocates as homeowners versus renters. Homeownership, of course, comes in many forms including single-family dwellings, condominiums, gated communities, etcetera. But the principle of home ownership is based upon autonomy and that is essentially the underlying principle of charter schools: control over your own destiny.

PATTERSON: It is helpful to think of charter schools as small businesses in this context. They will always have a certain failure rate; most will survive as they devise successful ways of identifying and meeting market demands. The winners in the process are the consumers. We should expect the emergence of "brand identification" and market consolidation as is usually the case in dynamic, expanding markets.

THE AUTHORS: Charter schools can be both permanent and temporary. It depends on the needs of a particular community—and how well charter schools respond to them. Until now, public schools have typically enjoyed a form of institutional immortality. Even failing schools are allowed to carry on. Man-made institutions should never be viewed as eternal. Charter schools will help us come to view schools as community responses to specific needs. Hard as this idea is to swallow, if and when those needs are met, the schools should declare victory and withdraw. We worry, though, about the contest between "mom and pop" charter schools and large franchise operations. If the latter obliterate the former, the charter movement will lose much of its character, variety, and popular appeal. The country is better off with both.

Can charter schools avoid re-regulation?

If forced into close conformity with conventional schools, they will lose their essential raison d'être. Freedom in return for results is the basic charter bargain. Yet there is ample evidence that the education system balks at giving schools real freedom and that, even in places where charters have wrested quite a lot of it, the danger of re-regulation is omnipresent.

BIERLEIN: Avoiding re-regulation can be done but it will be difficult, especially since most charter laws do not give the schools that much freedom to begin with. The driver will be the comprehensive accountability systems that some states are putting into place for all their public schools (i.e., rewards for success, corrective actions for failure to improve). This "real pressure" for results (such as is being felt in Texas, Kentucky, and elsewhere) is causing traditional educators to want the regulatory barriers removed. They are no longer paying lip service to this idea, but know that it is a matter of survival for many. We are a long way from having such accountability systems in all fifty states, of course, but the momentum is growing and this in turn will help charter schools with the re-regulation concern.

HART: "The price of freedom is eternal vigilance." The pressures for re-regulation are enormous. Special education and credentialing are a couple of areas we need to be especially concerned about. The best antidote in my view is a strong waiver law for existing regulations; this is one of the strengths of California's charter law.

PATTERSON: From the beginning, we have endured rhetoric about the "unfairness" of granting charter schools "special breaks"; the threat of re-regulation is today the major threat to the viability of charter schools. Our culture assumes (falsely) that increased governmental monitoring and oversight are effective remedies to a wide variety of perceived ills, and high levels of regulation "just happen" over the years. Charter advocates must use all the tools at their disposal to convince the public that increased regulation is really a poison that can kill charter schools or at least take away their reason for existence.

THE AUTHORS: Re-regulation is an ominous threat, the serpent pursuing the charter movement. Today, critics and journalists love to pounce on naughty charter schools when bad things happen and use them as arguments for re-regulation. But where are the groups patrolling for infractions against charter independence and ready to oppose and denounce over-zealous regulators?

Will charter schools accumulate enemies faster than friends?

Will today's opponents come to accept the charter movement, or will its successes cause them to redouble their efforts to halt it? Will "false" and "fair-weather" friends weaken the movement by throwing their support to wan versions with little true autonomy? We have in mind such obvious foes as teachers' unions, school board associations, and colleges of education. But the list is much longer. What about bond houses resentful of charters horning in on their capital monopoly? Private schools that find themselves losing market share to these tuition-free competitors? Advocacy groups fretful because some charter schools handle special education differently? And on and on.

As for allies, the issue is whether charter schools will garner support beyond those who found, attend, and work in them. Will foundations— usually risk-averse and tied into large "systemic" reforms—see this messy, grassroots movement as worthy of financial support? Will bankers view these schools as acceptable vehicles for loaned capital? Will venture capitalists support efforts to start companies to create and manage them? Will more than a few brave politicians take on the unions?

BIERLEIN: Having just recently attended the Education Commission of the States annual conference (which attracts many traditional-thinking educators and policymakers), I was amazed to see how the idea of charter schools is no longer being debated as an "evil." I heard numerous folks from across the nation use examples of what charter schools are doing in their state on any given issue. Many mainstream educators are beginning to see the possibilities, or at least they no longer see charters as the devil. (Vouchers occupy that spot!)

HART: In California, charter friends far outnumber enemies or even skeptics. Supporters include many traditional advocates for the poor (who tend to be liberal), many entrepreneurs and business folks (who tend to be conservative), and restless parents (who are across the ideological spectrum). This is a quite eclectic and powerful coalition of disparate interests and augurs well for charter schools. However, defenders of the status quo who are threatened by charters tend to be full-time (and well-paid) professionals and should not be underestimated. Their ability to interpret statutes and regulations in ways hostile to charter schools remains formidable. The devil is in the details, and the professionals are expert detail manipulators.

PATTERSON: This is precisely the reason why you want to "blast out" a charter school system and create as many schools as quickly as possible — to create a large, natural constituency of parents, teachers, and others who can recruit other friends, while putting foes on the defensive, particularly in trying to argue why their schools of choice should not be allowed to exist. I would like to see charters do a better job of forming associations with community groups, such as high-tech businesses and service clubs, who would be willing to make a substantial contribution to the educational mission of the school.

THE AUTHORS: Today, charter schools exist in a political microclimate that fosters their growth. Its soil is fertile for reform, and many discontented parents and teachers are willing to do a little watering to help the garden stay green. But the climate may change. Only the naïve would assume that any monopoly will welcome competition, that any entrenched system will gratefully receive so profound a transformation of its basic practices, or that truth alone can prevail against power. We agree with Tom Patterson. Charter schools cannot count on the permanence of favorable weather or the kindness of strangers. They need their own sources of power.

Will charter schools turn into another self-interested lobbying force, their own greedy, complacent establishment?

Will they seek to haul up the gangplank now that they have clambered aboard, and discourage messy new schools from coming into being (and perhaps vying for their students)? Closely related is the question of whether the charter movement will succeed at policing itself, imposing quality control on its own members, and tossing out its bad apples. Vested interests have a habit of defending all their members against criticism and punishment, no matter how venal or ineffectual some might be.

BIERLEIN: Human nature itself will ensure that charter schools will become part of a self-serving group within the education arena. However, I do not believe that they will become complacent since, despite concerns over accountability, most charter schools are indeed being required to produce results. The demand is so large for quality schooling that it will be quite some time until they are competing directly among themselves (although this is already happening in isolated areas). Finally, the diversity of charter school organizers is so vast (from the profit-seekers to the flower children of the '60s) that this will tend to prevent the immediate intimacy necessary to really implode on themselves.

HART: Self-policing is a good thing, and our statewide charter organization in California (CANEC) has already adopted a couple of resolutions (for example, a position statement on principles for non–classroom-based charter schools) that are modest self-policing steps. However, rigorous internal monitoring is always going to be limited, given human nature and the strong deregulation bias favored by charter advocates. Public hearings, media scrutiny, and, most important, parental choice are the best ways to maintain quality charter schools.

PATTERSON: Charter school operators tend to be overworked and to see themselves in a survival mode. What political involvement they make time for is often to help solve daily problems, especially related to funding. Too many are willing to trade freedom for dollars. It is critical as the movement matures for them to acquire a more global perspective with regard to self-policing, independent vendor status, and avoidance of regulation — issues on which their long-term survival depends.

THE AUTHORS: Besides needing its own power sources to stand up to the system's might, the charter movement needs to be transparent and self-critical. It should set a moral and educational example. That is one of the primary reasons we suggested a "transparent" approach to charter accountability. But the right attitude is also needed. The charter movement should move swiftly to condemn bad schools that cheat taxpayers or ill-serve students. In education as in so many domains, sunlight is the best disinfectant. Just as charter advocates want students held to higher standards, so must they demand the same of the schools themselves. This movement must hold itself accountable for refusing to accept mediocrity and failure. It should be its own toughest critic, its own best source of quality control.

Finally, will charter schools fall victim to their own success in stimulating education reform and be beaten back by a newly energized and more competitive "regular" school system?

BIERLEIN: Charter schools as a whole will not fall victim to their own success within my lifetime. Although some traditional systems are responding positively to the influence of charter schools in their community (by making significant improvements within their own systems), these events are still too few really to count. Charter schools are still very much in their infancy and will need their own lifetime of twenty years or more before being viewed as a mature reform effort.

HART: Charters are a means to an end: a more responsive educational system. If the education system becomes much more responsive and adaptive to charter-like ideas (I wouldn't hold my breath!), then charter schools can fold up their tents and quietly steal away.

PATTERSON: We charter school advocates should avoid seeing the charter movement as being in tension with the educational best interests of children. Otherwise, we occupy the intellectual and moral low ground now filled by public school apologists. It would be Paradise on Earth, educationally speaking, if charter schools were not necessary because other educational options had become so dynamic and effective. It's also not going to happen. In the meantime, eternal vigilance toward other threats to charter schools will be required if they are to fulfill their potential.

THE AUTHORS: We agree with our distinguished commentators that the optimal future would be one in which charter schools were no longer distinctive, not because they had been regulated into conformity with conventional schools but because all the other schools adopted the virtues of charter schools. The point, after all, is not to tout charter schools per se but to provide a first-rate education to all of America's children. Still, our commentators may be too glum about the prospect of this actually happening. As we illustrate in the next chapter, we can envision a future in which public education is itself reborn in the charter image.

12

WILL CHARTER SCHOOLS
SAVE PUBLIC EDUCATION?

WHAT MIGHT the future look like if the charter movement prospers and spreads? In this final chapter, we explore that future, guided by a suspicion that the ideas underlying that movement are those most likely to renew and replenish public education in America.

Critics will allege that our vision of public education reborn is really public education entombed. They will cite the Vietnam-era blunder of destroying something while claiming to save it. They will contend that charter schools are a grand specimen of what is wrong with contemporary education reform, not a prime example of how to do it right.

No book will end this profound dispute. But the time for bold thinking is at hand. Public education in the United States is in grave danger, its function still worthy but its structures rickety. Americans believe deeply in the principle but are dismayed by its performance.

So potent is the press for change that even some of public education's strongest defenders have acknowledged that it has only a limited time to get its act together. The late Albert Shanker recognized that "Time is running out on public education. . . . The dissatisfaction that people feel is very basic." Former Secretary of Health, Education, and Welfare David Mathews concludes that "Americans today are halfway out the schoolhouse door."[1] Veteran education writer Anne Lewis acknowledges that "For the past 30 years, much of the disappointment with public schools has come about as a result of their failure to educate all students equally well. . . . [T]his is what parents are running away from."[2] School reformers Marc Tucker and Judy Codding observe that "Increasingly, the public does not believe that the people who govern, manage, and staff our

[1] David Mathews, *Is There a Public for Public Schools?* (Dayton, Ohio: Kettering Foundation Press, 1996).

[2] Anne C. Lewis, "Politicians, Research Findings, and School Choice," *Phi Delta Kappan*, June 1998, 724.

schools can or will deliver."[3] Writes veteran critic Myron Lieberman, "[P]ublic education as we know it is a lost cause."[4]

Truth be told, public education *as we know it* probably *is* a lost cause. It resembles a termite-riddled building that retains its familiar appearance from afar yet is actually nearing collapse. But what is to replace it? Chaos? A completely private marketplace? Or a new model that affirms the public's obligation to educate the next generation but does not rely on a government bureaucracy to carry out that solemn duty?

What might such a new model look like? We can best sketch an answer by asking the reader to join us on one final tour. This one is imaginary. Let's have a look at education in Metropolitan City, U.S.A., circa 2010. Please watch your step as we travel. The footing is solid enough but it doesn't much resemble the places where you are accustomed to walking.

METROPOLITAN CITY, CIRCA 2010

Metropolitan City has a population of 300,000. With suburbs included, it is close to a million people, of whom 170,000 are school-age youngsters. Back in the late twentieth century, their predecessors attended some 260 public schools, run by a dozen separate systems, complete with superintendents, school boards, union locals, PTAs, and the rest, as well as forty private schools, mostly church-affiliated. In late 1999, however, the state of New Pensylina enacted a pilot charter school program that proved so popular that its cap on the number of charter schools was loosened in 2002, then lifted altogether in 2004, and the entire public education system was reconstructed in 2007.

Today, the Met City area boasts 500 schools, of which just two dozen are wholly private. These have declined to affiliate with New Pensylina's "Plan for Excellence in Public Education" (affectionately known as PEPE) because they prefer total independence. That means they must rely on tuition and philanthropy for their revenues, and some must struggle to maintain their enrollments. Though Republican legislators and a few pundits still murmur about vouchers, PEPE has satisfied most of the popular appetite for school choice, thanks primarily to the new schools it has brought into existence — and the formerly private schools that have opted in. Moreover, low-income families, as we shall see, qualify for "supplemental education certificates" that give them added after-school options and thus some of the benefit of vouchers.

The other 476 schools in and around Met City are "PEPE schools," which means they are publicly financed and publicly accountable, yet 450

---

[3] Marc S. Tucker and Judy B. Codding, *Standards for Our Schools* (San Francisco: Jossey-Bass, 1998), 18.

[4] Myron Lieberman, *Public Education: An Autopsy* (Cambridge, Mass.: Harvard University Press, 1993), 2.

of them are operationally independent. (We turn to the remaining 26 shortly.) Half have their own building-level governing boards and management structures. Typically started by parents or teachers, these closely resemble the charter schools of the late 1990s and we shall refer to them by that term. The other 225 PEPE schools operate under management contracts with various private firms and organizations. These we term "contract schools." The distinction between "charter" and "contract" schools is slowly disappearing, but it is still true in Met City in 2010 that charters are mostly indigenous, self-governing, and focused on single sites, whereas many contract schools are part of larger networks or chains, often with national name recognition, and the schools are run more like businesses or large-scale public services.

Contract schools are not invariably run for profit. The Core Knowledge Foundation and Modern Red Schoolhouse Institute are major nonprofit school operators with national reputations that have established large presences in Met City, as have the "Roots and Wings" and Accelerated Schools programs.[5] And after the Supreme Court's landmark decision of 2001, permitting public support for students in church-affiliated schools, several national religious organizations, such as the Roman Catholic Church, Muslims USA, and the Southern Baptist Conference, entered the field of public school management, as did Agudath Israel of America.[6]

In a development barely imagined by either supporters or opponents of such funding, ubiquitous school choice has also fostered many schools whose explicitly secular character is part of their appeal. Today, of the 476 publicly funded schools operating in the Met City area, only 63 include purposeful religious education (or "formation") in their curricula. They are obliged to make this known in their marketing and promotional mate-

---

[5] The Core Knowledge Foundation was founded by E. D. Hirsch, Jr., and is based on the ideas contained in his book *Cultural Literacy* (Boston: Houghton Mifflin Company, 1987). Its hallmark is a knowledge-heavy sequence of instruction. The Modern Red Schoolhouse Institute, based in Nashville, is promulgating the "Modern Red Schoolhouse" design developed at Hudson Institute with sponsorship from the New American Schools Development Corporation. It is a comprehensive school "reinvention" that combines contemporary ideas about technology and school organization with more traditional curricular priorities. Roots and Wings is another New American Schools project, based on the pioneering work of Robert Slavin in ensuring that disadvantaged children acquire basic skills. The Accelerated Schools Project follows the ideas of Teachers College professor Henry Levin, emphasizing that the surest way to succeed in educating disadvantaged children is not to "remediate" them but to enrich and intensify their learning.

[6] The issue, of course, is whether the "establishment of religion" clause of the First Amendment of the U.S. Constitution prohibits public dollars flowing via students to church-affiliated institutions. This has long been standard practice in higher education where, for example, federal grants and loans to students accompany them without challenge to such church-connected universities as Notre Dame and Yeshiva. But similar forms of aid to primary-secondary students (and, indirectly, to their schools) were under a constitutional cloud until the imaginary 2001 Supreme Court decision "referenced" here.

rials. Most other schools are equally candid that religious instruction is *not* part of their program, although some offer "release time" for students to obtain such lessons in nearby churches, and some make facilities available for religious groups wanting to conduct (voluntary) services or classes on campus. This sorting out of different kinds of schools has been surprisingly conflict-free. Of course, with New Pensylina's ambitious (and entirely secular) statewide academic standards hovering in the background, even a (state-aided) religious school must ensure that its students gain core skills and knowledge. Those that find this objectionable continue to take refuge in the private sector.

The great majority of PEPE schools obtained their charters or contracts from the Met City Regional Education Authority (MCREA), one of a dozen such entities created by the legislature in 2004. MCREA has replaced most of the former "local education agencies" in the area, though two suburbs opted to retain their own boards and superintendents. The hub of MCREA is a nine-member governing board. Five members are appointed by the governor and confirmed by the legislature; Met City area voters elect the other four, but candidates must be drawn from a nonpartisan slate nominated by the mayors of local municipalities. None may be a current or recent employee of a school or education organization. MCREA board terms last five years, so ordinarily it has one or two new members a year, but members may be removed by the State Court of Education Appeals if judged to be irresponsible, partisan, or subject to conflicts of interest. Service on the MCREA board has become a status-conferring civic responsibility, and an impressive array of talented, education-minded people have accepted the governor's appointment or the mayors' nomination. (Two or three also turned out to be dull time-servers, and one was removed when it was revealed that her investor husband owned part of a school management firm.)

MCREA appoints its own executive director, a job for which the prime qualification is dynamite managerial skills, not education credentials. The executive director, in turn, selects his or her own small staff whose principal duty is to issue and monitor the charters and contracts that are the chief constitutional documents of public education under PEPE.[7] (The school boards and superintendents of the two surviving suburban school districts have similar roles vis-à-vis the schools under their jurisdictions.)

In addition, there are "critical condition schools" (the remaining 26 schools referred to earlier): schools in trouble and in need of reconstitution, schools whose charters have been suspended or not renewed, schools between contractors, and other special circumstances calling for more ag-

---

[7] See Paul T. Hill, Lawrence C. Pierce, and James W. Guthrie, *Reinventing Public Education* (Chicago: University of Chicago Press, 1997), especially chapter 5, for an excellent and more detailed account of how this would work.

gressive engagement. MCREA's job is to turn them around or shut them down. It can do this through direct management, outsourcing, or dispatching a "crisis intervention" team. As of 2010, no school has remained under direct MCREA control for longer than two years. (Since MCREA has sweeping authority to replace personnel in schools under its direct control, those running PEPE schools have ample incentive to succeed under the terms of their charters or contracts.) Moreover, during this period of reconstitution, any family with a child in the school has priority in the lottery for entrance into other PEPE schools. No one is confined against their will in a "critical condition" school.

All PEPE schools with contracts obtained them from MCREA (or the two local school boards), but that is not the only route to a *charter* in New Pensylina. The state universities can also issue charters. Several—including the campus near Met City—have made good use of this option. Met State University has sponsored almost four dozen schools around the state, including eight in Met City and environs. Most of these focus on science, technology, and engineering, which are Met State's leading strengths.

All PEPE schools are schools of choice—and any New Pensylina youngster may attend any public school in the state. Municipal boundaries no longer define attendance zones. All schools are funded on the basis of enrollments, and $10,106 per pupil is the statewide norm in 2010, although extra moneys (including both state and federal dollars) accompany disabled youngsters and others with special needs.[8] In addition to the basic school payment, low-income parents may, upon request to MCREA, obtain "supplemental education certificates" worth as much as $2,000 per pupil, much of this deriving from the federal Title I program as it was restructured in the summer of 2000. Though families may not use these supplements for "regular" schooling—and PEPE schools may not charge parents for basic services—they may apply them to the costs of after-school programs, tutoring, weekend and summer programs, and suchlike. Many PEPE schools now offer these services, as do numerous private and nonprofit vendors.

School Shopping in Met City

PEPE schools do their own marketing, but MCREA provides ample public information, including the huge amount of data now inscribed on state-mandated "school report cards," particularly with regard to student achievement and other gauges of school performance. Several community organizations, including the local newspaper, have opted to supplement MCREA's efforts. Parents, in fact, are awash in information—in print, over the airwaves, and via the Internet—about individual schools. Dozens

---

[8] The $10,106 figure was calculated by projecting the 1997 per-pupil expenditure of $6,882 in a typical mid-sized city—we chose Cincinnati, Ohio—over thirteen years at an average annual inflation rate of 3 percent.

of people—employed by, or volunteering for, the Chamber of Commerce, the Society of Real Estate Agents, the NAACP, and the School Reform Alliance, to name a few—function as school selection advisors.

Four times a year, a giant "school fair" enables families to meet face-to-face with representatives of PEPE schools to learn more about them. A month or so after each fair, MCREA conducts a lottery for new students (and anyone wishing to change schools or sign up for a newly created school). On their preference card, parents are asked to note their three top choices and indicate any special circumstances, such as siblings already enrolled and geographic proximity.

The centralized lottery has been going for just a few years and remains controversial. Many schools would rather handle their own admissions, and MCREA has agreed that schools preferring to opt out of the lottery may do so next year, provided they agree to an external audit of their entrance procedures to ensure fairness and nondiscrimination.

Meanwhile, nearly 90 percent of area families get their first or second choice, and almost everyone gets one of their top three schools. One duty of MCREA is to find suitable slots for those who do not. Nobody has failed to be placed so far, and children who must attend a school that isn't one of their choices enjoy priority in the next lottery, should they wish to change.

The school supply is dynamic, not static. Oversubscribed schools often open additional campuses or turn faltering schools into branches. Also, many firms that operate contract schools watch the MCREA lotteries like hawks for evidence of what sorts of schools the public wants, so that more of these can quickly be furnished.

The menu of school options in Met City is impressive, including:

- "Alternative" programs for former dropouts, often with tech-prep curricula, internships, and other work experiences.
- "Back to basics" schools, many of them adherents of the Core Knowledge program but some modeled on successful inner-city schools led by Marva Collins and Thaddeus Lott.
- Experiential learning centers (e.g., Expeditionary Learning/Outward Bound).
- Other New American Schools designs, such as ATLAS and America's Choice.
- International Baccalaureate schools and high schools built around the Advanced Placement program.
- A number of well-known national "chains," including the Edison Project, Sabis Learning Systems, Beacon Schools, and Advantage Schools.
- Schools run by churches and religious organizations—Muslim, Lutheran, Jewish, Catholic, Baptist, even small Hindu and Buddhist schools.

- Schools run by civil-rights and minority groups, including the Urban League and the Council of La Raza. The National Council of Negro Women operates a popular single-sex school for African-American girls, and the Coalition of Black Professionals runs a highly regarded school for boys.
- Schools operated by educational and cultural organizations, including the Bill and Melinda Gates Foundation, the Carnegie Library, the Hewlett-Packard Museum of Natural History, and the Met City Symphony Orchestra.
- Schools launched by civil-society groups, including the Girl Scouts, YMCA, League of Women Voters, the Rotary Club, even the local American Legion chapter.
- Former private schools, now operating with charters.
- Several schools that specialize in the learning needs of home-schooling families, including two "virtual" schools and one part-time school where students come for specific classes and extracurricular activities.
- Schools located on the work sites of major employers, including private companies, large nonprofits (e.g., the Met City Medical Center), the nearby Air Force base, and a small contract-run primary school at the local AFL-CIO office that is attended mainly by the children of union executives. (All the employer-operated schools offer extended-day programs to meet the child-care needs of working parents.)
- Several dozen "mom-and-pop" charter schools of all stripes (traditional, progressive, comprehensive, etc.) initiated by clusters of parents or small teams of teachers.
- Schools specializing in English language acquisition and American acculturation for immigrants.
- Two residential schools for children from severely troubled families. (These institutions receive supplemental funding from the Met City United Way and the New Pensylina Department of Youth Services.)
- Ten schools (three of them formerly private) that specialize in the education of disabled youngsters, including programs designed around particular disabilities such as deafness, blindness, even autism.
- Magnet-like schools with themes focusing on leadership, theater, health care, public service, the environment, and foreign languages and cultures.
- Lots of "plain vanilla" schools that were once ordinary neighborhood public schools and still resemble them, though greater differentiation is visible every year as Met City's education marketplace grows sprightlier and people become more accustomed to selecting their schools.

School shopping is easier now that New Pensylina gives every student residing more than half a mile from school a "transit voucher," presently amounting to $773 a year. (If their parents drive them, families can pocket this money.) This has spawned a robust new school transport business as PEPE schools have engaged private van, bus, and taxi operators to bring their pupils to and from school, and community organizations have gone into the "get the kids to school" business. About three-fifths of children in the MCREA area currently qualify for this transit aid, meaning that almost $80 million per year is available in public revenues.

Viewed from the parent's perspective, all sorts of education combinations are now possible. Many opt simply to place all their children in a school — often a former neighborhood public school — that is convenient to their home or workplace. But it is also easy to mix and match. The *Met City Observer* recently profiled the Riley family, whose children are enrolled in four very different schools. Alexandra attends the Schubert Music Academy, a small charter school affiliated with the local symphony orchestra. Richard is in the college-prep course at Met City East, a large high school that also enables him to play interscholastic soccer. Rebecca has recently moved to the Children First School (a contract school run by the Met City Mental Health Center), where youngsters with emotional disabilities get special attention. And little Matt is in first grade at a school located within the Merrill Lynch office complex, where his mom, Heather Petrilli-Riley, is a broker.

Accountability in Action

Many factors now fertilize the flowering of education options in Met City: a wealth of information about schools, transportation funding, the snipping of red tape, and capital funding from state and private sources. But the trade-off is strict results-accountability, made possible by New Pensylina's strong academic standards and assessment system — and a steadfast commitment to reward success and intervene in cases of failure. For PEPE schools, accountability has come to mean both attracting and retaining clients and fulfilling the terms of their charters and contracts. But MCREA, though the state's chief enforcer, is not an autocratic bureaucracy that always enjoys the last word. Any school that believes it has been dealt an injustice can make its way to the State Court of Education Appeals. That court also operates a less formal "magistrate's office" where individuals — students, parents, teachers, whoever — can come if their dispute with a school was not handled to their satisfaction by MCREA, or if their grievance is with MCREA itself. (The magistrate's office must render a decision within sixty days.)

The mere existence of the Education Appeals Court helps keep MCREA on its toes (as does a host of watchdog groups that have made it their business to monitor the PEPE operation). In a typical year, fewer than a dozen disputes actually reach the court from the Met City area.

There is also more to PEPE accountability than "enforcement." Though the schools are not yet perfectly transparent, a library of information about them is available to anyone who wants to look. The state's school report cards contain much of it, but more is published in each school's annual report and is frequently updated on school web sites. One can, for example, download not only a detailed profile of a school's philosophy and curriculum but also ample data on its student and staff characteristics, what it spends its money on, its latest test scores, who serves on its governing board, the minutes of their meetings, and so forth. Timeliness in disclosing such information is factored into a school's ability to get its charter or contract renewed. And with enterprising journalists, researchers, parent groups, and others constantly scanning such information, school leaders realize that "everybody knows" what their school is and isn't doing—and will be rapidly alerted to any attempts at concealment.

School report cards and web sites furnish plenty of objective information about performance, but that is just the beginning of accountability. Every PEPE school also has an annual site visit by a team organized by its sponsor. Typically, these are two-day visits by teams of 4–5 people, usually including an education expert, a parent, a community representative (who may be a business person, civil-rights leader, clergyman, etc.), and a public official (often a legislator or city council member). The site visit yields immediate verbal feedback to the school operator as well as a written report that is shared with both operator and sponsor. Portions of that report are then published in the school's report card and placed on the Internet.

A school's charter (or contract) renewal, which occurs every five years, is quite a big deal, involving extensive efforts by school leaders to document its performance and rigorous external audits organized by the sponsor. There is ordinarily a public hearing, too, often taking the form of a "town meeting" with presentations by students, questions and challenges from the community, and explanations from school staff and board members.

INTERVIEW

Lyndon Hernandez (former executive director, MCREA)[9]

Lyn Hernandez was a surprise choice to lead MCREA during PEPE's launch phase. Former coach of the U.S. Olympic swim team, director of "Sink or Swim" (a sports mentoring program for inner-city youth), father of three, and lifelong resident of Met City, Hernandez brought dynamism and fresh ideas to MCREA's start. Today, he is founding CEO of a firm that operates contract schools for disadvantaged kids.

[9] As with everything else in this imaginary tour, this interview is fictional.

Do you have any educational heroes or mentors? How did you get involved with education reform? My eighth grade English teacher, Mr. Donahue, turned my life around. He's the one who got me out of trouble, into the swimming pool, and on the right track in life. I'll never forget what he did for me.

What are the principles of Met City's new educational marketplace? I wish you had asked us that when we first began! It took us a couple of years before we figured them out, but eventually we developed a mission statement with these key elements:

- The first priority of Met City students is learning. They will not advance to the next level until they have mastered the required material.
- Met City schools demand results. Schools that don't deliver don't last.
- An excellent education is provided for all students — regardless of race, religion, income, family background, or disability.
- Parents are treated as partners in their children's education and teachers are treated as professionals. If we don't value our parents and teachers, we will fail.
- Met City schools seek community involvement. Without community partners, our educational offerings suffer.
- Met City schools build upon cherished American values: enterprise, freedom, creativity, diversity, community, and competition.
- Every school is accountable to its customers (children and families) and to its sponsor. To succeed, it must be effective, efficient, and ethical.

What have been the greatest challenges posed by the PEPE system? Many people hadn't bought into the vision and therefore fought this at the start. Things almost fell apart when the state toughened its core academic requirements and, in response, we instituted the Met City "Sink or Swim Standards," in which no student was allowed to progress to the next grade without passing a mastery exam. A number of youngsters failed and had to attend summer school or repeat a grade. Most of the kids were actually fine with that, but some parents screamed. We almost had riots in my office. The other big crisis had to do with a power struggle with the State Court of Education Appeals. When we first began, we were building the plane while flying it, and everybody's roles hadn't yet been delineated. But eventually things fell into place.

Your greatest achievements? Test scores are rising. Schools are springing up all over and becoming more differentiated. This means kids with special needs — and every child has some kind of special need — will get an education that is matched to their temperament and interests, their strengths and weaknesses. It's amazing to me that we used to have basically one uniform system for 170,000 kids. Now we've got more like 500 systems for them. Maybe some day we'll have 170,000.

What advice would you give to other leaders considering such changes? Articulate a vision. Solicit community feedback. Work to get buy-in. Then empower people to do their jobs. And recognize that it takes time. When people stormed into my office demanding results, I had to eat humble pie and ask them to be patient.

Have there been any downsides to this new system? I didn't expect the private schools to rise up and give us hell. I didn't expect the charter and contract schools to develop their own lobbying group. And I didn't realize how much work all this would be.

Anything else to add? My pet project, the "Charter Lab," develops innovative education practices and then disseminates them once their efficacy has been proven. The Lab partners with non-education organizations for a cross-fertilization of ideas. In the old model, innovation was mostly the province of visionaries and mavericks. R&D was scarce. Now we bring surefire improvements to your doorstep.

The demise and reconstitution of schools also figure in the dynamism of the PEPE system. Though some oldsters rue what they call the volatility of education in Met City, most people have come to understand that a school need not last forever, and that if it is unable to produce sound education results, fulfill the terms of its contract or charter, and satisfy its clients, it has no inherent right to continue. Nor should it necessarily last forever if the people who made it tick—parents, teachers, whoever—move away or lose interest. The upshot is that, in a typical year, fifteen or sixteen PEPE schools in the Met City area—about one school in thirty—close down, lose their contracts or charters, or are reconstituted so thoroughly that they must be described as having been closed. Most of these were already on probation, but there are always surprises, four or five schools a year that gave few advance signals of distress. Because these are usually painful, the New Pensylina legislature recently authorized MCREA and its counterparts to gather more "distant early warning" data about schools. The theory is that the more transparent a school's operations (and finances, curriculum, etc.), the better able everyone will be to spot trouble early.

A Helping Hand

Freedom *cum* accountability is part of the formula for PEPE's dynamism, but just as important has been New Pensylina's commitment to boosting the "supply side" of education. The state has made grants (augmented by corporate and foundation gifts) to school incubators and technical assistance centers that help create new schools and troubleshoot when extant schools come in harm's way. (Part of the genius of PEPE is that the monitoring organizations for schools are not responsible for helping them succeed — only for determining whether they are in fact succeeding.)

Besides technical assistance, start-up money is available for new schools, as is access to the state revolving fund for capital expenses. PEPE schools cannot levy taxes or issue bonds directly, but they can tap a half dozen sources of long- and short-term capital loaned by investors and bankers whose risks are mitigated by a state guarantee program. (Schools operated by large national firms and generously endowed organizations have their own access to capital and start-up funds.) This means that a low-income community group or pair of teachers with a dream also can start a new school. Typically, they begin with a low-interest loan and start-up grant directly from the state and, after a few years, refinance with the private sector — often allowing them to move to a better facility — with the state's guarantee keeping the interest rate within bounds. (Enterprise has also seized the construction industry, and a number of PEPE schools now occupy striking facilities that do not much resemble yesterday's schools.)

As for Met City's existing stock of school buildings, after MCREA inherited them it held a grand real estate sale, with proceeds going into the capital revolving fund. Charter and contract school groups purchased some of these structures, private developers and investors many of the rest. Today, a lot of Met City schools own or lease those old buildings — their playgrounds and athletic fields are especially prized — even as many occupy different sorts of facilities.

A dynamic approach to school supply does not just mean incubating and housing new schools. It also means expanding and cloning successful ones and, sometimes, arranging for shaky institutions to be taken over. MCREA periodically runs a sort of school-operations auction at which charters or contracts that have gone sour, or reconstituted schools ready to be turned loose, are put out for bids. It's not mostly about money, though. The real competition is to see which prospective operator presents the best plan for that school's future.

MET CITY TEACHERS

PEPE schools are having a magnetic effect on teachers and would-be teachers. Now that it is possible in New Pensylina for almost any well-educated individual to become a provisional teacher with minimum red tape and no mandatory detour through a college of education, hundreds of people are lining up for classroom openings. Many think they want to teach for only a few years, and it remains to be seen how this will work out. Some astute school operators are experimenting with a two-tiered personnel system, in which a school with, say fifteen teachers, organizes itself into several teams, each consisting of a veteran teacher (earning $100,000 a year or so) and a few short-termers (earning perhaps $40,000 apiece). But all sorts of other variations are visible, including 45-year-old ex-Naval officers and plenty of vigorous retirees from other fields who know a lot and want to impart it.

Each PEPE school or school chain makes its own salary decisions, but all staff members have the right to participate in the state's generous teacher retirement system. Some PEPE schools try to cut corners on salaries, but the marketplace is lively enough that excellent teachers — and those in scarce specialties — have considerable leverage to negotiate solid compensation packages. Many schools in Met City pay competitive wages and also offer various incentives, bonuses, and performance-linked supplements..

Private philanthropists have joined forces to offer "Excellence in Teaching" awards that include monetary stipends. There are also "sabbatical" opportunities for teachers and many chances for professional development, including travel grants to study pedagogical models elsewhere in the United States, Canada, and overseas. (One of the technical assistance centers has established a professional development exchange program with cities in Ontario, Japan, Germany, and New Zealand.)

AND THEIR UNIONS

The teachers' unions are changing, too. Some of the teachings of the late Albert Shanker have sunk in, as have the "new union" messages of former N.E.A. chief Bob Chase (who now serves on the board of a Connecticut charter school). Partly because the grand merger of the two national unions never occurred, they have vied with each other to see which could modernize more successfully. Both seem to have taken as their text the perceptive 1997 book, *United Mind Workers*, which sketched a changed future for teachers' unions under a more decentralized and results-oriented regime of public education.[10] The introduction of PEPE in New Pensylina created a fine opportunity to try putting those ideas into practice. The most important shift, from the unions' standpoint, was from district-wide to school-based bargaining, but the changes have also included heavy emphasis on professional quality, productivity enhancement, and a new career ladder for teachers. The industrial-era model of union behavior has, for the most part, been put aside.

Both unions are striving to organize the PEPE schools. This means arduous building-by-building work and dozens of separate employment contracts shaped to the contours of individual schools. But the unions are

[10] Charles Taylor Kerchner, Julia E. Koppich, and Joseph G. Weeres, *United Mind Workers: Unions and Teaching in the Knowledge Society* (San Francisco: Jossey-Bass Publishers, 1997).

dogged — their future is on the line — and they have already managed to organize the instructional staffs at about two-thirds of Met City schools. Because the bargaining process operates school-by-school, because all teachers have chosen their schools, and because each PEPE school retains the absolute legal right (subject to "due process") to hire and retain only those staff members that it wishes — else it would not have the leeway to produce the results promised in its contract or charter — most of these contracts are flexible documents, more akin to the partnership agreements of a law firm than to the fruits of factory-style collective bargaining.

Besides organizing PEPE teachers as best they can, the unions are showing grudging acceptance of the changed education world of New Pensylina by, for example, themselves contracting to operate a handful of schools. Met City now has fifteen union-operated schools; most are former neighborhood schools that do not yet display strong innovative tendencies, but several serve as demonstration sites for fresh approaches to curriculum, instruction, staffing, and school organization.

None of this has deflected the unions from politics, to be sure. They tried hard to fend off the legislative changes of 2004 and 2007 and now they struggle to influence appointments to the MCREA board and the education appeals bench. They still haunt the state capitol, trying to persuade lawmakers to cap the profits that private firms can make from school operations or, better yet, to bar for-profit school operators altogether. That the American Federation of Teachers has succeeded in organizing teachers in 478 of the Edison Project's 611 U.S. schools is, however, causing second thoughts in that union's upper echelons concerning the evils of for-profit school operators. So is the popularity among teachers of school stock options and profit-sharing opportunities. Even the cautious New Pensylina Teacher Retirement Fund now invests in some of the more successful education management firms.

Other Players

Other organizations have changed, too. PEPE has had a big impact on teacher education. Public schools in New Pensylina must still employ "state certified" people, but licensure no longer hinges on completing a traditional teacher-training program. Now anybody can obtain a provisional certificate who comes up clean on a background check (good character references, no criminal record, etc.), holds a college degree, and passes a rigorous written exam that concentrates on subject-matter mastery. And one can get a "regular" certificate by teaching successfully, and receiving positive evaluations, for at least two years. (All certificates must, however, be renewed every ten years, at which time teachers' actual performance — and the achievement of their students — are appraised, first by their own schools, then by expert teams from the state professional licensing bureau.)

Since colleges of education no longer enjoy a monopoly on teacher preparation, some have gone out of business, and those that remain must compete by providing services that practicing teachers want. Many have
evolved into "departments of instructional skills" that work collab-
oratively with liberal arts colleges and specialize in helping on-the-job
teachers hone their techniques as they seek regular certification and recer-
tification. Some now also contract with individual PEPE schools to provide
specialized staff development, even helping MCREA and its counterparts
with the arduous task of reconstituting troubled schools.

The once powerful state school boards and superintendents' associations
are now vestigial, but the new "Association of School Operators" is a
force to be reckoned with at the capitol (and not always for good). It took
a public-relations drubbing in 2008, however, when it proposed amending
the New Pensylina constitution to guarantee that the state's per-pupil payments to schools would receive automatic inflation adjustments.

The state education department has shrunk to a fraction of its former
size. All it really handles these days is standard-setting, assessment, data-
gathering, and the issuance of school report cards. Since essentially all
state and federal dollars now accompany children to the schools of their
choice, there is scant need to administer and police "categorical" programs. Because the bureau of professional licensure now handles teacher
certification (and has outsourced both the background checks and the
teacher testing program), there is no further need for the education department to do that. And essentially all of its quasi-judicial functions have
been taken over by the Court of Education Appeals, which also handles
certain school-related civil-rights issues, though the federal Office for Civil
Rights remains involved on that front.

Even more interesting than the changes in traditional education entities
are the new outfits that have emerged. Besides the school operators themselves, dozens of private and nonprofit agencies now serve the education
enterprise. For example, several Met City accounting firms have opened
divisions that specialize in school budgeting. One of these has grown into a
full-scale "school business management" company that handles payroll,
benefits, purchasing, and sundry other business-related services for some
75 schools.

Private companies also specialize in school technology, including management information systems, computer networks, distance learning, and
web site maintenance. Some supply food or transportation, while others
furnish direct student services (e.g., psychological testing, violin lessons)
that the schools find more sensible to farm out. Purchasing cooperatives
have arisen among clusters of schools that find it more economical to obtain their erasers, desks and VCRs in bulk. Several enterprising people
have evolved into itinerant "school starters," typically contracting to direct
a new school for a year or so before recruiting a successor, handing over
the reins, and moving on to the next site. There is even a new cadre of

education leaders who specialize in turning struggling schools around— and a small band of "headhunters" who seek out crackerjack principals and teachers and try to woo them to change schools.

TAKING STOCK

How is all this working? The jury is still out. PEPE in its universal form is just four years old. New Pensylina's test scores are up nicely during that period but they remain significantly below where the state's standards (and those set by the National Assessment of Educational Progress) say they should be. Many students still do not reach the "proficient" level.

Yet dropout rates have plummeted, now that so many different schools are available to choose among. School violence is on the wane. The majority-minority achievement gap is narrowing as more minority families place their children in schools that work—and as unsuccessful schools get shut down or reconstituted. At last count, 78 schools in the area were "guaranteeing" that youngsters who attend regularly and do the prescribed work would meet the state's standards.

Economic development is going well, as more families and employers perceive that New Pensylina is serious about education innovation and excellence. Civil society in Met City is experiencing a renaissance, too, now that its many constituents—from neighborhood groups to churches and cultural institutions—can establish their own schools and provide this vital service to their communities or members.

A particularly bright spot on the education front is the enthusiasm shown for PEPE by parents of disabled children. The entire state has received a massive waiver from the regulations of the federal special education program, because so many schools are now going out of their way to serve these youngsters in innovative ways, including services made possible by the extra money that accompanies them to the schools of their choice. New Pensylina's arrangement with Washington is a part of an important national pilot project. The old system had become so rule-bound, litigious, and costly that Congress finally authorized the Secretary of Education to grant these mega-waivers to a dozen cities or states with particularly innovative and promising programs. Most people expect this approach to become the norm.

For the charter and contract schools that do not focus on special-needs children, private providers of special-ed services have been a huge boon. Dozens of schools now contract with such organizations, much as employers engage HMOs to meet the health care needs of their employees. Among the most successful providers of special education in the Met City area is the Sycamore Ridge Public Schools, one of the suburban systems that retained its separate identity. Long known for its excellent special-ed program, Sycamore Ridge now finds that it can generate revenue while helping more children by making its services available to other nearby

PEPE schools. (It even offers a special education "insurance" program for charter schools, much like the one pioneered by Douglas County, Colorado. See chapter 9.)

A handful of conservative legislators and anti-tax groups grump that PEPE isn't saving the state any money. Early evidence suggests that the overall rate of increase in New Pensylina's per-pupil spending has slowed just a bit, with efficiency gains offset by the generosity of the supplemental payments for poor and disabled youngsters. But more of the school dollar is making its way to the classroom. Whereas the old Met City school system and its surrounding suburbs employed a total of 8,500 non-teaching personnel, that number has dwindled to about 2,800, even though there are more schools than ever. To be sure, outsourcing such labor-intensive services as cafeterias and pupil transportation explains much of the decline in noninstructional staff, but so does actual shrinkage of bureaucracy and overhead. For example, the old "central offices" of Met City Public Schools and the nine suburban school systems that were absorbed into MCREA once housed a total of 875 employees. Yet MCREA itself employs just 47 individuals (not including those working in schools that it is reconstituting).

SCANNING THE HORIZON

Amid the generally positive news about education in Met City in 2010, we pick up two concerns for the future. The first is political: will the Association of School Operators, possibly in league with the teachers' unions, succeed in watering down the state's accountability system? Second, there is anxiety about the demise of private schools. The citizens of New Pensylina could one day awaken to find that education's only fully independent sector has been mortally wounded and that virtually every school in the state is now vulnerable to political interference or bureaucratic whim. PEPE schools, after all, are still *public* schools, with both the virtues and the hazards of that designation. A change in the legislature or governor's office could destabilize PEPE itself.

A handful of parents complain that they suffer from information overload and must make too many choices. The area's school selection advisors certainly have their hands full, ensuring that hundreds of youngsters from deteriorated families get placed in schools that suit them. A few politicians grouse that the unelected Court of Education Appeals has too much power—though nobody has been able to cite specific examples of it overstepping its bounds.

Education paradise has not reached Met City. But there is an unprecedented level of ferment and optimism, and early returns suggest that the new education arrangements are gaining traction and improving the lives of tens of thousands of youngsters.

EPILOGUE

WE BEGAN this book with the belief that the charter idea deserved examination and testing. We now conclude our effort to demystify that idea and show how schooling based on choice, autonomy, and accountability can undergird a new model of public education.

What makes charter schools appeal to so many families and teachers? What is distinctive about them? What can American education learn from them? In this Epilogue, we discuss ten elements that foster success in individual charter schools and ten larger lessons to be gleaned from the charter experience as a whole.

WHAT'S DISTINCTIVE ABOUT CHARTER SCHOOLS?

1. These schools are mission-driven, built around a unifying vision. Everybody associated with a school can see what it stands for and what it promises to deliver.

2. Charter schools are focused on academic achievement, not preoccupied with inputs and procedures. They have powerful incentives to produce results—and risk grave consequences if they fail to do so.

3. Charter schools, as schools of choice, are responsive to their consumers. Keeping clients satisfied is a hallmark of successful institutions, including most colleges and private schools, but it has not always been characteristic of public schools.

4. Charter schools are diverse. Their clients have widely varying needs and priorities. The schools' freedom to be different has helped them respond to these disparate demands.

5. Charter schools engage parents. Parents feel ownership. Some also feel that this school may be their youngster's last chance. And entrepreneurial schools must treat parents as a resource, not a nuisance.

6. Most charter schools have an intimate, family-like feel. Everyone knows everyone's face and name. Parents are welcome any time. That most charter schools are small surely helps. So does the sense of being in a lifeboat together, paddling through turbulent seas.

7. Charter schools build—and anchor—communities. They are communities unto themselves as well as sources of neighborhood stability and renewal. Many offer extra services to families and create strong partnerships with cultural, recreational, and business organizations.

8. Charter schools are infused with the spirit of innovation. While few are inventing brand-new education wheels, we found no charter school that isn't markedly different from conventional schools in its vicinity.

9. Charter schools foster teacher professionalism. Some teachers jump at the chance to work with like-minded colleagues in an entrepreneurial setting that affords them great autonomy. Many charters go "outside the box" when searching for staff, bringing able, eager people into public education who would not otherwise be there.

10. Charter schools are creating a new model of accountability. Deliver a quality product or you won't have students. Do what you said you would do — and produce the results you promised — or be shut down. It's as simple (and daunting) as that.

Though these qualities are important to school success, charter schools did not invent them. Some can be found in plenty of conventional public and private schools. It is fairly rare outside the charter movement, however, to find them at work simultaneously. We do not contend that every charter school accomplishes this feat, either. But when it happens, it's a potent recipe for a good school, and we have found it more often within the charter cosmos than in the traditional education universe.

CHARTER SCHOOLS AND PUBLIC EDUCATION

The charter movement recalls Solidarity, the courageous Polish trade union that stood up to an entrenched regime, exposed its inner weakness, and began to crack its hegemony. Like Solidarity, however, the present charter movement is not a full-scale alternative. It is more like a way of illuminating the power of different ideas about how education in America could work. It is what today's charter schools demonstrate, more than the concrete results of a thousand or so of them, that matters most in the long run. What is it, then, that they really show?

1. What we observed in "Met City" in 2010 — and can glimpse in a number of real places in 1999 — is more like an education ecosystem whose elements reinforce and depend on one another, than a bureaucratic system structured in typical government fashion. Much of its success derives from its freedom, its openness, and the flood of information that enables its inhabitants to signal one another. Yet it is not quite a free market, either. The state hovers in the background to make sure that individuals are not harmed.

2. This new system can still legitimately be termed "public," so long as one accepts the distinction between "public" and "government-run."

3. Schools take many forms. Nobody imagines any longer that there is, or ought to be, "one best system" for educating children. Instead, there is a generous supply of interesting, high-quality school options, and school operators have grown entrepreneurial and responsive to what people want.

4. Everyone is free, indeed expected, to select their children's schools, and mechanisms are in place to aid and abet the choice process. Many alternatives are available. More children's needs are being met. Yet the new system has enough structure, predictability, information, and accountability that, from a parent's point of view, it is not too risky.

5. The central accountability paradigm hinges on academic achievement and other indicators of performance, not on regulatory compliance or standardized procedures. Accountability operates at several levels and relies heavily on transparency and market forces as well as oversight by a school's sponsor.

6. Collateral institutions are adapting. There are still teachers' unions and colleges of education, for example, in the new ecosystem, but they behave differently. They, too, must become more entrepreneurial.

7. Successful innovations get passed around as rapidly as word of miracle drugs and discount airfares. There is a sizable competitive advantage in having the latest model — yet the accountability system is such that fads and hype cannot long substitute for concrete results. Novel methods are also devised to stretch the school dollar farther because there is advantage in having efficient schools that attract top-notch teachers, invest in technology, and provide coveted services.

8. The politics of education are changing. Instead of an insular policy arena dominated by traditional stakeholders, much authority is shifting to elected officials such as mayors and governors. The direct engagement of civic organizations in school operations widens the circle of interested parties. The fact that parents select their children's schools also deepens their interest in (and awareness of) education policies and practices. Education is still no peaceable kingdom, but many clashes are now decentralized — focused on individual schools — rather than system-wide. Charter schools turn out to foster a rebirth of local control and, with it, a strengthening of civil society.

9. The rest of the education world is reshaping itself to these new dimensions. Aside from academic standards and testing, little that the state is doing in the Met City 2010 scenario resembles what it was doing in 1999. Federal programs and policies, too, have been recast to support and complement this new delivery system.

10. Although the charter movement is no silver bullet for K–12 education in the United States, it is a relatively low-risk activity for a big country whose education system needs a thoroughgoing overhaul. It isn't an all-or-nothing proposition. Charter schools that falter will lose customers, and those that fail can be shut down without crippling the education system as a whole. Nor is the charter movement the only major change now underway. It coexists with all manner of "systemic" reforms as well as with other "choice," "contracting," and "schoolwide" innovations.

Perhaps one of the other reforms will prove more effective. But we are prepared to bet on the charter movement. We have seen its power to recreate the democratic underpinnings of public education and rejoin schools to a vigorous civil society. It preserves the features that Americans most value in public education (e.g., universality, equality), while reconstructing the institution itself around different assumptions and ground rules. Those new ground rules introduce other elements that U.S. society prizes (e.g., choice, efficiency, enterprise, standards, and accountability) but that are too seldom found in conventional public education.

It's a bet we are making, though, not a firm conclusion that we are drawing. Today, nobody can confidently assert that this new model is a "success." But it is off to a fine start. And if it succeeds, far from being the death knell of American public education, we judge that charter schools will provide a splendid example of how this vital enterprise can be reborn.

APPENDIX: SURVEY RESULTS
AND METHODOLOGY

TABLE A-1. Students' Comparison with Previous School[a]

	My Teachers			My Interest in School Work		
	Better	About the Same	Worse	Better	About the Same	Worse
All Students	60.7%	27.0%	4.8%	49.9%	35.4%	7.7%
Prior Public School Students	65.2%	24.7%	5.5%	52.4%	34.4%	8.4%
Prior Private School Students	48.5%	37.1%	6.6%	42.1%	43.7%	9.6%
Other[b]	52.1%	32.3%	1.9%	46.5%	37.2%	4.4%
White	64.9%	25.0%	4.0%	52.9%	34.9%	7.4%
Black	56.1%	26.3%	7.4%	50.5%	31.4%	8.1%
Hispanic	60.3%	25.0%	5.5%	49.8%	33.7%	8.5%
Asian	62.0%	29.3%	4.0%	50.0%	40.7%	5.3%
Native American	44.2%	47.7%	3.8%	37.6%	50.0%	7.8%

[a]"Sample A" student survey respondents from 39 charter schools across 10 states; N = 4,954 (February 1997); percentages may not add to 100 due to invalid and non-responses.

[b]"Other" refers to children who were home-schooled, previously attended another charter school, or did not attend school last year.

TABLE A-2. Parent Demographics[a]

			Highest Education Level	
Total Number of Children in Charter School	One	52.1%	Did not complete high school	12.0%
	Two	29.3%	High school, but no college	18.8%
	Three	10.0%	Some college, no degree	28.6%
	Four or more	4.1%	College graduate	18.7%
			Post-graduate/professional degree	12.2%
Length of Time At Least One Child In Charter School	First year	40.2%	Total Family Income	
	Second year	29.1%	Less than $10,000	11.0%
	Third year	12.8%	$10,000–$19,999	16.0%
	Fourth year or more	11.7%	$20,000–$39,999	26.0%
			$40,000–$59,999	18.0%
			$60,000–$99,999	13.0%
			More than $100,000	4.8%

[a]"Sample B" parent survey respondents from 30 charter schools across 9 states; N = 2,978 (February 1997); percentages do not add to 100 due to invalid and non-responses.

TABLE A-3. Parent Satisfaction with Charter School[a]

	Very Satisfied	Somewhat Satisfied	Uncertain	Not Too Satisfied	Quite Dissatisfied
Opportunities for parent participation	75.9%	17.7%	5.1%	1.1%	0.3%
Class size	75.2%	19.2%	3.0%	2.3%	0.3%
Curriculum	71.6%	22.9%	3.4%	1.9%	0.2%
School size	74.5%	18.6%	4.5%	1.9%	0.6%
Individual attention by teachers	70.8%	21.5%	5.2%	2.0%	0.5%
Academic standards for students	67.8%	22.4%	6.7%	2.5%	0.6%
Accessibility and openness	66.1%	23.6%	7.3%	2.2%	0.8%
How much school expects of parents	66.0%	23.2%	7.8%	2.2%	0.8%
People running the school	62.2%	26.4%	7.7%	2.7%	1.0%
Quality of teaching	56.6%	32.4%	8.1%	2.2%	0.8%
Technology	55.8%	24.6%	11.3%	5.9%	2.3%
School facilities	44.8%	34.1%	9.6%	8.5%	3.0%
Extracurricular activities	43.1%	28.9%	20.0%	5.7%	2.2%
Transportation to/from school	49.8%	22.9%	10.5%	10.0%	6.9%
Food	42.3%	27.4%	14.3%	9.3%	6.7%
Sports program	23.0%	37.0%	10.3%	22.8%	6.8%

[a]"Sample B" parent survey respondents from 30 charter schools across 9 states; N = 2,978 (February 1997); percentages do not add to 100 due to invalid and non-responses.

TABLE A-4. Parents' Rating of Charter School vs.
School Child Would Otherwise Attend[a]

	Better	About the Same	Worse
Class size	69.3%	16.3%	2.5%
Individual attention by teachers	69.9%	16.7%	2.7%
School size	68.6%	13.1%	4.4%
Quality of teaching	65.7%	19.7%	2.0%
Parent involvement	64.0%	21.3%	2.2%
Curriculum	65.0%	20.8%	3.1%
Extra help for students	64.3%	19.7%	3.3%
Academic standards	63.0%	22.2%	3.0%
Accessibility and openness	60.5%	23.0%	2.5%
Discipline	60.2%	23.6%	3.6%
Basic skills	58.8%	25.7%	2.4%
Safety	59.5%	24.5%	3.5%
School facilities	42.0%	27.1%	15.1%

[a]"Sample B" parent survey respondents from 30 charter schools across 9 states; N = 2,978 (February 1997); percentages may not add to 100 due to invalid and non-responses.

TABLE A-5. Charter School vs. School Child Would Otherwise Attend, Rated by Parents of Special Needs Students[a]

		Special Education[b]	Gifted[b]	LEP[c]
Curriculum	Better	64.5%	69.6%	75.4%
	About the Same	21.8%	18.3%	15.4%
	Worse	4.9%	3.0%	0.8%
Quality of Teaching	Better	67.1%	67.6%	61.5%
	About the Same	20.6%	19.5%	22.3%
	Worse	2.4%	2.4%	0.0%
Extra Help	Better	68.1%	65.9%	64.6%
	About the Same	17.6%	20.6%	18.5%
	Worse	4.3%	3.2%	0.8%
Parent Involvement	Better	65.0%	68.3%	52.3%
	About the Same	23.6%	19.2%	27.7%
	Worse	1.8%	2.4%	0.8%

[a]"Sample B" parent survey respondents from 30 charter schools across 9 states; N = 2,978 (February 1997); percentages may not add to 100 due to invalid and non-responses.

[b]"Special Education" students are those identified by parents as "not learning quickly, needing extra help," having a "physical disability," having "behavior problems," and/or having a "learning disability." "Gifted" students are those identified by their parents as being a "fast learner, often bored."

[c]Limited English Proficiency.

TABLE A-6. Parents' Rating of Child's Overall Performance[a]

	Previous School	Current Charter School	Change		Previous School	Current Charter School	Change
All				**Gifted[b]**			
Excellent	14.0%	24.5%	+10.5%	Excellent	26.9%	37.4%	+10.5%
Above average	20.0%	32.2%	+12.2%	Above average	33.3%	40.7%	+7.4%
Average	27.0%	30.3%	+3.3%	Average	26.5%	19.0%	−7.5%
Below average	12.0%	4.0%	−8.0%	Below average	8.4%	2.3%	−6.1%
Poor	5.3%	0.6%	−4.7%	Poor	4.9%	0.6%	−4.3%
Special Education[b]				**Limited English Proficiency**			
Excellent	5.9%	11.0%	+5.1%	Excellent	22.7%	27.6%	+4.9%
Above average	10.6%	26.8%	+16.2%	Above average	20.5%	35.3%	+14.8%
Average	36.8%	48.6%	+11.8%	Average	39.8%	28.4%	−11.4%
Below average	32.2%	11.8%	−20.4%	Below average	10.2%	7.8%	−2.4%
Poor	14.5%	1.8%	−12.7%	Poor	6.8%	0.9%	−5.9%

[a] "Sample B" parent survey respondents from 30 charter schools across 9 states; N = 2,978 (February 1997). Percentages may not add to 100 due to invalid and non-responses.

[b] "Special Education" students are those identified by parents as "not learning quickly, needing extra help," having a "physical disability," having "behavior problems," and or having a "learning disability." "Gifted" students are those identified by parents as being a "fast learner, often bored."

TABLE A-7. Students' Educational Challenges (Identified by Parents)[a]

| | Race/Ethnicity | | | | | |
	White	Black	Hispanic	Asian	Native American	Total
Interested in some subjects, but not others	38.5%	32.5%	34.4%	23.4%	26.9%	35.6%
Fast learner; often bored	34.5%	37.8%	24.2%	29.8%	26.9%	32.3%
No special challenges	27.7%	19.8%	29.4%	25.5%	15.4%	26.6%
Does not learn quickly; needs extra help	17.6%	27.9%	23.4%	17.0%	19.2%	20.9%
Too social; not academic enough	13.2%	18.3%	16.3%	6.4%	15.4%	14.7%
Behavior problems	9.1%	16.2%	15.0%	14.9%	7.7%	11.5%
Learning disability	10.4%	6.3%	7.7%	6.4%	19.2%	9.1%
Has few friends	7.9%	6.6%	7.6%	12.8%	11.5%	8.2%
Other	9.5%	6.9%	3.5%	8.5%	3.8%	7.3%
Does not speak English very well	0.7%	2.5%	15.0%	8.5%	3.8%	5.0%
Physical disability	1.8%	2.5%	1.5%	0.0%	0.0%	1.8%

[a]"Sample B" parent survey respondents from 30 charter schools across 9 states; N = 2,978 (February 1997). Percentages may not add to 100 due to invalid and non-responses.

TABLE A-8. Teacher Demographics[a]

Average Teaching	Public school	5.6 years
Experience of	Private school	1.7 years
Respondents	University/elsewhere	1.4 years
	Home-schooling	0.6 years
Certification	Certified in this state	71.6%
	Certified but not in this state	3.7%
	Working on state certification	17.0%
	Not certified/not working on it	7.7%
Current Member	Yes	23.6%
of Teachers' Union	No	75.6%
	No Response	0.8%
Previous Member	Yes	40.9%
of Teachers' Union	No	57.4%
	No Response	1.7%
Salary Level	Significantly higher here	16.1%
(compared with	Slightly higher here	18.7%
other job options)	About the same	27.5%
	Slightly lower here	20.3%
	Significantly lower here	17.3%
Likely Occupation	Teaching in another	
If Not Teaching	charter school	13.1%
In This Charter School	Teaching in a regular	
	public school	36.7%
	Teaching in a private school	8.6%
	Other	27.1%
	No/multiple response	14.6%

[a]"Sample C" teacher survey respondents from 36 charter schools across 10 states; N = 521 (February 1997); percentages may not equal 100 due to invalid and non-responses.

TABLE A-9. Teacher Satisfaction with Charter School[a]

	Very Satisfied	Somewhat Satisfied	Uncertain	Not Too Satisfied	Quite Dissatisfied
Fellow teachers	61.2%	33.2%	3.3%	2.1%	0.2%
Educational philosophy	61.6%	31.6%	4.3%	1.9%	0.6%
School size	59.1%	31.8%	5.6%	3.1%	0.4%
Students	50.9%	40.4%	5.4%	2.9%	0.4%
Challenge of starting new school	50.5%	33.5%	13.7%	2.0%	0.4%
Administrators	53.6%	31.8%	7.1%	5.3%	2.2%
Teacher decision-making	46.6%	31.9%	11.6%	7.4%	2.5%
Governing board	38.4%	32.2%	22.7%	4.1%	2.5%
Staff development	34.2%	38.9%	12.5%	11.9%	2.5%
Instructional materials	35.7%	37.3%	8.2%	15.3%	3.5%
Relations with community	21.3%	46.6%	23.5%	7.0%	1.6%
Parental involvement	26.8%	42.1%	9.7%	16.9%	4.5%
Salary level	25.5%	43.7%	9.2%	17.5%	4.1%
Non-teaching responsibilities	23.8%	36.0%	21.0%	14.7%	4.5%
Fringe benefits	24.6%	34.5%	19.4%	14.9%	6.7%
Physical facilities	23.0%	37.0%	10.3%	22.8%	6.8%
Relations with school district	12.1%	26.0%	40.7%	15.7%	5.5%
Relations with teacher union	9.7%	6.8%	69.3%	8.0%	6.2%

[a]"Sample C" teacher survey respondents from 36 charter schools across 10 states; N = 521 (February 1997); percentages may not add to 100 due to invalid and non-responses.

TABLE A-10. Teachers' Views on Charter School Success[a]

	Much Success	Some Success	Little or No Success
Providing for safety	66.3%	31.0%	2.7%
Providing for excellent educational alternative	62.4%	35.1%	2.5%
Positive influence on education in community	61.1%	36.4%	2.5%
Maintaining discipline	60.2%	34.6%	5.3%
Building high-quality staff	55.9%	40.6%	3.5%
Involving teachers in decision-making	56.9%	37.1%	6.0%
Raising student achievement	48.0%	49.6%	2.3%
Setting/maintaining high academic standards	46.6%	48.7%	4.7%
Strong curriculum, powerful methods	45.9%	49.4%	4.7%
Attracting the kinds of students it hoped to have	42.4%	53.8%	3.7%
Educating hard-to-educate students	40.1%	57.0%	2.9%
Keeping students in school	43.0%	50.9%	6.0%
Suitably assessing pupil performance	37.7%	57.4%	4.9%
Providing necessary teacher training	40.6%	50.7%	8.7%
Obtaining necessary resources	39.1%	52.9%	7.9%
Providing necessary instructional materials	42.2%	46.5%	11.2%
Running smoothly	33.7%	59.3%	7.0%
Involving parents	36.0%	54.7%	9.3%
Integrating technology	37.9%	47.0%	15.0%
Giving teachers adequate preparation time	31.7%	43.6%	24.7%

[a]"Sample C" teacher survey respondents from 36 charter schools across 10 states; N = 521 (February 1997); percentages may not add to 100 due to invalid and non-reponses.

METHODOLOGY

Our study yielded four sets of quantitative data, one each from students, parents, teachers, and schools:

- **Sample A:** student-reported data (n = 4,954 from 39 schools in 10 states, surveyed in February 1997). A "student" was a child enrolled in 5th grade or above. In ungraded or mixed-age schools, a "student" was someone 10 years or older. For the data to be included, at least 70% of a school's students were required to respond. Worth noting: 35.6% of these data come from California, 18.7% from Arizona, and 16.7% from Colorado.
- **Sample B:** parent-reported data (n = 2,978 from 30 schools in 9 states, surveyed in February 1997). A "parent" was a parent, guardian, or responsible adult with one or more child in any grade in the participating charter school. When siblings attended the same school, the parent completed one survey, using the oldest child as the "subject." For the data to be included, at least 40% of a school's parents had to respond. Worth noting: 49.2% of these data come from California, 15.4% from Michigan, and 12.7% from Colorado.
- **Sample C:** teacher-reported data (n = 521 from 36 schools in 10 states, surveyed in February 1997). A "teacher" was a full- or part-time professional instructional employee of the school, in any grade, teaching any subject. (This did not include aides, tutors, and parent volunteers.) For the data to be included, at least 80% of a school's teachers had to respond. Worth noting: 32.8% of the data come from California, 22.3% from Arizona, 14.0% from Michigan, and 12.9% from Colorado.
- **Sample D:** school-reported data on students and teachers (number of schools = 49; number of states = 9; number of students = 15,931; number of teachers = 1,005).

Samples A, B, and C were obtained by Hudson Institute and processed and tabulated by the Brookings Institution, while Sample D was obtained exclusively by Hudson Institute via self-reported data from the schools themselves. We excluded data that did not meet our response rates.

In a few instances, surveys were translated by schools so that parents not speaking English could participate. Individual identities of respondents were kept confidential. Surveys from Samples A, B, and C were coded. Hudson Institute never had access to the identity of any individuals filling out surveys. Each school assumed responsibility for internal confidentiality. Also, individual school data were kept confidential by authors and data analysts, although tabulations were provided to participating schools themselves.

Project Description

"Charter Schools in Action" was a multiyear study by the Hudson Institute, under the aegis of the Educational Excellence Network and supported by the Pew Charitable Trusts. Through extensive site visits, phone interviews, and surveys, the project team gathered and analyzed information about participating schools, communities, and states.

During the first project year (1995–96), site visits were conducted to 43 charter schools in 7 states: Arizona, California, Colorado, Massachusetts, Michigan, Minnesota, and Wisconsin. Detailed information was collected on 35 of them, a cross-section of the approximately 225 charter schools then operating nationwide. Over 700 interviews were conducted with individuals in these schools and their communities.

During the second year (1996–97), site visits were made to 45 charter schools in 13 states; 17 schools were visited for the second time; and 18 schools that had been visited in 1995–96 participated in follow-up interviews via telephone. The research team obtained direct information from 50 charter schools, a reasonable cross-section of the almost 500 charter schools nationwide at the time. (Three jurisdictions with operating charter schools were added in the project's second year: Florida, Texas, and the District of Columbia.) Visits were also made to New Jersey, North Carolina, and Hawaii to study the implementation of those states' new charter laws. Over 600 interviews were conducted in the second year, bringing the two-year total to well over 1,300.

During the second year, surveys were also administered to parents, students, and teachers in charter schools that agreed to participate. The project team developed the three questionnaires in consultation with charter experts and the Information Technology Services unit of the Brookings Institution. Results were tabulated from 4,954 students (fifth grade and older) attending 39 schools; from 2,978 parents of students attending 30 schools; and from 521 teachers in 36 schools.

Project staff during the first year were Hudson senior fellows Chester E. Finn, Jr., Bruno V. Manno, and Louann A. Bierlein. Joining the project staff in its second year was Hudson research fellow Gregg Vanourek. Copies of all the "Charter Schools in Action" reports, including additional data from the February 1997 surveys, can be found on the Internet at http://www.edexcellence.net.

INDEX

Academy of Charter Schools (Colorado), 179

Academy of the Pacific Rim: achievements of, 51–52; daily *gambatte* award of, 49; mission statement of, 47–48; revenue raising/operating costs of, 105, 106; statistics/information on, 46–47; teachers of, 49–50, 51

accountability. *See* charter school accountability

ACHIEVE (San Francisco), 134–35

Ackerman, Arlene, 173

Adams 12 School District (Colorado), 179

A.G.B.U. Alex and Marie Manoogian Charter School (Michigan), 161

Aitken, Judith, 97

Alice Deal Junior High School, 57

allegations against charter schools: as being elitist, 157; comparing them to vouchers, 167–68; as draining funds from public schools, 152–53, 173; high risk of, 153–55; on inviting profiteering, 165; listed, 151–52; on not going far enough to reform education, 168; as promoting segregation, 160–64, 185; regarding accountability, 155–56; on similarities of public and charter schools, 156

Allvin, Ron, 199, 200, 201

American culture: changes in corporate, 66–67; liberalization of, 69–70; parallel changes in education and, 70–72. *See also* civil society

American Federation of Teachers (AFT), 18, 175–76

American Prospect, The (Rothstein), 155

American Sign Language, 158

Andover, 55

APBA (Association for Performance-Based Accreditation), 133

Apple Tree Institute for Education Innovation, 199

Arizona Benefits Solutions, 33n.10

Arizona Career Academy, 202

Arizona Career and Technology High School, 136

Arizona charter law, 36, 104

Arizona charter schools, 75, 76, 129–30, 186–89

Arizona Instrument to Measure Standards, 75

Armisted, Clarise (fictitious name), 35

at-risk students. *See* disadvantaged students; minority students

Australian charter-like schools, 97

Balboni, Sheila, 234

balkanization charge, 160–64

Barnett, Harold, 214

barriers facing charter schools, 111, 240–41

"Basic" program (Sequoia), 31, 32, 34

Beacon Education Management, 92

Berger, Peter L., 225

Bierlein, Louann, 237, 238, 239, 240–41, 242, 243, 246

Bitar, Mike, 205

Blair, Tony, 96

Booth, Cordia, 153

Bossart, Marcia, 190

Boston Globe, The, 203, 218

Boston Latin, 55

Boston Public Schools (B.P.S.), 77, 95

Boston Renaissance School, 92, 184

boundary conditions, 164

Bowling Green Elementary School (Sacramento), 116

Boyd, Stacey, 47, 49, 51

Bronx High School of Science, 17

Brown, Jerry, 181

Brown, Linda, 118–19

Brown v. Board of Education, 19, 63

Bruns, Mickey (fictitious name), 79–80

Budde, Ray, 18

Bush, George, 64, 65

Byrd, Robert, 19

California charter law, 43, 155n.9

California charter schools, 76–77, 214–15

California High School Proficiency Exams, 92

California's independent study program (1993), 45

Canadian charter-like schools, 97–98

CANEC, 245–46

Carroll, John B., 62

Ceasar, James, 228, 235

Cellucci, Paul, 166

Center for Economics and Law Charter School (Philadelphia), 136

Center for Education Reform (Washington, D.C.), 152

Center for School Change (University of Minnesota), 75

Central Michigan University, 67, 96

Cha, George, 47

Chan, Yvonne, 94–95

character education program (NHA schools), 38n.16

charter-as-test-kitchen approach, 214

charter operators, 15–16

charter school accountability; in action, 131–34; allegations regarding, 155–56; in Arizona charter schools, 129–30; charter closures and, 135–38; dual nature of, 71–72; GAAPE and, 138–46; of hypothetical Met City schools, 255–56; in Massachusetts charter schools, 130–31; new ground broken by, 127–29; performance information used in, 133–34; as ticking bomb, 239–40

charter school achievement: demand for choice and, 96–98; of disadvantaged children, 79, 80–82; documentation on, 75–77; increased productivity/efficiency and, 94–96; by individual schools, 77–78; parental ratings on, 85–87; research and evaluation of, 98–99; school innovation and, 90–92; through school/parent partnership, 93–94; students' rating of their, 83; teachers and, 87–90; time horizons of, 78–79

charter school community: described, 227; interaction between civil society and, 234–36; "neighborhood" types of, 232–33; professional nature of, 231–32; profile on, 229; as self-governing, mission-driven, 228; as small and intimate, 229–31; as voluntary, 228–29

Charter School Development Corporation, 119

Charter School Expansion Act of 1998, 104, 186

charter school issues: accountability as ticking bomb, 239–40; barriers to entry as, 240–41; charter enemies/friends, 244–45; of charter lobbying, 245–46; of charter success, 246–47; evidence of superior education by, 238–39; re-regulation, 243–44; temporary or permanent status, 241–43

charter school lessons: on charter schools and public education, 266–68; on distinctive nature of charter schools, 265–66

charter school list: Academy of Charter Schools, 179; Academy of the Pacific Rim, 46–52, 105, 106; A.G.B.U. Alex and Marie Manoogian Charter School, 161; Arizona Career and Technology High School, 136; Boston Renaissance School, 92, 184; Bowling Green Elementary School, 116; Charter School of San Diego, 91–92; Chicago Preparatory High School, 163; Citizen 2000 Charter School, 137; City On A Hill, 53–54, 54, 73, 77, 89, 95, 202, 233; Clayton Charter School, 136; Colin Powell Academy (Detroit), 93, 106, 220–22, 236; Community Day Charter School, 158, 235; Crestone Charter School, 179; Dakota Open, 136; Douglas County Public schools, 109; El Puente Academy for Peace and Justice, 154; Excel Charter Academy, 37–42, 232; Fenton Avenue Charter School, 25–29, 121; Guajome Park Academy (California), 125; Healthy Start Academy, 163; HIS, 42–46; International Studies Academy (San Francisco), 109; Johnson/Urban League Charter, 136; Kingsburg, 199–202; Leadership High, 123–24, 126; Lowell Middlesex Academy, 163, 212; Marcus Garvey Charter School, 136; Medical Center Charter School, 125, 232; Metro Deaf Charter School, 158; Midway Elementary School, 136; Minnesota New Country School, 115; N.F.L.-Y.E.T. Academy, 161, 234; Pioneer Charter School, 213; Platte River Charter School, 195; Raul Yzaguirre Charter School, 161; Renaissance School, 77, 93, 194, 197; Rocky Mount Charter School, 207; San Carlos Charter Learning Center, 183, 211–12; Sankofa Shule, 161; Sequoia

School, 29–37; Seven Hills Charter
School, 100, 125–26; Texas Academy of
Excellence, 105, 107; Thomas Jefferson
Charter School, 190–91; Vaughn Next
Century Charter School, 115–16; West
Michigan Academy for Environmental
Sciences, 230–31; Windows Charter
School, 136
charter school political backgrounds: additional actors in, 180–82; fair-weather
friends and, 183–89; school boards/super-
intendents and, 179–80; stages of opposition leading to, 170–73; over state
charter laws, 171–73; teachers' unions
and, 174–78; over Washington charter
initiative (1995), 169–70. See also state
charter laws
Charter School of San Diego, 91–92
charter school ventures: access to technical
assistance/capital sources, 118; adaptations of, 103–4; adequate planning time
required for, 123; barriers facing, 111,
240–41; effective leadership required for,
122–23; enrollment problems and surprises, 110–11; environmental conditions
of, 117–18; finances of, 104–6; frantic
starts of, 110; government tiffs/manage-
ment frailties and, 109–10; illustrative
operating funds shortfalls, 108; lack of
business acumen and, 108–9; life cycle of,
113–17; political opposition and, 106,
108; pressure to imitate conventional
schools, 116–17; solutions to start-up
problems of, 117–18; staff burnout and,
115; start-up problems/issues listed 101–
11, 114; state charter laws and, 101–4;
worrisome test scores and, 115–16. See
also charter schools
charter schools: accountability of, 71–72,
127–47; arguments against, 151–68;
available public information on, 154–55;
boundary conditions for, 164; as communities, 227–34; cultural changes contributing to, 66–67, 69–70; cyberspace
"virtual," 92, 165; demand for, 96–98;
described, 14–17; diversity of, 23, 25;
evolution as educational alternative, 17–
18, 61, 63; global distribution of, 23; international movement toward, 97–98; life
cycle of, 113–17; origins of, 13–14, 18–
20; per-pupil facilities funding for (1999),
121; public, private, nonprofit allies of,

120; refugee spirit of some, 202; relationship between sponsor and, 117–18; state
distribution of, 23–24; state-level effects
of, 216–17; student likes/dislikes of, 84,
85. See also charter school list; charter
school ventures; teachers
Charter Schools in Action report (1997), 4
Charter Schools in Action research project, 3
Charter Schools Development Center (Sacramento), 175
charter sponsors: accountability of, 71–72;
charter application approval criteria for,
164; described, 16; GAAPE applied to,
142, 143–45; relationship between char-
ter school and, 117–18; vigilance of, 154.
See also charter operators
Chase, Bob, 260
Chelmsford Public Charter School (Massa-
chusetts), 92
Chelsea High School (Boston), 53
Chicago charter schools, 213–14
Chicago Preparatory High School, 163
Chicago School Reform Board of Trustees,
132
Chico, Gerry, 214
Choice 2000 On-Line Charter School in
California, 82
Christie, Jack, 216
Chubb, John, 66
Citizen 2000 Charter School (Arizona), 137
City Academy (St. Paul), 77
City On A Hill Charter School: academic
achievements of, 77; impact of, 73; ori-
gins of, 53–54; profile on, 233; refugee
spirit of, 202; spending per student by,
95; teacher empowerment in, 89
civil society: interaction between charter
schools and, 234–36; public education
and, 222–25; rekindled interest in vitality
of, 69; silent revolution and, 225–27. See
also American culture
Clark, Kenneth B., 63
Clayton Charter School (Colorado), 136
Clayton Foundation, 136
Clinton, Bill 13, 183
Clinton, Hillary Rodham, 211
Coalition of Essential Schools, 92
Codding, Judy, 248
Coleman, James S., 62
Coleman, Lynn, 153
Colin Powell Academy (Detroit), 93, 106,
220–22, 236

Colorado charter law, 96
Colorado charter schools, 75–76, 212–13
Colorado Department of Education, 216
Colorado Student Assessment Program, 75
Colorado Visionary Academy, 193
Community Consolidated School District #59 (Chicago), 191
community control movement (1960s), 226
Community Day Charter School (Massachusetts), 158, 234–35
competition: Arizona analysis on, 207; impact on selected public schools by, 208–9; positive impact of charter school, 204–6
competitive model of schooling, 65–66
Copeland, Paulette, 174
Core Knowledge Foundation (Met City), 250
"Core Knowledge" schools, 193
Coulson, Andrew J., 66
Crestone Charter School (Colorado), 179
Crew, Rudy, 180
cropping principle, 73
Cross, Janice (fictitious name), 82
crusaide for efficiency movement, 223–24
CTA (California Teachers Association), 175
culture of professionalism, 223
curriculum: "Basic" program (Sequoia), 31, 32, 34; for disabled students, 158; importance of academic, 155; Open Court, 40; "Project" program (Sequoia), 31; special education, 158–60; SRA phonics, 40; "Writing to Read" lab (Fenton Avenue), 29
cyberspace virtual chartering, 92, 165

Dakota Open (Minnesota), 156
Darling, Alberta, 174–75
Davis, Grey, 181
Dayton Daily News, 166
D.C. Charter School Resource Center, 119
DC CLAS (D.C. Charter League for Accountable Schools), 132
D.C. Public Charter School Board, 119
DCPS (Douglas County Public Schools), 109, 193, 196, 197, 198, 209. See also Douglas County charter district
Dearborn, Jennie (fictitious name), 42
Democratic Leadership Council poll (1997), 218
Denver charter schools, 212–13
Detroit Free Press, 154
DiLorenzo, Andrea, 177

disabled students, 157–60, 183, 185, 263–64
disadvantaged students: attending charter schools, 157; charter school achievement by, 79, 80–82. See also minority students
District of Columbia charter program, 119
District of Columbia Public Charter School Board, 132
Domino's Pizza, 57
Douglas County charter district: Golden Trails and, 197–98; increasing tension between DCPS and, 196–97; origins of, 192–93. See also DCPS (Douglas County Public Schools)
Drucker, Peter, 53, 57, 235

Eastin, Delaine, 29, 180, 181
Economist, The, 183
Edison Project, 92, 122, 166, 213
"Education by Charter" (Budde), 18
education management organizations, 17n.8
education reform: incrementalism of, 19; new solutions to, 20–22; shortcomings of privatization, 21–22. See also public education
education reform industry, 19
"Education Summit" (1989), 64
"Education's Big Gamble: Charter Schools" (PBS report, 1997), 153
Edutrain (Los Angeles), 137
effective schools research, 62–63
El Puente Academy for Peace and Justice (New York City), 154
Electronically Assisted Student Teaching (EAST) Program (California), 43–44
Elementary and Secondary Education Act (1965), 61
Ellis, Tim, 136
Engler, John, 78
English charter-like schools, 96–97
Equality of Educational Opportunity (Coleman), 62
establishment of religion clause (First Amendment), 250n.6
Evans, Jack, 173
Excel Charter Academy: education and entrepreneurship of, 39–41; interview of student from, 42; performance-based pay system of, 40–41; profile of parent from, 41; statistics/information on, 37–39; values community of, 232. See also NHA (National Heritage Academies)
Exeter, 55

factory model of schooling: assumptions of, 58–61; development of, 56–57
Fair, Harry, 109, 111–13
Fallon, Gayle, 176 213, 214
Family Development Charter School (Massachusetts), 212
federal education aid programs, 218
Fenton Avenue Charter School: accomplishments of, 28–29; launching of, 25–26; organizations giving assistance to, 121; statistics on, 25; unique characteristics of, 26–28
Fenton Charter Broadcasting (TV channel), 29
Fenway Middle College High School (Boston), 208
financial drain argument, 152–53, 173
First Amendment, 250n.6
Fisher, Donald, 122
Fisher, Doris, 122
Flake, Don, 30, 32, 34, 36
Flake, Floyd, 19, 66
Forrester, Jay, 92
Foster, Mike, 3, 237
Fowler, Donna, 176
Fox, Leonard, 153
Francis W. Parker Charter School (Massachusetts), 92
Friedman, Milton, 65, 182
Friends of Choice in Urban Schools, 119
Fukuyama, Francis, 223
Fuller, Howard, 66

GAAP (Generally Accepted Accounting Principles), 138–39, 140, 142
GAAPE (Generally Accepted Accountability Principles for Education), 138–46
Gaebler, Ted, 59, 68, 69
gambatte award (Academy of the Pacific Rim), 49
Ganado Unified School District, 33, 34
Gardner, John 175
Gaschler, Randy, 42–43, 45–46
GED (General Education Development) certificate, 91–92
Gillis, Paul, 160
Glenn, Charles, 160–161, 224, 235
Goenner, Jim, 67–68, 78–79
Golden Trails, 197–198
Goldsmith, Stephen, 68
Gould, Stephen Jay, 73
government: assumption of education management by, 58; GAAPE applied to, 142,

145–46; market education vs. education by, 66; public education as arm of, 224; reinventing, 68–69
Graham, Jack, 31
Grauman, Keith, 89–90
Grippe, Pat, 195
Guajome Park Academy (California), 125
Gude, Phil, 97

Haisman, Bob, 91
Hamilton, Scott W., 13, 130–31
Hanson-Harding, Brian, 190
Hansot, Elisabeth, 54
Harmon, Laura, 195
Hart, Gary K., 45, 75, 180, 181, 237, 238, 239–40, 241, 242, 243, 246
Hartley, Mary, 186–88
Haslip, Jim, 201–2
Hassel, Bryan C., 172, 215
Healthy Start Academy (Durham), 163
Heclo, Hugh, 69
Heffernan, Joan, 178
Hernandez, Lyndon (of hypothetical MCREA), 256–58
Higley School District, 33, 34
Hill, Paul T., 127
Hillel Academy, 17
Hip-Hop 101 (El Puente Academy), 154
Hirsch, E.D., 191, 193
Hirschman, Albert O., 202
HIS (Horizon Instructional System): as accreditation candidate, 46; legal battle by, 44–46; statistics/information on, 42–44; teachers of, 44
Hispanic students, 161–62. See also minority students
Holden, Karen J., 87
Holland Public Schools (Michigan), 205
Holmes, Rev. R. B., Jr., 162
Houston Federation of Teachers, 176, 213
Hoxby, Caroline, 209
Hudson Institute, 3
Hudson Institute survey (1997), 79, 84–85, 87, 89n.26, 113, 114, 158
Huizenga, John Charles (J.C.), 37, 40
Hunkapillar, Beth, 212

I.D.E.A. (for disabled students), 183, 185
IEPs (individual education plans), 158
International Studies Academy (San Francisco), 109

interviews: Doug Lemov (Academy of the
Pacific Rim), 50–51; Harry Fair (Renais-
sance Charter School), 111–13; James
Zaharis (Mesa Public School), 210–11;
Jennie Dearborn (Excel Charter Acad-
emy), 42; Keith Grauman (Guajome Park
Academy), 89–90; Linda Brown (Pioneer
Institute), 118–19; Lisa Graham Keegan
(Arizona State Superintendent), 129–30,
188–89; Lyndon Hernandez (hypothetical
MCREA), 256–58; Mary Hartley (Ari-
zona State Senator), 186–88; Richard
O'Connell (DCSD), 189; Scott W. Ham-
ilton (former Associate Commissioner),
130–31. *See also* profiles
Iowa Test of Basic Skills, 75, 163

Jackson Education Association, 205–6
Japanese charter-like schools, 98
Jasin, Claudia, 179
Jencks, Christopher, 65
Johnson, Lyndon, 61
Johnson/Urban League Charter (San Diego),
136
Junge, Ember Reichgott, 18

Kass, Sarah, 53, 57, 73, 89, 202, 212, 231,
233
KCAP (Kingsburg Community Assistance
Program), 201
Keegan, Lisa Graham, 74, 129–30, 188–89,
192
Keller, Paula, 197
Kerry, John, 218
Killian, Jacqueline, 194
Kingsburg (California), 199–202
Knapp, Mark, 176
Knoester, Bill, 38, 39
Kolderie, Ted, 58, 203, 204–205
Konkle, Mary Lou, 205
Kuhn, Thomas, 73
Kushner, Mark, 123–24, 126

Ladd, Everett Carll, 226
Lake, Robin, 127
Leadership High (San Francisco), 123–24,
126
learning: gap between resources and, 62; *A
Nation at Risk* report on student, 64. *See
also* public education
Lemov, Doug, 49–51
Levin, Henry, 65

Lewin, Nina, 229
Lewis, Anne, 248
Lieberman, Joseph, 13
Lieberman, Myron, 249
Likes, Larry, 34
Little, Carole, 122
Locke, Gary, 170
long-distance chartering, 92, 165
Los Angeles Unified School District
(L.A.U.S.D.), 95
Lott, Thaddeus, 211
Loveless, Tom, 170
Lowell Middlesex Academy (Massa-
chusetts), 163, 212
Lucente, Joe, 25, 26, 27, 28, 123, 202

Magden, Carol, 175
management revolution, 68–69
Mann, Horace, 54, 225
Marcus Garvey Charter School (Washing-
ton, D.C.), 136
Massachusetts charter law, 53
Massachusetts Charter School Resource
Center, 94, 118
Massachusetts charter schools, 77, 130–31
Massachusetts Finance Development
Agency, 125
Matheson, Kent, 205
Mathews, David, 223, 248
Matthews, John, 175
McGuinn, Patrick, 228, 235
MCREA (Met City Regional Education Au-
thority), 251–52, 253, 255, 262, 264. *See
also* Metropolitan City (circa 2010)
MEA (Michigan Education Association), 174
MEAP scores, 78–79
Medical Center Charter School (Houston),
125, 232
Merrow, John, 153
"Merrow Report" (PBS), 218
Mesa Public Schools, 30–31
Metro Deaf Charter School (Minnesota),
158
Metropolitan City (circa 2010): account-
ability of schools in, 255–56; achievements of PEPE schools of, 263–64;
additional players in, 261–63; concerns
for future of education in, 264; funding
of, 258–59; interview on PEPE schools
of, 256–58; PEPE schools of, 249–52;
school shopping in, 252–55; teachers of,
259–60; teachers unions of, 260–61

Michigan Association of Public School Academies, 67
Michigan charter law, 41
Michigan charter schools, 78–79, 205
Midway Elementary School (Georgia), 136
Minnesota charter law (1991), 18, 174
Minnesota charter school study (1999), 76
Minnesota Education Association, 174
Minnesota New Country School, 115
minority students: Academy of the Pacific Rim and, 47–48; allegation of charter segregation and, 160–64, 185; attending charter schools, 157; *Brown v. Board of Education* impact on, 19, 63; call for higher standards for, 63; charter school achievement by, 80–82; charter school achievement rating by, 83; estimated enrollment percentages of, 161–62; Native American, 33, 136–37. *See also* disadvantaged students; students
Mississippi charter law, 103
Missouri charter law, 81
Modern Red Schoolhouse, 134
Modern Red Schoolhouse Institute (Met City), 250
Moe, Terry, 60, 66
Montessori school (Mesa), 211
Moore, Karen, 212
Mormon seminary program, 33
Morrison Institute, 76
Moss, Reginald, 57
Mowen, Gregg, 206
MTEA (Milwaukee Teachers' Education Association), 174–75
Mulholland, Lori, 76

Nathan, Joe, 171
National Commission on Civic Renewal (1998 report), 226–27
National Commission on Excellence in Education, 13, 64
National Press Club (Shanker speech, 1988), 18
Nation at Risk, A, report (1983), 64
Native American school systems, 33
Native American students, 136–37
NEA (National Education Association), 88, 170, 175, 176, 231
NEA charter teacher survey (1998), 88, 89n.26, 93
NEA study (1998), 177, 178

NEA's Center for the Advancement of Public Education, 177
Neuhaus, Richard John, 225
New American Schools, 134
New American Schools Development Corporation, 65
"New Education Bazaar, The" (*U.S. News and World Report*), 181
New Jersey Monthly, 190
New Pensylina. *See* Metropolitan City (circa 2010)
New York State Charter School Resource Center, 162
New York Times, 57
New York Times Magazine, The, 181
New Zealand charter-like schools, 97
New Zealand's Education Review Office, 97
N.F.L.-Y.E.T. Academy (South Phoenix), 161, 234
NHA (National Heritage Academies), 38, 39–40, 41. *See also* Excel Charter Academy
Nisbet, Robert, 227
North Carolina charter law, 172–73
North Carolina charter movement, 206–7

O'Connell, Richard, 109, 193, 194, 195, 197, 198
Office for Civil Rights, 184
Ohio charter petitions, 156
Ohio Education Association, 166
"one best system, the," 55–56, 65, 226, 266. *See also* public education
Open Court curriculum, 40
opportunity space, 71
option value, 137
Osborne, David, 59, 68, 69

Pacheco, Marc, 166
PacRim. *See* Academy of the Pacific Rim
Pakistan charter-like schools, 98
parent profiles: Julie Veeneman (Excel Charter Academy), 41; Karen J. Holden (Renaissance School), 87. *See also* profiles
parents: charter school achievement role of, 93–94; charter school participation by, 265; charter school ratings by, 85, 87; charter school selection by income by, 86; school role of, 72; "sweat equity" by charter school, 95
Pataki, George, 180
Patterson, Thomas C., 137–38, 238–39, 240, 241, 242, 243, 245, 246, 247

Payzant, Thomas, 208
Pennsylvania Department of Education, 216
PEPE schools. *See* Metropolitan City (circa 2010)
performance information, 133–34
performance-based pay system, 40–41
Pew Charitable Trusts, 3
Pierce, Lawrence C., 127
Pioneer Charter School (Denver), 213
Pioneer Institute for Public Policy Research, 118
Platte River Charter School, 195
political battlegrounds. *See* charter school political battlegrounds
Porter-Obey funding, 183
Powell, Colin, 235–36
PPOR (per-public operating revenue), 194
Premack, Eric, 175
private schools: assumption of exclusivity of, 58–59; public education and, 56. *See also* charter schools; public schools; schools
privatization shortcomings, 21–22
professionalism culture, 223
profiles: ACHIEVE, 134–35; Clarise Armisted (fictitious name) [Sequoia School], 35; Janice Cross (fictitious name) [Charter School of San Diego], 82; Jim Goenner (Center Michigan University), 67–68; Karen J. Holden (Renaissance School), 87; Mark Kushner (Leadership High), 123–24; Mickey Bruns (fictitious name) [Lowell Middlesex Academy], 79–80; Nina Lewin (Chelmsford Public Charter School), 229; Sarah Kass (City On A Hill), 233; Vernon Robinson (North Carolina Education Reform Foundation), 206–7. *See also* interviews
profiteering allegation, 165
public accountability, 70
Public Charter School Program, 218
public education: as arm of government, 224; assumption regarding balance of power in, 60–61; charter school impact on, 211–19; charter schools as reinvention of, 16–18; civil society and, 222–25; crusade for efficiency movement and, 223–24; evolution of, 54–56; evolution of charter alternative to, 61; factory model of, 56–61; Great Society's strategy for, 61–62; in hypothetical Metropolitan City, 249–64; learning and resources gap

in, 62; lessons on charter schools and, 266–68; market vs. government, 66; new solutions for, 20–22; old assumptions on gauging, 59–60; "the one best system" of, 55–56, 65, 226, 266; parallel changes in society and, 70–72; positive competition with charter schools, 204–9; private schooling and, 56. *See also* education reform
public information availability, 154–55
public schools: at-risk youth in, 81; Australia's self-governing, 97; balance of power assumption in, 60–61; charter school and funding of, 152–53; government management assumption and, 58; impact of charter schools on, 211–19; near-monopolies assumption on, 58–59; reinventing, 70–72. *See also* private schools; schools
Putnam, Robert, 225

Rabinowtiz, Leonard, 122
Raul Yzaguirre Charter School (Houston), 161
Ravitch, Diane, 223
Reagan, Ronald, 64
Redford, Debbie, 37
Redford, Keith, 37
Reeves Elementary School (Edison Project), 92
refugee spirit, 202
Renaissance School (Colorado), 77, 93, 194, 197
re-regulation issue, 243–44
Ridge, Tom, 216
Riley, Richard, 217
Riordan Foundation, 29
Rittmeyer, Marilyn Keller, 190, 191
Robinson, Vernon, 163–64, 202, 206–7
Rockey Mount Charter School (North Carolina), 207
Rofes, Eric, 207, 215
Rothstein, Richard, 115, 155, 159
Ruppert, Pete, 39, 40

San Carlos Charter Learning Center, 183, 211–12
San Diego Teachers' Association, 175
Sancta Maria Middle School, 17
Sankofa Shule (Michigan), 161
Sarason, Seymour B., 181–82
SBM (site-based management), 64
Schneider, Mark, 230
school board opposition, 179–80

schools: importance of results by, 71–72; innovation and achievement link in, 90–92; new options available by, 70–71; new public accountability of, 70; reinventing, 70–72. *See also* private schools; public schools

SEED Public Charter School (Washington, D.C.), 123

segregation allegation, 160–64, 185

Sequoia College, 32

Sequoia School: community educational environment and, 30–31; future challenges of, 35–37; options available within, 31–32; profile of student from, 35; search stability by, 34–35; statistics on, 29–30; stormy start of, 32–34

Seven Hills Charter School, 100, 125–26

Shalvey, Don, 212

Shanker, Albert, 18, 57, 248

Silber, John R., 53, 166

silent revolution, 225–27

Sindelar, Tim, 158

Sixty Minutes (TV show), 95, 218

Sizer, Nancy, 92

Sizer, Theodore, 65, 92

Smith, Pastor Ellis, 220–22, 235–36

Smithson, Clark, 32

Solidarity movement (Poland), 266

Spady, Fawn, 169–70

Spady, Jim, 169–70

special education issues, 157–50, 184, 263–64

Springpeace, Deborah, 100, 125, 126

SRA phonics curriculum, 40

staff burnout, 115

Stanford 9 test, 75, 76, 133

state charter laws: charter impact on, 217; common features of strong, 102; common features of weak, 101–2; importance of strong, adaptive, 117; legislative compromise and weak, 171–72; Washington charter initiative (1995), 169–70; weakest in the nation (Mississippi), 103. *See also* charter school political battlegrounds

Steinberg, Jacques, 57

student interview (Jennie Dearborn, fictitious name), 42. *See also* interviews

student profiles: Clarise Armisted (fictitious name) [Sequoia School], 35; Janice Cross (fictitious name) [Charter School of San Diego], 82; Mickey Bruns (fictitious name) [Lowell Middlesex Academy], 79–80. *See also* profiles

students: charter school achievement rating by, 83; charter school likes/dislikes by, 84, 85; disabled, 157–60, 183, 263–64; disadvantaged, 79, 80–82, 157; Native American, 33, 136–37. *See also* minority students

subsidiarity principle, 228

Sumida, Irene, 27, 28

superintendent opposition, 179–80

"systems thinking," 92

TAAS (Texas Assessment of Academic Skills), 75, 76

Tacoma New Tribune editorial, 170

Taylor, Frederick Winslow, 223

Taylorism, 223–224

teacher profile (Mark Kushner), 123–24. *See also* profiles

teachers: of the Academy of the Pacific Rim, 49–50, 51; burnout of charter, 115; charter school achievement and, 87–90; at HIS, 44; of hypothetical PEPE schools, 259–60; "looseness as to means" applied to, 72; performance-based pay system for, 40–41; professional nature of charter, 231–32; school role of, 72; as stakeholders, 64; tenure of charter, 89n.26. *See also* charter schools

teachers' unions: charter opposition by, 174–78; of hypothetical PEPE schools, 260–61

technical assistance access, 118

tenure (charter teachers), 89n.26

test scores: California High School Proficiency Exams, 92; Iowa Test of Basic Skills, 75, 163; issue of worrisome, 115–16; Stanford 9 test, 75, 76, 133

Texas Academy of Excellence, 105, 107

Texas State Board of Education, 216

"third way," 222n.1

Thomas Jefferson Charter School (Chicago), 190–91

Thompson, Tommy, 175

Thurgood Marshall Middle School, 179

tight-loose strategy, 66–67, 68

Time for Results reports (1986), 64

"Time Stands Still in Some School Boiler Rooms" (Steinberg), 57

Title I funding, 109, 183, 185

Toch, Tom, 165

Tocqueville, Alexis de, 17, 223, 225

Tolkoff, Ann Connelly, 53, 57, 73, 202

Total Quality Management, 68
Toussaint, Brunel, 57
Tucker, Marc, 248
TURN (Teacher Union Reform Network), 178
Turtle Island (Michigan), 136
Tyack, David, 54, 55

United Federation of Teachers (New York City), 180
United Mind Workers, 260
United Teachers of Los Angeles, 27
University of Minnesota, 75, 76, 77
University of Minnesota study (1998), 88
Urban Magnet School of the Arts, 17
Urbanski, Adam, 177–78, 208
U.S. Department of Education, 98, 158, 160
U.S. News and World Report, 165, 181

Vaughn Next Century Charter School, 115–16
Vaughn Street Learning Center (California), 94–95
Veeneman, Julie, 41
Venerable, Lawndia White, 137
"virtual" charter schools, 92
Visionary Academy, 195
vouchers, 167–68

Wade, David, 30, 32, 34, 36
Wall Street Journal, 209
Washington charter initiative (1995), 169–70

Washington Post, 159
WEA (Washington Education Association), 169, 170
Weingarten, Randi, 180
Wells, Amy Stuart, 182
Welsh charter-like schools, 96–97
West Michigan Academy for Environmental Sciences, 230–31
WestEd Regional Education laboratory study, 77
Western Association of Colleges and Schools, 46
Western Placer Unified School District, 43, 45, 46
Whittle, Christopher, 65
Wide Range Achievement Test, 51
"wild west" of charter schools. *See* Arizona charter schools
Williams, Anthony, 173
Williams, James A., 166, 213
Wilson, James Q., 67
Windler, Williams, 216
Window Rock School District, 33, 34
Windows Charter School (San Diego), 136
"Writing to Read" lab (Fenton Avenue Charter School), 29

"Yellow Pages test," 68
Yoder Community Resource Center, 232

Zaharis, James, 30–31, 210–11
Zollers, Nancy, 159